SOTHEBY'S
CONCISE ENCYCLOPEDIA OF
GLASS

SOTHEBY'S
CONCISE ENCYCLOPEDIA OF
GLASS

GENERAL EDITORS
DAVID BATTIE • SIMON COTTLE

LITTLE, BROWN AND COMPANY
BOSTON · TORONTO · LONDON

First published in 1991 by Conran Octopus Limited,
37 Shelton Street, London WC2H 9HN

First U.S. edition

ISBN 0-316-08374-7

Library of Congress Catalog Card Number 91-52939

Library of Congress Cataloging-in-Publication Data
Sotheby's concise encyclopedia of glass / general editors, David
Battie, Simon Cottle. – 1st U.S. ed.
     p.   cm.
Includes bibliographical references and index.
ISBN 0-316-08374-7
     1. Glassware–Collectors and collecting.   I. Battie, David.
II. Cottle, Simon.   III. Sotheby's (Firm)

NK5104.S66   1991
748.29–dc20   91-5293

10 9 8 7 6 5 4 3 2 1

Printed in Great Britain

The publisher would like to thank Roy L. Davids, Ronald Varney, Lauren Tarshis, Ken Adlard,
Sarah Battie, Katie Klitgaard, Christina Smale, Jill Thomas-Clark,
Sandy Shepherd, Mary Davies, Susan Egerton-Jones, David Lee, Servis Filmsetting Ltd and the
Department of European Ceramics and Glass, Sotheby's London, for their help with this book.
Thanks also to Mallett and Son Antiques Ltd, Mallett at Bourdon House Ltd,
Sheppard and Cooper Ltd, Designers Guild and The Gallery of Antique Costume and Textiles
for lending items for photography.

ILLUSTRATIONS ON PAGES 1–12

Page 1: Dutch goblet engraved by Frans Greenwood, 1745
Page 2: English drinking glasses, mid 18th century
Page 4: Water lamp of 'Celeste blue' lead glass, Frederick Carder, 1920s
Pages 4–5: Group of English coloured bottles, mid 19th century
Page 6: Designs for wine glasses, Richardson's of Stourbridge, mid 19th century
Page 9: Pâte-de-verre vessels, Argy-Rousseau, 1920s
Page 10: Detail from a still life, Gerrit Willensz, c.1620
Page 12: Group of coloured glassware, 18th–19th century

CONTENTS

THE CONTRIBUTORS

PATRICIA BAYER
Between the Wars
(Twentieth-Century Developments)

Patricia Bayer is an American freelance writer specializing in 19th- and 20th-century decorative arts. She is the author of *Art Deco Source Book*, 1988, and *Art Deco Interiors*, 1990, and the co-author of *The Art of René Lalique*, 1988, and *Lalique Perfume Bottles*, 1990. She was a contributor to *Sotheby's Concise Encyclopedia of Furniture*.

SIMON COTTLE
Fakes and Forgeries
Care and Conservation

Simon Cottle worked in the museum profession in London, Newcastle-upon-Tyne and Glasgow for ten years before joining Sotheby's London in 1990 as an Expert in European glass and 18th-century British ceramics. He has organized a number of large-scale exhibitions of glass, notably on Beilby enamelled glass (about which he has also published several articles), on Sowerby glass – together with a book – and, more recently, on Scottish contemporary glass. He has contributed to numerous reference works and lectures widely on the decorative arts.

BARBARA DEISROTH
American Art Nouveau
(Arts and Crafts and Art Nouveau)

Barbara Deisroth is Senior Vice President and Director of the 20th Century Decorative Works of Art Department at Sotheby's New York, which she joined in 1971. The Department, which was formed in 1973, includes Victoriana, Arts and Crafts, Art Nouveau and Art Deco. Ms Deisroth lectures frequently on the Art Nouveau and Art Deco styles and is familiar with the major private and institutional collections in this field around the world.

OLIVER FORGE
Pre-Roman Glass

Oliver Forge is a Deputy Director of Sotheby's London and has worked in the Antiquities Department since 1980. He first began cataloguing ancient glass in about 1982 and now has responsibility for this area.

PHILIPPE GARNER
Emile Gallé
(Arts and Crafts and Art Nouveau)

Philippe Garner is a Director of Sotheby's London, responsible for sales of Decorative Arts post-1880 and of photographs. He also organizes sales in London and Monte Carlo. He has written extensively on aspects of design and the decorative arts and on the history of photography. His definitive biography of Emile Gallé was published in 1976.

MALCOLM HASLAM
European Art Nouveau
(Arts and Crafts and Art Nouveau)
Post-War: 1945–70
(Twentieth-Century Developments)

Malcolm Haslam was an antiques dealer for several years before becoming a writer and lecturer specializing in the decorative arts. He is a regular contributor to magazines and the author of several books, including *English Art Pottery 1865–1915*, *Marks and Monograms of the Modern Movement*, *In the Nouveau Style* and *Arts and Crafts Carpets*.

JEANETTE HAYHURST
Continental Glass
(The Nineteenth Century)

Jeanette Hayhurst trained as a photographer at the Victoria & Albert Museum and in 1969 joined Sotheby's London. While there she became an avid researching glass collector. In 1980 she 'retired' to form her own company, selling glass of all periods. She also researches, writes and lectures on the techniques and history of glass.

MARTIN MORTIMER
British Glass
(The Eighteenth Century)

Martin Mortimer joined the antiques dealer Delomosne & Son Ltd in 1948. Their specialities include English china and glass. He has made a particular study of period glass lighting and lectures and writes articles on these and allied subjects. He is honorary advisor to the National Trust on their English glass light fittings.

MARTINE NEWBY
Roman Glass

Martine Newby studied Archaeology at Southampton University and joined the British Museum in 1985 working on *The Glass of the Caesars* exhibition. In 1988 she was awarded The Rakow Scholarship from The Corning Museum of Glass to study the Medieval glass from Farfa, Italy. She currently works for Sheppard and Cooper Ltd, dealers specializing in ancient and antique glass. She has written several articles on Roman and Medieval glass and has edited a book of seminar papers on Roman glass.

DAVID PRIESTLEY
Chinese Glass
(The Eighteenth Century)

David Priestley was educated at New College, Oxford. He read Chinese, and, in his final year, studied Chinese ceramics under Mary Tregear, the Keeper of Eastern Art at the Ashmolean Museum. He joined Sotheby's Chinese Department in 1984 and is a Director of Sotheby's Hong Kong. He is also a Deputy Director of the Chinese Department at Sotheby's London.

SARA ROSSI
Paperweights
(The Nineteenth Century)

Sara Rossi has worked for Spink & Son Ltd, Britain's leading dealer in paperweights, since 1984, and has travelled thousands of miles around the world as dealer, researcher and lecturer. She is the author of *The Letts Guide to Collecting Paperweights*, 1990.

CHRISTOPHER SHEPPARD
The Renaissance Period

Christopher Sheppard was educated at Trinity College, Cambridge, where he became interested in the whole field of glass, particularly the Roman and Renaissance periods. He has published numerous articles and two recent catalogues: *Glass from the Restoration to the Regency* and *Engraved Glass, Masterpieces from Holland*. Since 1974 he has run Sheppard and Cooper Ltd.

J. GARRISON STRADLING
American Glass
(The Nineteenth Century)

J. Garrison Stradling is an author, lecturer and antiques dealer in partnership with his wife Diana, based in New York. Specializing in ceramics and glass, The Stradlings are known for their expertise in 18th- and early 19th-century American glass. Mr Stradling served for 11 years on the Board of Trustees of the Jones Museum of Glass & Ceramics in Douglas Hill, Maine.

IAN WOLFENDEN
British Glass
(The Nineteenth Century)

Ian Wolfenden is a Senior Lecturer in the Department of History of Art, University of Manchester, and runs a postgraduate course in Art Gallery and Museum Studies. He has published articles on 19th-century British glass in academic journals and collectors' magazines and also lectures on the subject. A founder member of the Glass Association, he is Editor of its *Journal*.

DAVID WHITEHOUSE
Islamic Glass
Medieval Glass

David Whitehouse is Deputy Director of The Corning Museum of Glass and Editor of the *Journal of Glass Studies* (USA). He directed excavations at the deserted Medieval port of Siraf in the Persian Gulf, and later became Director of the British Institute of Afghan Studies in Kabul and of the British School at Rome. Dr Whitehouse writes and lectures about Roman, Islamic and Medieval European glass.

PERRAN WOOD
Continental Glass
(The Eighteenth Century)

Perran Wood was the Head of the Glass Department at Sotheby's London from 1977 to 1984 and a Founder Fellow of The Corning Museum of Glass. He is now a consultant in glass to a number of institutions, including Sotheby's, and has published articles and contributed to various publications on the subject.

FOREWORD

For a great part of the twentieth century glass was something of a Cinderella among the arts, although Edward Dillon's Glass, published in 1907, introduced the subject to an English-speaking audience with an understanding and a breadth of scholarship unrivalled at the time. He stood on the shoulders of previous English writers who had made their individual contributions to the subject: Alexander Nesbitt with his cataloguing of the glass in the South Kensington Museum (1878) and the Felix Slade Collection in the British Museum (1871), and Albert Hartshorne with his specialized study of English glass (1897). Our knowledge of the general history of the subject was transformed by Robert Schmidt's great compendium Das Glas, published in 1922; but those who could only manage English had to wait until 1946 for a general survey, in W.B. Honey's Glass, A Handbook (Victoria & Albert Museum). Since that time, knowledge has mushroomed in all areas, thanks to archaeology for the earlier stretches of time, and to the general expansion of our horizons by research, the systematization of knowledge by modern methods and publication in such specialized periodicals as the Journal of Glass Studies, now some thirty years old. In particular, the voluminous sources for nineteenth- and twentieth-century glass are now being thoroughly plumbed. The combined weight of all this knowledge has made it virtually impossible for a single author to update the works of Dillon and Honey. In this volume a band of contributors, each a specialist in his or her own field, has put together a comprehensive review of the subject, from the very beginnings of glass-making in Mesopotamia, by way of Rome and the glass industries of Byzantium, the Sassanian Near East and Medieval western Europe, to Renaissance Venice and all that flowed from its epoch-making contribution. Special attention is focused on the nineteenth and twentieth centuries, with much new information and fresh insights.

ROBERT J. CHARLESTON

INTRODUCTION

'*For now we see through a glass, darkly . . .*'. Paul, writing this now well-known passage in his First Epistle to the Corinthians, *would have been familar with the curious 'liquid stone' known as glass. In his day it was, for the most part, a misty, grey tinged material used as a holder for unguents and oils or moulded into dishes and bowls. But the* Book of Revelation *is rich in similes suggesting the translucent nature of glass: '. . . before the throne there was a sea of glass like unto crystal'; 'the city was pure gold, like unto clear glass', the latter passage then continuing with a list of precious stones. It was during the lifetime of the early saints that glass-making was revolutionized by the discovery of glass-blowing.*

Glass is made from sand melted with a flux such as soda or lead oxide. The resulting mass – known as the metal – is in reality a liquid in solid state at normal temperatures. In fact, throughout its life it will continue to flow, as can be seen in Medieval glass windows, the panes of which are thicker at the base than at the top. For the first millennium and a half, glass use was restricted to beads, the first vessels appearing in about 1500 BC. Centuries of refinement and experimentation led to a near colourless metal comparable to rock crystal. From as early as the eighth century BC solid lumps of glass were treated as hardstones and ground by abrasion to form vessels; some, later, of miraculous complexity: the diatreta, *or* cage cups.

The extraordinary capacity of glass to refract light has been exploited by colouring it with oxides, by enamelling or wheel-cutting, and by using it as prisms in chandeliers and candelabra to increase the wavering flame of candle-light.

This book tracks the development of glass from its discovery until modern times in ten chapters written by fifteen authors, each a specialist in his or her field. The photographs, all in colour, have been chosen to mirror the wide diversity of the world of glass.

PRE-ROMAN
GLASS

The exact origins of glass are lost in the sands of time, but it is likely to have been developed from experiments with glazes in western Asia about 3000 years before Christ. As is common throughout much of the history of glass-making, the earliest pieces were made as substitutes for precious and semiprecious stones, since glass could be cut and polished with greater ease than the harder natural materials.

In Egypt under the Pharaohs, faience, a material akin to both glass and ceramic, was used to make figures and inlays for furniture. This in turn led to a profitable glass-making industry. Along with objects made of other materials, glass vessels were among the numerous items buried with the dead for their use in the afterlife; glass amulets and inlays, as well as scarabs, were also made for this purpose. Beads, cups, bowls and bottles for ointments and scents were all formed in glass before the dawn of the Hellenistic period. Coloured mosaic glass appeared from the third century BC, and glass tableware was made to exacting standards by skilled craftsmen.

As the Hellenistic period drew to a close under the Roman onslaught, glass-making continued and new techniques were developed.

DETAIL OF A HELLENISTIC MILLEFIORI BOWL, 3RD–2ND
CENTURY BC

The technique of slicing canes to create a mosaic effect was known in Roman times, and has continued to be used to the present day.

THE BRONZE AGE
c.3000 TO 1200 BC

'There is a story that once a ship belonging to some traders in natural soda put in here and that they scattered along the shore to prepare a meal. Since, however, no stones suitable for supporting their cauldrons were forthcoming, they rested them on lumps of soda from their cargo. When these became heated and were completely mingled with the sand on the beach a strange translucent liquid flowed forth in streams; and this it is said was the origin of glass'. This rather fanciful description of the discovery of glass was written by Pliny the Elder (AD 23–79) and is indicative of the mystery that has long surrounded the origins of this fascinating substance.

It would be difficult today, as indeed it was in ancient Rome, to imagine everyday life without glass, and one reason for this must be due to the invention of glass-blowing. For many centuries before that discovery, the most beautiful glass vessels were created by highly skilled craftsmen using intricate, almost impossible to imagine, methods. Cut and ground like lumps of stone, shaped in moulds like pottery or metal, luxury glassware was being produced by techniques that rivalled the more sophisticated ones of the much later glass factories which led to modern mass production.

MESOPOTAMIA
c.3000 TO 1200 BC

For a long time the earliest evidence of the existence of glass has been dated to the third millennium BC, its place of origin most probably Mesopotamia, in western Asia. Glass more than likely came about as a direct result of experimenting with the different coloured glazes which had previously covered many small objects. The earliest known glass occurs in the form of beads, pendants, cylinder seals and inlays, probably made to imitate the more expensive and rarer semiprecious and precious stones. The usual colours were blue and green, and the technique involved cutting the glass into the desired shape, which was then polished.

Around 1650 BC the 'core-formed' technique evolved, which was used for the manufacture of glass vessels. In this method a core consisting of a mixture of sand, clay, mud and other organic materials was formed into the required shape around a metal rod. This was dipped into molten glass which was wound around the core until the entire surface was covered. It would then be rolled, or 'marvered', on a flat surface, decorated on the outer surface with different coloured spiral threads and 'marvered' again. The rims, handles and bases were added and, finally, the metal rod was removed and the core scraped out. This technique required considerably more skill than had previously been necessary and established glass-making as a respected and valuable craft. The shapes, based on contemporary pottery, were straight-sided beakers, bottles with tall necks and pointed bases and, occasionally, bowls. The core-formed technique, which was to dominate glass-making up until the Hellenistic age, most likely originated in northern Mesopotamia. Examples have been found in the ancient sites of Assur, Nineveh and Nuzi.

Another important technique invented in Mesopotamia (c.1500 BC) was that of casting mosaic glass for making goblets and bowls. Cut segments of monochrome or polychrome mosaic canes were placed in a shaped mould to form a pattern and heated until the canes fused; the mould was subsequently removed and the vessel polished and ground. Many examples, mostly fragmentary, have been found at Agar Ouf near Baghdad and Nuzi and Hasanlu in northwestern Iran.

A variety of small objects was also produced from about 1600 BC onward, such as plaques used to decorate royal palaces, inlays for furniture, seals, pendants, amulets of gods and goddesses, and a selection of jewellery. They were made either by the method of casting in a mould or by using the core-formed technique.

The now independent and profitable glass-making industry inevitably spread throughout the Ancient World. Soon additional workshops were established and glass became a commodity worthy of export to other important areas.

EGYPT
c.1540 TO 1200 BC

There is little evidence of extensive glass manufacture in Egypt before the New Kingdom (c.1540 BC). Prior to this, glass had been used, as in western Asia, as a glaze on beads; a small number of these have been found in graves dating back as far as the Pre-Dynastic Period (c.3200 BC). The next stage in the evolution of glass in Egypt was the discovery of faience. Faience is a mixture of quartz sand and an alkaline substance covered by a vitreous glaze which, once mixed, can then be moulded, cast or even thrown on a wheel. Although bearing the same name, it is unrelated to the tin-glazed faience of Europe. Scientifically, glass is almost the same as faience, so it is surprising that it took such a long time for glass to be discovered in Egypt. This might indicate that the highly successful Mesopotamian glass industry had not yet reached Egypt.

After the expulsion of the Hyksos, the tribes that had previously dominated Egypt, and the founding of the New Kingdom in the Eighteenth Dynasty (c.1540 BC), Egypt regained its political, economic and artistic prominence throughout the Ancient World. Pharaoh Tuthmosis III (ruled c.1504–1450 BC) is believed to have returned to Egypt with Asiatic glass-makers after waging war in Syria, and there are examples of flasks inscribed with his royal cartouche which might substantiate the theory that he was in some way responsible for the introduction of the core-formed technique in Egypt. Other glass appearing in Egypt at this time resembled the vessels from the Near East. Early examples were all very different in their shapes, sizes and decoration, and it was not until the reign of Amenhotep II (c.1450–1425 BC) that they began to become more standard in form and more prolific in

EGYPTIAN CORE-FORMED *KRATERISKOS*, FROM MEMPHIS, NEW KINGDOM, *c.* 1290 BC (H8.7cm/3½in)

The dark blue glass body is decorated with opaque white, yellow and turquoise coloured spiral trailing combed into a festoon pattern. The shape is one of the most popular of the New Kingdom. The foot and handles were applied later.

EGYPTIAN CORE-FORMED VESSEL IN THE SHAPE OF A *BULTI*-FISH, NEW KINGDOM, 18TH DYNASTY, *c.*1353–1336 BC (L14.5cm/5¾in)

An extremely good example of core-formed glass, this vessel was found in El-Amarna.

production. In contrast to the burial places of his predecessors, the tomb of Amenhotep was filled with many glass vessels. The vessels of this period came in about a dozen forms and many different sizes, and included beakers, jugs, *krateriskoi* (vases), pomegranate flasks, jars, kohl tubes and *amphoriskoi* (small vessels for oils or unguents); the most popular colour was blue. Many of the shapes were derived from the more traditional pottery and metalwork forms, which were containers for oils, ointments, scents and kohl; some had covers while others were sealed with linen and wax or papyrus wads. The decoration on certain types of vessels became more elaborate, with opaque coloured trailing combed into festoons, zigzags or spiral patterns with horizontal bands of glass wound above and below. Although glass was now being produced in larger quantities it was still considered to be a luxury item and may well have been distributed only at court.

By about 1400 BC glass was being used as inlays for furniture. For a long time semi-precious stones, ivory, faience, gold and silver had been employed for this purpose, but in glass artists discovered a practical and

EGYPTIAN CAST BLUE GLASS HEAD OF A KING, POSSIBLY AMENHOTEP II, NEW KINGDOM, 18TH DYNASTY, *c.*1435–1415 BC (H4cm/1½in)

Most surviving royal portrait heads seem to have come from figures made of other materials, but this head was probably attached to a glass figure.

economical material that could be moulded into any shape. Once polished it provided exceptionally beautiful ornamentation for even the grandest of furniture. An example of this can be seen on the famous throne of Tutankhamun (ruled *c.*1334–1325 BC), with its inlays of gold, calcite, faience and different coloured glass. Many such inlays can also be found on reliefs on the walls of temples and tombs, simulating the skin, headdress and clothing of the figures. Also produced in Egypt at this time were enormous quantities of glass beads, pendants, amulets and other types of jewellery.

EASTERN MEDITERRANEAN
*c.*1400 TO 1200 BC

During the late Bronze Age the glass industry reached certain regions of Syria and Palestine, as well as islands such as Crete, Cyprus and Rhodes. Whether glass was actually manufactured at these places or was imported from Egypt is still an unanswered question. Few examples have been found, but surviving vessels closely resemble those types produced in Egypt. However, in some instances the shape, form and decoration differ. There are, for example, core-formed jugs with pad feet and spouts, and pomegranate flasks with nipped rather than rounded foliation. This suggests that a relatively thriving industry existed outside Egypt, but whether it resulted from importing raw glass or making the vessels *in situ* is unknown.

THE AEGEAN
c.1400 TO 1200 BC

Glass was also found in the Aegean, in particular in central Greece and Crete, but, unfortunately, even fewer examples have survived than from the eastern Mediterranean. What has turned up as a result of excavations from Mycenaean sites are small glass objects, in particular rectangular, thin 'tablets' with ribs and perforations, known as 'appliqués'. They are mostly cast, and many are of the dark blue glass characteristic of the Near East. These appliqués were decorated with a variety of Mycenaean motifs, such as rosettes, palmettes, flowers and scrolling, and they were mainly used for decorating clothing or for personal adornment. As well as these appliqués, beads, pendants and inlays were produced. The glass may have come from the east in ingot form and been worked locally.

THE IRON AGE
c. 900 TO 400 BC

The collapse of the glass-making industry in the late Bronze Age (c.1200 BC) was a direct result of the continual war throughout the Near East and eastern Mediterranean world. The Mycenaean and Minoan cultures disappeared completely, Egypt was drastically weakened by constant battle and Mesopotamia rapidly declined. As always in an economic crisis, the production of luxury goods suffered, and the glass-making industry was no exception. There appears to be no significant glass made between 1200 and 900 BC.

LATE MINOAN OR MYCENAEAN DARK BLUE AND AQUAMARINE GLASS NECKLACE, FROM CRETE OR THE PELOPONNESE, c.1400–1250 BC

This necklace consists of 15 rectangular glass beads decorated with a roulette of rosettes and interspersed with 16 faience beads.

From about 900 BC a new age of expansion, civilization and culture began in the Ancient World. The Assyrian Empire was created in Mesopotamia and remained prominent until the rise of the Achaemenid Empire under Cyrus the Great in 539 BC. The powerful Achaemenid Empire expanded through most of western Asia and the Aegean. Syria emerged as a powerful force, as did Greece. Italy and the western Mediterranean were drawn into this new civilization by trade connections with Greece. An important contribution to this new era was the development and creation of new forms of art that re-established the almost extinct glass-making industry.

WESTERN ASIA
9TH TO 6TH CENTURIES BC

Glass first began to re-emerge in northern Syria and Assyria in the form of inlays on ivory plaques that were used on furniture.

The first group of vessels, which appeared around the eighth century BC, comprised monochrome cups and bowls of differing shape and size. Probably made to imitate rock crystal, they were mainly of translucent colourless or green glass, cast in a mould and then ground and polished. Many were simply decorated with wheel-cut horizontal ridges although examples exist with elaborate decoration such as diagonally cut grooves or engraved figures and flowers.

In 1850 in the Northwest Palace at Nimrud in Assyria, an important group of cast vessels was discovered, which included the famous Sargon Vase, now in the British Museum. This squat *alabastron* (bottle for ointment, scent or body oil) bears a cuneiform inscription with the name of King Sargon II (722–705 BC). Vessels such as this were cut from blocks of raw glass and then drilled, ground and polished. The locations where many of these vessels were found indicate that these luxury goods were distributed throughout the Near East. The sites of their manufacture have never been ascertained, but they probably came from Phoenicia or Assyria.

NEAR EASTERN YELLOW-GREEN CAST, CUT AND POLISHED VASE, FROM MESOPOTAMIA OR SYRIA, *c*.750–600 BC (H19cm/7½in)

This vase, related to the Sargon Vase, was probably carved from a solid lump of glass. (LEFT)

ACHAEMENID COLOURLESS CAST AND CUT BOWL, LATE 5TH CENTURY BC (D16cm/6¼in)

This bowl is an example of Persian glassware at its best and is closely related to metal prototypes. It is said to have come from Gordion. (BELOW)

PUNIC CORE-FORMED HEAD-BEAD, FROM CARTHAGE OR THE SYRO-PALESTINIAN COAST, 5TH–3RD CENTURY BC (H3.4cm/1¼in)

formed technique. Core-formed vessels soon followed, some pieces decorated with spiral threads, others with distinctive applied, pinched prunts. *Alabastra, oinochoai* (small jugs) and *aryballoi* (flasks for bath oil) were the more standard forms and usually were made in green, brown or blue glass. Most likely the Etruscans drew their inspiration from glass-makers in Mesopotamia or Phoenicia. However, production from northern Italy, although important to its own culture, contributed little to the now thriving glass-making industry.

Core-formed glass re-emerged during the eighth century BC. Unlike cast and cut glasses, they were not considered items of value or importance. Indeed, they were rather uninspiring in form and decoration if compared to earlier core-formed vessels.

ACHAEMENID EMPIRE
7TH TO 4TH CENTURIES BC

With the defeat of the Assyrians by the Persians in 612 BC glass-making in the Near East once again almost entirely disappeared, only to return in the fifth century BC, when glass became, more than ever, a luxury. The Achaemenid Empire produced beautiful vessels, many in the form of bowls, beakers, rhytons and shallow bowls known as *phiales*, all based on elaborate forms of contemporary metalwork. They were often cast in colourless glass and polished in imitation of rock crystal. In 450 BC Aristophanes wrote that after gold vessels those of glass were the most expensive. Examples have been found in Iran, Iraq, Turkey and other areas of the

Mediterranean, which might indicate that glass of this quality was greatly valued. Perhaps this is why this type continued after the collapse of the Persian Empire and through to the Hellenistic age.

Core-formed and rod-formed glass was manufactured from the sixth to fourth century BC. Rod-forming, a similar technique to core-forming in that it involves glass being wound around a metal rod, was employed particularly to make square or cylindrical glass tubes used for kohl, examples of which have been found in graves in northwestern Iran, eastern Turkey and Iraq. Decorated with spiral trailing, they often had applied 'eyes' and shoulder knops.

ETRURIA
8TH TO 7TH CENTURIES BC

Glass began to appear in northern Italy at about the beginning of the eighth century BC. At this early stage, it was very basic: beads, bracelets and other small objects of blue or green glass were made using the rod-

PHOENICIA AND CARTHAGE
c.7TH TO 2ND CENTURIES BC

During the seventh century BC, numerous rod-formed beads or pendants, mostly in the form of grotesque heads, began to appear in the Mediterranean area. Many were bearded, with applied coloured details and a loop at the top for suspension. The exact area of manufacture is not known but it is assumed there were distribution centres in Phoenicia and at Carthage. Rod-formed pendants in the form of birds and animals were also made at this time.

EGYPT
7TH TO 4TH CENTURIES BC

After the end of the New Kingdom (*c*.1075 BC), the highly successful Egyptian glass-making industry fizzled out, and during the Iron Age only decorative inlays seem to have been made. As before, these were used on coffins and household furniture and were produced on a very large scale.

MEDITERRANEAN
6TH TO 2ND CENTURIES BC

Without doubt the largest and most successful glass to be produced during the Iron Age were the core-formed vessels from the Mediterranean area. Based on existing pottery prototypes such as *alabastra*, *oinochoai*,

of more varied shapes than seen previously. Their applied handles and feet, as well as their decoration, are more elaborate. The core-formed vessels of Group III (mid second century BC to early first century AD) comprise fewer forms than the two previous groups. The decoration, handles and lugs used resulted in a less appealing vessel.

Soon other smaller kingdoms began to break away and establish independence. The Attalids formed such a kingdom at Pergamum, which grew in power until it overshadowed most of western Asia Minor. The influence on these domains was largely Greek and as a result Greek culture reached boundaries far wider than ever before.

HELLENISTIC CORE-FORMED LENTOID ARYBALLOS, EASTERN MEDITERRANEAN, MID TO LATE 4TH CENTURY BC
(H13.3cm/5¼in)

Decorated with opaque yellow and white spiral threads, this vessel has a particularly unusual form. (RIGHT)

HELLENISTIC CORE-FORMED ALABASTRA, EASTERN MEDITERRANEAN, 6TH–4TH CENTURY BC

Decorated with opaque white and yellow spiral trailing combed into zigzag and festoon patterns, these two vessels are fairly typical examples of core-formed glass of the Mediterranean Group II. (LEFT)

amphoriskoi, *aryballoi*, *hydriae* (containers) and *stamnoi* (small jars), they were used for scents, ointments and oils.

Much research has been done on the Mediterranean core-formed vessels, resulting in their division into three chronological groups. In each group the shapes, with differing types of foot and handle, and the area of manufacture and distribution are taken into account. The vessels in Group I (mid sixth century to early fourth century BC) are usually of average size (8–10 cm/3¼–4 in), and their applied handles closely resemble those seen earlier in Mesopotamia. Those in Group II (mid fourth century to late third century BC) are larger and made up

HELLENISTIC AGE

*c.*330 TO 30 BC

The empire of Alexander the Great embraced the whole of Greece, Anatolia, Egypt, the Near East and parts of India. After his death in 323 BC this vast area immediately became a battlefield between his successors, and it was more than thirty years before it was broken up to form three main dynasties: the Antigonids in Greece, the Seleucids in Babylonia, Syria, Asia Minor and northwestern India, and the Ptolemies in Egypt and parts of Greece.

Egyptians, Arabs, Jews, Indians, Syrians and Babylonians were among those who fell under Greek influence and formed part of this Hellenistic civilization and culture.

One of the significant features of the Hellenistic age was the enormous wealth enjoyed by the monarchs and aristocracy, and the extravagance of the lives they led. Trade in many kinds of products between the varying states and cities from the Aegean and all along the Mediterranean resulted in the growth of new cultural centres at such places as Alexandria, Antioch, Damascus and Ephesus. Cloth, papyrus, jewels, incense, gold, silver and ivory, as well as glass, were valuable commodities.

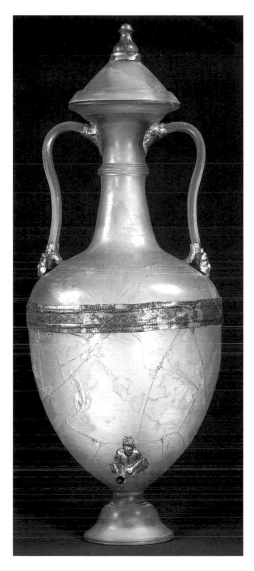

HELLENISTIC CAST AND CUT
AMPHORA AND COVER, EASTERN
MEDITERRANEAN, LATE 2ND–1ST
CENTURY BC (H59.6cm/23½in)

This large glass vessel, supposedly found in Olbia, Sardinia, was made in two parts joined together by a copper-gilt strip. (FAR LEFT)

HELLENISTIC CAST AND GROUND
FOOTED BOWL, POSSIBLY FROM
EGYPT, MID TO LATE 3RD CENTURY
BC (D21.9cm/8½in)

This Canosa Group bowl, reputedly found in Italy, is a fine example of Hellenistic craftsmanship. (LEFT)

HELLENISTIC
CAST GOLD
SANDWICH
GLASS BOWL,
FROM CANOSA,
LATE 3RD
CENTURY BC
(D19.3cm/7½in)

This Canosa Group bowl was made with considerable skill. The gold leaf decoration is an eight-petalled rosette with leaves and other floral details. (LEFT)

MONOCHROME AND MOSAIC CAST VESSELS, 3RD TO 1ST CENTURIES BC

The earliest Hellenistic cast glassware found on archaeological sites has become known as the Canosa Group. Many examples have come from the cemeteries outside Canosa in southern Italy, while others have been discovered in different areas of southern Italy, including Sicily. The most frequent forms are plates, dishes, cups, bowls and *skyphoi*; all were influenced by contemporary pottery or metalwork and were made as luxury tableware by highly skilled craftsmen for wealthy patrons.

The technique used was to cast the vessel in a mould, remove it, grind it on a wheel and then polish it to an extremely high level. The pieces were green, blue, purple or aquamarine in colour, and their decoration usually consisted of horizontal lathe-cut grooves of varying widths. In some instances vessels were painted or gilded with floral or geometric motifs.

One of the most skilled and extremely rare techniques used to make Hellenistic glass resulted in 'gold sandwich glass' – a precursor of eighteenth-century Bohemian *Zwischengoldglas* – examples of which are found among the Canosa Group. This process involved two similarly shaped glass

vessels placed together, with an applied layer of patterned gold leaf in between. The two vessels would then be lightly fused together and the rims ground smooth. The result was a very beautiful and desirable object.

Once again there is a question as to the source of these vessels. It has been thought that the Egyptian city of Alexandria, founded by Alexander the Great in 332 BC, was the source of many top-quality luxury objects during the Hellenistic period, but archaeological evidence does not necessarily support this theory. Since so many of the vessels were discovered at Canosa it might be assumed that there were factories with skilled artisans in southern Italy, but that does not explain why other pieces of this glass were found elsewhere. It is most likely that glass-makers in several places, including Alexandria, were responsible for the production of the Canosa Group.

Mosaic glass existed in Assyria from the ninth to fourth century BC. Although some vessels survive, mosaic glass was mostly in the form of inlays, plaques and strips. Possibly Asiatic workers introduced the technique to Alexandria when they established themselves there and it was during that period when the production of mosaic vessels came into prominence, contributing greatly to the overall success of the Hellenistic glass-making industry.

Although mosaic glass was produced up until the Roman period, Hellenistic mosaic vessels can be distinguished by their canes. These were usually of two standard designs, spiral or star-shaped, and set within translucent coloured backgrounds. A characteristic

mosaic vessel of the time was decorated with a 'network' cane pattern, achieved by winding opaque white and yellow threads around a larger strand of colourless glass, then fusing them all together on a colourless ground. The result gave a 'lacy' appearance to the vessel. Almost all of the vessels were edged with a spirally twisted cane or coil intertwined around one or two white or yellow threads, a feature found on both Hellenistic and Roman mosaic glass.

Between 218 and 201 BC, the Levant, an area along the Syro–Palestinian coast, was taken over from the Ptolemies by the Seleucid kings, resulting in the re-establishment of two important glass-making industries. The first produced the group of core-formed glass vessels described earlier as the Mediterranean Group III. The second produced a group of cast drinking vessels of relatively simple form. These can be divided into two groups based on their shape, either conical or hemispherical, both types having convex bases and tapering sides. The dimensions and colour vary enormously but the form always remains the same. Often they were decorated with simple wheel-cut grooves of varying width either on the inside or the outside. The technique used differed from the Canosa Group vessels in that the cooled glass was put over an open mould until it formed the shape of that mould. It was then ground and polished.

Examples of these have been found all over the Ancient World, including Dura-Europos in Syria, Ephesus in Asia Minor, Athens, Carthage in North Africa and parts of Spain, and they were made in great quantities. Although similar to the core-formed vessels in terms of mass production, they differ in that distribution was more widespread than had ever been known before. There are also examples of this type decorated with cut flutes, a form of decoration used previously

by the Achaemenids and continued by Hellenistic artisans on metalwork and pottery as well as on glass.

The final stage of the Hellenistic age saw the gradual influence of Rome undermining the supremacy of the Hellenistic kingdoms. In 133 BC Pergamum fell to the Romans, and by 146 BC the Greeks and Macedonians had surrendered. Between 70 and 60 BC the Seleucid strongholds in Asia Minor, Syria and Palestine also succumbed to the Romans. Surprisingly, such drastic intervention did not have a serious effect on the production of glass, which continued to be made with the same enthusiasm as before.

The ribbed bowls which began to appear around the first half of the first century BC were related to the conical and hemispherical bowls described earlier; they also seem to have been produced in Syro-Palestinian workshops. This form continued to be popular up to the first century AD. The main colours are yellow, green and brown, and the ribs were of differing size and spacing and not as crisp, well-defined or symmetrical as on the Roman examples.

Mosaic glass vessels also continued to be produced during the late Hellenistic period. Although related to the earlier examples, they were now made with different rims and stood on 'base-ring' feet. These were distributed all over Greece and Syria.

A new pattern was introduced at this time: different coloured canes were laid in rows, then fused together to form a striped design. Like standard mosaic bowls they had twisted rims and stood on 'base-ring' feet.

GOLD-BAND MOSAIC ALABASTRA
c.1ST CENTURY BC

The gold-band method was used in the first century BC for scent-containing *alabastra*. It involved taking bands of gold sandwich glass and blending them with bands of glass in three or four different colours (usually purple, blue, green and brown). Little is known of the distribution of these vessels and although originally thought to be Roman, geographical evidence shows a similarity with other luxury Hellenistic glass.

EGYPT
4TH TO 1ST CENTURIES BC

Since the late Bronze Age, Egypt had produced an enormous number of small objects in various materials. This continued throughout the Hellenistic era (roughly equivalent to the period of Ptolemaic rule, 323–30 BC), and the articles made took the form of inlays, plaques, amulets and beads.

The inlays of the Ptolemaic period are usually in the form of human details, such as eyes and eyebrows; figures or parts of figures, such as torsos, limbs, faces and clothing; animals; mosaic bars, either with human masks or typical Egyptian motifs; stripes; and hieroglyphic symbols. As in the late Bronze Age, all were used on religious and household furniture and mummy masks. Possibly the most complex type of inlay is the mosaic bar in the form of a human mask, in which two equal halves – each showing half a mask – would be joined to make up the complete head.

Egyptian glass amulets had been produced since the New Kingdom (c.1540 BC) and continued to be made in great quantities

during the Ptolemaic period, beginning in the third century BC. They varied in quality and took many different forms, which included animals, gods and goddesses, and scarabs. All were mould cast and based on amulets made out of other materials.

Plaques are also found, decorated with one of about a dozen types of local flowers and plants with a translucent blue, green or grey ground. The technique is similar to that used in the production of mosaic vessels, with mosaic glass canes being fused together into a matrix. Other plaques were decorated with fish and assorted marine life. As with the floral tiles, these plaques have been found in many areas of Egypt, particularly in Alexandria and Bahnasa.

Vessels produced in Ptolemaic Egypt represented an important, highly decorative contribution to Hellenistic glass. They combined the mosaic technique with that of fusing inlays into the background. The inlays took the form of flowers, birds, fish and animals, all familiar from everyday Egyptian life.

By the end of the Hellenistic age glassmaking had become a widespread industry.

EGYPTIAN GLASS INLAY OF A ROYAL FIGURE, PTOLEMAIC PERIOD, 304–30 BC (H13.9cm/5½in)

The face and torso are made to imitate jasper while the crown is meant to resemble lapis lazuli. This inlay would have been used on either domestic furniture or a funerary object. (ABOVE LEFT)

GROUP OF MOSAIC GLASS FRAGMENTS, 1ST CENTURY BC–1ST CENTURY AD

Floral designs predominate in this group of highly decorative fragments. (ABOVE)

No longer was it confined to isolated areas and made exclusively for wealthy patrons. Factories had now been established all over the Mediterranean region, and glassware was slowly becoming available to many more people. The age of Imperial Rome was an important time for glass manufacture and continued many of the traditions of the Hellenistic glass factories, which in effect laid the foundations for the eventual success of Roman glass-making.

ROMAN GLASS

During the early Roman period the glass-making techniques of the Greeks were continued, but new colours were introduced. Production was increased to such an extent that glass objects were no longer luxuries, so it is not surprising that, despite its fragility, large quantities of Roman glass have survived. Much of this has acquired an attractive lustrous patination through burial, an iridescence much prized by collectors.

Glass became a medium through which a political message could be transmitted across the Roman Empire, as well as fulfilling a more mundane use as containers for oils and unguents. The finest glass vessels for court use were miracles of glass-cutting, either double-walled cage cups or cameo pieces, such as the famous Portland Vase. The new technique that made these objects possible was glass-blowing, which revolutionized the industry. Blowing into a mould meant that quantities of identical bottles could be produced. Colour came in to and went out of fashion, replaced by colourless glass on which the engraver or enameller could display his skills.

As the Roman Empire faded in the fifth century AD, so did fine glass-making: cutting deteriorated, and the metal itself was flawed.

GROUP OF VARIED ROMAN VESSELS, 2ND–4TH
CENTURY AD

———

*Each object displays a rainbow-like iridescence, the natural result of attack by
salts in the soil during burial.*

THE LYCURGUS CUP, 4TH CENTURY
AD (H16.5cm/6½in)

*Made in dichroic glass, this cage cup changes from
green to red in transmitted light.* (BELOW)

FINDS OF BURIED GLASS

The amount of Roman glass to have survived to the present day is surprisingly large – greater, in fact, than that of any other period including the late seventeenth and eighteenth centuries, when the Venetians were mass-producing glass for their own consumption and for the European export market. Archaeological excavations on Roman sites throughout the empire have produced large quantities of glass vessels but they are almost always in fragments. Intact vessels do survive, however, and have been retrieved from several sources, including abandoned and buried cities, most notably Pompeii and Herculaneum. The majority of these complete objects come from cemeteries, where they were buried as grave goods or functioned as cinerary urns containing the ashes of the deceased. In nineteenth-century

Europe, when towns which had been built over Roman settlements expanded outside their Medieval walls, builders unearthed quantities of glass from cemeteries along the old Roman roads.

Most buried Roman glass is covered by varying thicknesses of iridescence, which has the same rainbow-like effect on the surface of the glass as petrol on water. It is caused by a reaction between naturally occurring chemicals leached from the soil and those in the glass.

In a few extraordinary survivals, such as the Lycurgus Cup in the British Museum and the engraved purple situla (bucket-shaped container for holy water) now in the Treasury of St Mark's, Venice, glass objects may not have been buried but remained above ground as heirlooms and works of art. During the last hundred years, detailed study of surviving objects has rendered it possible to chart their history, development and distribution, even though some links are still missing.

SHORT HISTORY

After the death of Alexander the Great in 323 BC, his empire was divided among his generals, who founded separate 'Hellenistic states'. Simultaneously in the west, the Romans were becoming increasingly influential, expanding their frontiers so that by 201 BC they had defeated the Etruscans and conquered the entire western Mediterranean. During the second and first centuries BC they began to take over the Hellenistic states, conquered Gaul and invaded Britain. This expansion culminated in 31 BC, with the victory of Octavian over Mark Antony and Cleopatra at the Battle of Actium, which brought Ptolemaic Egypt, the last Hellenistic state, into the Roman Empire.

In 27 BC, Octavian, at the age of 36, became the emperor Caesar Augustus. He built up Rome to become a worthy centre for an empire that now extended across the

GROUP OF PURPLE- AND AMBER-
COLOURED GLASS, 1ST–4TH CENTURY
AD (Jug: H25cm/9¾in)

*The two small cups or bowls in the foreground date
to the 1st century AD and are more intense in colour
than the later vessels behind.* (LEFT)

TWO RIBBED BOWLS, ITALY/EASTERN
MEDITERRANEAN, SECOND HALF 1ST
CENTURY AD (Smaller: H5.9cm/2¼in)

These Rippenschalen, *decorated with spiralling
white threads, were marvered flush before the ribs
were formed by pincers.* (BELOW)

GROUP OF LATER
ROMAN GLASS,
2ND–4TH
CENTURY AD

*The group comprises a
pale bluish-green
candlestick*
unguentarium *and a
variety of flasks with
straight necks and
flaring mouths.*

entire Mediterranean and northward into central and western Europe. The newly established peace and the lack of frontiers enabled the uninhibited movement of peoples across the empire, and the merging of people, their products and their technical skills resulted in a common culture. It also promoted the rapid development of manufacturing and commerce on a large scale, as well as a great demand for luxury goods. In particular, the glass industry was transformed, with important glassworks being established in Rome and elsewhere in Romano-Italy.

Glass, like silver, gold and other materials, began to be used to promote the cult and image of the emperor throughout the Roman Empire and beyond its frontiers. Such was the purpose of the small press-moulded glass parade medallions bearing Julio-Claudian busts set in bronze frames. Even the Portland Vase, in the latest interpretation of its two scenes, is thought to be a piece of private imperial propaganda. On one side the figures are believed to depict Paris, his mother Hecuba and the goddess of love, Venus, the alliance with whom led to the fall of Troy, while on the other, Augustus, also with his mother, Atia, and the god of the sea, Neptune, symbolize the rise of Rome under Augustus and the new 'golden age'.

During the second century the Roman Empire reached its zenith under the emperors Trajan, Hadrian and Marcus Aurelius. Material prosperity ensured the uninterrupted expansion of manufacturing and trade. Prevailing glass fashions of the late first century continued into the second and glass became ever more widely available to all levels of society. Ordinary everyday domestic table and storage wares were for the most part made in plain, undecorated glass, and a wide range of shapes was produced: dishes and plates; bowls, beakers and cups; bottles, jars and jugs of all sizes; and occasionally ladles and spoons, lamps and inkwells. Gradually new types of mould-blown vessels were introduced, as well as new types of decoration on free-blown glass. The applied snake-threads and abraded or engraved geometric and figural motifs originating in the east were adopted and developed in the west.

The third century, by contrast, was a period of great political instability with several independent kingdoms being established within the empire. The glass produced, still mostly table and storage wares, displayed more regional variations. At the end of this period, stability was restored by Diocletian and maintained by Constantine the Great and his sons before the empire finally divided. Christianity was adopted as the official religion. The major centres of glass production survived but the standard shapes, decoration and colours employed changed. Thinly blown table and storage wares in pale shades of yellow, green, olive and brown predominated, but finer luxury wares were also produced, including gold glass and intricate cage cups (*diatreta*).

WALL FRESCO
OF A GLASS
BOWL FILLED
WITH FRUIT,
POMPEIIAN,
SECOND STYLE

*Peaches, quinces, green
almonds and twigs are
contained in the glass
bowl. The fresco is
from a bedroom in the
villa of Publius
Fannius Synistor, near
Boscoreale, Italy. The
villa was constructed
between 40 and 30 BC.*

MOSAIC GLASS
FISH, LATE 1ST
CENTURY BC–
1ST CENTURY AD
(L17.2cm/6¾in)

*Red and yellow
anatomical details
appear on the blue
fish, which was inlaid
into a tile and probably
decorated a wall.*

TECHNIQUES

During the Hellenistic period glass was produced at Rhodes, Alexandria, Sidon and other sites along the Syro-Palestinian coast. Contemporary writers have provided information as to the locations of the first Roman factories. In *De Geographica*, written at the end of the first century BC, Strabo mentions two major production centres in the eastern Mediterra-nean which had earlier traditions: Alexandria and Sidon. He also attributed the invention of glass itself to the Syro-Palestinian region. Pliny the Elder called Sidon '*artifex vitri*' (the maker of glass) and in his *De Natura Rerum* also mentioned the Campanian industry, remarking that the sand from the banks of the River Volturnus was excellent for glass-making. He went on to say that glass production spread from Italy into Spain and Gaul (excavations at Cologne have revealed evidence of a glasshouse there, dating from the mid first century AD).

Strabo also wrote that the glass-makers at Rome so reduced the production costs that 'a drinking cup could be purchased for a copper coin'. This reduction in cost and the speed at which glass became common in Rome are also mentioned by Seneca and Petronius. In the latter's novel, *Satyricon*, the nouveau-riche character Trimalchio complains that he would have preferred a glass cup to one of gold had glass not lately become so cheap and ordinary.

CAST GLASS

The first glass pieces in the reign of Augustus were cast and harked back to the late Hellenistic tradition. The glass factories which appeared in Romano-Italy were founded by Hellenistic glass-makers from the eastern Mediterranean, who may have come as freed men or prisoners of war. It is not surprising, therefore, that the laborious, slow and resultingly expensive techniques of casting and sagging mosaic and monochrome glass vessels continued to be employed. Tableware was still heavily influenced by ceramic and silver styles. Late Hellenistic forms included monochrome, flat-bottomed ribbed bowls, generally in golden-brown or greenish-yellow translucent glass, and small hemispherical mosaic-glass bowls, some with flared rims. The Romano-Italian industry continued to produce similar glass, but generally in much brighter colours that did not go out of fashion until AD 60 to 70. They even introduced new colours to their repertoire such as 'emerald' green and 'Persian' or 'peacock' blue. New mosaic patterns were introduced in which the colours, composition and configuration employed were far more complex and diverse, and a gradual shift away from copying pottery and metalwork created new forms more suited to the methods of manufacture.

Sixteen major classes of cast tableware have been identified and can be divided into six distinct groups based on their form, colour, mosaic patterns, decoration and refinement of technique:

1. CAST RIBBED BOWLS were either broad and shallow or hemispherical, and were produced both in mosaic and monochrome glass. Colours used were dark and cobalt blue, golden-brown and, more unusually, naturally coloured bluish-green, opaque white, opaque light blue and colourless. These bowls are of a higher quality than their Hellenistic precursors, with evenly spaced and shaped ribs producing a symmetrical pattern. The ribs were either long (extending underneath the vessel) or short, while their height and sharpness depended upon the length of time the blank was sagged in the furnace.

2. MOSAIC CAST BOWLS WITH APPLIED RIMS occur in four principal forms: broad shallow bowls, small hemispherical bowls or beakers, small concave-sided bowls and *pyxides* (covered, box-like containers), and

different canes arranged in triangular or wedge-shaped quadrants to create a symmetrical pattern) and meandering strips (huge cane sections formed from coloured strips wrapped around each other in serpentine, curvilinear or concentric strips).

3. CAST MONOCHROME VESSELS were usually made in one of four vivid translucent colours: emerald green, peacock blue, deep or cobalt blue, and aquamarine; very occasionally they came in golden-yellow or colourless. They were also made in opaque glass: white, light blue, red, several greens and even pink. They occur mainly as bowls and plates with carinated (ridged) profiles that were influenced by Arretine pottery, silver and bronze wares. Other forms include cylindrical *pyxides*, rectangular trays, stemmed *skyphoi* and boat-shaped vessels. Unlike the two preceding groups, which were formed by sagging a circular blank over a former mould, they were cast in the space between two or more interlock-

COLOUR-BAND AND GOLD-BAND BOTTLES, PROBABLY ITALIAN, EARLY TO MID 1ST CENTURY AD
(Taller: H9cm/3½in)

The colour-band mosaic bottle has a piriform body, and the small, globular gold-band mosaic bottle was formed from serpentine lengths of canes.

MOSAIC GLASS *PATELLAE*, PROBABLY ITALIAN, c.25 BC–AD 25
(Tallest: H4.3cm/1¾in)

Two cups comprise mosaic canes, one is cast in opaque red glass. (LEFT)

occasionally large bowls, flat plates and cylindrical dishes. They were made from lengths of striped and/or network (*reticelli*) canes with further network canes attached as rims. These canes were arranged into a variety of designs: parallel rows of composite canes (using no more than two or three different canes formed by fusing several coloured strips, often interspersed with single lengths of network canes), parallel rows of *reticelli* canes, short cane strips resembling parallel rows, quadripartite (usually a dozen

ing moulds. Once cold they required cutting and polishing on all surfaces.

4. CAST MOSAIC VESSELS were carinated or else they appeared as broad plates, broad shallow bowls, hemispherical bowls and beakers, tall beakers and occasionally *pyxides*. They were made from uniform small cane sections with tiny opaque and translucent elements in a translucent matrix, usually of purple, medium or dark green, or aquamarine, in a variety of patterns.

5. GOLD-BAND MOSAIC VESSELS were first introduced by Hellenistic workers in the form of *alabastra* and as bowls from Canosa. They were manufactured by one or more complicated techniques involving serpentine lengths of pre-formed canes of dark blue, purple, aquamarine, golden-brown, emerald green and gold sandwich glass. They occur in three basic shapes: lidded *pyxides*, globular and carinated bottles, and also small bowls, broad shallow bowls, hemispherical beakers and *trullae* (ladles).

6. COLOUR-BAND GLOBULAR BOTTLES comprised lengths or sections of pre-formed mosaic canes which were gathered on a blowpipe and inflated. This technique forms a link between casting and blowing.

BLOWN GLASS

The industry changed dramatically with the discovery that glass could be blown. The new process of inflation, developed during the second half of the first century BC, was quickly adopted so that within a hundred years factories had been set up throughout the whole Mediterranean basin and in almost every outlying Roman province. It was now possible to produce glass vessels quickly, cheaply and in large quantities and a wide variety of forms. Glass also had the advantage of being impermeable, easily cleaned and reusable, and, for the first time, it was treated as a substance in its own right, no longer dependent on other materials such as pottery and silver for its repertoire of shapes. Glass vessels were widely used for eating, drinking and storing all kinds of products from cosmetics to wine and oil. In fact, the new popularity of glass among all levels of society brought it into direct competition with the ceramics industry, even resulting in the demise of Italian thin-walled pottery. By the end of the first century AD free- and mould-blown glass had superseded other manufacturing techniques.

The exact location of the invention of glass-blowing still remains obscure. Indeed, it could have been made simultaneously at several centres along the Syro-Palestinian coast, one of the oldest glass-producing regions of the world. There must have been a period of experimentation before glass-blowing became well understood and accepted by glass-workers, but within twenty or thirty years of its invention all the requisite tools and techniques for the new process had been developed. For the most part, however, they have remained unaltered to the present day.

The earliest evidence comes from two Jewish sites. The first lies in the centre of the Jewish Quarter of the Old City of Jerusalem, where glass-working refuse was found discarded in a disused ritual pool, later covered by a paved road built by Herod the Great between 37 and 34 BC. Among the glass waste, which also included fragments of late Hellenistic conical and hemispherical cast bowls, were fragments of glass tubes. Some of these tubes appear to have had one end pinched shut before being inflated into oval bulbs. They were, of course, not 'true-blown' (with the use of a blowpipe) but they represent the period of experimentation that must have taken place before the technique was perfected. It was in a grave at Ein Gedi, an oasis on the western shore of the Dead Sea, that the earliest datable true-blown glass bottle was found. The cemetery itself went out of use in c.31 BC, shortly after Herod came to the throne in c.40 BC.

In essence, glass-blowing is simple, but it demands the greatest skill and dexterity. Usually a team of four workers with a master blower, or gaffer, at its head works together. The gaffer first gathers a gob of molten glass from a pot in the furnace on the end of the blowpipe, actually an iron tube about 0.9–1.5 m (3–5 ft) long. After slightly inflating the gob he manipulates it into the desired shape by blowing and swinging it, rolling it on a flat surface (the marver) or shaping it with tools. The partially blown piece may be reheated and blown repeatedly to modify its shape. It is then removed from the blowpipe and attached to a pontil rod with a seal of glass so that the vessel's neck and rim can be finished and handles applied. Finally, it is placed in the annealing oven. The process of annealing is of great importance, for although the act of blowing a vessel takes only a matter of minutes the finished article has to be cooled very gradually and evenly throughout its thickness over a day. This reduces the internal strains caused by the continual reheating and manipulation during manufacture that would otherwise cause the vessel to shatter spontaneously. Glass furnaces would probably have been enclosed in order to maintain the high temperatures required.

GROUP OF EARLY
ROMAN VESSELS,
1ST–2ND
CENTURY AD
(Tallest: H21cm/8¼in)

These vessels include a beaker, storage jar or cinerary urn, shallow 'pillar-moulded' bowl and square-handled bottle. (LEFT)

MARBLED GLASS
FLASKS, 1ST
CENTURY AD
(Tallest:
H14.8cm/5¾in)

This collection displays the variety of shapes and forms of marbled flasks that were used to contain perfumes and unguents. (RIGHT)

CAMEO GLASS

The most spectacular examples of luxury glass of the early Roman Empire are those made of cameo glass. This group includes the Portland Vase, one of the most famous of all antiquities. Glass cameos were made in imitation of objects in banded stone such as onyx, and as virtually the same techniques were employed to cut, carve and polish them it is probable that the same craftsmen worked with both materials. Because some inflation is involved in their manufacture cameos form a bridge between vessels made by casting and fully developed blown glass.

To achieve a two-layered blank, usually opaque white over dark blue, three different techniques were employed. Recent experiments in New York have shown that the Portland Vase was probably formed by the first technique: 'flashing'. Here a gob of blue glass is repeatedly dipped in molten opaque white glass to build up the outer layer before being further inflated. The second technique was 'casing', in which a gob of the inner glass (blue) was inserted into a previously cast, but still hot, cup-shaped blank of the outer glass (white). The two were inflated to the desired shape to ensure the two layers had fully fused together. In the third method the white overlay was applied as a thick coil around the vessels and then reheated.

The finished blank was then given to the gem-cutter, who with great precision and patience cut away the outer white layer to leave the decoration standing in relief against the dark background. On several plaque fragments as many as six superimposed layers were used to create a multi-coloured scene. The scenes on the 17 complete or reconstructable vessels and several hundred fragments which have survived include Egyptian and classical myths.

For a long time it was thought that cameo vessels were first manufactured in Alexandria, primarily because of the Egyptian city's strong lapidary tradition. However, most have been found in Italy, especially at Pompeii, and were presumably either made nearby or at Rome.

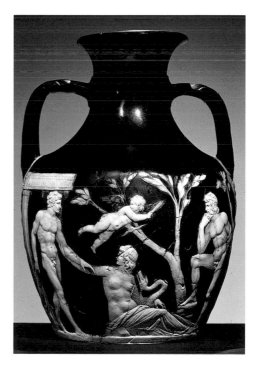

THE PORTLAND VASE, POSSIBLY
CARVED BY DIOSKOURIDES, 30–20 BC
(H24.8cm/9¾in)

MOULD-BLOWN GLASS

For a long time it was believed that the invention of mould-blowing preceded or was contemporary with that of free-blowing. Mould-blown vessels actually first appear some seventy years later on sites dating from *c.* AD 25 in both Italy and the Syro-Palestinian region. The technique of blowing a bubble of glass into a prepatterned mould was invented and developed when the prevailing fashion was for brightly coloured wares, usually decorated in high relief. These new mould-blown objects, therefore, probably initially served as cheaper alternatives to the more costly cut and cameo glass, and stone and metal vessels.

During the third quarter of the first century AD, Roman taste changed to colourless wares. Colourless glass – far more difficult and therefore more costly to produce – was increasingly used for facet-cut glass, which exploited its natural refractive quality. Mould-blown glass, which did not reflect light in the same way, decreased in popularity. During the later Roman period mould-blowing was used largely for utilitarian purposes to produce particular shapes or decoration, but no longer, it appears, purely for its own sake.

No moulds have survived from the first century AD, a lack of evidence explained by the high temperatures required to blow glass, which destroy the design on the inside of the mould. Moulds were made out of fired clay, which was fragile, or metal, probably a copper alloy, which could be melted down and reused. It is certainly possible that moulds were also made from stone and fine gypsum plaster.

Unlike clay vessels, glass does not shrink as it cools, and so it cannot be easily lifted out of its mould. To overcome this problem moulds were made in two or more parts. The joins between these mould pieces appear as vertical seams on the finished vessel and these were often incorporated into the designs of the better pieces. Usually there are two opposing seams (two-part moulds), but sometimes additional vertical mould pieces were added in order to accommodate the shape and facilitate the removal of the vessel from the mould.

The moulds were probably taken from originals of fired plaster, pottery, clay, wax or wood, which in turn could have been copied from another glass. From the archetype a clay or copper-alloy mould may have been made. Multiple moulds would have permitted simultaneous production of identical vessels at several centres and itinerant glass-blowers could have travelled throughout the empire supplying regional or specialized markets. Individual examples could also have travelled long distances as personal possessions (especially among the military) rather than as items of trade.

It is thought that the first glass mould-blowers came from Sidon in Syro-Palestine, but there is no direct evidence to confirm this. On the thumb rests of his free-blown two-handled cups Artas stamped both his name and that of his home town, 'Seidon', in both Greek and Latin characters. The Greek Aristeas is the only mould-blower who signed his work with his name and place of origin, which he arranged in three lines in a rectangle with handles.

Other names that occur on mould-blown vessels include those of Ennion, Jason, Meges, Neikaios, M. Licinius Diceus and C. Caesius Brigaddus. These names could refer to the original maker, the mould-maker or the glass-blower, or even appear as an advertisement for the workshop. On contemporary Roman moulded, decorated pottery it is generally accepted that the prominently displayed names were advertisements for the factory owner. Some of the names and inscriptions found on mould-blown vessels indicate that the makers or purchasers of the glass were of Levantine origin. For instance, Ennion is a Hellenized Semitic name, while the inscription, 'Let the buyer be remembered', which occurs on two signed Ennion cups, was a version of a blessing that is still found in contemporary Semitic languages.

It has long been assumed that these 'Sidonian' workers founded the Romano-Italian industry and that Ennion first worked in the Levant at Sidon, later migrating to northern Italy, perhaps near Aquileia or in the Po valley. At the former location he was thought to have produced jugs, *amphoriskoi*, hexagonal flasks and globular bowls and at the latter, cylindrical cups. Recent archaeological evidence is beginning to question this assumption but some sort of link must have existed between Syro-Palestinian glass-workers and those in Italy, though that connection is not yet fully understood.

TYPES OF VESSELS

First-century mould-blown glass vessels can be divided into six distinctive groups, although they all share many similar features in their decorative motifs and forms:

1. A series of cups and bowls bear Greek inscriptions, including drinking slogans: ΚΑΤΑΙΧΑΙΡΕ ΚΑΙ ΕΥΦΡΑΙΝΟΥ ('Rejoice and be merry'); complimentary greetings: ΕΥΦ ΡΑΙΝΟΥ ΕΦΟ ΠΑΡΕΙ ('Be glad that you have come'); and ΛΑΒΕ ΤΗΝ ΝΕΙΚΗΝ ('Take the victory'). Also inscribed are the names of the glass-makers Ennion, Jason and Meges. These vessels, dating to the early first century AD, are found in Italy and along the Syro-Palestinian coast.

2. This group, closely related to the first, was probably produced in the same factories and comprises small jars, jugs, flasks and *pyxides*. Often hexagonal in shape, they are decorated with a variety of emblems, the significance of which is no longer understood.

3. A group of naturally coloured cups and ovoid jars, decorated with scenes of gladiatorial combat, chariot racing and other sporting events, was in fashion for a comparatively short time. They were made in the third quarter of the first century AD and are to be found almost exclusively in the Roman legionary encampments of the Upper and Lower Rhine and in Britain. The most common are chariot cups with four

MOULDED CONICAL BEAKER, 1ST
CENTURY AD (H13.2cm/5¼in)

This piece was blown into a two-part mould. (RIGHT)

COLCHESTER CIRCUS CUP, MID 1ST
CENTURY AD (H7.9cm/3in)

*This vessel belongs to a group of cups depicting
chariot racing or gladiatorial combat.* (BELOW)

OPAQUE WHITE 'SIDONIAN' MOULD-
BLOWN *PYXIS*, 1ST CENTURY AD

*After removal from the mould the pyxis was
decorated with yellow and blue splashes. It forms a
link between early mould-blown vessels and free-
blown glass with splashed decoration.* (BELOW)

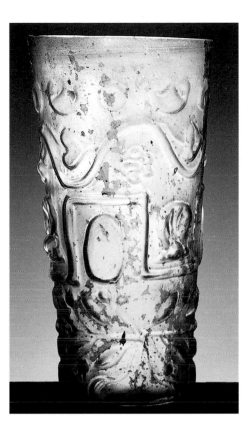

quadrigae (four-horse chariots), whose decoration is divided into three horizontal bands,
the topmost with the names of the chario-
teers and the lowest with chariots. The
middle band illustrates the familiar features
of the central barrier: turning posts, statues,
trophies, altars, obelisks and two types of lap
counters (eggs on spikes and seven upended
dolphins). A jar with gladiators from
Sopron in Hungary also bears a Latin
inscription by the maker, '*M. LICINIVS
DICEVS F(ECIT)*'. The four gladiators on the
vessel are each identified by name:
PETRAITES, PRVDES, ORIES, CALAMVS.
Petraites is mentioned on an inscription at
Pompeii and is known to have been fighting
during the reign of Nero.

4. Truncated conical beakers which appear
in the latter half of the first century AD are
found at Pompeii and Herculaneum. The
high-relief decoration on these vessels
includes almond-shaped, oval or circular
bosses arranged in staggered rows. They also
have combinations of the following motifs:

rings, peltas (shaped like a type of shield),
meanders, scrolls, shells, lattice, spirals,
foliage, bunches of grapes and vine leaves.

5. Truncated conical beakers with more
complex designs of mythological scenes are
contemporary with the preceding group,
and like them are found throughout the
empire. They typically have four figures,
male and female, representing gods and/or
the seasons and standing between columns
beneath leafy garlands or niches with
pointed pediments.

6. Prismatic bottles were introduced in the
first century AD and remained popular
through the second century. They were
made in thick, naturally coloured bluish-
green glass, the shade determined by the
amount of iron oxide occurring in the sand.
Most were blown into four-sided square or
rectangular moulds, but they can have as
many as 13 sides, while others are cylindrical. The neck and rims were formed afterward and the majority were given handles

that do not project over the sides or above
the rim so that they could be packed easily
and safely into boxes for transport around
the empire. Their transparency enabled their
contents to be easily checked. Often the
bases have moulded geometric designs,
generally concentric circles which might
represent trademarks or their contents.
Others have Greek or Latin inscriptions that
usually identify the maker, such as Fronti-
nus, who worked in northern France.

During the second and third centuries AD
the head flask, a new form of mould-blown
decorated ware, was introduced. A few blue
and opaque white examples, however,
would appear to date from the end of the
first century AD. In the form of a face, often
with curly hair, some head flasks represent
images of gods, Negroes or grotesques,
while others have two faces. Throughout
the rest of the Roman period jars, sprinklers
(for containing bathing oils), jugs and bottles were blown into moulds with ribs or
geometric designs and then further inflated
to reduce the sharpness of the decoration.

GROUP OF COLOURED AMPHORAE, ITALY/EASTERN
MEDITERRANEAN, 1ST CENTURY AD (Smallest: H9.2cm/3½in)

*Left to right: small purple amphora with blue handles, blue amphora and pale
purple amphora with yellow, white and blue splashed decoration.* (BELOW)

THE MASTERPIECE, COLOGNE,
SECOND HALF 3RD CENTURY AD
(H27.5cm/10¾in)

*This flattened bottle is the most spectacular known
example of applied snake-thread decoration with
white, red, blue and some gilded trails.* (ABOVE)

DECORATION
ON GLASS

The first century AD was a great
period of invention, innovation
and experimentation in the decorative techniques of glass. It must always be
remembered, however, that the majority of
Roman glass produced was naturally coloured and undecorated. Decoration could
be applied while the vessel was hot, or it
could be executed once the piece was cold.

APPLIED DECORATION

The decoration of a glass vessel while hot can
take several forms, the simplest being
applied trailing. The decoration is dropped
on to the vessel from a gob on the pontil and
drawn out into a trailed pattern, usually in
the form of a line spiralling around the body
either in the same or in a contrasting colour.
Multiple vertical or spiral ribs can be formed
and left in relief or marvered flush. Most
decorative are 'snake-threads': applied
coiled threads in either coloured (opaque
white, yellow, blue, red or gilt) or colourless
glass, left smooth or with tooled ridges and
arranged in serpentine trails across the bodies
of a wide variety of shapes. This technique
originated in the eastern Mediterranean and
reached its peak in the early third century in
the Cologne workshops. On a series of late
Roman animalistic flasks in the shapes of fish
or mice, applied trails were used to delineate
detailed anatomical forms. On other vessels,

thick coils were used to build up a cage
around the vessel.

Decoration could also take the form of
blobs and speckles. The hot, partially blown
vessel was rolled on a flat surface covered
with small chunks or fragments of glass. The
pieces picked up by the warm vessel were
either left in relief or marvered flush and
then sometimes spread by further inflation,
as in the northern Italian 'splashed' wares of
the first century AD. In the fourth century
individual blobs were dropped on to the
surface either in horizontal rows or in
triangular groups.

On other vessels, especially jugs dating
from the first and early second centuries,
press-moulded medallions, like those on
contemporary silver vessels, were attached
below the junction of the handle to the
body. Occasionally these medallions were
signed, such as the group with Medusa heads
inscribed '*AMARANTHVS F(ECIT)*' (from the
Burgundian region of France). Pre-formed

DIATRETA HANGING LAMP, c. AD 300
(D12.2cm/4¾in)

This colourless cage cup, cast or blown as a thick blank, has been wheel-cut. The attachments are of copper alloy. (RIGHT)

FACET-CUT OVAL DISH, ITALY, SECOND HALF 1ST CENTURY AD
(L27.3cm/10¾in)

*After the blank was made by the glass-maker (*vitrearius*), it was passed to the glass-cutter (*diatretarius*) to be facet-cut.* (BELOW)

POPULONIA BOTTLE, ITALY, LATE 3RD–EARLY 4TH CENTURY AD
(H18.4cm/7¼in) (BELOW)

applied decoration was also used in the late third and early fourth centuries, as attested by a small group of beakers with fish and shellfish applied in rows to the outside.

CUTTING AND ENGRAVING

During the latter half of the first millennium BC the art of cutting and engraving, grinding and polishing on glass and hardstone gems had been fully developed in such centres as Alexandria. The glass-cutter was now able to satisfy any demand made by prevailing fashions during the Roman period. Glass-cutters of the early first century followed traditional silver designs with floral and figural work in relief. During the second half of the first century AD deliberately coloured wares fell from favour and the finer glass was all intentionally decolourized by adding manganese oxide to the batch.

True colourless glass permitted a glass-cutter to take full advantage of the material's optical quality with faceting and engraving. The facets in the upper rows tend to be hexagonal while those toward the bottom are diamond-shaped. The glass-cutters also experimented with abstract patterns, lines and circles. During the second century they combined faceting with engraved details to create figural designs that were mythological (Diana and Actaeon) or scenic (Nilotic), or depicted pastimes (boar hunting, gladiatorial combat) or natural subjects (shellfish).

In the third century there appeared abraded or engraved geometric (shallow circular or oval faceting, crosshatching and interlocking circles) and figural motifs, sometimes with Greek or Latin inscriptions. In the late third to early fourth century a series of bottles was produced with pictorial maps of two coastal resorts – Baiae and Puteoli – generally found elsewhere and not at the two sites depicted on them. In the fourth century several new types of engraving and abrading appeared: straight lines with superficial strokes, broad abraded hollows and Greek inscriptions in double parallel lines. A very fine group of vessels, engraved with a variety of motifs, also exists, and was probably made in Rome.

CAGE CUPS

Cage cups, or *diatreta*, were *the* luxury vessels of the late Roman Empire. Cast or blown thick-walled blanks, sometimes incorporating coloured bands, were laboriously carved in relief and then undercut, leaving the decoration usually in the form of a net or cage attached to the main body of the vessel only by small, hidden bridges.

A recently discovered hemispherical bowl, with its bronze attachments still in place, shows that at least just before it was buried it was used as a hanging lamp. These vessels would have taken months to produce and were therefore available only to the uppermost echelons of society.

PAINTED GLASS AMPHORA, EASTERN
MEDITERRANEAN, AD 50–70 (H20cm/8in)

*From Kerch (Panticapeum) in southern Russia, this
amphora is decorated with vine tendrils, ivy leaves
and birds.* (RIGHT)

GOLD SANDWICH GLASS PORTRAIT
MEDALLION, ITALY, 3RD CENTURY AD
(D3.6cm/1½in)

*The gold glass medallion contains the portrait bust
of a young woman, with the Latin inscription 'To
Anatolius, with thanks'.* (BELOW)

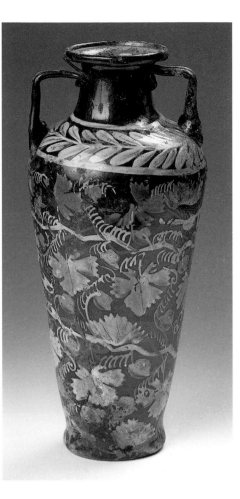

GOLD GLASS

The earliest known Roman gold sandwich glass, dating from the third century, is a group of portrait medallions in which the gold leaf was attached to a disc of blue glass. The decorated gold leaf is protected by a second layer of colourless glass. Minute incisions were made to reveal the background colour, creating an effect of light and shade. Those of the fourth century belong to the bases of bowls and cups and were, for the most part, made in colourless glass. They bear portraits, or mythological, Jewish and Christian scenes, often with painted details. Most have been preserved in the catacombs outside Rome, where they were deliberately broken away from the vessel. Those with wedding scenes were probably broken and inserted into the plaster after being used for the last time at a funerary banquet.

PAINTED GLASS

Painting, like mould-blowing, was one of the techniques introduced to northern Italy by Syrian workers during the first century AD. Bright colours were painted on to the outside of the vessel and then fired in the furnace so that the colours would fuse to the glass. The western examples, usually bowls, are decorated with naturalistic scenes (birds in foliage and other wildlife) and even a battle between pygmies and cranes. In the east another group, both painted and gilded with mythological and genre scenes, is known from Begram in Afghanistan. These are closely related in shape to tall faceted glasses and were probably made in the same first-century factory.

Painting in unfired pigments is rare and usually occurs on the underside of the vessels, where it is best protected. A group of

first-century lidded jars from Cyprus has painted on the underside of each lid a design in dark outline, sealed by an applied whitish ground. In the case of the Paris Plate (late third or fourth century) in The Corning Museum of Glass, some colours were superimposed over others.

LATE ROMAN
AND EARLY
BYZANTINE
GLASS

In AD 330 Constantine the Great transferred the capital of the new Christian Roman Empire from Rome to Constantinople, the site of ancient Byzantium. The empire was divided into east and west and this division became permanent after the accession in AD 395 of Honorius in the west and his brother Arcadius in the east. This, however, did not result in the end of the manufacture of Roman glass. In the west some styles continued into the tenth century, when potash from bracken and other woodland plants replaced soda as the source of alkali used in glass-making. The greatest impact on the industry, however, was due to the fifth-century barbarian invasions of Europe. The cultural break which resulted brought a decline in production standards, such as an increase of bubbles and black impurities in the metal and less varied decoration.

In the east the break came with the Arab conquests in the early seventh century. Little is known of glass-making during the early Byzantine Empire, though glass-workers were actively encouraged. In AD 337 Constantine exempted glass-makers (*vitrearii*) and glass-cutters (*diatretarii*) from all public levies and Theodosius II, a century later, discharged them from paying personal taxes. The high-quality colourless and deliberately coloured glass of the third and fourth centuries was replaced with naturally coloured green or bluish-green vessels. These containers were also made in yellow and brownish metals and were often decorated with dark blue glass.

New shapes were introduced, such as flasks with very tall necks and amphorae and unguent flasks with elaborate handles. To this group belong the ostentatious *balsamarii*, with double or quadruple compartments buried under two- or three-tiered handles, and thick serpentine animalistic vases, in the form of a droopy-tailed quadruped supporting a spherical or cylindrical body surrounded by a cage made up of tiers of zigzag trailing. Lamps were made in three new forms: beakers with deep kicks (indentations), cups with three handles applied at the rim so that they could be suspended and conical lamps, often decorated with applied blue blobs arranged in horizontal rows or in triangular groups.

Mould-blown jugs, flasks and jars were made with a variety of geometric patterns. Perhaps the best known are hexagonal or octagonal jugs and squat bottles from the sixth and early seventh centuries, decorated with both Christian (crosses, lozenges or scenes from the Bible) and Jewish (menorah, shofar and incense burner) religious motifs. These vessels were sold to pilgrims in Jerusalem, where they were used as containers for holy oil or holy water.

In the sixth century Jewish glass-makers are said to have moved to Constantinople, probably bringing with them the technique of gold sandwich glass that was used to great effect in church wall and vault mosaics. There is also a small group of tiles with geometric patterns in gold leaf; these are believed to have come from a Byzantine monastery in Syria and have been assigned dates ranging from the sixth to twelfth century AD.

MOULD-BLOWN JUG WITH STYLITE SAINT, EASTERN MEDITERRANEAN, 5TH–7TH CENTURY AD (H14.2cm/5½in)

The Stylites were a group of saints – the most famous being Saint Simeon Stylite – who spent many years on top of a column in prayer and meditation. (LEFT)

FLASK WITH CHRISTIAN SYMBOLS, *c.* AD 300–400 (H.7.6cm/3in)

The dark yellowish-brown pilgrim flask is decorated in blue trails with a cross and two X's. (BELOW)

GROUP OF LATE AND POST-ROMAN GLASSES, 4TH–6TH CENTURY AD

The handled large and small jars, bottles and double cosmetic tubes are much cruder in design and execution than earlier pieces.

ISLAMIC GLASS

*B*etween the decline of Roman glass-making and the emergence of the Venetians as the world's leading glass-makers at the end of the Middle Ages, the finest glass vessels were made in Islamic countries, such as Egypt and Iran. Islamic glass-makers inherited some of the forming and finishing techniques of the Romans and the Sassanians. They developed these, rediscovering 'lost' Roman techniques, and made at least one original discovery: the manufacture of lustre.

Between the eighth and the eleventh centuries, glass-makers in Egypt and western Asia produced a wide range of luxury objects. In addition to vessels painted with lustre, they made mosaic glass, gold glass and glass with decoration cut on the wheel. The most accomplished wheel-cut vessels are made of colourless glass and are decorated in relief. A handful of these have a coloured overlay, most of which has been removed to create a cameo effect.

In the thirteenth and fourteenth centuries, glass-makers in Syria and Egypt decorated drinking vessels, mosque lamps and other objects with gold and enamel. Although the Romans produced gilded and enamelled glass, and enamelled glass was made by Byzantine and western European craftsmen in the Middle Ages, Islamic glass-makers used gilding and coloured enamels more extensively than any of their predecessors or contemporaries are known to have done.

THREE ISLAMIC VESSELS OF CONTRASTING FORMS,
9TH–16TH CENTURY AD

———

A flared wine glass, 16th century; jug, 9th–10th century, and drinking horn,
12th–13th century. Each displays signs of burial, but has ornamental
details that are still quite apparent.

SASSANIAN GLASS

The Sassanian dynasty ruled a large part of western Asia from AD 224 to 651. From their power base in southern Iran, the Sassanians conquered the rest of Persia, Mesopotamia (Iraq) and what are now Afghanistan and parts of Soviet Central Asia.

In the seventh century, the Sassanian Empire was overwhelmed by the Arabs. Indeed, within a hundred years of its proclamation by the Prophet Mohammed in AD 622, the Islamic religion had spread from the Arabian Peninsula to the Indus River in the east and to Morocco in the west. Later, it reached parts of Southeast Asia and sub-Saharan Africa. The Arabs conquered three regions with long traditions of glass-making: the Syro-Palestinian area, Egypt and the Sassanian Empire.

Although most Sassanian glass in public and private collections has no archaeological pedigree, there is little doubt that much of it comes from Iran. Finds from excavations support this conclusion, and also show that similar glass was made in other parts of the Sassanian Empire, such as Mesopotamia. Although experts have a fairly clear impression of what Sassanian glass looked like, the shortage of finds from archaeological excavations has resulted in only a sketchy knowledge of its chronology.

Sassanian glass is usually pale green and transparent, or almost colourless but with a grey or brownish tint. Glass-makers formed their products by blowing and (less frequently) by casting and pressing. They decorated them both while the glass was hot (by manipulation and the application of blobs or trails) and while it was cold (by cutting, grinding and polishing).

Sassanian glass decorated while it was hot includes cast or pressed pendants, ribbed vessels blown into moulds, vessels with applied trails or knobs made by pinching the wall and pulling the glass outward, and conical lamps with blue blobs. Lamps with blue blobs, however, were also produced in the Roman Empire, and it is not clear how many of the vessels that are said to have been found in Iran were actually made there.

The best-known types of Sassanian glass decorated while they were cold are cups made from thick-walled blanks, which were finished by cutting, grinding and polishing. Most of these objects belong to one of three groups. In the first, the decoration consists of an overall pattern of circular or hexagonal facets. Among the datable (or apparently datable) objects of this type are two finds from Japan: a bowl from the tomb of Emperor Ankan (ruled 531–5) in Osaka Prefecture, and a similar vessel in the Shōsōin at Nara, which is believed to have been donated by Emperor Shōmu in 752. In the second group, the decoration is cut in relief and consists of circular or oval bosses, often with concave surfaces. The last group comprises vessels decorated with bands of geometric ornament, in which broad, shallow cuts and facets predominate.

ISLAMIC GLASS

Until recently, the study of Islamic glass was based almost wholly on stylistic criteria, aided by information from a handful of archaeological excavations. Foremost among the excavations was the German work at Samarra, Iraq, between 1911 and 1913. Samarra was the capital of the Abbasid caliphs from 836 to 883, and for years scholars mistakenly assumed that almost every find from the site was made in the period of caliphal occupation. More recently, excavations have taken place at Fustat in Egypt, Siraf in Iran, Serçe Limani in Turkey and other sites. These discoveries, when published in full, will add considerably to the history of Islamic glass-making.

7TH AND 8TH CENTURIES

In the first two centuries after the Islamic conquest, glass-makers in the Syro-Palestinian region, Egypt and the Sassanian Empire followed existing traditions.

Applied decoration on glass occurred widely. In the Syro-Palestinian region, for example, glass-makers adapted the Roman tradition of forming double or quadripartite cosmetic tubes by reducing their size and placing them on the backs of glass 'camels' made by manipulating the hot glass and adorning them with trails. These 'dromedary flasks' were extremely popular, and examples have been found in Egypt, Syria, Iraq and Iran. Another type of glass consisted of spherical bottles and egg-shaped flasks decorated with blobs of glass which, while still hot, were drawn out in four simple movements until they resembled a stylized animal skin on a flat surface.

At the same time, glass-makers experimented with pincered and stamped decoration. The former was achieved by using an instrument resembling tongs, the two jaws of which were decorated with the same pattern so that the design – often an inscription or a zoomorphic motif – can be seen on the inside and outside of the vessel.

The most common variety of early Islamic stamped glass consists of small, disc-like 'coin weights', which were produced in Egypt in huge numbers between the eighth and fifteenth centuries, and were used to establish the weight of coins. The earliest known Islamic coin weight bears the date (AH) 90, which is equivalent to parts of AD 708–9. Stamped appliqués bearing the name of the ruler or official who issued them and the capacity that they guaranteed were attached to vessels used to measure quantities of specified substances. Meanwhile, glass-makers in western Asia produced vessels with stamped medallions adorned with Sassanian-type human heads, birds and winged horses.

8TH TO 11TH CENTURIES

Glass continued to be widely used, and the repertoire of objects made in this period ranges from simple utilitarian vessels, some with applied or mould-blown ornament, to exquisite luxury items. Among the latter are scratched and wheel-cut glass, mosaic glass, gold glass and lustre glass.

COSMETIC
BOTTLE, 8TH–
9TH CENTURY
(H10.7cm/4¼in)

*This small bottle,
which is surrounded by
a 'cage' of openwork
trails, rests on the back
of a camel. Bottles of
this type were made in
the Near East during
the early Islamic
period.* (RIGHT)

SCRATCH-
ENGRAVED
BOTTLE,
PROBABLY 9TH
CENTURY
(H20.7cm/8in)

*The finely drawn
decoration, which is
characteristic of this
group of early Islamic
vessels, was probably
scratched with a
diamond.* (FAR RIGHT)

objects are cut in what is known as the
'bevelled' style, in which outlines are cut on
a slant, often with no distinct second plane
forming the background.

The bevelled style was employed by
craftsmen in many media and enjoyed

The group with scratched decoration
consists of vessels with geometric or vegetal
ornament, sometimes accompanied by
inscriptions, which was scratched with a
point, possibly a diamond. Many such
vessels are of translucent deep blue glass.
Recently, new light was thrown on the
chronology of these vessels by the discovery
of examples in the 'crypt' of the Buddhist
temple at Famen, west of Xian in Shaanxi
Province, China. The crypt was sealed in
874 and the glass, therefore, very probably
belongs to the ninth century.

Wheel-cutting, which had been practised
extensively by the Sassanians, was revived in
the ninth century. Between the ninth and
eleventh centuries, it was used to produce a

wide variety of objects, which include some
of the finest achievements of Islamic glass-
making. The wheel-cut glass of the Abbasids
and their successors has been divided into
several styles. The most elaborate Abbasid

widespread popularity. A second style consists of relief-cutting, in which the background is removed, leaving the ornament in
high relief. Numerous examples of relief-cut
glass have been found in northern Iran.

VESSEL WITH
PINCERED
DECORATION,
8TH–9TH
CENTURY (D10cm/4in)

*Objects with pincered decoration
were made in Egypt and the Near
East. They display inscriptions, or animal
or geometric motifs.*

BOTTLE WITH RELIEF-CUT
DECORATION, POSSIBLY NISHAPUR,
9TH–10TH CENTURY (H14cm/5½in)

THE CORNING EWER, LATE 10TH OR
EARLY 11TH CENTURY (H15.5cm/6in)

*This is the supreme example of Islamic cameo glass
and one of the greatest achievements in glass-cutting
of any period or culture. A colourless parison was
covered with a translucent green overlay. Most of
the overlay was then cut away, leaving the
ornament in relief.* (LEFT)

GOLD-GLASS BOTTLE, LATE 8TH
CENTURY (H15cm/5⅞in)

*This rare bottle, in the collection of the British
Museum, is highlighted with blue enamel. Made in
either Egypt or Syria, it was reputedly found at
Nishapur.* (RIGHT)

Scholars often associate the style with the
city of Nishapur, which flourished under the
Persian Samanids, who ruled it from 874 to
1001. It is highly unlikely that Nishapur was
the only place of production (if, indeed,
relief-cut glass was made there at all), and
other centres almost certainly existed elsewhere in western Asia and in Egypt.

A logical extension of wheel-cutting is
the cameo technique, in which a layer of
glass of one colour is applied to all or part of
an object of a different colour. Subsequently, most of the outer layer is removed
by carving, grinding or cutting, leaving the
decoration in relief. Cameo glass was made
by the Romans, but there is no reason to
suppose that production persisted into the
Islamic period; it is much more likely that
the technique was rediscovered in western
Asia or Egypt in the ninth or tenth century.

Islamic cameo glass usually combines
translucent coloured decoration with a colourless background. It may be divided into
two groups. In the first, blobs or trails of
coloured glass were applied to the vessel and

marvered. After the vessel had been
annealed, the overlays were cut on the
wheel. This 'padding', or 'marquetry', technique allowed the glass-maker to produce
objects with small, isolated designs. It was
inadequate, however, for schemes which
took up the entire surface. For these, the
vessel had to be almost completely covered
with an overlay. Objects of this type are
rare; perhaps the earliest surviving piece is a
bottle in the David Collection, Copenhagen, decorated with birds and vegetal

motifs. Other examples include a ewer at
The Corning Museum, a bowl in the
Museum of Islamic Art, Cairo, and a cup in
the L.A. Mayer Memorial Institute for
Islamic Art, Jerusalem.

The Corning Ewer shares with one or
more of the other vessels the occurrence of
printies (decorative cut patterns) on the
bodies of the birds and animals and the
presence of nicks or hatching on the raised
outlines. The ewer, the pitcher and the cup
reputedly came from Iran and their forms

MOSAIC-GLASS
PLATE, PROBABLY
9TH CENTURY
(D20.2cm/8in)

*The Romans formed
vessels by assembling
and fusing coloured
rods, and it is likely
that Islamic glass-
makers rediscovered it
in the 9th century.*

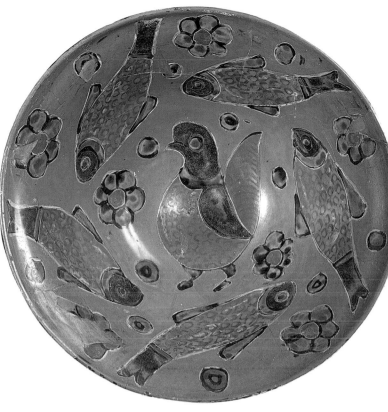

BOWL WITH
LUSTRE
DECORATION,
9TH–10TH
CENTURY
(D15.8cm/6¼in)

*The technique of
making lustre was
probably discovered in
Egypt in the 8th
century. Islamic
craftsmen used it to
decorate both glass and
ceramics.* (LEFT)

have numerous parallels among glass, pottery and metal objects from the same country. The Corning Ewer, however, is closely similar to rock crystal ewers attributed to workshops in Fatimid Cairo, one of which bears an inscription that names the Caliph al-Aziz Bi'llah (ruled 975–96).

Among the finds from Samarra are fragments of multi-coloured mosaic glass tiles. Finds from other sites include plates, cups and perfume bottles, many of which are formed from canes with 'bull's-eye' motifs (that is, with a cross-section that has a circle of one colour at the centre and an outer ring of another colour).

Gold glass was extremely rare and only seven examples are known to exist. Three of these objects are enlivened with spots of blue enamel. None of the objects is dated or comes from a datable archaeological context. An estimate of their date, therefore, depends on stylistic criteria. A fragment in the David Collection in Copenhagen and another fragment in The Corning Museum of Glass are each decorated with bands of

pseudo-Kufic (an early form of Arabic) writing. The closest parallels for the writing occur in tenth-century manuscripts and none of the other motifs is inconsistent with the belief that the vessels were made in the tenth century. The fragment in the David Collection came from Iran and a bottle in the British Museum is similar in shape to Iranian wheel-cut glass; a western Asiatic provenance, therefore, is probable.

Another rare type of Islamic glass is decorated with lustre. This shiny effect was obtained by painting the surface with a suspension of finely powdered copper oxide or silver oxide and then firing the object in oxygen-free conditions at a temperature of about 600°C (1112°F). This temperature was high enough to fuse the metal to the surface but insufficient to soften the glass and cause the object to collapse. The lustre is generally translucent and it may be brown, yellow, green or red, used either singly or in combinations. Islamic potters used the same technique to decorate glazed earthenware.

Lustre painting seems to have been

applied to glass before it was applied to pottery. A fragment of lustred glass from Fustat bears the name of a governor who ruled in 772–3, and a fragment in the Islamic Museum at Cairo is dated (AH) 163 (AD 779–80). A bowl at The Corning Museum has an inscription stating that it was made at Damascus between AD 718 and 814. Unfortunately, it is not known whether Damascus was the only place of manufacture or how long lustre painting on glass was practised before and after the dates on these objects.

11TH TO 13TH CENTURIES

Among the most distinctive products of this period are bottles, bowls, zoomorphic vessels (usually birds), gaming pieces and other objects formed from coloured glass and decorated with opaque white trails. The most popular colours for the base glass were deep purple, blue and green. The vessels were decorated by winding an opaque white trail around the parison and marvering it until the trail was flush with the surface.

Occasionally, after reheating, the parison was further inflated in a mould, which produced a ribbed effect. Frequently a feather-like design was made by dragging the trail up and down with a pointed instrument. In a few cases, the trailed decoration is accompanied by gilding.

Glass with mould-blown decoration continued to be made. Among the best-known objects are bottles, jugs and other coloured glass vessels that are often attributed to northern Persia. Among the decoration are ribs, made by inflating the parison in a ribbed dip mould, pattern moulded honeycomb and lattice motifs, and vegetal ornament and inscriptions.

The relief-cut and cameo vessels from the eighth to eleventh centuries represent the high point of Islamic glass-cutting. With one exception, the 'Hedwig beakers', later products were not cut in relief and the decoration tends to consist either of facets or of linear motifs. The progressive simplification of the ornament is well illustrated by the finds from Serçe Limani, where the wheel-cut decoration consists mainly of geometric, vegetal and animal motifs.

The most puzzling group of Islamic glass (if, indeed, it is Islamic) consists of the Hedwig beakers, so called from the legendary association of one example with St Hedwig (d. 1243), the patron saint of Silesia. Most of the 13 Hedwig beakers that survive intact were preserved in church treasuries or aristocratic collections in Europe; fragments of four others have been found in excavations in Italy, the Soviet Union and Germany. All these beakers are of colourless or almost colourless glass, often with a smoky topaz tint, and decorated with lions, griffins or eagles in high relief. Hedwig beakers are widely believed to be Egyptian and of the twelfth century, but neither the place of manufacture nor the date is certain.

13TH AND 14TH CENTURIES

The most spectacular Islamic glass of the thirteenth and fourteenth centuries is decorated with gilding and brightly coloured enamels. The gilding was either applied as

gold leaf or as a fine powder suspended in an organic medium. The enamel consisted of powdered glass, or frit, applied in paste form. The heat required to fuse the enamel (normally 650–750°C, or 1202–1382°F) was lower than the temperature at which the vessel would have begun to soften (about 850°C, or 1562°F). The same technique was used to produce enamelled metal objects and overglaze-painted mina'i earthenware.

Gilt and enamelled glass was made in Syria and Egypt. In 1930, Swedish scholar Carl Johan Lamm divided it into six groups, for which he suggested dates and places of manufacture, such as Aleppo, Raqqa and Damascus. Lamm's attributions were almost completely intuitive and his chronology leaned heavily on two historical events: the

sack of Aleppo and Raqqa by the Mongols in 1259–60 and the capture of Damascus by Timur (Tamerlane) in 1400. Later, Danish scholar P.J. Riis proposed a revised classification, which dissociated several of Lamm's groups from supposed places of manufacture, for which no positive evidence exists.

It is sometimes said that gilt and enamelled glass was a natural development from the lustre-painted glass of an earlier period. This hypothesis can neither be proved nor disproved. What seems to be certain, however, is that some of the earliest gilt and

BOTTLE, PROBABLY 12TH CENTURY (H25.8cm/10¼in)

The body was blown in a two-piece mould. The decoration includes an Arabic inscription which means: 'And to the owner happiness and blessing and joy'. (ABOVE LEFT)

HEDWIG BEAKER, PROBABLY 12TH CENTURY (H14cm/5½in)

Beakers of this type are among the most puzzling objects in the history of glass-making. Although closely similar to one another, they are unlike any other vessels made in the Middle Ages and their origin and date are open to debate. (ABOVE)

enamelled vessels are decorated with figural and architectural scenes, the style of which suggests that they were made in northern Syria in the early thirteenth century. After about 1250, figural scenes declined in popularity and were replaced by heraldic devices and, later, by lotus blossoms, phoenixes and other motifs of Chinese inspiration. In the fourteenth century, the forms decorated with gilt and enamel included bottles, basins, jugs, beakers and cups. Hanging lamps, used to illuminate mosques, survive in large numbers, especially in Cairo.

15TH TO 19TH CENTURIES

TURKEY. Glass was produced in Turkey under the Ottoman dynasty, which emerged in the fourteenth century and ruled from Constantinople (modern Istanbul) between 1453 and 1923. No examples of fifteenth- to eighteenth-century Ottoman glass have been recognized, although evidence for its manufacture exists in manuscripts. The *Surname-i Humayun*, for example, an illuminated manuscript of about 1582, depicts a parade of glass-makers in

IRAN. Knowledge of glass-making in Persia (Iran) during the Safavid dynasty (1501–1736) and its successors is comparable with that of Turkey under the Ottomans. Between the sixteenth and eighteenth centuries, records show that Venetian glass was exported to Persia, and Safavid manuscripts are illustrated with paintings which include bottles and tumblers used for wine. The Ali Qapu pavilion in Isfahan, which was restored by Shah Abbas I (ruled 1588–1629), contains ceilings with cavities that once held displays of glass. It is not clear, however, how much of this glass was made locally and how much was imported.

The French traveller, Jean-Baptiste Tavernier, who visited Persia in the mid seventeenth century, noted that Shiraz had several glass factories, and many eighteenth- and nineteenth-century glass vessels from Iran are believed to have been made there. They include plain and mould-blown sprinklers, bases for *kalians* (the bottoms of water pipes, or *huqqas*) and flasks.

INDIA. During the Mughal period (1526–1857), glass was widely used by the imperial family and the nobility, as inventories, accounts by European visitors and commercial records attest. The *A'in-i Akbari*, compiled in 1596–7, notes the manufacture of glass in Bihar and near the Mughal capital at Agra. Later sources mention factories outside the Mughal Empire, in Gujarat and other parts of western India. Most of the surviving Mughal glass, however, dates from between the late seventeenth century and the mid nineteenth century. The eighteenth-century vessels include numerous bell-shaped *huqqa* bases, and contemporary products from Gujarat include *huqqa* bases and flasks made in imitation of imported Dutch gin bottles. Many of these objects have elaborate gilt and enamelled decoration. A completely different type of glass was produced at Kapadvanj, near Ahmadabad in Gujarat. It consists of blue, green, brown and purple sprinklers, tumblers and spouted vessels. Production ceased in the nineteenth century, when English lead glass captured the local market.

GILT AND ENAMELLED VASE OR DISH, MID 14TH CENTURY (D31.8cm/12½in)

Vessels of this shape are rare in the Islamic world. This is the only known gilt and enamelled example. It belongs to a group of objects with similar decoration that were made in Syria in the 14th century

Islamic gilt and enamelled glass enjoyed a high reputation far beyond its countries of origin. The fourteenth-century Italian travellers Niccolò of Poggibonsi and Giorgio Gucci noted the quality of the decorated glass of Damascus, and examples of Syrian glass were exported to Europe and China.

The deportation of the glass-makers of Damascus by Timur in 1400 supposedly put an end to the production of gilt and enamelled glass in western Asia. Brascha of Milan, who visited the Holy Land in 1480, recorded that the captain of his ship 'sent from Jaffa to Damascus glass vessels from Murano'. The golden age of Islamic glass-making had ended. Venice was a major supplier, and later Islamic glass was strongly influenced by imports from Europe.

Constantinople. In the seventeenth century, Ewliya Celebi (d. 1679) recorded that there were glass factories established in four districts of Constantinople. The best-known Ottoman glass of the eighteenth century consists of colourless vessels which are decorated with opaque red marbling.

During the reign of Selim III (1789–1807), a local artisan returned from Murano and set up a glass-making workshop at Beykoz, 17.5 km (11 miles) north of Constantinople. This factory produced objects with gilt or gilt and enamelled decoration, in which floral motifs were prominent. Another workshop, opened at Incirköy in 1846–7, produced *Çesm-i Bülbül* glass, which is decorated with stripes of opaque white and translucent coloured glass.

MEDIEVAL GLASS

*I*n *Europe most vessels produced between the fifth and the seventh centuries were of bubbly, pale green glass. A few objects were formed in moulds and others were decorated with trails, but the majority of 'Dark Age' vessels were plain.*

The manufacture of luxury glass began again in the eighth century. Between the ninth and the eleventh centuries, the most sought-after vessels made in western Europe were either brightly coloured, sometimes with gold leaf appliqués, or decorated with reticella rods.

In the twelfth and thirteenth centuries, Byzantine glass-makers continued their tradition of producing coloured cubes for mosaics. They also made vessels with gilded or gilded and enamelled decoration, medallions with religious scenes, and perhaps painted window glass.

In western Europe the most significant development in the twelfth century was the extensive use of pictorial stained-glass windows. In the late thirteenth and early fourteenth centuries, glass-makers in Italy, on the upper Rhine and in other parts of Europe began to produce colourless glass which they made by carefully selecting the raw materials or decolourizing the batch with manganese.

The number of glasshouses and the use of glass vessels increased substantially in the fourteenth and fifteenth centuries. Technology, however, seems to have stagnated until, in the second half of the fifteenth century, the Venetians perfected colourless cristallo and established themselves as the continent's leading producers of luxury glass.

INTRODUCTION

The glass of the Middle Ages falls into two groups that have been studied and appreciated in significantly different ways. The first group consists of stained-glass windows, of which thousands survive. Their study has generated a vast literature and in many regions the history of stained glass is known and recorded in considerable detail.

The second group comprises glass vessels, which until recently suffered from almost total neglect. This is because relatively few Medieval glass vessels have survived above ground. Consequently, knowledge of the range and quality of the glass vessels of the Middle Ages depended not only on the objects themselves but also on descriptions and illustrations in Medieval manuscripts. In Germany, this information was summed up in 1933 by Franz Rademacher in his monograph *Die Deutschen Gläser des Mittelalters*. In France, James Barrelet performed a similar service in *La verrerie en France de l'époque gallo-romaine à nos jours*, which appeared in 1953. Elsewhere, existing evidence usually failed to attract attention.

Today, the situation is changing rapidly. Archaeology (which has already transformed the study of Roman and pre-Roman glass, and is poised to do the same for early Islamic glass) is changing the way scholars think about the use of glass in the Middle Ages. Excavations in all parts of Europe, from Paris to London, and from Plzeň in Czechoslovakia to Lübeck and Konstanz in Germany, have transformed contemporary scholarship of Medieval glass-making. This transformation has been apparent to readers of specialized literature for some time; it became apparent to a wider public in 1988–90, thanks to two spectacular exhibitions. First, in 1988, the Rheinisches Landesmuseum in Bonn and the Historisches Museum in Basel mounted *Phönix aus Sand und Asche, Glas des Mittelalters*: a breathtaking exhibition that focused attention on Medieval glass-making in Germany and adjoining regions. Later, in 1989–90, the

Musée des Antiquités de Seine Maritime in Rouen organized *à travers LE VERRE, du môyen âge à la renaissance*, an equally eye-opening exhibition of Medieval and Renaissance glass made in France.

The effect was startling. The conventional picture based on Rademacher and Barrelet disappeared. Instead of row upon row of pale green *Waldglas* ('forest glass'), there was glass of almost every size and description. Suddenly, there was a wealth of information, mostly provided by archaeologists, that revealed a new image of later Medieval glass-making: versatile, innovative and technically assured. Venetian glass-makers led the world in the year 1500; but a century earlier there was very little the Venetians could have taught the glass-makers of southern Germany, and a hundred years before that glass-makers in eastern France were making mould-blown objects of superlative quality.

Despite these advances, however, information on Medieval glass-making is still very patchy; next to nothing is known about the glass used in Constantinople, the largest and richest city in Europe, and knowledge of glass in Spain and Portugal, as well as in Greece and the Balkans, is minimal. There are several reasons for the gaps. Firstly, after

the conversion of Europe to Christianity in the late Roman and early Medieval periods, very few objects were placed in graves (one exception to this 'rule' occurred in southwestern France in the twelfth and thirteenth centuries, when glass bottles occasionally accompanied burials). Secondly, documents show that in many parts of late Medieval Europe broken glass was collected for recycling; glass, therefore, is significantly underrepresented in the archaeological record. Thirdly, most of the glass made in Europe after the ninth or tenth century contains potash as a flux. This makes it more vulnerable to decay, especially in acidic soil conditions, than Roman glass (which contains soda or natron).

CLAW-BEAKER, PROBABLY 6TH CENTURY (H16.7cm/6½in)

The 'claws' were made by applying blobs of hot glass to the wall and inflating them. (FAR LEFT)

CONE BEAKER, 5TH–EARLY 6TH CENTURY (H23.5cm/9¼in)

This beaker was found in Yorkshire, but made on the Continent. (LEFT)

THE DARK AGES

At the end of the Roman period, glass-making declined in western Europe. In Italy, for example, the production of luxury glass ceased in the late fourth century. After this date, most vessels were made of bubbly, pale green glass. The repertoire of forms was considerably reduced and the occurrence of glass on archaeological sites declined sharply (in the fifth- to sixth-century cemetery at Vicq, southwest of Paris, only fifty of the two thousand graves contained glass vessels). The repertoire of techniques, too, declined: engraving, wheel-cutting, gold sandwich glass and dichroic glass disappeared. Almost every early Medieval glass object was blown (but rarely in a mould and seldom with applied ornament); casting disappeared. In the sixth or seventh century, a workshop functioned at Torcello, near Venice, and this produced cubes for making mosaics, bottles and goblets with a hemispherical or half-ovoid bowl, stem and splayed foot. More or less contemporary workshops in central Italy made goblets, bottles and drinking horns, some of which are decorated with coloured trails. Similar goblets were also made in southern France.

In the Rhineland and the area between the lower Rhine and the Loire, as in Italy and southern France, the production of glass continued in the Dark Ages. Here, too, however, the quality of the products declined. The glass makers' repertoire became restricted to beakers, bottles, bowls and hemispherical cups, most of which were made of transparent green or brown 'naturally' coloured glass. The most elaborate form was the *Rüsselbecher*: the trunk- or claw-beaker, which has superimposed rows of 'trunks' or 'claws' made by applying blobs of hot glass that melted the wall of the vessel at the point of attachment; the fact that they melted and pierced the wall allowed the blower to inflate not only the vessel but also the blobs, which were pulled out and manipulated with tools.

In the seventh century, glass-makers in western Europe began to expand their repertoires. *Reticella* canes, which are made by twisting together two or more rods of different colours, came into use. They were applied to vessels datable to between 550 and 650 at Valsgärde and Eketorp in southern Sweden, and they were used elsewhere to decorate beads and pendants.

In England, the occurrence in seventh-century contexts of distinctive vessels that do not appear on the Continent suggests that one or more workshops existed in Kent, perhaps near the king's residence at Faversham. At the same time, English and Irish jewellers and metalworkers used (and perhaps made) mosaic-glass canes and coloured enamels to produce polychrome ornament. In northern England, however, Benedict Biscop was compelled to import Continental craftsmen to glaze the windows of his church at Monkwearmouth in 674, and Cuthbert of Lindisfarne also turned to the Continent for glass-makers in 685.

THE CENTRAL AND LATER MIDDLE AGES

Throughout this period, glass-makers in the Mediterranean regions and in northern Europe used different types of furnaces. The 'southern' or 'Mediterranean' furnace was a circular structure with three superimposed chambers. The lowest chamber contained the fire. Above this was a chamber with several 'glory holes', through which the gaffers gathered molten glass from the pots and inserted partly formed objects for reheating. The uppermost chamber was used for annealing. The earliest European evidence for furnaces of this type is an illustration in a manuscript of Hrabanus Maurus's *De Universo*, which was made in 1023 and is preserved at the abbey of Monte Cassino, in Italy. Although larger, Italian furnaces of the fifteenth and sixteenth centuries were of the same general type. The 'northern' furnace, on the other hand, had the three chambers on the same level. The shape and the arrangement of the chambers were variable. According to Theophilus, a Benedictine monk sometimes identified as Roger of Helmarshausen (active in the early twelfth century) and the author of a manual known as *De Diversis Artibus* ('On the Various Arts'), the three chambers formed a composite furnace with a single fire trench running through it. A *c*.1420 Bohemian manuscript of the *Travels* of Sir John Mandeville, on the other hand, contains a drawing of a glass furnace in which the heat was transmitted laterally to the subsidiary annealing oven.

9TH TO 11TH CENTURIES

From the first stage of Medieval glass-making luxury items and very little else are extant. In western Europe, most evidence comes from trading settlements ('emporia'), which passed on luxury goods from one kingdom to the next, and from monasteries. One of the best-known emporia is the Viking site at Birka in Sweden. Here, the custom of placing objects in the graves of the dead survived longer than it did in western

BEAKER WITH *RETICELLA* CANES, 9TH OR 10TH CENTURY (H10.3cm/4in)

This beaker, found at Birka in Sweden, belongs to a group of early Medieval glass vessels decorated with coloured trails and reticella rods. Although such rods decorated jewellery in the 7th century, their occurrence on Medieval vessels seems to be restricted to the 9th and 10th centuries. (ABOVE)

Europe. Among the finds from the cemeteries at Birka is a beaker decorated with blue and yellow trails, and with vertical ribs made by applying spirally twisted *reticella* canes of opaque white, yellow and colourless glass. These canes, which resemble the spirally twisted canes of the Hellenistic and early Roman periods and which appeared in the seventh century, seem to have enjoyed wide popularity in the eighth and ninth centuries. Examples have been found in many parts of Europe, from Scandinavia to southern Italy. Other luxury objects that had a wide distribution were blue glass vessels decorated with applied gold triangles. Fragments have been found at Helgö in Sweden, Niedermünster and Paderborn in Germany, Dorestad in the Netherlands and Liège in Belgium. At present, these luxury glasses raise more questions than they answer: where were they produced; were they made in one place, then traded and used at others; who owned the finished products?

Other types of glass from northwestern Europe and the British Isles include beads, 'slick stones' or 'linen smoothers' (disc-shaped objects that may have been used for smoothing textiles), and mirrors, which occur in ninth- or tenth-century contexts at Birka and Haithabu in Denmark.

Very little early Medieval window glass survives and scholars depend on written information for much of what is known about the origins of 'stained' glass (none of which, in this period, was actually coloured by staining). Stained-glass windows are composed of pieces of colourless and coloured glass, usually with details painted in vitreous pigments, held together by strips of lead, known as 'cames', and set in an iron frame. The *Liber Pontificalis*, the official chronicle of the Popes, records the presence of coloured-glass windows in several churches in Rome during the pontificate of Leo III (795–816). Among the earliest remains of Medieval coloured windows are the numerous colourless, blue, green, amber and red fragments found at Jarrow in northeastern England, which date from some time between 682 and *c*.870. None of them bears any trace of painting. Indeed,

there is no unequivocal evidence for painted windows until the ninth century, when the *Life of Ludger* recounts the miracle of a blind pilgrim who spent a night at the saint's tomb, and the next morning 'could distinguish the images painted on the windows', and when the Irish monk Sedulius Scotus described a decorated window in the bishop's palace at Liège, Belgium, in about 840. Although fragments of Carolingian painted window glass survive, the earliest windows preserved *in situ* probably date from about 1095 and are in Augsburg Cathedral, Germany.

Among the monastic sites where glass has been found in ninth- and tenth-century contexts are Farfa in central Italy, which yielded fragments of painted window glass, San Vincenzo al Volturno in central Italy, where window glass, lamps and other vessels were manufactured, and Glastonbury in England. All three were Benedictine abbeys, and one wonders what role the Benedictines may have played in the preservation and dissemination of glass-making technology. (The earliest records of glass-making in Venice, from 982 and 1083, are documents connected with the Benedictine abbey of San Giorgio Maggiore.)

Very little is known about glass in the Byzantine world. In fact, the aspect of Byzantine glass-making about which the most is known is the production of tesserae,

GILDED AND ENAMELLED BOWL, PROBABLY 10TH CENTURY (H17cm/6¾in)

The bowl appears to be black, but is in fact a deep reddish purple. The decoration consists of seven medallions, each containing figures from classical mythology and legend. Inside the rim is a pseudo-Kufic inscription. It is probable that this object was made in or around the 10th century.

the pieces of coloured glass from which mosaics are made. Huge numbers of tesserae were required for the mosaics that covered the walls and ceilings of Byzantine churches, and (to a lesser extent) for icons known as 'portative-mosaics' or 'micro-mosaics'. Mural mosaics may have been made continuously in the Byzantine world since late antiquity, but there is no record of major construction or of the renovation of existing buildings at Constantinople between the early seventh century and the later eighth century. Among the greatest achievements of Byzantine mosaicists after this apparent hiatus are the mosaics in the cathedral of Hagia Sophia (tenth to thirteenth century) and in the Kariye Camii (thirteenth century), both at Constantinople, and in the monasteries of Daphní (*c*.1100) and Hosios Loukás (eleventh century) in Greece. The earliest surviving portative-mosaic was produced in the 1060s.

Mosaicists from Constantinople – and their tesserae – were in demand even outside the Byzantine Empire. The Moslem caliph, Hakam II (ruled 961–76), employed Byzantine craftsmen to decorate the mihrab of the Great Mosque at Cordoba, in southern Spain; in the Ukraine, Prince Vladimir of Kiev (ruled *c.*978–1015) imported Byzantine craftsmen to build and decorate with mosaics the Church of the Tithe in his capital; and tesserae, if not mosaic-makers, were probably imported to decorate churches in Sicily and Italy.

The treasury of St Mark's Cathedral in Venice contains a number of glass vessels, which were brought from Constantinople in 1204. They include a bowl of purple glass decorated in coloured enamels with figures from classical mythology. Similar figures occur on Byzantine ivories of the tenth and eleventh centuries, and there is little doubt that the bowl, too, is Byzantine. Among the other glass vessels are hanging lamps and a cup. They are made of colourless glass and have relief-cut ornament consisting of discs, some of which have pointed bosses at the centre. One lamp has an eleventh-century gilt bronze mount. Some scholars maintain that the objects were made in Constantinople, others suggest that they are Sassanian.

12TH TO MID 13TH CENTURIES

Knowledge of Byzantine glass of the twelfth and thirteenth centuries is somewhat better. In the early twelfth century, Theophilus recorded that 'Greeks' made gilded and enamelled glass. In all probability, Theophilus was referring to a group of bottles and other forms made of dark blue and other coloured glass, with gilded or gilded and enamelled decoration. The most common form is a cylindrical bottle with a short, narrow neck. Regardless of the form, the decoration consists of combinations of friezes, squares and roundels, which contain vegetal motifs, birds, animals and geometric elements. All of these objects are closely similar and it seems likely that they were made at one place in one relatively short period. Most of the places where the glass

was found are in the eastern Mediterranean, but single specimens have been found at sites in Italy, the United Kingdom and the Soviet Union. Paphos in Cyprus, Corinth in Greece and Novogrudok in the USSR have yielded both examples of gilded and enamelled vessels and evidence of glass-working, and all have been proposed as places where the objects were made. It is also possible that the workshop that produced them was situated in Constantinople.

Byzantine craftsmen may also have produced painted-glass windows in the twelfth century. Two churches at Constantinople (Istanbul) – the Kariye Camii (the former St Saviour in Chora, rebuilt between 1077 and 1081, and extensively remodelled in the early twelfth century) and the Zeyrek Camii (the Church of the Pantocrator, built in 1120–36) – contained painted-glass windows. It is not yet clear, however, whether the windows were installed when the churches were built, or are additions dating from the Latin occupation of the thirteenth century. The case for regarding them as Byzantine is strengthened, perhaps, by the twelfth-century windows decorated in Byzantine style at the monastery of Studenica in Yugoslavia.

Byzantine glass-makers continued to produce tesserae for mosaics. These included pieces which have a layer of gold leaf sandwiched between two layers of glass. The same technique was employed to make a group of square plaques 9cm ($3\frac{1}{2}$in) across, made of yellowish glass that is decorated with triangles of gold leaf arranged in a cruciform pattern and covered with a colourless overlay. The National Museum at Damascus, Syria, has eight such plaques, which are said to have been found at Ma'arat an Nu'man, 50km (30 miles) north of Hamáh. The plaques appear to come from a single building, and are variously dated between the sixth and the twelfth centuries. The motif they bear has analogies in a twelfth-century palace, now known as the Tekfur Saray in Istanbul (Constantinople), and also in the cathedrals of Monreale and Cefalù in Sicily. It is likely, therefore, that the objects date from the twelfth century and are Byzantine in origin.

BOTTLE, *c.*12TH CENTURY
(H17.5cm/7in)

This bottle was found at Ellwangen, Baden-Württemberg, Germany. It is made of yellowish-green glass. The parison was decorated with opaque red trails. It was then inflated to the desired size and shaped with tools, after which the yellowish-green trails were added.

In western Europe, glass began to have a wider currency in the twelfth century. It was used for both vessels and stained-glass windows. In many parts of western Europe, glass occurs on sites of all kinds for the first time since the Roman period. The range of forms, however, was small. In Germany, the excavated material includes beakers and biconical flasks with trailed decoration. In France, bottles with tall necks were common in the south, while in the north the most widespread form was a cup with a ribbed body and a hollow conical foot.

Mirrors also became more common. The frequency of literary references to mirrors, first attested in the ninth century, greatly increased in the late twelfth century. The first recorded transactions involving mirrors date from shortly afterward; in 1215, for example, Arnulf of Basel in Switzerland sent glass to Germany for making mirrors. A recent study suggests that Germany in general and Nuremberg in particular were regarded as Europe's leading mirror makers in the later Middle Ages, and mirror cases that were made of ivory, wood and leather had a wide distribution.

The most significant development in the twelfth century, however, was the emergence of stained glass as a vehicle for communication. In the mid twelfth century, the Gothic system of construction made possible the installation of windows that were larger than those used in the preceding Romanesque structures. Wall painting, previously employed to teach Bible stories to the largely illiterate population, declined, and pictorial stained glass began to take its place. Twelfth-century stained glass was designed to fill the tall, narrow lancet windows that were a hallmark of early Gothic architecture. The designs were either large single figures or series of small narrative scenes. They employed a wide range of coloured glass and extensive grisaille painting. Among the most important twelfth-century windows are those installed by Abbot Suger (1081?–1151) in the abbey church of St-Denis, Paris.

Early Gothic cathedrals have a tall nave flanked by lower aisles. Rows of windows run along the aisles, there is often an upper row of windows at gallery level and (above the level of the roofs of the aisles) the wall of the nave has a third row of clerestory windows. Beginning in the early thirteenth century, detailed narrative windows were restricted to the windows in the aisles, where they were most easily seen, and windows with single figures were placed in the gallery and clerestory. In general, windows were larger than before and glaziers became concerned with the quality of illumination in the building. Ambitious programmes of windows were designed. Colours became deeper and this effect was sometimes heightened by applying a coat of grisaille to the back of the glass. A freer, more naturalistic style of rendering the figures emerged. Notable examples of early thirteenth-century stained glass include windows in the cathedrals at Bourges, Reims and Amiens in France. The windows of Ste-Chapelle,

THE ALDREVANDIN BEAKER, SECOND HALF 13TH CENTURY–EARLY 14TH CENTURY (H13cm/5⅛in)

This beaker, in the British Museum, takes its name from its Latin inscription: MAGISTER ALDREVANDIN ME FECI[T] *('Master Aldrevandin made me').*

which Louis IX constructed in his palace in Paris in 1243–8, are an outstanding glazing programme from the middle of the century.

Two methods – known as the cylinder and crown techniques – were used in the Middle Ages to manufacture the flat glass used by glaziers. The cylinder technique, which was known in Roman times and is described by Theophilus, involves elongating the parison by swinging it. The end of the parison is then reheated, opened and widened so that the parison now consists of an open-ended cylinder. This is detached from the blowpipe and annealed. After annealing, the cylinder is transferred to a preheated furnace, where it is split open longitudinally and flattened. The last stage in the process is the annealing of the sheet. Although the crown technique is often said to have originated in Normandy in the fourteenth century, from around 1200 it

seems to have coexisted with the cylinder technique. Crown glass is made by spinning the parison after an opening has been made at one end of it. The centrifugal force generated by the spinning converts the hollow parison into a flat disc which, after annealing, can be cut into panes of the desired shape.

LATE 13TH AND 14TH CENTURIES

In many parts of Europe, glass-making developed rapidly in the late thirteenth century. The most widely discussed vessels made in this period are enamelled beakers known as the Aldrevandin Group. The group takes its name from a celebrated example in the British Museum, which bears the inscription: MAGISTER . ALDREVANDIN . ME . FECI[T] ('Master Aldrevandin made me'). It is decorated in coloured enamels with coats of arms. Other beakers in the group are decorated with religious figures, secular scenes, birds and animals, and heraldic motifs. An example from Tartu in Estonia is signed by MAGISTER PETRVS and at least two beakers from London are signed by MAGISTER BARTOLOMEVS. In the early 1980s, beakers of this type were rare; now almost every large-scale urban excavation in Germany or Switzerland produces fragments.

The Latin inscriptions, Christian figures and heraldry are all emphatically European. The method of decoration (enamelling), on the other hand, is not; at the time, as far as glass is concerned (the Aldrevandin Group apart), it was largely – perhaps exclusively – Islamic. For this reason, scholars such as Carl Johan Lamm looked to the eastern Mediterranean for the origins of the Aldrevandin beakers. Indeed, Lamm developed the hypothesis that they were made for Western patrons (hence the Christian iconography) in Jerusalem (hence the Islamic technique). More recently, they have been attributed to Venice, partly because of their rarity at sites in the Islamic world and partly because of references in the Venetian archives to local production of painted beakers in the thirteenth century. The archives also demonstrate a close connection between Venetian glass-makers and the eastern Mediterranean. References to the importation of Levantine cullet begin in 1233, and in 1255 the first mention is made of imported *allume catino*. This was a soda-rich plant ash, obtained mainly at Tripoli in Lebanon and Alexandria in Egypt, which became the standard fluxing agent for generations of Venetian glass-makers.

This 'Venetian hypothesis' may be correct. There is, however, a strong German-speaking lobby which points out that fragments of only three Aldrevandin beakers have been found in Italy (at Verona, Lucera and Palermo), but dozens north of the Alps. Perhaps there is room for both hypotheses. Stylistically, the objects are far from homogeneous and it may be that the Aldrevandin Group was made in Venice and imitated (conceivably by Venetian émigrés) at one or more places in Germany. Again, chemical analyses might come to the rescue, enabling scholars to determine whether the group was made either in one locality or in several.

There is little doubt that the skills existed in German glasshouses to accomplish the work. Indeed, recent excavations have revealed the high level of expertise achieved in parts of central and western Europe in the late thirteenth and fourteenth centuries. One of the largest collections of such material was found at Konstanz in Baden-Württemberg. Here, excavations yielded thousands of fragments of late thirteenth- to fourteenth-century glass vessels. While the majority of the fragments were made from transparent pale green *Waldglas*, which was often decorated with prunts, many others are colourless and have prunts, ribs and dark blue trails. Thanks to its rich archives and the reflected glory of the products of its Renaissance glass-makers, Venice dominates the literature about late Medieval glass. Nevertheless, the best pieces from Konstanz and other sites in Germany and adjacent regions rival the finest objects attributed to Venice.

The glass-makers of Switzerland and southern Germany had never made glass of this quality before, and their achievement raises the question: where did they acquire

CUP, 13TH–EARLY 14TH CENTURY (H6.7cm/2⅝in)

This is the finest surviving example of a group of cups with applied decoration and a single ring handle that were probably made in Germany at around the turn of the 13th century.

BEAKER WITH APPLIED ORNAMENT, MID 13TH–MID 14TH CENTURY (H10.2cm/4in)

The vertical trails on this beaker were attached to the bottom of the wall, drawn up to the top and then extended downward in a series of loops. It was probably found at Speyer in Germany.

BEAKER WITH APPLIED DECORATION, LATE 13TH–EARLY 14TH CENTURY (H15cm/5⅞in)

This elegant beaker belongs to a group of objects that combined simple blue trails with pinched colourless trails and were found in Switzerland and southern Germany. Its workmanship is remarkable.

PRUNTED BEAKER, 13TH OR 14TH
CENTURY (H12.6cm/5in)

*Until recently, colourless beakers with prunted
decoration were attributed to Venice. In the last few
years, however, similar objects have been found in
Switzerland and southern Germany, and it now
appears that colourless glass may have been made
both in northern Italy and immediately north of the
Alps at around the turn of the 13th century.* (RIGHT)

BOTTLE, PERHAPS 13TH CENTURY
(H11.6cm/4⅝in)

*Ribbed bottles had a wide distribution in the 13th
and 14th centuries. This example may have been
made in Italy or Yugoslavia.* (BELOW RIGHT).

BEAKER, 13TH OR EARLY 14TH
CENTURY (H9.5cm/3¾in)

*Such beakers have been found at sites on the upper
and middle Rhine, and in adjacent areas. Similar
vessels occur in Italy and Greece.* (FAR RIGHT)

BOTTLE, *c.*14TH CENTURY (H22.7cm/9in)

*The ribbed decoration on this bottle was made by
blowing the parison into a dip-mould before
completing the inflation.* (ABOVE)

their expertise? In 1982, the accepted view was summed up in the exhibition in Venice *Mille anni di arte del vetro a Venezia,* and in the catalogue that accompanied it. This view took a number of archaeological discoveries and arranged them in a logical sequence of events. The first discoveries had taken place in Germany and neighbouring countries and consisted of drinking vessels and other forms of greenish *Waldglas,* sometimes decorated with prunts. None of these early finds was from a closely datable context and consequently they were attributed, somewhat vaguely, to the fourteenth and fifteenth centuries. The second discovery took place in Greece in 1937. This consisted of the remains of two glass-makers' workshops in the Byzantine city of Corinth. Among the vessels made at Corinth were prunted beakers, beakers with vertical ribs and cups with mould-blown patterns of diamonds, ovals and hexagons. Coins and other finds from the vicinity of the workshops led to the conclusion that they operated in the eleventh and twelfth centuries. The prunted beakers and other objects, therefore, were assumed to be typical Byzantine products of the period between about 1000 and 1150. A third group of discoveries came from Italy, where vessels very like the finds from Corinth began to appear in the 1960s, as Medieval archaeology became established. Whenever these objects were found in datable contexts, they belonged to the thirteenth and fourteenth centuries. Although many of them are made of transparent yellowish glass, the best are almost colourless: a quality achieved by the careful selection of raw materials and, later, by the addition of manganese to the batch.

The conclusion seemed obvious: by one means or another, the Byzantine tradition of glass-making found at Corinth was introduced to Italy in the twelfth or thirteenth century, flourished there and was transmitted across the Alps in the fourteenth century. Indeed, a connection between Constantinople and Venice already existed in the form of thirteenth-century stamped glass medallions decorated with scenes from the lives of Christ and the Virgin, the Evangelists, apostles and saints. The medallions fall into two groups: those made of translucent glass with images of Orthodox saints and Greek inscriptions, and those made of opaque red glass that have inscriptions in both Greek and Latin. The first group is generally thought to be from Constantinople, while the second group seems to be Venetian.

Today this conclusion is open to doubt. It appears now that the finds from Corinth are both untypical of the Byzantine world and difficult to date (it is not clear that the eleventh- and twelfth-century coins were associated with the remains of the glassmakers' workshops sufficiently closely to provide a date for the glass). It is known, too, that the finds from Italy, Switzerland and Germany form a broadly coherent group, which probably came into production in the thirteenth century and quickly developed regional characteristics that allow scholars to separate the glass made in one area from the glass made in another. Thus, while there is still a great deal to be learned about European glass in the thirteenth and fourteenth centuries, it is reasonable to suppose that in all probability it was *not* inspired by Byzantine glass from southern Greece; that the

DISH WITH APPLIED DECORATION, MID 13TH–MID 14TH CENTURY (D25.6cm/10⅛in)

This spectacular dish was probably found in Germany, where fragments of other such vessels have come to light. Similar objects were made in southern France.

driving force behind the new developments was not necessarily Venice; and that glassmakers in Germany were every bit as skilful as their Italian counterparts. The prunted beaker – the standard drinking vessel in Italy, Switzerland and Germany in the thirteenth century – could have been developed in any one of those countries, although at present Italy may have the strongest claim to be the area in which these developments began.

One of the largest collections of Medieval glass from a closely dated archaeological context in Italy was found at Tarquinia, 75km (45 miles) northwest of Rome. The glass vessels, which were buried with other refuse from a wealthy household in about 1390, consisted almost exclusively of tableware: bottles for serving wine and a variety of prunted, ribbed and mould-blown beakers. The other objects included urinals (perhaps used mainly for uroscopy, a form of medical diagnosis practised in the Middle Ages), large bottles for storing liquids and part of a still (which could have been used either for distilling or for alchemy). There was very little window glass at Tarquinia, but written evidence shows that by now

glass panes had replaced oil-soaked parchment in the homes of the affluent Italians.

One thirteenth-century innovation that may have been Italian was the production of colourless plaques and medallions decorated on the back with gold leaf bearing scratched designs. Among the earliest datable examples are plaques which decorate the pulpits designed by Nicola Pisano at Pisa (in 1260) and Siena (in 1267–8), and two discs in the tomb of Pope Clement IV (d. 1268) at Viterbo. The method of making these plaques was described in the fourteenth century by Cennino Cennini in a manual entitled *Il libro dell'arte*. The artist prepared a piece of colourless glass by rubbing it with charcoal and lye, and rinsing it. Next, he painted the surface with glair (an adhesive made from white of egg) and applied the gold leaf. The design was scratched with a needle and, finally, the object was backed, usually with a material painted black. The popularity of these forerunners of *verre églomisé* declined in the fifteenth century with the rejection of the International Gothic style in favour of more realistic images.

The influence of Italy is evident in the Balkans. Dubrovnik, on the Adriatic coast,

BEAKER WITH APPLIED DECORATION, BEFORE 1470 (H9.5cm/3¾in)

This beaker was used as a reliquary in the chapel at Grambek, Schleswig-Holstein, Germany. (ABOVE)

GOBLET, LATE 14TH CENTURY (H17.8cm/7in)

This goblet was found in 1949 in the Church of the Augustinians at Rouen, France. During the demolition of the church, which had been badly damaged during the Second World War, workmen discovered it in a niche, which had been closed with a stone. Records show that it was customary in Normandy for masons to conceal glasses of wine in the buildings where they worked. (ABOVE RIGHT)

GERMAN BEAKER WITH APPLIED DECORATION, 14TH–EARLY 15TH CENTURY (H14.1cm/5⅝in) (RIGHT)

became both a producer of glass and a major distributor of vessels imported from Venice. The glass-makers of Dubrovnik, as revealed in Medieval documents, came from Venice and other parts of northeastern Italy. Among the archaeological sites that have yielded material of this period are Split and the fortress at Belgrade, both in Yugoslavia. The finds from these sites and the information preserved in archives suggest that Venetian glass-makers may have produced glass specially designed to appeal to local taste in the Balkans during the fourteenth and fifteenth centuries.

Elsewhere in Europe, distinctive local styles began to emerge. Finds from Plzeň and Prague in Czechoslovakia, for example, include few of the forms that were current in Germany. The most common drinking vessel used in the mid to late fourteenth century was a tall, slender flute decorated with numerous, very small prunts. In the Netherlands, Belgium and northern France, on the other hand, the repertoire of drinking vessels was dominated by cups standing on tall conical feet and goblets with ribbed bowls, tall, slender stems and low conical or bell-shaped feet. In southern France, colourless cups or lamps, sometimes decorated with deep blue trails of glass, were common; they were produced at La Seube, one of the few Medieval glasshouses that have been excavated in this region.

Glass-makers were active in England by 1240 but the earliest excavated glasshouses, in Surrey and Sussex, date from about 1330. They produced bottles, drinking vessels, lamps, urinals and vessels used for alchemy and distillation. Excavations in London, Southampton, Winchester and elsewhere have revealed the presence of both *Waldglas*, presumably produced locally, and colourless glass, including beakers of the Aldrevandin Group, imported from the Continent.

The art of stained glass continued to develop in the late thirteenth and the fourteenth centuries. Windows in Gothic churches became even larger than before, and now consisted of vast expanses of glass divided into vertical panels by mullions. In addition, glaziers took advantage of changes

KRAUTSTRUNK, LATE 15TH–EARLY
16TH CENTURY (H11.8cm/4⅝in)

*This is an outstanding Krautstrunk ('cabbage
stalk') beaker. The form evolved from the prunted
beakers of the Middle Ages and is so called because
of its resemblance to the stalk of a cabbage after the
leaves have been detached. This beaker is unusual,
being made of colourless glass with colourless, green
and blue prunts.* (FAR LEFT)

GOBLET WITH APPLIED RIBS AND
OPENWORK FOOT, EARLY 16TH
CENTURY (H14cm/5½in)

*This goblet, formerly in the Strauss Collection, is
an excellent example of the late Medieval vessels
that were made in the tradition of the ribbed beakers
of the 13th and 14th centuries.* (LEFT)

in glass technology. They were able to use
thinner sheets of glass (which weighed less
and could be assembled with fewer cames),
glass flashed with a second colour through
which a design could be scratched and the
deep yellow glass that was produced by the
application of silver stain.

In France, the Netherlands and England,
grisaille windows, consisting mostly of clear
glass with decoration painted in grey,
became increasingly popular, and in general
the appearance of stained glass was lighter
than before.

In Germany and Italy, however, the rich,
multi-coloured windows continued to be
made as in the thirteenth century. The
tendency toward greater naturalism continued. Figures were carefully modelled and
scenes contained a profusion of plants and
animals. The naturalistic trend reached its
apogee in the International Gothic style
between about 1380 and 1430. Outstanding
examples of windows decorated in this style
exist in Bourges Cathedral in France and
York Minster in England.

15TH AND 16TH CENTURIES

According to the written evidence, the
number of glasshouses and the use of glass
vessels increased in the fourteenth and
fifteenth centuries. However, although the
industry itself certainly expanded, glass
technology was going through a period of
stagnation. Colourless glass appears to have
been less common than before, and there
were fewer innovations. Indeed, glass of this
period is dominated by green and yellow-
brown forest glass. Tooling was widely
used; prunts and simple mould-blown patterns are common.

In Germany, beakers with broad, flat
prunts (the so-called *Krautstrünke*, or 'cabbage stalks') became the standard type of
drinking vessels in the late fifteenth and early
sixteenth centuries. Some were used as
reliquaries, and their wax seals with stamps
or scratched inscriptions provide valuable
evidence for the dates of particular forms. A
late development of the prunted beaker, for
instance, has a trailed openwork foot, and

this development is also seen on beakers with
vertical ribs. During the sixteenth century,
some of these drinking vessels assumed wild
and extravagant forms as well as types of
decoration, from overgrown flutes to *Krautstrünke* to claw-beakers.

In France, three types of drinking vessel
predominate in this period, and all of them
originated earlier. They are: beakers, which
may have vertical or swirled mould-blown
ribs; glasses with a conical or egg-shaped
body and a hollow foot, many of which
have moulded or applied decoration; and
goblets. Flasks and bottles also occur in large
numbers. Some of these objects show clear
Venetian influence, and one group is decorated with enamel.

By this date, however, Venetian glass-
makers had come into their own; they were
the best in Europe and their products, where
available, graced the tables of the rich from
one end of the Continent to the other. Very
soon, glasshouses all over Europe were
making colourless *cristallo*, which they
worked in the *façon de Venise*.

THE RENAISSANCE
PERIOD

*T*he rise of Venice in the fourteenth century as the major trading nation of Europe brought unparalleled wealth to the city. Merchants achieved the highest ranks and spent fortunes on their collections. Chinese porcelain, spices and textiles were imported, painting and sculpture flourished, and there was a resurgence of the ancient art of glass-making. Venetian glass, concentrated on the island of Murano, was known throughout Europe and its glass-makers have been producing almost continuously ever since.

Influences spanned Chinese porcelain, which was imitated in glass, Roman mosaics and Byzantine hard stone carvings. Vessels were exported to such far-flung outposts as Britain, Constantinople and Syria. These export pieces were made in locally acceptable shapes with gilt and enamelled decoration. The trade was sophisticated enough for special commissions, for example, vessels commemorating marriages, to be produced.

The excitement and inventiveness of the period are well displayed by the glass-makers. The flair with which they created extraordinarily complex forms and their use of trapped air bubbles, coloured canes and gold flecking, have never been surpassed.

VENETIAN DRINKING GLASSES, 17TH CENTURY

These elaborate, convoluted stems are the ultimate demonstration of the glass-maker's ability to manipulate his material. Their delicacy implied refinement in the user and thus made them popular with the merchant classes.

VENICE

VENETIAN STANDING BOWL, *c*.1533

The bowl is decorated in gilding and enamel with the arms of Catherine de' Medici, who married Henri II of France in 1533 at the age of 14.

Of the enormous cultural inheritance in the applied arts that has been handed down by the Most Serene Republic of Venice, glass is arguably its most famous bequest. 'Crystal', a term used by glass-makers to describe the purity of their products, comparing them with the mineral known as rock crystal, has become a synonym for fine glass because of the Venetians. The word *cristallo* is first documented in relation to objects made from glass in the year 1409, but we do not have any extant clear glass of provable Venetian origin until the mid fifteenth century (although there are some wonderful clear glass vessels dating from the thirteenth century that may have been produced in Venice). Certainly Venetian glass was already famous – and in use – outside Italy in the early fifteenth century: for example, the French Duc de Berry's inventory of 1416 included examples of '*voirres faiz à Venise*'.

The glass-making trade was highly important to both the populace and the economy of Venice and this fact was recognized by the authorities, who closely regulated the industry with exact codes. These rules were defined in 1441 in the *Mariegola dell'Arte di Verieri da Muran*. The glass industry had already been banished in the thirteenth century to the island of Murano from the main islands because of the risk of fire. Murano is about an hour by rowing boat from Venice itself, and it was on this island that the great production of glass took place. The huge output went all over the world from the mid fifteenth century until 1797, when Napoleon destroyed the guilds and disbanded the glasshouses, many of whose owners were Venetian descendants of the fifteenth-century glass-makers.

FIFTEENTH CENTURY

Fifteenth-century Venetian glass was a luxury made for the wealthy. Inventories often record prized pieces of glass individually, and they were sometimes prized as much as precious metal.

ENAMELLED AND GILDED GLASS

Much of the glassware from this period was coloured. Vessels usually had gilded and enamelled borders, and enamelled decoration that could be figurative or armorial. Henry VIII of England is known to have had 'iiii standing Cuppes of blewe glasses w^f covers to theym paynted and guilte'.

Many of the colours of the vessels were made to imitate precious and semiprecious stones, and in addition to clear *cristallo* vessels, examples exist in blue, purple, emerald green, turquoise, opaque turquoise, opaque white and brown marbled to imitate chalcedony. The glass pieces were first blown to the desired form, then gilded and fired in the furnace, and subsequently enamelled and fired again. Finally, if handles were

VENETIAN SAPPHIRE BLUE STANDING CUP, *c*.1475 (H16.5cm/6½in)

The scene on the bowl of this footed cup depicts the Triumph of Venus.

required on a piece they were then fixed while the vessels were still warm. A contemporary traveller, the Swedish priest Peder Månsson, observed glass being gilded in about 1510; he described how the gilded glass was returned to the furnace for firing before it was slowly annealed to prevent cracking. The enamelling and gilding processes on glass were also described by Vannoccio Biringuccio in *De la Pirotechnia*, the first printed book on the subject, published in Venice in 1540. He wrote of how the glasses were 'truly' gilded with fine gold leaf and decorated with patterns of scales, scallops and leaves and of how, if desired, they could be ornamented with paintings and a variety of fine enamels.

The tradition of enamelling on glass had originally come to Venice from the great Syrian workshops of Aleppo and Damascus (the Romans, too, had practised this craft), and every Venetian painter on glass would have been aware of the superb gilded and enamelled eleventh-century Byzantine cup in the Treasury of St Mark's, probably brought back to Venice after the sack of Constantinople in 1204 and listed in the inventory of 1325. The influence of Syrian enamelled glass may have come through Spain where these *vidres de Damas* may be found in inventories of the fourteenth century. King Martin I of Aragon (ruled 1395–1410), for instance, was the owner of a mounted enamelled-glass serving dish, and an order of 1387 from the city council in Tortosa, Spain, directed a painter to buy a glass lamp either of Damascus manufacture or an imitation (*obrada o contrafeta de Damasc*), which suggests that there were local products available at that time. There is also the problem of the so-called Aldrevandin Group of fourteenth-century enamelled glass objects, which may have been made in Venice or elsewhere in Europe.

Proof that the *cristallo* was being refined in the mid fifteenth century can be found in the patent that was granted to Angelo Barovier and Niccolo Mozetto in 1457 to make *cristallo* by a new method at a time of year (summer) when the furnaces were usually closed. Angelo Barovier was credited with being 'the best Venetian maker of cristalline vases' on his death in 1460, and the family name is recorded many times in subsequent generations of glass-makers. The earliest datable clear glass is the beaker depicted in the central panel of the Adoration of the Shepherds, from the famous altarpiece started after 1468 and completed before 1476 by the Flemish painter Hugo van der Goes. It was painted for the Italian merchant and representative of the Medici family, Tommaso Portinari, in Bruges. The glass is a brilliant small *cristallo* beaker with a vertical mould-blown ribbed body, a pinched base ring and strong kick from the pontil. Another glass of this general type is illustrated by the Master of Mary of Burgundy on a leaf in a *c.*1480 Book of Hours in the Bodleian Library, Oxford, depicting the Adoration of the Magi. There are at least

SPANISH
ENAMELLED
GOBLET, *c.*1500
(H 20.3cm/8in)

This blue goblet of Gothic form was probably made in Barcelona and displays a style of decoration more Oriental than Venetian. (ABOVE)

DETAIL FROM
*THE PORTINARI
ALTARPIECE*,
HUGO VAN DER
GOES, 1468–76

From the central panel of the Adoration of the Shepherds, the detail shows a ceramic vase and a ribbed cristallo *beaker on a pinched base-ring.* (RIGHT)

two clear glass beakers of this form surviving, one in the Museum of Decorative Arts, Prague, the other formerly in the Biemann Collection, Zürich. Three other fragmentary examples dated *c*.1500 have been found in Southampton, England.

The fact that the Portinari beaker had made its way to Bruges to be depicted in an altarpiece shows how Venetian glass was already travelling. The majolica *albarello* (drug-jar) in the same painting is of a Hispano-Moresque type (dating from *c*.1460) and was clearly a revered object in this household. Further evidence of Venetian glass travelling outside Italy can be found in the imitation pearls for the cross in the Prince of Viana's Chapel in Barcelona in 1461, which was described as *contrafetes de Venecia*. The Treasury of St Peter's Church in Salzburg was said to have had gilded Venetian glasses in 1477.

VENETIAN FLARED BEAKER, *c*.1500

The vessel is decorated at the base of the body in gilding and enamel with an unusual motif that resembles flames. (LEFT)

VENETIAN *LATTIMO* GLASS JUG, EARLY 16TH CENTURY (H21.5cm/8½in)

The jug is decorated with two groups of marine grotesques derived from an engraving by Girolamo Mocetto, Frieze with Tritons and Nymphs. The piece once had a pewter lid. (BELOW)

SMALL VENETIAN GOBLET, *c*.1500

The fantastic animal figures are typical of Italian decoration of this period. (RIGHT)

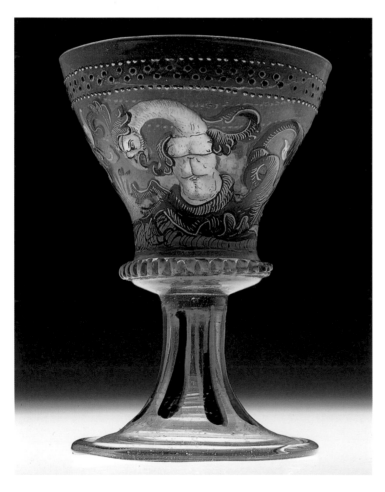

LATTIMO GLASS

One of the costly imports into Europe was Chinese porcelain, which the Venetian galleys brought from the Near East. This much-prized ware had also been used as ambassadorial gifts to several of the doges in the fifteenth century; for instance, the twenty pieces of porcelain that were given to Doge Pasquale Malipiero (d. 1462) by the Sultan of Egypt in 1461. The Venetian glass-makers imitated this porcelain after 1475, when a patent was granted for making 'porcellano'. The opaque white glass was called *lattimo*, from the Italian word for milk, *latte*. Unfortunately, only about fourteen pieces are recorded from the late fifteenth and early sixteenth centuries. It is known that the Duke of Ferrara's agent purchased seven bowls of '*porcellana contra-facta*' in Venice in 1504. These must refer to glass copies as the first European porcelain factory was not in production until the 1570s in Florence, under the patronage of the Medici. Henry VII of England had a *lattimo* vase (and a turquoise one) with his profile bust on one side (now in the British Museum). One of the finest extant examples is the small bowl with a bust of a young man and the inscription, 'I am your servant', from the Rothschild Collection (now in The Corning Museum of Glass). This was made in about 1500 and has a parallel in (or is one of a pair with) the bowl decorated with a bust of a young woman in the Kunsthistorisches Museum, Vienna. The profile busts on these bowls are derived from paintings by the popular Venetian artist, Vittorio Carpaccio (c.1465–c.1525).

Even rarer, to judge by surviving examples, is the wonderful goblet of Gothic form from Waddesdon Manor, now in the British Museum, in opaque turquoise glass painted with two scenes of lovers amid a richly gilded and enamelled surround. Apparently, there are only four other opaque turquoise Venetian glass pieces to have survived from this period: a gilt and enamelled tazza and the Fairfax Cup (which is also dichroic), both in the Victoria and Albert Museum, a jug with a *latesin* (a form of *lattimo*) body,

which has handles and a foot in opaque turquoise, in the Musée du Verre, Liège, and the handle of the *latimo* jug from Toledo. The antecedent for this type of glass may be found in an Islamic ninth to tenth century opaque turquoise glass bowl cut in relief with animals in the Treasury of St Mark's, Venice, and listed in the inventory of 1571.

CALCEDONIO GLASS

Venetian glass-makers could also look to St Mark's Treasury for classical and Byzantine agate and sardonyx vessels to inspire them in the production of popular *vetro calcedonio*. There are numerous references to these, as well as a number of extant examples, like a Gothic goblet in the Wallace Collection, London, and a ewer in the British Museum.

MOSAIC GLASS

Roman mosaic glass provided the inspiration for flamboyant millefiori ('thousand flowers') glass, of which only a few examples have come down from the fifteenth and sixteenth centuries. Notable among these are a flaring goblet and two miniature ewers

VENETIAN *CALCEDONIO* GOBLET, LATE 15TH CENTURY (H18cm/7⅛in)

This swirling coloured glass was made by Venetians to satisfy the fashion for gemstone vessels, which were often mounted in precious metals. (LEFT)

VENETIAN GOBLET OF GOTHIC FORM, LATE 15TH CENTURY (H18.9cm/7 7⁄16 in)

Opaque turquoise glass was much rarer than opaque white during the Renaissance period. (BELOW)

VENETIAN
DRINKING
TAZZA, SECOND
QUARTER 16TH
CENTURY

This cristallo *drinking
tazza has a rare
millefiori glass knop.*

in the British Museum, as well as a rare tazza with a millefiori knop of *c.*1530 in the Ashmolean Museum. In 1496 Maria Barovier, presumably a relation of Angelo, was recorded as being a maker of the canes for millefiori glass, perhaps in the furnace that she sought permission to build in 1487.

EXPORTS AND COMMISSIONS

Venetian glassware was selling throughout the trading world in the second half of the fifteenth century. There are a series of gilt and enamelled mosque lamps in the Topkapi Palace in Istanbul; these presumably date from after 1479, when Sultan Mehmet II, with whom Venice had been at war constantly since the fall of Constantinople in 1453, agreed to a treaty. This was subsequently and more favourably confirmed by his son Bajazet II in 1481. Related to these lamps is a group of five *cristallo* beakers, found in a Jewish cemetery in Syria. The fact that the Venetians were making glass of special shapes (such as lamps) for an export market is significant. In the sixteenth century they expanded into other areas, particularly in Germany and northern Europe, to cater to localized tastes. The export of Venetian enamelled glass to the Near East is also proof that the great Syrian enamelled-glass industry had finally run its course.

THE BEHAIM MARRIAGE BEAKER,
*c.*1495 (H11.5cm/4½in)

The cristallo *beaker was made to commemorate the marriage of Michael Behaim and Katerina Lochnerin. It is the earliest recorded extant piece of Venetian export glass.*

The commissioning of glass for special occasions, often decorated with armorials, became common both in Italy and elsewhere in Europe at the end of the fifteenth century. A number of early datable glass pieces exist, notably a fine pair of clear glass pilgrim flasks housed in the Museo Civico, Bologna, with the arms in enamel of Alessandro Bentivoglio and Ippolita Sforza, who were married in 1492. Also extant is a goblet of Gothic form in the Civic Museum of Wrocław (Breslau), Poland, with the arms of Hungary and Bohemia, probably for Matthias Corvinus, King of Hungary (1440–90), and there are fragments of a goblet from the Royal Palace, Budapest, with the arms of his queen, Beatrice of Aragon (1457–1508), who received Venetian glass from Ferrara in 1486. Indeed, the Spanish royal family were avid collectors of glass. A crucial pair of Venetian clear glass vessels, the marriage beakers for Michael Behaim and Katerina Lochnerin of 1495, came to light in the sale of the Robert von Hirsch Collection in 1978. One, now in The Corning Museum of Glass, is enamelled with the figures of St Catherine and St Michael for the bride and groom and the arms of Behaim. The Behaim family were wealthy merchants from Nuremberg and these glasses are the earliest with exact dates that may be found exported from Venice. The clarity of the *cristallo* in these glasses is such that it recalls the rock crystal objects in St Mark's Treasury with which the glassmakers would probably have been familiar.

The Spanish court bought large quantities of Venetian glass, as well as patronizing Barcelona factories. In 1503 King Ferdinand (ruled 1479–1516) sent Queen Isabella 148 glass objects from the Spanish city to join the 260 already at her palace at Alcalá de Henares. Her lady-in-waiting, Violante de Albion, wrote extensive descriptions of this glass in 1503, but, unfortunately, did not differentiate between Venetian glass and that produced in Barcelona. She refers to *calcedonio*, agate and onyx glasses, and she mentions some made of white, presumably *lattimo*, and turquoise enamel. Others are purple, blue and green, sometimes of more than one colour, and they are frequently described as having covers. These covers rarely survive, but there is a covered goblet decorated with coloured spiked prunts in the Victoria and Albert Museum (perhaps made for the German market) and a fine clear wrythen goblet and cover with a gilt and enamelled border of fifteenth-century date in the British Museum. Some are described as enamelled with white, purple, red, yellow, green and blue. She particularly discriminates between two types of gilding: *dorado*, comprising apparently solid areas of applied gold, and *dorado de oro molido*, with gilt flecks (fired copper) on the glass. Violante reported that numerous pieces bore armorial devices, and many had painted figures.

PAINTERS AND ENAMELLERS

A large number of hands may be detected on the enamelled glass of the fifteenth and sixteenth centuries. Some of these were undoubtedly independent decorators who may or may not have been directly employed in the glasshouses. Giovanni Maria Obizzo (fl.1488–1525) was one painter who in 1490 had had over a thousand pieces of enamelled glass fired by Bernardino Ferro (apparently without a licence), including large numbers of *lattimo*. In 1911 the scholar Robert Schmidt attempted to define the hands at work and the subject sources of Venetian enamelled glass, and in a 1974 article on *lattimo* glass T.H. Clarke provided

many more sources. Reference to Carpaccio has already been made, and Schmidt and Clarke have shown that prints and woodcuts were essential sources for Venetian glass painters. The artists and engravers of these sources include Girolamo Mocetto, Andrea Mantegna, Benedetto Montagna, Francesco Colonna and frequently Vittorio Carpaccio, particularly for profile busts.

SIXTEENTH CENTURY

The popularity of Venetian glass continued, while the glass-makers experimented with new techniques to encourage their markets. For reasons of finance and prestige, many rulers tried to entice them (and other Italian glass-makers) to set up glasshouses outside Venice.

FILIGRANA

As the sixteenth century progressed Venetian glass became lighter and less coloured, although Gothic shapes continued to be made until about 1525, when enamelling (with the exception of armorials) became less popular in Italy (but not north of the Alps). In 1527 the brothers Filippo and Bernardo Serena, who were Muranese glassworkers, applied for a patent for a new method of working with glass canes. This was the beginning of the famous Venetian glass that was worked with opaque white and sometimes added coloured canes, described in 1540 by Biringuccio as 'twisted

MONUMENTAL COVERED GOBLET, EARLY 16TH CENTURY (H25cm/9¾in)

Decorated with Krautstrunk *prunts, the goblet was made in Venice for the German market.* (ABOVE)

VENETIAN MOULDED EWER IN *VETRO A RETORTOLI*, LATE 16TH CENTURY (H27.4cm/10¹³⁄₁₆in)

After the canes were incorporated into the glass, the vessel was blown into a mould with armorial double-headed eagles for the German market. (LEFT)

designs of thorn branches and other criss-cross inlays'. They were known as *vetri a filigrana* and were made in several designs. Canes were laid down on the marver and then the blown bubble of *cristallo* was rolled on to the canes, which, being hot, collected them and then absorbed them in the regular shapes that had been laid out to provide the striped patterns. Simple *filigrana* was described as *a fili*, but the canes could also be rotated to make *filigrana a retortoli*.

The glass-blowers' imagination and technology finally ran riot with the wonderful *vetri a reticello*, in which the crisscrossed bands of *lattimo* actually trap bubbles of air between them to make an elaborate net in the glass. These *filigrana* glasses were in fashion for nearly two hundred years and

FOUR VENETIAN
FILIGRANA
VESSELS, LATE
16TH–EARLY
17TH CENTURY
(Largest:
H27cm/10⅞in)

The goblet, reliquary, drinking tazza and ceremonial goblet display the wide variety of canes used in this type of decoration.

VENETIAN
LOBED *RETICELLI*
BOWL, *c.*1600

This bowl is unusual in that it combines red and blue stripes with the usual opaque white lattimo. (ABOVE)

imitated in other countries, sometimes with painted stripes instead of bands incorporated in the glass. There is a 1533 painting by Bonifazio de' Pitati in the Galleria dell'Accademia, Venice, showing a beggar holding a glass bowl decorated *a fili* in his hand. Henry VIII had 'xii bolles of glass wth one cover to theyme all wrought up wth Diap worke

white' before 1542, indicating that the glass had become fashionable far from Venice quite soon after it had been perfected. The technique patented by the Serena brothers, who were working in Venice, had classical antecedents: both the Hellenistic Greeks and the Romans employed *filigrana* to decorate their glass vessels.

ICE GLASS

Another popular glass type originating in Venice was ice glass. In this technique the glass was marvered on to pieces of haphazard glass fragments or even lightly rolled over water to cool instantly while being blown. This produced irregular cracking and a distortion of the clarity. Parts of the glass alone might be decorated in this way, the remainder being plain or gilded. In 1537 the poet Garcilaso de la Vega bought 32 pieces of Venetian glass in Toledo, 'some engraved, others frosted [ice glass] and yet others plain'. Philip II very greatly admired this type of glass and in 1564 had 65 fine Venetian examples in his palace of El Pardo, his collection including a variety of covered goblets, flutes and decanters. In the Österreichisches Museum für Angewandte Kunst in Vienna three examples of ice glass from Schloss Ambras are preserved, two of which also have blue and white filigree *a retortoli*; these were purchased from Venice on the orders of Archduke Ferdinand II (1520–95) of the Tyrol in 1568.

diamond-point a date, name or inscription. In 1549 Vincenzo di Angelo dal Gallo applied for a patent for a certain technique of engraving glass with a diamond point, which he alleged he had been practising for fifteen years. In 1562 Pastor Johann Mathesius, who was a friend of Martin Luther, preached a sermon in Bohemia in which he described how 'nowadays all sorts of festooning and handsome lines are drawn by diamond on the nice and bright Venetian glasses'. There are a number of fine dishes with gilt and *a fili* rings which are diamond-engraved around with fanciful Mannerist beasts and engraved in the centre with the arms of the Medici Pope, Pius IV (1559–65), or, as in examples in the British Museum, with the papal insignia in the circular

ENGRAVED GLASS

Engraved glass – *vetri intagiate* – was for sale in Toledo by 1537. It would have been engraved with a diamond or sharp corundum. There is little commercial engraved glass known before about 1530, but prior to this amateurs sometimes scratched in

decoration. The earliest extant dated professionally diamond-engraved glass is a beaker of 1566 with the arms of Vienna, in the Museum of Decorative Arts in Prague. Shortly afterward there are numerous diamond-engraved glasses decorated by Venetians in Venice or in the many glasshouses by this date operating in Europe.

HALL-IN-TYROL AND VENICE

A large amount of Venetian glass has been attributed to Hall and Innsbruck in Austria, partly on the basis that pieces have been found there and they are often cold-painted and gilded as well as diamond-engraved. However, many of these types also survive

COVERED ARMORIAL GOBLET, *c.*1580–90

Decorated in gilding, diamond-point and cold-painting with the arms of Archduke Ferdinand II of Austria, the goblet is perhaps by Antonio Montano.

in Venetian and old Italian collections with long provenances, and great care must be taken in attribution. A diamond-engraved and cold-painted reliquary dating from about 1580 in the Frari, originally from another Venetian church, is identical to glass ascribed to Innsbruck. However, it cannot be an import as during the sixteenth century there were strict rules about this. Part of the confusion arises because Muranese glass-workers using identical materials were operating in Innsbruck for Archduke Ferdinand II under licence from the Venetian Republic. Moreover, in the wreckage of the ship carrying glass to Constantinople (sunk off the Dalmatian island of Gnalić in 1583), there are several fragments with similar diamond decoration.

WHEEL-ENGRAVING

Wheel-engraving on glass was unknown in Venice until the eighteenth century. This may have been partly due to the thinness of the glass, rock crystal being a more suitable medium for engraving. The best workshops for rock crystal were in Milan, particularly those of the Saracchi and Miseroni families, some members of which worked in Prague in the court of the Emperor Rudolf II.

The Venetian export market developed rapidly as the sixteenth century passed, and the Venetian authorities took an increasing interest in a glass industry which was contributing heavily to the republic's treasury with foreign payments. At this time many European courts and rulers were setting up their own glasshouses with imported Venetians. The Venetian authorities, unhappy with the loss of specialist skills and technical knowledge to the new glass-houses, adopted a 'stick and carrot' approach to their emigrant workers. On the one hand, the recalcitrant glass-makers were threatened with fines, hard labour in the galleys and even death if they did not return to Venice and, on the other, they were promised wealth and privileges if they did. It did not, however, prevent glasshouses manufacturing glass *à la façon de Venise* being set up in Altare, Florence, Vienna, Barcelona, Antwerp, Hall, Innsbruck, Montpellier, Kassel, London and other places by the end of the sixteenth century. Worse for the Venetian authorities was the fact that glass made in Antwerp was being sold in Spain as 'Venetian' and, together with Spanish glass, was being sold in the New World as the real product. Many of these glasshouses had difficulty producing glass of Venetian standards because they could not get raw materials of the right quality. Spanish barilla was considered the best potash for making Venetian *cristallo*, and this was offered by Duke Cosimo de' Medici to his prospective Muranese glass-maker by way of an inducement in 1570.

Venetian exports of glass were large in the sixteenth century. The agent of King Philip II of Spain ordered that Venetian glass

should be shipped to Spain with his paintings by Titian in 1561 and by 1564 he had 320 *vidrios de Venecia* in his palace, El Pardo. The manufacturers varied their products to take account of the markets they were selling to. The trade in enamelled glass to the Near East in the late fifteenth century went on into the next century. An analysis of the cargo of the Venetian cargo ship wrecked off the Dalmatian coast in 1583 provides a fascinating time capsule of trade of the time. This ship, probably the *Gagiana*, was bound for Constantinople with, among other things, a large cargo of glass. It was insured in Venice and part of the cargo was salvaged while the remainder was abandoned. In 1967 it was rediscovered and two cannons, dated 1582, were recovered together with a large quantity of glass, mostly of familiar shapes. There were also, however, numerous Oriental-type painted sprinklers for rose-water that were familiar in Islamic glass but not in European, and blue bottles with tall necks with a fold at the top that were reminiscent of Islamic bottles of the thirteenth and fourteenth centuries.

FUNCTIONS OF GLASS

Undoubtedly some similarly shaped vessels had different uses in different countries. The fine wrythen tazza in *Bacchus*, the *c.*1594–5 painting by Caravaggio in the Uffizi, is clearly being used to imbibe red wine. These tall tazzas fulfil a similar role in the monumental 1563 painting, *The Marriage at Cana*, by Paolo Veronese (in the Louvre). However, in northern Europe similar pieces seem to have been used for sweetmeats or even fruit, as may be seen in seventeenth-century still-life paintings by Jan Davidsz de Heem, in which red wine is usually seen in a tall flute glass, traditionally Dutch in style.

A number of shapes were made specifically for the northern market. These would include *Scheuer* glasses made north of the

DETAIL FROM
BACCHUS,
CARAVAGGIO,
c.1594–5

*The boy holds a tazza
filled with red wine,
illustrating that these
vessels were used for
drinking.* (RIGHT)

VENETIAN
GOBLET WITH A
SCENE FROM THE
COMMEDIA
DELL'ARTE,
SECOND HALF
16TH CENTURY
(H19.2cm/7⅝in)

*Enamelled on the
vessel are Pantaloon
fighting Harlequin,
and the peacemaking
Doctor.* (BELOW)

*FAÇON-DE-
VENISE* GILT
AND ENAMELLED
STANGENGLAS,
DATED 1580
(H26cm/10¼in)

*Decorating the vessel
are an armorial and the
inscription.* SVSSANA
KLAMERIN GEBORNE
KLAINHANSIN. *It was
probably made in Hall-
in-Tyrol.* (BELOW)

Alps of green *Waldglas*, which have a spur as a handle and were in common use in Germany in the late fifteenth century. A good example, in Venetian *cristallo* decorated with the arms of Reich von Reichenstein, dating from about 1520, is in the British Museum, but this form is rare. A monumental early sixteenth-century covered goblet with *Krautstrunk* (cabbage-stalk) prunts is in the Victoria and Albert Museum. Less than half a dozen of this type are extant.

Figural enamelling and the customary gilt and enamel dotted borders went out of fashion in Italy in the middle of the sixteenth century. This was not true north of the Alps, however, where there was a ready market for *Stangengläser*, which were tall, cylindrical beakers, often on raised feet, used for beer. The accustomed gilding and dot patterns are often retained, and an example in the British Museum, dating from the second half of the sixteenth century, has the surely Venetian subject of Pantaloon fighting Harlequin from the commedia dell'arte. Other examples are sometimes dated, such

GLASS DESIGN FROM AN ILLUSTRATED LETTER, *c.*1670

The page of drawings with instructions is from the correspondence of John Greene of the London Glass Sellers' Company with Alessio Morelli of Venice.

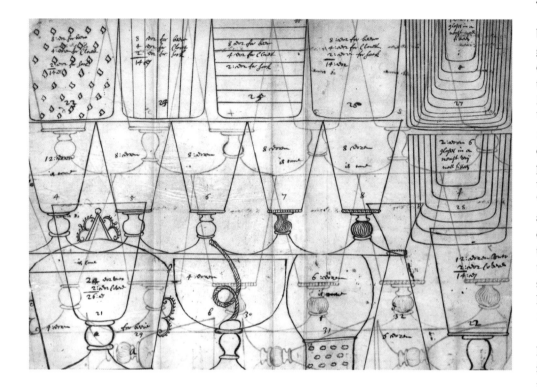

Venetian glass. In England, first Giacomo Verzelini in the sixteenth century, then Sir Jerome Bowes and, during James I's reign (1608–25), Sir Robert Mansell were given monopolies to make and sell *cristallo* (thus also controlling Venetian imports).

Some indications of the close relationship between the importer and the supplier of glass can be gleaned from the fascinating correspondence between two members of the London Glass Sellers' Company, Michael Measey and John Greene, and the Venetian Alessio Morelli between 1667 and 1673. The Englishmen were constantly emphasizing the need for quality in the products, 'That all the Drinking Glasses bee verij well made' and that they should be of 'verij cleer whit sound mettall'. These letters are illustrated with nearly five hundred drawings of glasses to be provided, many of these in the English taste, and separated into various sizes for each of the different wines, such as claret and sack. Robert Charleston has pointed out that the order of August 1668 was for 5400 objects, a sizable business.

Glass of the seventeenth century was lighter and more flamboyant, not so much in colour as in decoration. Goblets acquired wings and frills, and sometimes they had figures in glass moulded as part of the stem, sometimes in the form of a horse. Ultimately the wings and complications became hugely exaggerated, as seen in the extra-ordinary goblet in a still-life painting of 1716 by Gabriele Salci. This conforms closely to the eccentricities of the glass provided for King Frederick IV of Denmark and Norway in 1708–9, housed in the Rosenborg Castle. The tall shape is still definitely for the northern market but the flamboyance is quintessentially Venetian. There was even a revival of dichroic *lattimo* glass for the northern market: *vetri di girasol*, or opal glass. This seems to have been a favourite of the Scandinavian king and he bought many pieces. The beaker and cover in this type of glass from the Waddesdon Manor Collection in the British Museum is interesting as it is mould-blown with the Triumph of Neptune. Whether it was made by Venetians in or out of Venice is an open question.

'OPAL' COVERED GLASS BEAKER, SECOND HALF 17TH CENTURY
(H23.5cm/9¼in)

Mould-blown with the Triumph of Neptune in relief, this beaker was made by Venetians, perhaps in Dresden.

as the one in the Biemann Collection, Zürich, which is inscribed 'SVSSANA KLA-MERIN GEBORNE KLAINHANSIN' and is dated 1580. This has the familiar qualities of Venetian glass, but Axel von Saldern has attributed it to Hall. There is another glass in the same collection dated 1588 and yet another with the early date of 1558. In the British Museum are a pair of *Stangengläser* gilded with figures taken from Titian's woodcuts published in 1590 and with the arms of Jacob Praun of Nuremberg and Clara von Roming, whom he married in 1589. Undoubtedly some of these *Stangengläser* were made north of the Alps, but many are likely to have been Venetian.

This large export trade continued into the seventeenth century, with fiercely competitive local markets vying for the Venetian business and protecting themselves through monopolies in an attempt to keep out

THE VENETIAN INFLUENCE

STILL LIFE,
PIETER CLAESZ,
1630

*This oil painting on
copper illustrates,
among other things,
fish, bread, a watch
and two glass vessels: a
Roemer at left and a
fallen goblet at rear.*

FAÇON-DE-
VENISE TALL
BEAKER, *c*.1600
(H19cm/7½in)

*The vessel is made of
vetro a fili with
opaque white and blue
threads and features
applied gilt lion's-head
masks and prunts; it is
probably from the
Netherlands.*
(BELOW LEFT)

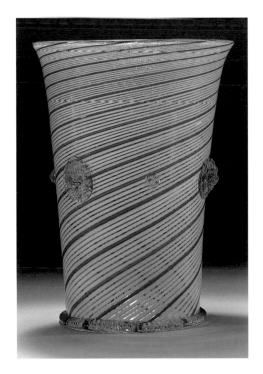

Post-Medieval glass in Europe falls into two basic categories: imitations of rock crystal and examples of German *Waldglas*. The first group includes deliberately coloured vessels which were inspired by other hard gemstones, such as emeralds and amethysts. This practice had its roots in high-quality, finely coloured Hellenistic and Roman glass, some of which was characterized by great clarity. In the German *Waldglas* (forest-glass) tradition (just as in ordinary Roman glass), the naturally occurring ferrous oxides present in the sand were allowed to dominate the colour structure of the glass, thus rendering it varying shades of green. Manganese oxide was added to the batch, to neutralize this greenish hue with a pink tint. The dual tradition is still present today in the differentiation between bottle glass, which is green or brown, and crystal, which is clear. This distinction was also true in the sixteenth century. In northern Europe some of this *Waldglas* was of high quality, but in Italy, southern France and Spain it tended to be of a more rustic nature.

ALKALI

The differences in shades of green and in weight between glass from the north and that from the south are partly due to the type of alkali used in the batch. Alkali was added to the raw materials to serve as a flux to reduce the fusion point of silica (from the sand or pebbles) and, therefore, the temperature required in the furnace. It was obtained as potash from the ashes of burnt beechwood and other woods in the Germanic states, and from bracken and ferns in France. South of the Alps, in Spain and Italy, soda from the ashes of barilla, a salt-marsh plant (known colloquially in English as 'glasswort') was used as an alternative to the potash.

Italian green glass, usually described as *toscana*, often has the lightness of Venetian *cristallo* but without its clarity or smoothness. Much of it is similar to Spanish provincial glass, and it is not always easy to differentiate between them. The *Waldglashütten* also produced deliberately coloured glass vessels, particularly in blue and opaque red, but these do not possess the refinement of the Venetian pieces. There was a scramble to recruit Venetian glass-makers throughout the sixteenth century because of their skills in blowing *cristallo*, resulting in a wide variety of *façon-de-Venise* products.

SPAIN

Spanish glass does not have the same origins as glass from other parts of Europe. The Romans had conquered and left their influence in many parts of Europe, but there is a stronger Islamic influence in Spain than anywhere else (with the possible exception of Venice). This can be seen in the architecture of southern Spain and the designs used in metalwork and textiles. Moreover, there are many references to Damascus enamelled glassware in Medieval inventories. Indeed, there was already a thriving glass production in Barcelona at the end of the fifteenth century, a source of much local pride. A certain Jerónimo Paulo wrote to Paolo Pamphili from Rome in 1491 that 'Barcelona glass was much esteemed at the Roman court and rivalled that of Venice'.

Barcelona glasshouses enjoyed serious royal patronage. In 1503 King Ferdinand sent 148 pieces of glass from Barcelona to Queen Isabella at Alcalá de Henares. Some of these objects were enamelled with 'Moorish' letters, as on a double white-handled vase of greyish glass in the Barcelona Museum of Decorative Arts. The opaque

white, green and red enamel decoration on a blue Gothic goblet is far more Oriental in treatment than on comparable Venetian pieces and it also lacks the typical Venetian gilding. It cannot date much after 1500 and could be twenty years earlier. This displays a sophistication and strength not possible in any other place, apart from Venice, in the late fifteenth century.

Enamelling continued to be fashionable in Spain, as in France and Germany, for much longer than in Venice. There are a number of vessels, enamelled in greens, yellows and opaque white, which were produced in Barcelona or perhaps on the island of Mallorca from about 1560 to 1590. The glass is not of the same calibre as Venetian but its enamelling has a naïve charm. Venetian styles, too, were imitated

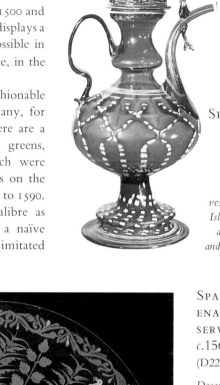

SPANISH EWER, LATE 16TH CENTURY (H23.3cm/9⅜in)

The shape of this vessel displays strong Islamic influence and also occurs in silver and enamelled objects.

SPANISH ENAMELLED SERVING TAZZA, *c.*1560 (D22cm/8¹¹⁄₁₆in)

Decorated in polychrome enamel with three groups of figures among vegetation, the tazza was probably made in Barcelona, or perhaps Mallorca.

in the late sixteenth century, sometimes in fantastic and spectacular forms, as in the impressive ewer with *lattimo* stripes in the Musée du Verre, Liège. The clear glass in this piece is slightly more yellow than its Venetian counterpart would have been. By the

seventeenth century the standard of Spanish glass had deteriorated and the mass-produced pieces fell far short of the standards of excellence achieved by the Venetians, though they did retain Venetian elements, such as *filigrana* canes.

OTHER CENTRES IN ITALY

One of the historical mysteries of glass is the production of Altare near Genoa. Glass-making had been practised there since at least the ninth century. By the mid fifteenth century it was a flourishing business made up of special guilds which, unlike their counterparts in Venice, actually encouraged glass blowers to go and work in other countries. There are numerous references to this centre in the sixteenth century which record apparently strong links with France. Unfortunately, there is not one piece of extant glass which can be said with certainty to be the produc-

COLD-PAINTED TAZZA WITH JUDITH AND HOLOFERNES, 1551

The glass is façon de Venise, the decoration perhaps Swiss. As the pigments are unfired, it is rare for a piece to be in such good condition.

tion of Altare, and it therefore must be assumed that the glass is so close to that of Venice that experts are unable to distinguished between them.

Of Florentine glass, however, more is known. Cosimo de' Medici was anxious to produce glass in the Venetian style and was already negotiating in 1567 with a Muranese, Luigi Bertolo, to establish a glasshouse under his patronage. This proved to be fruitless and negotiations were renewed in 1570. However, it was not until 1579 that the glasshouses came into full production, at a time when the first European porcelain factory had also begun production in Florence under Medici patronage.

Further evidence of Florentine interest may be seen in the elaborate designs for glass created by Giacomo Ligozzi (c.1547–1627), who had arrived in Florence by 1578. Even more fantastic designs were published by Giovanni Maggi (1566–1618) in 1604 and dedicated to Cardinal Francesco Maria Del Monte, who was the Medici chief representative in Rome. Del Monte was also the patron of the artist Caravaggio and the first recorded owner of the Portland Vase. Some of Maggi's designs are so extravagant that they may be regarded as imaginary; if they were not, then little has survived to this day. Others are of familiar forms from Spain, Venice or Antwerp, or perhaps Hall or Innsbruck. It does suggest that highly sophisticated glass was being made in Florence at this time.

Additional proof of the importance of Florence as a glass centre in the early seventeenth century is the publication there in 1612 of Antonio Neri's *L'Arte Vetraria*. Neri was a chemist and a priest who had had experience working in glasshouses both in Antwerp and Florence. His was the first printed book on the chemistry and technique of glass-making. The publication was profoundly influential on glass-makers in other countries in the late seventeenth century and afterward, when it was translated into English (1662), Latin (1669), German (1679) and French (1752).

There were also glasshouses in Rome and Naples but, like those of Altare and Florence, their production is difficult to identify. Robert Charleston has tentatively attributed to Naples a group of seventeenth-century coloured bowls and vases with base metal mounts, a number of which are in Waddesdon Manor.

FRANCE

Verre de fougère (named after the burnt ferns used as an alkali, corresponding to German *Waldglas*) was made in profusion and has been found in many Medieval and post-Medieval excavations, indicating its extensive use.

Whether fine glass was made extensively in France in the early sixteenth century is another open question. In 1443 a 'Signor Ferro' from Altare was working at a glasshouse in Goult, Provence, for the Duke of Anjou, but nothing is known of this production. In 1511 Matthieu de Carpel was making glass in Lyon *à la façon de Venise*, but none of this glass can be identified. Henri II patronized an unsuccessful attempt at St-

FRENCH ENAMELLED GOBLET, MID 16TH CENTURY (H22.4cm/8⅞in)

The chalice-shaped goblet was possibly made by Venetians or Altarists working in France.

Germain-en-Laye in 1551 to make glass in the Venetian style. It is not, however, until the third quarter of the sixteenth century that there is a recognizable group of fine French-made glass with Venetian inspiration. There were competent enamellers on glass in Montpellier during the latter part of the sixteenth century. Both the French Prince de Condé and Catherine de' Medici owned vases of Montpellier enamelled glass in the late 1580s. A magnificent flared beaker enamelled with three halberdiers, in the Musée de la Renaissance, Ecouen, France, is the pinnacle of a group of glass with French inscriptions. The gilded band is decorated with the words, 'En – la Seuur [Sueur] – de ton visage – tu mangeras – Le payn' ('With the sweat of your brow you will eat bread'). It dates from *c.*1560 and is as fine an example of enamelled glass as any produced in Venice or elsewhere at the time. There is a beaker of similar form and quality in the Victoria and Albert Museum. Whether these glass pieces were made in Montpellier or elsewhere is unknown.

From 1603 glasshouses were established in Nevers by Altarists. Nevers became well

DETAIL OF A STILL LIFE, SEBASTIAN
STOSSKOPF, *c.*1643

Illustrated is a wicker basket filled with façon-de-
Venise *goblets and wine glasses.*

known as the centre for glass figures, some of which were elaborately set into grottoes to depict a story, often of a religious nature. One of these glass-makers, Bernard Perrot (d. 1709), later moved to Orléans where, with another of Italian origin, Nicolas Massolay, he made opaque white glass to imitate porcelain in 1668.

There were undoubtedly large numbers of crystal vessels being made in France and imported there in the late sixteenth and early seventeenth centuries. Bernard Palissy, famous for his pottery, has been quoted in the late sixteenth century as complaining that 'glasses had become as numerous and their prices so low that the makers could not command a decent living, and that the glasses were hawked through the streets by those who sold old hats and scrap iron'. A painting by Sebastian Stasskopf in the Kunsthalle, Karlsruhe, was painted in France in about 1643 and shows a basket of *façon-de-Venise* glasses that may well have been made in France. The superb diamond-engraved dish in The Corning Museum of Glass with the monogram of Gaston, Duc d'Orléans (1608–60), shows the high standard that the French glass-makers could achieve.

THE LOW COUNTRIES

The *Waldglas* tradition was strong in the Netherlands, but the European craze for Venetian glass arrived there as well at an early period. The Colinet glasshouse at Beauwelz (near Mons, Belgium) was founded under the patronage of Margaret of Austria (regent of Emperor Charles V) in 1506, while a glass-maker named van Helmont had a glasshouse at Antwerp making *du verre cristallin à l'instar de Venise* in about 1535. The Netherlands were part of the Spanish Empire until the north (Holland) revolted in 1598. A relationship probably existed between glass-makers there and those in Barcelona.

In 1541 Jean Michel Cornachini set up a glasshouse in Antwerp with Muranese workers. The Colinets were still working at Beauwelz and designs of glass made by them from 1550 to 1555 survive in the Library of Raymond Chambon. Familiar Venetian shapes to be made in *cristallo*, *verre cracquelé* (ice glass) and *filigrana* are illustrated, as well as the usual *Waldglas* shapes of *Berkemeyers*, *Roemers* and *Stangengläser*. One illustration is of a glass *Nef*, an elaborate table ornament in the form of a ship. It is interesting to note that one of these was presented to Emperor Charles V and his son, Philip, while visiting the glasshouse in 1549. *Verre de Venise Liègois* was being made in 1571 by Nicolas Francisci

THREE GERMAN GLASSES, SECOND HALF 16TH CENTURY

The red jug with silver mounts, like the tall prunted Stangenglas, *comes from the Rhineland. The enamelled jug with contemporary pewter mounts is dated 1580.*

VENETIAN '*NEF*' EWER, SECOND HALF 16TH CENTURY (H34.3cm/13½in)

The bowl in the form of a boat, its spout forming a prow, was made for the centre of a table display.

and glasshouses were set up in Brussels, Middelburg and Amsterdam during the sixteenth century.

A tradition of diamond-engraving on glass became extremely fashionable in the last quarter of the sixteenth century – the earliest extant dated Netherlands beaker is of 1581 – and this led directly to the practice of personalizing pieces of glass, carried out by Anna Roemers Visscher and Willem van

Queen Elizabeth's reign (1559–1603), although there were Venetian glass-makers in London between 1549 and 1551. An extraordinary tankard with London silver-gilt mounts of 1548–9 may have been made there or imported from Venice or Antwerp. It was not until 1567 that a Frenchman, Jean Carré, came from Antwerp to make glass windows and glass vessels in the Venetian style at Crutched Friars in London, shortly

utionary coal-burning furnaces took over from wood-burning ones, thus industrializing production and enabling furnaces to reach higher temperatures. The new developments encouraged the building of glass-houses in coal-mining areas, especially near Newcastle-upon-Tyne and Bristol. The fine glass produced was still in the Venetian idiom, but its manufacture did not prevent entirely the importation of Venetian glass.

Heemskerk. However, the Dutch engravers frequently tended to prefer to engrave green *Roemers* and bottles made out of *Waldglas*, as opposed to the clear *façon-de-Venise* glass vessels.

ENGLAND

Henry VIII had over six hundred glass objects in one of his inventories. Forest glass had been made in the Weald of Kent in both the fifteenth and sixteenth centuries, but fine glass does not seem to have been established until

followed by other Venetians, including Giacomo Verzelini. Ten glass pieces survive with diamond engraving dating between 1577 and 1586 that have direct English connections. A 'graver in puter and glasse' called Anthony de Lysle, of French origin, has been credited with all the engraving of this group of *façon-de-Venise* glass. An eleventh glass by this hand, dated 1578, is in the Musée de la Renaissance, Ecouen, and was apparently made for a French couple from Poitou. This also appears to be from Verzelini's Crutched Friars glasshouse, but has sometimes been attributed to France.

In the seventeenth century, during the time of Sir Robert Mansell's patent, revol-

FAÇON-DE-VENISE JUG WITH ENGLISH SILVER-GILT MOUNTS, LONDON, 1547–8 (H12.8cm/5in)

This small jug is the only one recorded with a combination of turquoise, green and white vetro a fili. (ABOVE LEFT)

FAÇON-DE-VENISE DIAMOND-ENGRAVED DRINKING TAZZA, DATED 1578 (H16cm/6¼in)

Perhaps engraved by Anthony de Lysle for another compatriot with the arms of Marthe Mansion de la Pommeraya, the tazza was probably made in England by Giacomo Verzelini. (ABOVE)

GERMANY

There are many problems in differentiating between glass made in Venice and that made across the Alps in Austria in the late sixteenth century. In the north the princes of Germany wanted their own glasshouses, and the earliest was established in Vienna as early as 1486. Others soon followed, including Laibach in 1517, Hall in 1534 and Innsbruck in 1570. Elsewhere, *façon-de-Venise* glass was produced in Kassel, Dresden, Augsburg, Munich and Nuremberg. This imported industry, however, never entirely superseded the traditional local one, as it did elsewhere in Europe. In the fifteenth and sixteenth centuries there were an enormous number of glass furnaces in the forests of Hesse, Silesia, Saxony, Bohemia, Thuringia and the Schwarzwald. Spessart appears to have been a particularly important centre. These areas not only retained their *Waldglas* traditions, but they also developed their own clear glass. Their output was not in the Venetian idiom, but was more robust and suitable for heavy enamelling.

ENAMELLING

Enamelling on glass was a decorative art particularly practised in Bohemia. Thus from the *Stangenglas* developed the *Humpen*, a large cylindrical beaker, often enamelled with elaborate coats of arms or representations of a variety of subjects that might be be toasted. Some of the *Humpen* are enormous, holding up to a gallon of liquid. The most common decoration is the *Reichsadler*, the arms of the Holy Roman Emperor, the earliest extant example of which appears on a glass dated 1571 (although Bohemian enamelled glass is referred to in literature in 1561). This toast to the *Römische Reich* was a tradition lasting into the eighteenth century. Another subject

was the *Kurfürsten* – portraits of the kings and princes (either on horseback or seated) who held feudal land from the emperor. *Humpen* also commemorate guilds and trades, individual families, marriages, hunting, religious subjects, fables, musicians, armorials, the ages of man and occasionally erotic subjects. Other types of vessels were decorated in this manner, such as a Bohemian enamelled jug with pewter mounts dated 1580 (presumably for a marriage). A Bohemian goblet in the Toledo Museum of Art is decorated *a retortoli* and has a pale green tint; it dates from *c.*1600, and the enamel painting depicts the sacrifice of Isaac. The continuing use of gilding covered by

KURFÜRSTENHUMPEN OR ELECTORS' *HUMPEN*, DATED 1607 (H43.9cm/17⅜in)

These tall glasses with scenes of the Holy Roman Emperor and his electors were used to toast and to show allegiance to the ruler. (ABOVE LEFT)

ENAMELLED GOBLET WITH *LATTIMO* STRIPES, *c.*1600 (H20cm/7⅞in)

The scene on this Bohemian glass is that of Abraham preparing to sacrifice Isaac. (ABOVE)

BEAKER WITH
GYPSY
PROCESSION,
JOHANN
SCHAPER, 1666
(H10.5cm/4⅛in)

*The Nuremberg three-
footed beaker was
painted by Schaper
with a scene taken
from Jacques Callot's*
Les Bohémiens, *of
1621. It is initialled
'J.S.' and dated.*

enamel dots around the rim is an indication of the prevailing influence of Venetian glass styles in Bohemia.

Enamelling on glass with *lattimo* stripes continued during the seventeenth century: a Saxon example with the arms of Johann Georg II in The Corning Museum of Glass is dated 1662. Franconia was also a noted enamelled-glass region in the mid seventeenth century. Many of the subjects are taken from engravings; for instance, the early *Reichsadlerhumpen* with a Crucifixion portrayed in the centre are painted from an engraving by Hans Burgkmair of 1507. This tradition continued throughout the seventeenth and eighteenth centuries and passed into folk art, particularly on flasks.

There were also enamellers of a higher quality who worked outside the factories decorating pottery, porcelain and glass. Referred to as *Hausmalers* (home or free-lance decorators), they were often itinerant. One of the best of these was Johann Schaper

(1621–70) of Nuremberg, who painted many glass vessels, particularly in *Schwarzlot und Goldmalerei* (black and gold). He occasionally painted in polychrome, as on a beaker from the Ernesto Wolf Collection in the Stuttgart Museum depicting a gypsy procession; it is signed and dated 1666. Other *Hausmaler* artists of the seventeenth century who decorated glass were Johann Keil (1642–1719), Hermann Benkert (1652–81), Abraham Helmhack (1654–1724) and Johann Faber (*fl.*1678–97).

ENGRAVING

Diamond engraving in the Venetian tradition can be found on glass produced by Sebastian Höchstetter's workers at Hall from about 1560 and at the Hofglashütte in Innsbruck from 1570. Fine diamond engraving was practised by

Georg Schwanhardt the Elder, as may be observed on a covered goblet dated 1635 in the collection of the Germanisches National Museum in Nuremberg.

Wheel-engraved decoration on glass originated in Germany, from where it spread to the Netherlands. It was achieved by creating power to drive wheels of different sizes (usually made of copper), which rotated with an abrasive to cut the glass when contact was made. Foot treadles were often used, but in big workshops water mills would drive the wheels. Different wheels were used to achieve clear areas, opaque areas, high relief or intaglio of different sizes. In 1588 Emperor Rudolf invited Ottavio Miseroni from Milan to his court in Prague, where he became the court engraver of precious stones. In the same year Caspar Lehmann also came to Prague from Uelzen. Lehmann has been credited with being the first wheel-engraver on glass (which is softer to cut than most gemstones), substituting it for the rock crystal that the Miseroni family engraved upon. However, in 1569 an 'Adam der Glasschneider' is recorded, but whether he was a wheel-engraver is open to doubt. Before moving to Prague Lehmann may have learned his craft in Munich, where he must have seen the marvellous rock crystal of the Saracchi and Annibale Fontana (still preserved today in the Schatzkammer) in the court of Wilhelm V of Bavaria. Lehmann's beaker in the Museum of Decorative Arts in Prague depicting allegories of Power, Nobility and Freedom is signed and dated 1605. There are also a number of panels attributed to him.

Lehmann's pupil Georg Schwanhardt the Elder moved from Prague to Nuremberg in 1622, where he established a dynasty of glass engravers, although others – Hans Wessler, Georg Krig, Hans Müller and Heinrich Knopf – had practised the craft before with their gem engraving. The Schwanhardt family, namely, two sons (of which Heinrich is the more famous), three daughters, a daughter-in-law and even the maid all engraved on glass. There is a superb covered beaker in the Rudolph von Strasser Collection of *c.*1632 by Georg Schwanhardt the

LOW COUNTRIES
DIAMOND-
ENGRAVED FLUTE,
c.1655–60
(H50cm/19⅝in)

*The figure on
horseback is that of the
five-year-old Willem
III of Orange, taken
from an engraving of
1655 by Hendrick
Rokesz.* (RIGHT)

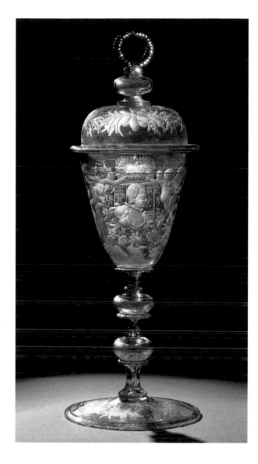

Elder depicting the Judgement of Paris, with
Venus fully clothed in seventeenth-century
dress. The fine goblet of the Emperor
Leopold I from the Ernesto Wolf Collection
is attributed to Johann Wolfgang Schmidt
and dates from about 1685. Nuremberg
engravers typically chose to decorate goblets
and beakers and these were probably made
there by the Dutch glass-blowers known to
be at work in about 1650. These glasses were
lighter than other German glass and usually
had covers. Schmidt, like his contemporary,
Hermann Schwinger, was one of a group of
Nuremberg-based engravers indebted to
George Schwanhardt the Elder.

Wheel-engraving was also practised in
Tambach in Thuringia in the mid seventeenth century and in Bohemia in the latter
part of the century. In Bohemia a thicker
glass imitating rock crystal was engraved,
but few engravers' names are known until
the end of the century. At this time the
brothers Friedrich and Martin Winter were

engraving and cutting rock crystal glass at
Hermsdorf, Silesia, for the glasshouse of
Count Schaffgotsch. A group of beakers
originating from Bohemia are referred to as
being by the Master of the Koula Beaker.
This engraver produced fine glasses with
polished engraving, often depicting classical
figures in a landscape.

In about 1645 wheel-engraving also
spread from Nuremberg to the Netherlands,
and scholar Pieter Ritsema van Eck has
drawn attention to an interesting group of
Dutch pieces which clearly show German
influence. A recent find is a fine covered
goblet engraved with the profile bust of the
Emperor Charles II of Spain, and showing
arms that were borne by him only between
the years 1665 and 1668.

The German tradition of wheel-engraving on glass continued into the eighteenth
century in many centres, and although engraving in the Netherlands was considered
the best in Europe, its origins were German.

WHEEL-ENGRAVED NUREMBERG
GOBLET, c.1685 (H43.5cm/17 3/16 in)

*The portrait of Leopold I was engraved by Johann
Wolfgang Schmidt and is perhaps based on a
numismatic likeness.* (ABOVE CENTRE)

LOW COUNTRIES ENGRAVED
COVERED GOBLET, c.1665
(H32.7cm/12⅞in)

*The profile bust is that of Charles II of Spain and
the Indies, with arms borne by him only between
1665 and 1668. He was sovereign of the Spanish
Low Countries.* (ABOVE)

THE EIGHTEENTH
CENTURY

The seventeenth century in Europe saw unparalleled changes in both the decoration of glass and in the metal itself. The ancient Roman technique of cutting was reintroduced, making its way from gem-cutters on to the newly developed, stronger glass. To facilitate deeper carving, water power was harnessed to drive the grinding wheels. A better understanding of chemistry and constant experimentation heralded the introduction of colour, particularly ruby red, and new processes led to large sheets of glass to create larger windows and mirrors of unflawed glass.

The strength of European glass-making moved northward from Venice to Germany and Bohemia. In England George Ravenscroft developed a metal that revolutionized glass-making – lead crystal. A major contribution made of the latter was the flamboyant chandeliers, which developed from the 1730s and were reflected in the multi-faceted borders of mirrors, thus bringing a new sense of light to dark interiors.

In the Low Countries the Venetian and German influences combined and a school of engravers arose which produced both wheel- and diamond-engraving of superb quality. British makers concentrated on drinking vessels that relied on subtle variations of form to make an impact. Others were engraved, painted in enamels or had colour-twist stems.

DETAIL FROM *STILL LIFE WITH PARROT*, GABRIELE SALCI, 1716

The artist has placed a fine example of a Venetian Mannerist goblet, which
was in great demand in the 16th and 17th centuries, beside a small, clear-glass
tumbler engraved with scrolls in the new fashionable 'Bohemian' style that was
sweeping through Europe.

CONTINENTAL GLASS

The latter part of the seventeenth century was not only a time of technical experimentation in many European glass-making centres, but also a rich period in the decorative arts. Glass-makers in northwestern Europe were shrugging off the influences of Italy, and their output began to manifest the first stages of distinctive, indigenous styles.

The late seventeenth-century Baroque style, favoured by the court of Louis XIV, was one of theatricality and grandeur. In the mid eighteenth century the Rococo style developed as a reaction to the earlier movement. This lighter, more sophisticated approach, epitomized by Madame de Pompadour and paintings by François Boucher, was gradually eclipsed by a less feminine, colder and more academic style in the third quarter of the century, one of the repeated revivals of interest in the classical world that became known as Neoclassicism.

These movements and trends are reflected in glass-making over this period. From the late sixteenth century table glass stopped being a luxury article only available to the rich and the courts, a material either imported from Venice or produced with difficulty locally with the help of Italians. Quite suddenly in the 1670s, in response to local demand, an outburst of research in more than one European centre resulted in locally manufactured glass, often of better quality than anything previously available.

POTASH-LIME GLASS

As part of the general movement toward producing indigenous luxury glassware, glass-makers and chemists in England, France and the German lands were seeking ways of producing a more 'crystalline' metal. Spurred on by the 1612 and 1679 publication of treatises on glass-making by, respectively, Antonio Neri (1576–1614) and Johann Kunckel (c.1630–1703), Bohemian glass masters such as Louis Le Vasseur d'Ossimont and Michael Müller (1639–1709) experimented by adding chalk to the potash flux, which resulted in a robust metal, closer in weight and refractive powers to the admired qualities of rock crystal. D'Ossimont had been attracted from the Lorraine estates of Count von Buquoy (1781–1851) to the glassworks on his southern Bohemian property. In Bohemia (now part of Czechoslovakia) at this time, local magnates encouraged the establishment of glassworks on their estates, mainly to help create agricultural land by clearing inaccessible forests.

It cannot be coincidental that a more robust metal was developed in the German centres of Bohemia, the Electorate of Brandenburg and Silesia (now part of Poland) just as the art of wheel-engraving on glass was in the process of overtaking all other methods of decoration in popularity.

EARLY NUREMBERG GLASS

The progression from carving and engraving hardstones and rock crystal to engraving on glass has traditionally been credited to Caspar Lehmann (1563/65–1622), attached to the court of Emperor Rudolf II in Prague. Whatever the case, Lehmann's most celebrated pupil, Georg Schwandhardt (1601–67), moved in 1622 from Prague back to his native city of Nuremberg, where he founded the most important workshop of Germanic glass-engraving, which survived for more than a century. During the last quarter of the seventeenth century and the first quarter of the eighteenth, many excellent engravers were working in Nuremberg, and signed examples of their work exist. This is in contrast to the anonymous output of the Bohemian and Silesian centres. The most important engravers working in Nuremberg included Johann Wolfgang Schmidt (d. 1710), Paulus Eder (fl.1685–1709) and Georg Friedrich Killinger (fl.1694–1726).

The two most common forms of glass decorated by the Nuremberg school at this time were the tall goblet and cover and the beaker on bun feet. The goblet, thin-walled and fundamentally of the façon-de-Venise type, usually has a generous rounded bowl set on a stem composed of a series of flattened hollow knops separated by discs or collars. The foot is wide and low with a Venetian-style folded rim, and the finial of the ovoid cover matches the stem. The bowl is decorated with the main engraved details while small decorative elements such as a wreath or border may appear on the foot and cover. In addition to the conventional engraved subjects of the period, which include portraits such as those of the emperor and important civic and religious officials, Schmidt's repertoire included armorials, allegories, emblems, and biblical and mythological images. He specialized in battle scenes in woodland settings which achieve dramatic effects, placing groups of cavalry with tightly packed rows of lances to contrast with the enclosing forest, all surmounted by the smoke and dust of battle. It is not known if these scenes, which included naval engagements, are based on engravings of historical battles but early engravers seldom seem to have worked without reference to a print, even if details were altered or elements from more than one engraved source were combined on the same glass.

Killinger and the slightly younger Anton

period. These heavier Bohemian glasses encouraged deeper intaglio engraving.

Some of the most imposing Nuremberg pieces were partly coloured, with either dark blue, emerald green or more rarely purple bowls and covers, colourless stems and cover finials and coloured feet. The Nurembergers also used the recently perfected *Rubinglas*, or ruby glass, whose almost alchemical secret of manufacture the chemist Johann Kunckel, working in the Drewitz and Potsdam glasshouses of the Brandenburg elector, claimed to have rediscovered by adding gold to the batch. The technique soon spread to other centres such as Bayreuth, Freising and Munich, where Hans Fiedler produced it for the Bavarian elector, Maximilian II (1662–1726). By the second quarter of the eighteenth century Nuremberg declined as a centre of engraving and other areas, such as Silesia and Bohemia, came to the forefront.

HIGH BAROQUE IN BOHEMIA AND SILESIA

The glass master Michael Müller, working in the Helmbach glasshouse (in the Winterberg region of southern Bohemia), perfected the potash-lime recipe, resulting in a thicker, more ductile glass. The stage was set for an explosion of glass-making activity in Bohemia, the Riesengebirge and Silesia. Over the eighteenth century there was hardly a place in the West that escaped the influence of Bohemian glass, this being due both to imports and imitations.

At the turn of the seventeenth century three centres produced some of the most grandiose and dramatic essays in 'sculptural' glass-making ever seen. From 1680 Christoph Labhardt (1641–95) had been active at the court of the landgrave of Hesse-Kassel as a carver of gems, hardstones and glass. A water-powered cutting mill had been built

SOUTH GERMAN RUBY-GLASS, SILVER-GILT MOUNTED TANKARD, *c*.1700 (H21cm/8¼in)

Rubinglas *was considered a luxury glass.* (TOP)

NUREMBERG ENGRAVED BEAKER, JOHANN WOLFGANG SCHMIDT, *c*.1700 (H11cm/4¼in) (ABOVE)

NUREMBERG PART-COLOURED ENGRAVED GOBLET AND COVER, LATE 1600s (H46cm/17⅞in) (ABOVE RIGHT)

Wilhelm Mäuerl (1672–1737) both produced highly sophisticated wheel-engraving, sometimes combined with diamond-point detail, and made frequent use of the contrasts between polished engraving (*Klarschnitt*) and matt work (*Mattschnitt*). In the 1720s Killinger and other Nuremberg engravers favoured simple baluster goblets, probably imported from Bohemia, for their work, which included chinoiseries, Chinese-inspired decorative devices whose usage reached its apogee during the Rococo

to produce the power to grind, carve and engrave through thick areas of glass, facilitating the production of increasingly three-dimensional effects. Franz Gondelach (1663–1726), Labhardt's famous pupil, was to outstrip his master in this technique, producing sculptural goblets and other ceremonial wares with figural finials and boldly raised borders of acanthus leaves.

Among the loose hegemony of states comprising the Holy Roman Empire, there were at this time strong links between Hesse-Kassel and Brandenburg, where the Elector Friedrich III (later King Friedrich I of Prussia) had married the daughter of Landgrave Karl of Hesse-Kassel in 1689. The chemist Johann Kunckel was carrying out experiments for the Brandenburg elector at Drewitz and it is thought that Kassel possibly sent to Potsdam for its glass. A water mill was also set up in the 1680s in Potsdam for Martin Winter (d. 1702), who produced highly engraved work (*Hochschnitt*) for the Prussian court. His brother Friedrich (d. *c*.1712) was concurrently working as *Glasschneider* (glass-cutter) and *Glasschleiffer* (glass polisher) for the Silesian magnate Count Christoph Leopold Schaffgotsch at Petersdorf, who was conducting a correspondence on technical matters of glass-making with the elector. There, water power was also used in the production of glass carved to resemble rock crystal with a success not to be surpassed until the end of the nineteenth century. Friedrich Winter specialized in producing covered goblets in the form of cornucopias with raised acanthus leaves (often embellished with the Schaffgotsch arms or fir-tree crest). This fashion for heavy monumental parade goblets was to last barely two generations.

Martin Winter's nephew, Gottfried Spiller (1663–1728), continued in this tradition at Potsdam, producing massive goblets with matt raised decoration and brilliant renderings of the Prussian coat of arms. A sign of changing fashion, however, was Spiller's figural engraving. Spiller's legacy of incorporating engraved putti in his goblets, either as supporters or engaged in activities such as dancing or bacchanalian

sport, would endure in Brandenburg – and wherever its influence was felt – well into the next century. Gondelach's influence, though, soon dissipated, although it is possible that Johann Moritz Trümper (1680–1742) may have been responsible for a few surviving glasses, their stems carved into rather static and etiolated sculptural forms.

Although Friedrich Winter died in about 1712, it is possible that his studio continued production into the 1730s, when a small group of *Pokale* (covered goblets) was made

with *Hochschnitt* decoration, these with more of a Régence/Rococo feeling. There is also the extraordinary anomaly of the carved Augustus Rex goblet in the Stuttgart Museum, produced by an as yet unidentified master in 1731 for Augustus the Strong in the Dresden glasshouse. The proportions are monumental, but the form is classically symmetrical. The conceit of the cover in the shape of an electoral cap (with finial in the form of raised royal monogram) recalls

early objects made for the Swedish royal family at Kungsholm in the 1680s.

Bohemian glass of the experimental *fin de siècle* tended to be rather heavy, and its engraved decoration crude. A series of thick-walled beakers and heavy baluster goblets based on metal prototypes dates from this period. Already, though, there is evidence of the use of faceting and printies (circular or oval polished depressions, *Blankschnitt* in German) around the rim and on the base, a decorative technique effected

SILESIAN *HOCHSCHNITT* GOBLET, WORKSHOP OF FRIEDRICH WINTER, *c*.1700 (H19.7cm/7¾in) (ABOVE LEFT)

The glass is carved to resemble rock crystal.

POTSDAM ROYAL ARMORIAL BEAKER AND COVER, ENGRAVED BY GOTTFRIED SPILLER, LATE 17TH CENTURY (H22cm/8¾in) (ABOVE)

by the *Kugler*, a specialist cutter whose method of creating contrasts with the engraving lightened the overall effect. Engraving at the beginning of the century was also not of high quality, with little use of polished detail and the employment of large, coarse foliate motifs.

An anonymous engraver whose circle in the Riesengebirge had considerable influence at this time was the so-called Master of the Koula Beaker, whose idiosyncratic style involved the use of deep, often polished engraving. Subject matter tended to be mythological and based on engraved sources. This often provincial style was to change quite abruptly at the beginning of the second decade, as the influence of the new Régence style in France spread across Europe, mainly in the form of plates of

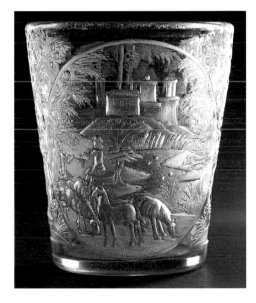

BOHEMIAN ENGRAVED BEAKER, ATELIER OF THE MASTER OF THE KOULA BEAKER, LATE 17TH CENTURY (H11.2cm/4½in) (ABOVE)

BOHEMIAN (RIESENGEBIRGE) ENGRAVED GOBLET AND COVER, EARLY 18TH CENTURY (H28cm/11in)

This piece features allegories of the Four Seasons. (ABOVE RIGHT)

engraved ornament by Jean Bérain and his German imitators, such as Paul Decker (1677–1713). This new decorative vocabulary involved the use of grotesques, arabesques and symmetrical arrangements of foliate scrolls and strapwork, known in German as *Laub- und Bandelwerk*.

In the meantime glass engravers' guilds were being established, particularly in northern Bohemia, at centres such as Steinschönau (now Kamenický Šenov) and

Reichenberg (Liberec), which became one of the main nerve centres of the Bohemian glass trade. This was carried out with such vigour that it resulted in Bohemia capturing the European glass market during the first half of the eighteenth century. Journeyman engravers and traders travelled with barrows, paniers or carts, peddling glass all over Europe, sometimes carrying out simple engraved commissions on the spot. In Spain, the Bohemians established entrepôts for the further distribution of their glass as far afield as the Black Sea and Mexico.

The best Bohemian glass consisted of well-proportioned goblets and covers set on faceted baluster stems, sometimes enclosing red and gold swirling threads, which also appear in the cover. The decoration often takes up a large proportion of the bowl with central motifs such as armorials, monograms, hunting scenes, religious figures or the ever-popular emblems and allegories, surrounded by scrollwork, cornucopias, baskets of fruit and flowers, lambrequins and putti. Unfortunately, there was a tendency for some exponents to dilute the effect of their work in a plethora of tiny decorative details. Sweetmeat glasses in the form of shells or cornucopias and tall flasks were also important elements on the dining table. The use of covered *Pokale* seems to have been ubiquitous in polite society, although it is not clear to what extent they were made in sets and whether they were only used on the most formal social occasions, when drinking consisted of rounds of formal toasts.

In contrast to Bohemia, where the quality of engraved decoration on glass varied quite considerably, the important Silesian centres produced work of a consistently high standard and continued to do so for several decades after Bohemian engraved decoration was in decline. Workshops tended to be near the area's abundant hot springs and spas, one of the most important of which was Warmbrunn (Cieplice), where 42 engravers are recorded in 1742, supplying visitors and the German fairs, such as those at Leipzig and Frankfurt. The Silesian workshops had also taken up the Régence scroll and arabesque, but tended to control it more

tightly than their Bohemian counterparts, making much use of polishing to highlight motifs and achieving in their best work decoration of great sophistication.

An event of great impact on Silesia – and much celebrated by glass decorators – was the seizure of the province from Maria Theresa by Friedrich II of Prussia (Frederick the Great) in 1740. Numerous glasses have survived which are decorated with a portrait of the Prussian monarch adapted from contemporary medals. Frederick's victories over the French and Austrians at Rossbach, Leuthen, Liegnitz and Torgau during the Seven Years' War (1756–63) were commemorated on Silesian glasses with bird's-eye views of the battlefield.

Toward the middle of the century Rococo motifs began to be adopted in glassware – not only asymmetrical scrolls, but shellwork and scales. One of the most influential Warmbrunn engravers at this time was Christian Gottfried Schneider (1710–73). A number of contemporary paper imprints of his work have survived, indicating how in the 1750s and 1760s styles had become looser, compositions less static and figures unashamedly elegant. The only other Silesian artist whose work can be identified is Caspar Gottlieb Langer (*fl.*1749), whose signed goblet depicting a group of carousing members of the Leipzig Chamber of Commerce is in that city's

Historical Museum. Particularly favoured by the Silesian engravers were subjects with putti, often after prints by the master Jacques Stella (1596–1657); also popular were pastoral subjects. In the late 1750s and 1760s foliate scrolls and shells began to make their appearance as large raised motifs on bowls and covers, either finely polished or gilded, confining and separating the areas of wheel-engraved decoration.

THE COURT GLASS ENGRAVER

Bohemia and Silesia were exceptional in that glass-making and decoration there were not oriented toward the court of a prince. Elsewhere in Germany patriotic decoration tended to be the norm and a number of engravers and their studios were attached to the many large and small German courts as *Hofkristal-schneider* (court glass engravers).

DRESDEN

Over a long period the Saxon electors had been passionate collectors of 'curiosities', none more so than Augustus the Strong (1670–1733), who was also king of Poland.

A glasshouse had been established in 1699 near Dresden, and a group of late but important *Hochschnitt* goblets was produced there, including the example carved with Augustus the Strong's monogram. Other glasses, probably from the same workshop, are recorded, such as the goblet with a relief portrait of the monarch with Potsdam-type acanthus decoration (now in The Corning Museum of Glass). It is known that glass engravers were employed to engrave the arabesques on early Böttger stoneware and that the technique of applying moulded glass-paste portrait medallions to royal Saxon and Potsdam goblets was probably developed in the workshops supplying Dresden's treasury, the so-called Green Vaults. Besides his work in the manufacture of true porcelain, Johann Friedrich Böttger (1682–1719) is also credited with producing *Rubinglas* at Dresden, applied as a red layer on clear glass. Certainly there are a number of objects, including miniature teapots decorated with the royal Saxon-Polish arms and Dresden silver-gilt mounts, which could be the fruits of his work.

An engraver who had an important workshop from c.1717 to 1744 was Johann Christoph Kiessling (d. 1744). He produced high-quality engraving of mainly hunting scenes in a combination of matt and polished cutting. His work is found on typical Saxon goblets of this period, which comprise a deep funnel bowl on a faceted baluster stem with shoulder knop. Apart from court commissions it received from Dresden, the Glücksburg glasshouse at Wittenberg in Saxony produced large numbers of more pedestrian glasses. These included goblets with marked thistle bowls and inverted baluster stems, on which the everted base of the bowl and the whole stem are cut with tiny horizontal sets of facets.

BRANDENBURG

Gottfried Spiller, his workshop and its successors of the next generation were not influenced by delicate Bérainesque ornament and continued producing substantial goblets and beakers with figural scenes of

SAXON RUBY-GLASS MINIATURE
TEAPOT, *c.*1715 (H9.6cm/3¾in)

This tiny object, featuring c.1730 Dresden mounts, is unlikely to have been made for use. (LEFT)

POTSDAM ROYAL PORTRAIT GOBLET
AND COVER, *c.*1735 (H31.6cm/12½in)

The gilded engraved detail creates a sumptuous impression on the goblet, which is decorated with a portrait of Queen Sophia Dorothea of Prussia. (BELOW LEFT)

POTSDAM ENGRAVED GOBLET, ELIAS
ROSBACH, *c.*1735 (H21.8cm/8½in)

Rosbach's workshop carried on the Potsdam tradition. (BELOW).

either large putti, often in bacchanalian disarray in the Winter tradition, or scenes with figures of Greek deities such as those favoured by Elias Rosbach (1700–65) and his circle, first at Potsdam and after 1736 at Zechlin. Other goblets of drawn-funnel form are decorated with portraits of the reigning monarchs in Prussia, Friedrich I and Sophia Dorothea. Here the engraving is

LAUENSTEIN
ARMORIAL
GOBLET AND
COVER, c.1770
(H31.3cm/12¼in)

*Lauenstein glass-
makers included lead
oxide in their recipe
and as a result their
simpler, well-balanced
glasses are often either
crizzled or splendidly
cristalline. This goblet
bears the arms of the
Prince of Schwarzburg,
the pontil is engraved
with a lion and the
letter 'C'.*

gilded to create a sumptuous effect. Gilt borders and highly polished cutting featured on *Pokale* made from the 1740s to the 1760s at Zechlin, where armorial engraving predominated.

As a result of the experiments of Johann Kunckel in the 1670s, gold-ruby glass was also produced at Potsdam, whose output included impressive, High Baroque covered goblets. The ruby metal was particularly deep and rich, and engraved details such as the Prussian royal coat of arms tended to be gilded as well. Potsdam also produced simpler polygonal flasks and bottles, as did southern Germany and Bohemia.

THURINGIA

From 1723 Andreas Friedrich Sang (*fl*.1719–60), a member of a considerable clan of engravers, became court glass engraver to the dukes of Sachsen-Weimar. A few glasses signed by him exist, from which it is possible to obtain a good idea of his style. He produced scenes with putti or the infant Bacchus astride a barrel, very much in the Potsdam style, worked on typical Thuringian goblets with a deep ogee bowl and a moulded pedestal stem, a form which would be taken up in England and elsewhere. There

are also pear-shaped goblets on which Sang traced arabesques incorporating busts and landscapes. Johann Heinrich Sang (*fl*.1745–55) followed in his father's footsteps, working in the High Rococo style with florid shell- and scrollwork.

Georg Ernst Kunckel (1692–1750) was a fine engraver who became *Hofglasschneider* to Friedrich II of Sachsen-Gotha at his court in Coburg in 1721. Kunckel settled nearby in Eisenach and stylistically his work reveals links with the Nuremberg school, with Killinger and above all with Mäuerl. His grasp of line is always extremely elegant and, like Mäuerl, he was adept at the contrapuntal positioning of polished and matt engraved details.

Another central German glasshouse was at Lauenstein, which experimented with the English lead-glass recipe. Some Lauenstein glasses are crizzled, but in general the metal has the lustrous quality of lead glass and tends to be blown into less tightly controlled forms, more in the manner of an English baluster. There is simple faceting on the base of the bowl and on the heavy baluster stem. The foot is high with a thick folded rim, and the rims of both bowl and cover are usually embellished with plain gilt lines.

Although engraving never died out completely in the German centres, its popularity waned temporarily from about 1770, as the use of the heavy, elaborate and formal *Pokal* and cover died out. The emphasis on cut wares grew in importance with the spread of the Neoclassical Anglo-Irish style.

OTHER FORMS OF DECORATION

The technically exacting process of creating gold sandwich glass (*Zwischengoldglas*) probably had its roots in reverse-glass painting and engraving in the seventeenth century. Johann Kunckel mentioned the technique in his *Ars Vitraria Experimentalis* in 1679. The great majority of surviving *Zwischengoldglas* was

made in Bohemia during the first half of the eighteenth century. The bowl of a goblet or the body of a beaker consists of two parts. There is an inner glass, usually with slightly flared sides, on the outer surface of which gold or, more rarely, silver foil was applied and engraved with a needle to create a frieze of decorative motifs such as hunting and garden scenes, religious subjects and armorials. Over this an outer glass layer was slumped to fit exactly up to a flange a few millimetres below the rim, and the two pieces were glued together. A medallion, consisting of a gilt or silver motif on a red lacquer ground, was inserted into the base and the outer layer was cut with vertical facets. The effect is decorative and luxurious.

Exactly where in Bohemia these glasses were produced is still not known. At one time they were thought to be the products of workshops attached to monasteries, an attribution based on a famous beaker depicting the interior of a church with Father Kligel (d. 1746), a priest from the monastery of Haindorf (Hejnice) in northern Bohemia, near Friedland (Frýdlant), in the pulpit. This is one of the few *Zwischengoldglas* pieces with a personal reference on it. In view of the large number produced and evidence that they were also made for export, it seems more likely they originated in workshops closely connected with glass-making centres. Variations on the gold and silver foil decoration include a small thick-walled group with sides painted in *faux marbre*, a group with polychrome-lacquered details on a silvered ground and another with polychrome-lacquered, engraved scenes. A further variant was the insertion of *Zwischengoldglas* medallions or plaques into a conventional goblet, flask or beaker.

Certainly this technique must have influenced the work of two consummate artists working in the last quarter of the century. In Warmbrunn Johann Sigismund Menzel (1744–1810) produced a series of Neoclassical urn-shaped goblets and covers embellished with *Zwischengoldglas* medallions with black portrait silhouettes. Any other decoration is minimal, with a little faceting, gilt-line borders and occasionally

some discreet engraved detail. In Gutenbrunn in Lower Austria, Johann Joseph Mildner (1763–1808) produced some of the most technically proficient and beautiful work using this technique ever to have survived. Working mainly on beakers, he set medallions into the sides, fillets into the rims and medallions into the bases. Besides full-scale polychrome portraits of the Austrian royal family and of his patron, Count Fürnberg, Mildner also produced silhouettes, monograms, armorials and local views and figures. He seems to have had no followers and with him the technique died out until it was revived toward the end of the nineteenth century.

The strong tradition of decorating glass in polychrome enamels in the German lands, a technique inherited from the Venetians that reached its peak in the seventeenth century, continued in certain centres almost to the end of the eighteenth century. In Saxony a number of workshops continued to provide enamelled vessels for the court cellar and apothecary, while in Franconia guild *Humpen* and glasses painted with views, such as that of the Ochsenkopf

Mountain, continued to be produced in the 1730s and 1740s. In Bohemia enamelling was adapted to the Rococo style in the 1760s, particularly on *Milchglas* (opaque white glass) wares such as punch sets, decanters and tankards, on which the painting was similar to that on porcelain, with ladies and gentlemen in landscapes with classical ruins enclosed within scrollwork. In general, this technique declined during the century to that of a peasant craft, as can be seen from the innumerable schnapps flasks which have survived, painted in a limited palette with stereotyped motifs. The Nuremberg *Hausmaler* ('house painter') tradition, founded by Johann Schaper (1621–70) in the seventeenth century, was carried on in Breslau (Wrocław) and Kronstadt (Kunštát) in Silesia by the Preissler family, father Daniel (1636–1733) and son Ignaz (1676–1741). The latter worked for the Kolowrat family at Schloss Reichenau (Rychnov) in eastern Bohemia, producing skilled painting in black and red enamel washes (called *Schwarzlot*) on glass, *Milchglas* and porcelain. His subject matter ranged from large mythological scenes, such as a flask in the Victoria and Albert Museum, London, with Diana and Actaeon, townscapes in the Nuremberg style with Bérainesque borders and a large number of wares decorated with chinoiseries, featuring Eastern potentates and philosophers, exotic buildings and birds.

THE LOW
COUNTRIES

As a great trading, seafaring and mercantile region, the lowland countries of Belgium, Luxembourg and the Netherlands had for a long time been the site of a flourishing glass-making industry, founded in the sixteenth century by the Italians. As soon as the conflict with Spain was resolved by the Treaty of Westphalia in 1648, the northern Protestant United Provinces were free to

develop their trading empire worldwide. The southern, predominantly Catholic, provinces remained under the control of Spain and later, in the eighteenth century, they came under Austrian rule. By the end of the seventeenth century Liège had overtaken Antwerp as the glass-making centre of the southern Netherlands.

Throughout the Netherlands the *façon-de-Venise* style of glass-making continued into the early eighteenth century, when influences began to spread from centres such as Nuremberg on the one hand and on the other hand England, with its new lead-glass fashions. In the Dutch Republic the rise of a powerful urban middle class had encouraged the unique phenomenon of a strong tradition of entirely amateur decorators on glass, of which the most celebrated were the Visscher sisters of Amsterdam, Anna (1583–1651) and Maria (1594–1649), and Willem van Heemskerk (1613–92) of Leiden, all of whom specialized in calligraphic inscriptions in diamond-point.

In the next century engraving was to develop along pointillist-like lines at the hands of the innovative Frans Greenwood (1680–1761), who practised his art in Dordrecht. This stipple-engraved technique involved tapping on the surface of the glass with a sharp point, the degree of density of dots creating light and shaded effects. Of the 47 known signed pieces by Greenwood, ranging from the earliest (1720), which is entirely in line, to his mature work of the 1740s, in which virtuoso displays of stippled shading were achieved, the subject matter tended to be culled from prints or paintings of the previous century and therefore give a particularly composed and painterly impression. Greenwood's work stimulated a whole group of engravers in the next generation, of whom the most important were Aert Schouman (1710–92) and the three artists whose work had until recently been placed under the umbrella of David Wolff (1732–98). All three concentrated on Rococo scenes, such as putti borne on clouds and music-making children, and presumably must have been closely associated in some form of workshop situation.

DUTCH STIPPLE-ENGRAVED GOBLET, FRANS GREENWOOD, 1745
(H25cm/9⅞in)

The Dutch excelled at amateur engraving on glass in the 17th and 18th centuries, and the pointillist technique of stippling on glass was perfected by Greenwood from 1720 onward. The subject on this piece is a Dutch 17th-century engraving and is worked on a typical light baluster goblet. (BELOW)

DUTCH ENGRAVED GOBLET, JACOB SANG, c.1760 (H15.9cm/6¼in)

Jacob Sang, a member of a German family of glass engravers, was one of the most adept artists using the wheel in the mid 18th century in the Netherlands. The popular engraved subject on this glass depicts the 'mothering' chamber, with infant, nurse and an inscription around the rim wishing good health to the mother and child. (RIGHT)

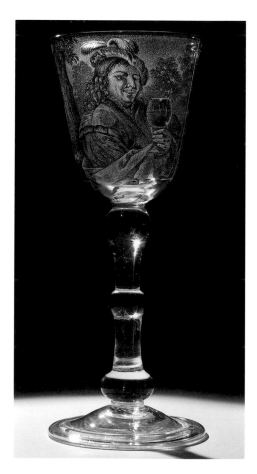

VENETIAN *LATTIMO* RED-ENAMELLED PLATE, MIOTTI GLASSWORKS *c.*1740 (D22.5cm/9in)

By the 18th century Venice was reduced to catering for tourists. Sets of these white plates with views of Venice, after etchings by Luca Carlevaris, were produced for foreigners on the Grand Tour, including Horace Walpole, who had a set at his Twickenham home, Strawberry Hill. (LEFT)

Numerous glasses were wheel-engraved with a multitude of subjects, including toasts – such as to friendship, the pregnant wife, silver anniversaries, the Fatherland and the House of Orange, all decorated below with the relevant symbols or subjects. Many of the best engravers of the time, such as Jacob Sang (d. 1783) and his brother Simon Jacob, members of the illustrious Weimar family of engravers who were working in Amsterdam from the early 1750s, used English light baluster wine glasses, favouring the softer, less brittle finish of the English lead glass for their delicate and precise work.

The subject of glass production during the eighteenth century in the Netherlands is at present confusing. Traditionally all glass of lead was ascribed to England and it was thought that so many pieces bore Dutch engraving because of the strong trade links between the countries. However, more recent research has revealed that lead glass was certainly made in Middelburg, the Netherlands, and in Namur, Flanders. Whatever the origins of Dutch-decorated glass, the impetus to embellish it had largely died out by the end of the eighteenth century.

VENICE

The heyday of Venetian glass-making was over by the end of the seventeenth century, as fine *cristallo* began to be manufactured elsewhere in Europe and the new Bohemian chalk glass grew in popularity. An interesting cross section of the products of Murano from the first decade of the century survives in the Glass Cabinet at Rosenborg Castle, Copenhagen, the result of a visit by King Frederick IV of Denmark and Norway to Venice in 1708–9. All the skills of the seventeenth-century Muranese artists are still evident, in the use of filigree, lampwork flowers and trailing, and a considerable emphasis on wares in a soapy opalescent glass (*vetro a girasol*). But they also include colourless wares that were blown and engraved in the Bohemian style.

Venice could not compete with Bohemian dominance of the European glass market and increasingly resorted to the production of glass for tourists. Glass-makers such as the Miotti family at the Al

ARRANGEMENT OF THE GLASS CABINET, ROSENBORG CASTLE, COPENHAGEN, 1714; ENGRAVED IN 1867

Gesù Glassworks seem to have produced mainly opaque white wares, tea bowls and saucers decorated with low-fired gilding and enamels, as well as sets of opaque white plates finely painted in reddish enamel with views of Venice after Canaletto and Guardi,

VENETIAN ENAMELLED FLASK, WORKSHOP OF OSWALDO BRUSSA, SECOND HALF 18TH CENTURY (H13.9cm/5½in)

among others. An enameller, Oswaldo Brussa, painted charming bird and floral motifs on glass with faint echoes of Islamic decoration.

Giuseppe Briati (1686–1772) is credited with developing the Venetian chandelier in about 1739, one of the most extraordinarily exaggerated glass objects ever produced. The main elements were blown, the rims often trailed in a colour and the whole embellished with lampwork flowers and fruits to create an effect when lit like an exploding firework. These were extremely popular abroad and helped to establish local production in the Holy Roman Empire and

France. The Venetians also specialized in elaborate mirrors, a fashion developed in France but adapted by the Muranese with their own brand of fantasy. Frames were divided up and bevelled to reflect thousands of facets of light, as well as engraved with figures and scrollwork in Bohemian style.

FRANCE

France was in the forefront of fashion in the decorative arts during this period, its court aped by royalty in many other European countries. However, unlike in the German lands, there does not seem to have been as strong an interest in table glass in France as there was in architecture, furniture and various other furnishings. It was in architectural glass that the French made the greatest contributions. To furnish the vast and grandiose palaces for the French court, Jean-Baptiste Colbert (1619–93), Louis XIV's minister, had grasped the importance of encouraging home industries rather than relying on foreign imports, for which purpose various factories and workshops were set up.

In 1689 Bernard Perrot (d. 1709), an Altarist from Orléans (where a glasshouse was founded in 1662), was granted a patent by the Académie des Sciences for the production of flat glass by the revolutionary method of casting. A manufactory was founded to produce it at St-Gobain in the forest of La Thiérache in northern France, and French mirror glass rapidly took the lead in the markets of the time. Using this technique, much larger pieces of flat glass could be produced, which had a revolutionary effect on huge Baroque reception rooms where the windows, often from floor to ceiling, were now composed of large panes with few imperfections and set in wooden, not lead, glazing bars. In the room itself the use of large mirrors became feasible and fashionable, and the windows were often set opposite each other to create 'perpetual' reflections, further enhanced by the illuminations of the new cut-glass chandeliers.

Ordinary domestic glass was made throughout the eighteenth century in the traditional glass centres of Lorraine and Normandy, but their output seems to have been restricted to simple tableware with mould-blown decoration. It was only in the 1780s that the glasshouse at St Louis, near the Rhine north of Basel, experimented with lead crystal while making cut glass in the Anglo-Irish manner, a fashion rapidly gaining popularity on the Continent.

FRENCH ENGRAVED TUMBLER, ST LOUIS, 1775 (H7cm/2¾in)

SPAIN

In Spain glass-making during this period divided itself into two distinct types. On the one hand, the glass centres of Andalusia and Castile continued creating glass in the strong local traditions evolved over the previous two centuries, producing it in an unrefined soda metal using soda from the barilla plant as a flux. The types of wares they made included the *cántir* (a two-spouted jug), *porrón* (a long-spouted wine vessel) and *almorratxa* (a four-spouted rosewater sprinkler), idiosyncratic pieces which were unique to Spain.

Glass for the court and upper classes was produced at the royal glassworks of La Granja de San Ildefonso, southwest of Segovia, founded in 1728. Its wares reflected the influence of the Bohemians, who in fact had strong links with Spain, specifically Cadiz. Goblets, bowls, case bottles and flasks were produced in a decolourized metal with shallow polished facets and flutes, often gilded, in the second half of the century; these reflected the classical taste.

SPANISH ENGRAVED AND GILT VASE AND COVER, LA GRANJA DEL SAN ILDEFONSO, c.1780 (H51cm/20in)

SCANDINAVIA

A glasshouse was established in 1676 at Kungsholm, Stockholm, by a Muranese glass-maker, Giacomo Scapitta. Surviving glasses suggest a high percentage of royal commissions in the form of *façon-de-Venise* goblets engraved with the royal cipher, some with stems with the royal monogram in free-standing letters. As in other centres at this time, such as Potsdam and the Riesengebirge, the Swedish glass recipe was chemically imbalanced and Kungsholm glass has tended to crizzle. Also

in Sweden, glass was produced showing influences from Lauenstein, Thuringia and Saxony.

Norway's first important glass-making centre was established in 1741 at Nøstetangen, where glass was initially made in German potash-lime metal and later in English glass of lead. Stylistically, Germanic and English influences mingled to produce a distinct indigenous glass in which both influences are clearly visible. From 1755 James Keith (*fl.*1750–87), from Newcastle-upon-Tyne, worked at Nøstetangen, introducing elements of the English glass-making vernacular: loving cups, candlesticks, goblets, punch bowls and tankards were produced with moulded flame-like decoration, as well as a type of anachronistic 'nipt-diamond-waies'. Variants on the 'English' twist-stemmed wine glass were also made. The most important decorator at the factory was Heinrich Gottlieb Köhler, who was brought to Norway via Copenhagen from Silesia. At first he restricted himself mainly to royal portraits and armorials in a robust German Rococo style, but later his subject matter included local landscapes and crafts in the Dutch manner. The other engraver whose name has survived from this period, just before engraving fell out of fashion in the 1770s, is Vinter, who worked in the Germanic style on wares from Nøstetangen as well as Hurdal.

RUSSIA

A s in Sweden, the earliest Russian glass-making activities were tentative and in the Venetian tradition. The first glasshouse of note was founded in 1668 at Izmailovo near Moscow under the patronage of Czar Alexis. By the beginning of the next century the ubiquitous Bohemian style of engraved, colourless glass was appearing under the influence of immigrant Bohemians. Glass from Izmailovo was mainly intended for the court and was engraved with royal symbols. Goblets in the Saxon style were also produced, many with

engraved portraits of the empresses Elizabeth and Catherine II (these often of poor quality). Glass-making expanded rapidly during the eighteenth century as centres were established to manufacture bottles, plate glass and mirrors.

It was only toward the end of the century that glass of any quality was produced in Russia, mainly at the St Petersburg Glassworks, founded by Peter the Great in the early eighteenth century. The firm

RUSSIAN GLASS AND ORMOLU TABLE, IMPERIAL GLASSWORKS, ST PETERSBURG, c.1807 (H79cm/31in)

expanded and was renamed the St Petersburg Imperial Glassworks in 1792. Influenced by the Neoclassical style sweeping through Europe, the factory produced wares in vivid colours as well as marbled shades. Large vases and urns in the French Neoclassical style were made, as well as sophisticated versions of local wares, such as eggs, painted by artists with links to the Imperial Porcelain Manufactory. Large table services were produced, such as the 'Orlov' service in colourless glass with gilt decoration, which illustrated the growing 'international style' of this time. Indeed, the service could just as well have been made in Bohemia, France or England.

BRITISH GLASS

RAVENSCROFT'S GLASS OF LEAD

Continuing research has upheld the reputation of George Ravenscroft (1618–81), although he is no longer credited with the actual invention of lead glass. Nevertheless, there is no doubt that it was his experiments that eventually provided England with the finest examples of vessel-glass in the world during the following century.

Ravenscroft was typical of the educated entrepreneurs of his time, involved in trade yet deeply interested in the emerging sciences. His connections with Venice (his brother was at one time in partnership with the English Consul there) indicate lasting interest in at least one aspect of glass: he was an importer of looking-glass plates. Aside from this, he had established a glasshouse in the Savoy, London. His experiments were aimed at achieving a new recipe for vessel-glass, heavier and more brilliant than variants of the hitherto universal soda metal. He explored the use of flints, and of lead oxide as a flux, an ingredient already used in Italy in the manufacture of 'paste' jewellery.

In 1673 he was granted a patent for a new glass, and was retained by the Glass Sellers' Company for further experiments at a new glasshouse provided for him at Henley-on-Thames. The Glass Sellers' Company, long dependent on Venice, was acutely anxious to improve the quality of glass manufactured domestically. Initially the new glass deteriorated rapidly after cooling, its surface becoming fogged by innumerable microscopic cracks, a condition known as 'crizzling'. By 1676, however, Ravenscroft advertised that these early problems were solved (which they were not), and the following year the Glass Sellers' Company agreed that vessels made of the improved material might bear a raven's-head seal. That the problem of crizzling was far from overcome is clear, since all known sealed Ravenscroft pieces have deteriorated, some to a marked degree.

Identifying what was made in the new material is, disappointingly, no easy task. The Glass Sellers' 1677 agreement with Ravenscroft lists glasses of various sizes for various purposes, together with bottles and cruets, but few of the known sealed exam-

ples fit the list. Among sealed Ravenscroft pieces are posset pots, none of which is included in the 1677 list. In addition, once one sets aside early lead glasses with actual seals one is into the difficult area of attribution between the products of England and the Netherlands, for the Dutch experimented with lead as well. By the late 1680s England virtually had a Dutch court, with all its attendant stylistic preferences, so although it is possible to date glasses on style within broad brackets, it is not always easy to pronounce on national provenance.

Nevertheless, it is clear that the manufacturers took the new material to their hearts, with glasshouses advertising 'flint' glass increasing in number. Fine things were made, including large *Roemers* which were copied from Central European originals, with hemispherical ribbed bowls and wide hollow stems set with prunts, and many ceremonial covered cups, generally embellished with pincering, trailing and other types of applied ornament. This elaborate decoration, together with diamond moulding ('nipt diamond waies') and gadrooning, bore witness to the remaining, if somewhat distant, influence of Venice. Coins were sometimes included in the hollow knops of these prestige pieces, but are generally less than helpful in dating them.

GADROONED POSSET POT, GEORGE RAVENSCROFT, c.1677 (H7cm/2¾in)

At the base of the spout is the seal of George Ravenscroft, who is credited with the introduction of glass of lead to England. (ABOVE LEFT)

DRINKING GLASS WITH HEAVY RETICULATION, c.1680–5 (H15.3cm/6in)

The rich decoration shows that many fine makers retained a devotion to Continental styles. (ABOVE)

DRINKING GLASSES

The twenty remaining years of the seventeenth century saw the gradual elimination of England's dependence on Venice as a stylistic influence. Not only did makers appear to find the more ductile nature of lead glass conducive to more substantial designs, it is as if they put away, perhaps with some relief, the delicacy and 'foreignness' of Central European styles in favour of a thoroughly English vigour. Their forms were clearly based on contemporary fashions in silver, and indeed in furniture making, with a firm emphasis on turnery and strength. In drinking glasses (probably the most numerous class of glass vessel, hence the generic term), there developed the family of glasses known as balusters. The word refers to the architectural form used, to begin with, upside down as the principal feature in the stem of a glass.

At first stems were simple, but gradually a considerable vocabulary of forms was built up and, as the years went by, elaboration increased. By 1725 stem forms could be quite complicated, and makers also played with the shapes of the bowl and foot. Later generations have given a host of names to the different components of the stem known as 'knops' – from acorn, egg, melon and mushroom, to annular, bobbin, hollow and winged – and collectors compete avidly for glasses which include the rarer examples. There were good and bad makers, of course, but given the happy combination of an experienced gaffer and a good batch of glass, the resulting product could be a miracle of balance and gleaming light, the design competently gauged and successfully achieved. Indeed, assessment of these glasses relies on whether or not it is evident that the maker has achieved his aim in terms of design. If, clearly, he has, and if he has been fortunate enough (and at this date luck was a weighty ingredient) to have produced a good metal, and if time has been kind and the surface has escaped wear and the original

FIVE GLASSES OF BALUSTER TYPE, *c.*1715–25
(Tallest: H20.6cm/8⅛in)

The variety of stem forms was almost limitless. One glass is neatly engraved with the name 'ROBERT BUXTON' *and* 'OXFORD INN EXON'.

PORTRAIT OF THE EARL OF LINCOLN AND THE DUKE OF NEWCASTLE AT THE KIT CAT CLUB, LONDON, BY SIR GODFREY KNELLER, *c.*1721

Each sitter holds an 18th-century baluster drinking glass, known as a 'Kit Cat glass', identified from this painting.

fire finish has survived, the glass may then justifiably be considered a work of art.

Contemporary with the great balusters are similar glasses with moulded pedestal stems. Instead of being manipulated by the gaffer at the chair, the stems were cast in moulds which gave them four, six or eight facets, as well as decorations on the

in balustroids. The features of a 'Newcastle' glass are increased height at the expense of width and, in many cases, undeniable elegance. The group received its name by virtue of the existence of a very small number of vessels that were decorated in white or coloured enamels in the workshop of brother and sister William and Mary

ground that the reverse is the case and by far the larger number of glasses of 'Newcastle' character – lead or not – were made in such centres as Liège. Indeed, some of these might have been sent to Newcastle, since the Beilbys certainly enamelled some glasses with Dutch armorials. No doubt future research will shed more light on this subject.

shoulders, such as diamonds. The mould could provide for other details as well, illustrated by a series cast to celebrate the 1715 coronation of George I, with crowns on the shoulders or a variety of toasts, such as 'God Save King George'. This stem form was popular in Silesia (it is usually called the Silesian stem), and it is no accident that its use in England coincided with the arrival there of the House of Hanover. Its life was relatively short in terms of wine glasses (*c*.1715–30), but it survived in increasingly debased form in candlesticks and tazzas (or waiters) well into the nineteenth century.

'NEWCASTLE' GLASS

A decorative feature in the stem of a baluster glass was a tear of air. Ideally, this retained a central position in a knop during the turning of the stem. Soon, makers trapped multiple tears of air within the stem of the glass. These are prominently seen in the extensive range of so-called 'Newcastle' light balusters and

Beilby in Newcastle-upon-Tyne; some of these pieces are signed. Many more of the glasses are decorated with fine engravings, these generally of a Continental character, often with Dutch inscriptions and occasionally signed by known Dutch exponents. Since there are occasional dated examples, some of which are engraved with paired armorials recording dynastic marriages, it is clear that this large class of glasses stretched from the 1730s right up until the end of the eighteenth century.

Frequently found armorials include those of Princess Anne, daughter of George II, who married Prince William of Orange in 1734, but David Wolff (1732–98), the best known stipple-engraver, and others used these glasses as vehicles for their painstaking work even at the very end of the century. The long-held theory survives that the Dutch, who nurtured brilliant schools of engraving, preferred glasses of lead crystal for their work and sent to Newcastle for them. However, the suggestion is gaining

BALUSTROIDS

The term 'balustroids' was coined to bring together a considerable variety of light-weight drinking glasses of debased baluster form. These were often tall and thin, generally with multiple knopping, and it seemed illogical to class them with balusters, which bear clearly defined knopping. The balustroids comprise a large, mixed collection; although occasionally there are good ones, most are mean. From the beaded knop, frequently a feature of elegant 'Newcastle' glass, it was but a short step to the simplest air-twist stem, achieved by drawing out the gather, with its symmetrical bubbles, and twisting it while still molten. The simple result is known as a multi-spiral air-twist (MSAT to glass experts). Another, known as 'mercurial', called for threads of air of flat rather than circular section, resulting in a glittering increase in the reflection of light. Soon more complex variations appeared, such as the double series, wherein one

complete stem type was combined with another of a different pattern. The addition of opaque white threads in about 1760 produced the most elaborate of the twist stems. At first simple, these became amazingly intricate and were often made with extreme accuracy. While the common form of air-twist is of single series only, most opaque-twists were double series, with the single rarer; the rarest of all, and often difficult to identify, are those with a triple series. Occasionally one finds a mixture of air-twist with opaque white threads and sometimes, in this group, makers added an element of colour. Parallels to these glasses exist on the Continent, specifically in the Low Countries and in Norway, but they seldom approach those that were made in England in terms of technical virtuosity.

Glasses with plain stems were made alongside those with twists, and they appeared in the same forms. Many of them retain the folded foot that protects them against chipping, a feature dispensed with

for more refined glasses in the middle of the century. They were cheaper than their lacy cousins, and were intended for use in rougher situations. Wine glasses with cut stems were made from the time of the introduction of cutting, but only came into popular favour in the third quarter of the eighteenth century. It was formerly believed that the various stem types had their specific periods, but undoubtedly they were available together. When Thomas Betts, the prominent London glass-cutter, died in 1767, his estate was in dispute and an inventory had to be taken of all his stock in trade as well as household effects. Among his stock were some 10,000 drinking glasses. Their descriptions included 'hollow', 'wormed' (air-twist), 'enamell'd' (opaque-twist), 'twisted' (probably incised), 'plain' and 'cut'. The only stem pattern not specifically mentioned is 'incised'. This technique involves drawing a stem from a deeply ribbed gather to give it convex grooves, then twisting and drawing it.

There were of course times when fashion dictated a preference for each of these styles, and it is unlikely that any period other than the 1760s would have produced such a range. Twist-stemmed glasses seem to have fallen from favour in the 1770s and cut stems gained ground. Cutting comprised varied patterns on the stems and sometimes it spread over the bowls and even on to the feet. Soon drinking glasses reduced in height, and as the chaste 1780s and 1790s unfolded, there was a preponderance of simple glasses with plain conical bowls, perhaps a little fluting and some delicate Neoclassical engraving of festoons. Always available in sets, there came about an increasing demand for suites, until by the early nineteenth century whole services in one pattern were available, with glasses in five sizes, tumblers, decanters in three or more sizes, claret jugs, water jugs, ice plates and finger bowls. The service could be cut in one of an almost limitless number of patterns, and in a richness to suit the fashion of the day – and the depth of the buyer's pocket. The reduction in stem height continued into the early nineteenth century.

DECORATION AND COLOUR

Basic decoration took the form of mould-blowing in the glasshouse. Bowls of wine glasses and other vessels could be blown into moulds which produced shallow fluting or reticulation (diamond moulding) halfway up the bowl. Sometimes the bowls were blown into a second gather carrying heavy fluting, or blown on to the top border of such a gather, resulting in double- or single-wall gadrooning, a residual feature of Venetian glass. Gadrooning survived in wine glasses into the 1760s, and in mugs and loving cups much longer. It was back in favour for custard cups and some wine glasses in the 1830s. The surface decoration most frequently used was engraving. At first much of the engraving on English glass was probably done in the Netherlands, and if not there, then by Continental craftsmen newly settled in England. However widely and deservedly English glass of lead was admired, its vernacular engraving was undeniably bad, at least throughout most of the eighteenth century.

ENGRAVED GLASS

There are exceptions, of course, including a small group of early eighteenth-century baluster glasses engraved in diamond-point with various toasts, such as 'God Bless Queen Anne' and 'Prosperity to the Church of England'. The work on these balusters is extremely neat. There is also a series of glasses made in the middle of the century that share various features, such as multi-spiral air-twist stems with central swelling knops; double ogee or pan-topped bowls, and often polished-out pontil marks. They are engraved with wreaths of fruit and flowers, sometimes of Jacobite significance, horizontal hops-and-barley ears for strong ale, or fruiting apple or pear for cider or perry. Again the work is exceptionally fine. But largely the run-of-the-mill fruiting vine borders, birds in flight and hops-and-barley glasses are simply executed.

Glasses were often engraved to commemorate national and political events. This was spasmodic through the eighteenth century but became common in the early nineteenth. Glasses were engraved to record civic events such as engineering feats, coaching, sport and many other subjects. Perhaps the most extensive group of commemorative glass was that provided for the toasting of the Stuart royal house after the arrival of the Hanoverian dynasty. The Jacobites were those who desperately longed for the return of what they continued to see as the rightful royal line. Even after the brutal defeat of the second rebellion in 1746 by the Duke of Cumberland at Culloden, Jacobites continued to toast the Pretender. Glasses were engraved with emblems of open or discreet loyalty. The heraldic rose of England was the principal motif, with one or two buds to remember the Old and Young Pretenders. The Cycle Club was the most extensive of the Jacobite groups and its motto, 'Fiat' ('May it happen'), appears on many glasses. Other, less common mottoes include 'Redeat' ('May he return') and 'Revirescat' ('May he be reborn'). An extensive group of flowers is supposedly of Jacobite significance, including honeysuckle, carnation and lily-of-the-valley. Opinions vary as to the

TABLEWARE, SECOND QUARTER 18TH CENTURY (Decanter jug: H21.6cm/8½in)

The influence of silver forms is evident in the decanter jug, and readily apparent in the tripod salt. The two short glasses, one of which is handled, were for jellies.

precise meaning of these botanical references, but emblems such as the oak leaf, recalling Charles II's concealment in the Boscobel Oak after the battle of Worcester, and a star denoting hopes for the future are more easily interpreted.

Rarest of all Jacobite glasses are those of the so-called 'Amen' series. These carry verses of the national anthem and occasionally other sentiments, inscribed in diamond-point within elaborate borders. The whole layout descends to a point at the base where the word 'Amen' terminates the toast. The glasses are normally plain drawn trumpets, a common enough type; the calligraphy is naïve, and ever since the publication of large-sized photographs in specialist books early this century, there has been increasing concern about some specimens that have emerged. Later copies indeed exist, so the provenance of a piece is critical.

ENAMELLED AND GILDED GLASS

Aside from engraving, glass decoration at this time included enamelling and gilding, but both are quite rare. The temperature needed to fire the enamels was very close to the melting point of the glass, with the result that glasses so decorated frequently slumped in the kiln. It is not uncommon to find wine glasses enamelled by the Beilby family in Newcastle-upon-Tyne leaning perilously. The Beilbys seem to have had a virtual monopoly with their enamelling process. Few examples of the technique appear which cannot be attributed to them. Their delicate landscapes with garden buildings or sporting subjects, as well as the more common borders of fruiting vine or festoons of flowers, were all carried out in the ductile medium which, with delicate flourishes of acanthus, was the very essence of Rococo.

A large proportion of the work used white enamel only, but there are a few coloured examples, principally armorial goblets for local families. There is also the splendid series of royal armorial goblets, which comprise bucket bowls on opaque-twist stems and carry the royal arms on one side with the plumes of the Prince of Wales on the other. This feature goes far to confirm the theory that they were enamelled to celebrate the birth of the prince in 1762. This

DECORATED GLASS, THIRD QUARTER 18TH CENTURY
(Decanter: H27.5cm/10¾in)

The three gilt pieces display the house style of James Giles, although the subject on the decanter – horsemen, perhaps representing the King of Prussia and his attendants – is unrecorded. The little tumbler is known as a pony. (ABOVE)

NAVAL TUMBLER AND MASONIC GOBLET, *c*.1800
(Goblet: H13cm/5⅛in)

The tumbler records the victorious admirals of four naval battles. The goblet, with 'lemon-squeezer' foot, is engraved with masonic emblems. (ABOVE LEFT)

THREE BEILBY WINE GLASSES WITH ENAMEL DECORATIONS, *c*.1765–70 (Tallest: H16.8cm/6⅝in)

These glasses illustrate arcadian landscapes and a diaper ornament. (ABOVE)

OPAQUE WHITE
VASE, *c*.1755–60
(H14.6cm/5¾in)

*Imitation of Chinese
porcelain appears to
have been a principal
aim in the minds of the
makers of opaque white
glass.* (RIGHT)

PAIR OF
CANDLESTICKS
WITH OPAQUE
WHITE GLASS
BASES, *c*.1780–5
(H30.5cm/12in)

*The gilding on the
white glass follows the
house style of James
Giles (though he was
bankrupt by 1775).
The lemon-coloured
drops add a rich
tint to these superb
candlesticks.* (RIGHT)

date is extremely early in the life of the Beilby studio and it is surprising that such sophisticated works should have been attempted at that time. Against this, some of the goblets are more successful than others, with clearer, less muddy colours and, where called for, more sophisticated gilding. Nine are known, of which four are signed; there is also a decanter. The signed example in the Beves Collection at the Fitzwilliam Museum, Cambridge, is typical.

By far the largest body of eighteenth-century gilded glass is attributed to the workshop of James Giles (1718–80) in London. He was principally a decorator of porcelain bought in the white from various sources, mostly from Worcester, but he worked on glass as well, obtained from the Falcon Glassworks and William Parker, both in London. A popular motif he employed was fruiting vine, emblematic of wine, but there were also delightful bouquets of flowers and insects. After 1770 a group of his glassware appeared with Neo-classical subjects, some based on details taken from objects in Sir William Hamilton's first collection of antique Greek vases, found in and around Naples. Most, but not all, of these later decorations were carried out on opaque white glass. Opaque white glass evolved in the 1750s and was manufactured in several locations. That much of it emanated from the areas of south Staffordshire renowned as centres for the manufacture of vitreous enamels is no accident; parallels in decoration of early examples abound, and attempts were made to emulate the popular copies of Chinese export porcelain, which was itself arriving from the Far East by the boatload. English opaque white or enamel glass was dense and solid and owed its opacity to the addition of arsenic, rather than the more normally used tin; it is quite opaque and does not opalesce in transmitted light. Not surprisingly, opaque white glass failed in competition with the emergent porcelain factories, but nonetheless it continued in intermittent production for some fifty years, finding its place in decorative objects such as scent bottles and candlestick bases. Its closest relative, of course, is the enamel which is found on clock dials.

COLOURED GLASS

Consideration of white glass leads to the coloured variety. Nearly everything that was made in colourless glass in the eighteenth century was also produced in colour, although sometimes very rarely. There are some curious anomalies in this regard, however. At the end of the century there was a fashion for coloured decanters and glasses. The decanters had gilt labels, generally for spirits, and for this reason were normally of pint capacity. Green and blue were the most popular colours, but while there is an abundance of green glasses there are comparatively few green decanters and, more extraordinarily, there are numerous blue decanters, but a blue wine glass is an extreme rarity. The whole group fills wine lovers with horror and the usual defence is that they were all used for spirits rather than for wine. As well as blue and green (the latter ranging from emerald to turquoise), amethyst is sometimes seen, and there is even solid yellow recorded in the above-mentioned inventory of Thomas Betts, although only one such piece is listed. Only two pieces of this date (1765), both of an olivine tint, are known at present.

The term 'solid' in relation to colour is used to separate pieces coming from a single-coloured batch from those which were cased (overlaid with a second colour) or stained (sometimes called 'flashed', i.e., superficially coloured by chemicals). The latter two processes came into increasing use in the nineteenth century. Yellow-stained pieces, brilliantly cut before processing, can be found dating from the 1820s, and by the mid-1830s colour was back in full favour, the usual tints (blue, green, amethyst, amber) being joined by red. Indeed, red glass constitutes a special case. Gold-ruby glass was made on the Continent in the early eighteenth century – its added element was, as its name implies, gold – but apparently it was not produced in England at that time. Indeed, there is practically no eighteenth-century English red glass. Intriguingly, however, a patent exists taken out in 1756 by a gentleman (presumably of German extraction) named Mayer Oppenheim, for a recipe for red glass. The process is complex in the extreme, but what pieces were made in the material have yet to be established.

The English did make colour-twist wine glasses in which clear red was a common inclusion. There is also a series of small lamp glasses in red, generally reticulated and with folded rims. These would have socketed into elaborate sanctuary lamps and the few that are known are of a solid colour. But this seems a meagre inheritance indeed from the 21 years that spanned the granting of Oppenheim's patent until his bankruptcy in 1777.

It is well known that the most precise controls were needed in the manufacture of red glass, or else it went completely black. Even in the 1830s, when colour really 'arrived' in English glass, it was controlled by single or double casing. Thus a vessel

would be blown in clear glass and encased in a thin layer of red (a thick, or solid, layer would produce too dark a colour). If the piece was to be cut, a second casing was applied, of colourless crystal, which would – if great care were exercised – carry the cutting without piercing the intermediate layer of colour. Of the extensive group of

WATER JUG WITH SULPHIDE INCLUSION, *c.*1820 (H18.4cm/7¼in)

The technique of including moulded ceramic plaques in the walls of glass vessels was imported from France by Apsley Pellatt. (ABOVE LEFT)

TWO VASES OF PAINTED GROUND GLASS, FIRST HALF 19TH CENTURY (Taller: H17.2cm/6¾in)

The vases in the Etruscan taste are decorated in enamel colours. (ABOVE)

DECANTER AND GLASSES OF COLOURED GLASS, *c.*1770 (Decanter: H26cm/10¼in)

The amethyst decanter and the cut stem cordial are exceptional rarities; the green glass, perhaps for champagne or mead, is less so. (ABOVE)

heavy, handsome and richly coloured pieces of cut glass produced in the 1830s, it is probable that only red had to be treated with such caution. Among the solid colours are blue, amethyst, green of various shades, yellow (both amber and a vivid, almost fluorescent, lemon) and a pale 'electric' blue.

DESSERT DISH AND CLARET JUG, c.1820–30
(Jug: H26cm/10¼in)

The octagonal dish is step, or prismatic, cut, a pattern repeated on the neck of the claret jug. Red, the hardest shade to control, came into use with the revival of many colours in the 1830s.

and attached to the sides of the principal plates, the joints being masked by bridging pieces, these often in colour. Much of the 'cutting' was carried out horizontally (as was the finishing of the 'cast' plate itself) by painstaking rubbing with graded abrasives, but wheel-cutting was employed as well.

Much research is still needed in this field to clarify the methods and machinery used, but it is relatively easy to separate the two techniques. A considerable quantity of early cutting takes the form of flat planes, which would have been cut with bevelling equipment. Hollows require a revolving wheel.

THE DEVELOPMENT OF CUTTING

A great deal of glass-making activity was taken up in the production of looking-glass plates. George Ravenscroft himself imported mirror-plates from Venice, but John Greene, writing in 1671, stated that 'as well as drinking glasses, looking-glass plates are made in England better than any that come from Venice'. It was in the workshops of the makers of looking-glass plates that the craft of cutting was born. Plates were frequently bevelled, both for mirrors and for the new sash windows, in which plate was sometimes used. Bevelling increased in complexity with the dawn of the new century, and borders were contrived in varying shapes, and of both concave and convex section. Borders were also made in separate pieces

CHANDELIERS

The ability to decorate glass by cutting it allowed plate-glass makers to expand into other fields. Among the earliest of their products were chandeliers. Here the stem pieces only were cut, principally in flat planes, the arms presumably being considered too fragile to withstand work. The English glass chandelier was born when the glass-makers made their first branches. Hitherto, virtually everything was made on the rod or pontil, its weight thus disposed evenly about its centre. The glass arm was a load-bearing structure. The first arms had integral candle tubes and drip pans; although comfortably within the competence of a

maker of baluster drinking glasses, the construction was unnecessarily complex. The heat of a candle left to gutter would crack the tube and a whole new unit would be required. Soon detachable pans evolved, which rested on a shoulder provided beneath the candle tube. The chandelier in the Chapel of Emmanuel College, Cambridge, donated in 1732, is a good example from this early stage of cutting. Most of the cutting on its stem pieces is in flat planes.

Glass-cutting developed rapidly thereafter, and somewhere along the line the twin crafts of cutter and scalloper evolved, the former dealing with surface treatment, the latter with borders. The lap was used for flat faceting, as in jewellery. The lap is a horizontal turntable of stone, wood or lead, fed with requisite abrasives and water, on which a skilled craftsman could produce facets of geometrical accuracy, brought up to such a degree of polish that no marks of abrasion survived. Chandeliers, the most complex, and among the most costly, products of the industry, are sometimes datable, either as gifts or from accounts, and thus serve to fix changes of style in cutting patterns. These increased in complexity as techniques and equipment improved, but were always geometrically arranged and accurately carried out. The most common motif was that of a large flat diamond with crosscuts over the angles. This was used for some 25 years after 1750, usually in combination with other details, and is almost invariably seen on the central balls of chandelier stems. During this time pendent ornaments of great variety were added to chandeliers as personal demand dictated. These added movement and an appealing twinkling effect as draughts or the heat of lighted candles caused their gentle movement. With these drops, and increasingly elaborate arm profiles, chandeliers reflected the Rococo style.

The Neoclassical style, first seen in the chandeliers that William Parker of London supplied for the Assembly Rooms, Bath, in 1772, soon brought both the design and craftsmanship of English glass chandeliers to a peak. A classic example at the end of the

TWO-TIER CHANDELIER IN THE CHAPEL OF EMMANUEL COLLEGE, CAMBRIDGE, PRESENTED IN 1732

This chandelier has been valuable in dating similar fittings, whose characteristics combine simply cut stems and uncut arms. No other example with two tiers of arms is at present known. (BELOW)

SINGLE-LIGHT CANDELABRA, c.1775 (H53.4cm/21in)

These charming creations have generally suffered over the years. It is unusual now to find candelabra in substantially original condition, as these are. (BELOW)

CHANDELIER FOR SIX LIGHTS, c.1820 (H104cm/ 3ft 5in)

This chandelier is of simple construction and outline. Its components, however, are far from simple, each drop being cut with innumerable facets to produce brilliant prismatic colours when caught by the sun. (BELOW LEFT)

century would have a vase-shaped central feature, canopies above and below, plain six-sided arms, drip pans and sconces with 'Vandyke' rims (so called after the elegant lace collars of the Stuart gentry), and all dressed with delicate graded chains of pear-shaped drops. Examples may be seen at Arbury Hall at Nuneaton, home of the FitzRoy Newdegate family, who ordered a pair of chandeliers from William Parker in 1788 for the dining room and another, of similar form but larger, on the completion of the saloon in 1804.

The festoons of glass chains which so enhanced the last of the Neoclassical chandeliers developed in density after 1800. Soon the structure became subservient to the dressings, so that the whole form of a chandelier could be composed of closely packed chains and fringes of long finial drops. Each chain might include some thirty drops in perhaps six or eight graded sizes, and each drop might have 32 facets on each side. Costs soared. The chandeliers that Parker supplied at Bath, forty arms each and

3 m (10 ft) high, cost about £100 each in 1781. By 1820 a chandelier of comparable size could easily cost as much as four or five thousand pounds, some much more, the rise being brought about by the enormous amount of handwork required. There is a splendid pair of typical Regency chandeliers of this type at Saltram in Devon.

OTHER LIGHTING DEVICES

To complement chandeliers an inexhaustible range of supporting lighting was available, from candlesticks and candelabra to wall brackets and, later, lamps. These followed, as closely as their purpose allowed, the evolution of chandeliers. In the case of candlesticks, stem forms echoed those of baluster drinking glasses, with tears and knopping of comparable style. Many eighteenth-century examples carried moulded pedestal stems, again accompanied by teared knops. These were on occasion inverted, and of true baluster form, a variation almost never seen on a drinking glass.

From the 1750s on, stems were generally cut. Contemporary terms covering these lighting devices are confusing: a chandelier can be called a branch or a lustre; candelabra can be branched candlesticks or girandoles; and wall brackets are called sconces, particularly if backed by looking-glasses.

DECANTERS

Glass was widely used during the eighteenth century, apart from drinking glasses and lighting. In the late seventeenth century wine was seldom served in an intermediate vessel between bottle and glass, but decanter jugs, handled and sometimes stoppered, appeared in the early eighteenth century. These could carry some residual moulded gadrooning, and were often of varied section, of which the most popular for a while was octagonal (again following the fashion in silver). Handles were soon dispensed with and made

to have evolved to facilitate the cooling of wines by immersion in ice after decanting. The presence of a single collar high on the neck is presumably an indication that wine was sometimes stored in them, the ring permitting a firm grasp to tie down a cork. It is possible that these were used for sparkling wines. These decanters had a long neck, slightly flaring at the top, on a comparatively short body with vertical sides. They date from about 1725 to 1730 and there are a few cut with facets at the neck and flat planes on the side. Two-bottle cruets with similar cutting are found in hallmarked silver stands.

The so-called shaft-and-globe form followed, and these are normally stoppered, either with a ball containing multiple tears or with the first of the spire stoppers. In the 1760s came the shouldered group, wider at the shoulder than at the bottom and often fitted with spires, sometimes with the first vertical disc stoppers cut with triangular flat facets on the border. The mallets followed in the 1770s; wider at the base than the

to the end of the century. Apparently it was difficult to grasp when full, so rings were added on the neck, and the lip was enlarged to a sizable flange to prevent the wine running down. The ship's decanter, sometimes known as a 'Rodney' (after Admiral Lord Rodney), also emerged at this time; its great basal width ensured stability at sea.

As for decoration, cutting is rarely seen before the debut of the shouldered family of decanters, but it appears in some richness on mallets. Many of the shouldered and mallet decanters were engraved with labels (based on silver examples) bearing the names of the bottles' contents. Rings continued on the necks of decanters well into the nineteenth century, particularly for plain and lightly cut examples. Richly embellished decanters might have step or prismatic cutting up the neck. Aside from prismatic cutting, there was by then a huge variety of surface patterns. Among the most common are diamonds (plain, strawberry and hobnail), pillars and flutes (flat, hollow and mitre).

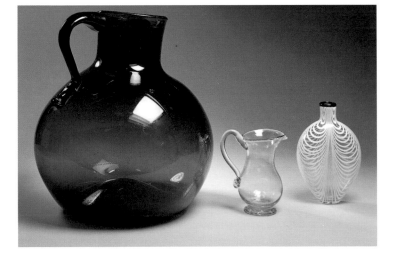

GIANT FLAGON,
WINE JUG AND
FLASK, EARLY
19TH CENTURY
(Flagon:
H37cm/14½in)

The un-decolourized jug is provincial, the flask a characteristic Nailsea-type product.

only rare appearances for about a hundred years, surfacing once more in the early nineteenth century on claret jugs. A large family of mould-blown decanters was seen in the second quarter of the eighteenth century, with sections of varied complexity. They offered a large surface area and are said

shoulder, these had vertical disc stoppers of great variety. Decanters of Indian-club shape continued into the 1780s, by which time they were yielding to tapers. The tapered decanter with pear-shaped stopper, notched or plain and still with only a vestigial lip, continued to be made through

BOTTLES

Bottles of glass emerged in the fourteenth century, often ribbed or wrythen and with a shallow kick. The standard form of bulbous body and tapering neck scarcely altered before the 1650s, by which time a neck-ring had been introduced to allow the tying down of a stopper. Retail sale of wine was illegal in Britain, and it was the practice for buyers to provide their own bottles for the importer to fill. They needed identification, and a glass wafer, or 'seal', moulded with the owner's initials was applied. By the end of the seventeenth century corks were in use as stoppers, following the invention of the corkscrew, or bottle screw.

English factories produced vast numbers of bottles for the domestic and Continental markets. Necks became shorter, bodies wider and the kick higher, but, during the eighteenth century, bottles gradually became more cylindrical, presumably to assist in storage. The use of seals continued into the nineteenth century and collecting interest lies mainly in the rarity of their details: dates, crests and initials of City of London companies and families tell of their drinking habits over two centuries.

In the nineteenth century, a degree of automation was introduced with the inven-

ENGLISH WINE BOTTLE, 1690 (H14cm/5½in)

As well as the date, the seal bears the initials of Richard Walker, tenant of the King's Head tavern, Oxford, flanking a bust of the reigning monarch, William III.

until 1780 that these restrictions were relaxed, enabling the industry to flourish. Factories opened at Waterford and Cork in 1783, and others soon followed in Dublin. Although labour and management were drawn from English glass-making centres, pieces of a uniquely Irish character were produced from the mid-1780s through shortly after 1825, when an excise duty was imposed. Irish glass from this period is eagerly sought today, both for its particular forms and delightful surface patterns.

Irish glass of this time is not only of the traditional dark blue-grey tint, but, due to casual control of ingredients, it can also assume green and yellow shades. Waterford imported much of its sand from King's Lynn, Norfolk, so there was no special ingredient giving that factory's products superiority over the output of others. The word 'Waterford', therefore, should be used sparingly and cautiously.

In around 1800, Irish factories introduced the technique of blowing vessels into patterned moulds that would imprint patterns

rare marked vessels (of which decanters are the most numerous). Popular, too, are oval and round pedestal fruit bowls, sometimes with turn-over rims. Oval bowls were also set on square or fluted cast feet. Such feet and the turn-over rim are almost exclusively Irish, as is the glass piggin, its shape deriving from the wooden dipper for lifting milk or cream, with one or two longer staves acting as a handle.

Lighting equipment made of Irish glass is comparatively rare. The few known important chandeliers formerly considered Irish are mainly English, although the one in the Old Parliament House, Dublin, is embellished with Irish parts. Possible exceptions are the fitting in the City Hall, Waterford, and half-chandeliers that hang in front of oval mirrors with borders of moulded multi-coloured glass 'jewels'.

Much Irish glass was exported, a great deal to the United States. After 1820, steam power and improved training and equipment allowed glass-makers to produce fine, complex cutting of the highest quality.

tion of a butterfly mould, by Thomas Ricketts of Bristol. The hinged mould enabled the glass-blower to produce a fully finished pouring lip and groove for a cap at the bottle's top, together with a moulded kick beneath. The opportunity was taken to incorporate the maker's name in the bottom mould. The result was little different from the bottle in use today.

IRELAND

The subject of Irish glass – Waterford in particular – is bedevilled by myth and misattribution. While there is a corpus of exclusively Irish designs, it is only a small part of a very large industry.

Throughout the eighteenth century, the English government – Ireland was then under British rule – imposed severe duties on the import and export of glass. Production was limited and sporadic, and it was not

around the base. Such moulds also included the factory name. The addition of crimped neck-rings, a press-moulded stopper and sketchy engraving yielded a finished product of reasonably decorative value with little effort and without cutting equipment.

Collectors compete for these relatively

VARIOUS PIECES OF IRISH TABLE GLASS, *c.*1785–95 (Decanter: H28.5cm/11¼in)

The soft cutting on these pieces is characteristic of Irish glass of the last 15 years of the 18th century. The mould into which the lower part of the water jug was blown carried the factory name.

CHINESE GLASS

Chinese glass made before the Qing Dynasty (1644–1912) is rare. This is surprising, considering that glass-making technology (as revealed by archaeological finds) existed in China from as early as the Warring States period (481–221 BC). The reasons for this rarity are complicated, but one of the central factors is the traditional Chinese attitude toward glass as a material. They felt that its principal quality was the ease with which it could be made to mimic other substances. Opaque pale blue glass, for example, made a good copy of the mineral turquoise, was easier to work into small items of personal adornment than the stone and was considerably less costly. By contrast, the Western and Near Eastern traditions of glass-making have sought, through a vast range of techniques, to emphasize the interplay of glass with light and sometimes to produce objects of great delicacy and beauty. The effect of this rather limited Chinese attitude was that in the pre-Qing period glass was viewed not so much as something precious but as a rather low-status material.

All this changed with the accession to the throne of the Kangxi emperor (1662–1722). Most likely he had seen and admired examples of Western glass brought to court, and in 1696 he established as part of the extensive Palace Workshops – the Zaobanchu – a specialized glass workshop to be run, at least at first, by Jesuit missionaries. The balance between Western and Chinese technology used in the glass workshop is not clear, but the fact that much early eighteenth-century Chinese glass is crizzled (an instability caused by an excess of alkali) in the same way as some contemporary European glass suggests that a flawed recipe from Europe was in use. This is certainly true regarding the manufacture of the clear red and blue glasses, which were the most popular early products of the imperial workshops. The technique of fusing the foot to the body in a separate piece

and the re-emergence of blown vessels are further suggestions of a strong European influence on Chinese glassware.

Technical advances were made during the succeeding reign periods of Yongzheng (1723–35) and Qianlong (1736–95), but the basic repertoire was established early on. The main categories were plain clear or opaque glass in a range of colours; carved glass, its surface decoration achieved by traditional lapidary techniques; cased or overlay glass, with one or more colours of glass applied to the glass body and then carved through to reveal the different colours; and enamelled glass, in which the glass body was treated as a surface for painted decoration, much like a porcelain body.

ENAMELLED GLASS

To judge from the style and superlative quality of the painting on enamelled glass of the eighteenth century, it is clear that the decorators were the same as those who more often applied their skills to the finest imperial porcelain and copper-bodied vessels. The thick milky glass used as the base for the enamels resembles highly translucent porcelain, and when lit from the back the glass imparts an extra glow to the colours that could never have been achieved if the enamels had been applied to a copper body. Perhaps because these superb wares were the results of a collaboration between different workshops, however, they were among the most adversely affected by the weakening of imperial patronage in the nineteenth century. Some fine enamelled-glass vessels made in private workshops in Peking appeared in the first few years of the nineteenth century, but apart from these the technique seems almost to have died out, except for some examples in various debased forms.

IMPERIAL ENAMELLED POUCH-SHAPED VASE, QIANLONG PERIOD, 1736–95 (H18.8cm/7⅜in)

OVERLAY GLASS

Overlay, or cased, glass, by contrast, was manufactured wholly in the glass workshop. From restrained beginnings in the eighteenth century, generally employing rich translucent red glass over clear or 'snowflake' glass, the technique expanded during the nineteenth century to include almost every imaginable colour pairing, from blue on yellow to red on black to green on toffee brown. Many of these combinations allude to other wares and other types of decoration. Blue on white, for example, suggests blue-and-white porcelain; red on yellow is reminiscent of carved hornbill; and black on red resembles certain kinds of lacquer. The old Chinese predilection for treating glass as a substitute for other materials had not disappeared, but instead had become a source of decorative inspiration.

Elaborations on the basic overlay method included multiple overlay, wherein more than one layer of different coloured glass was applied to the body, and multi-coloured overlay, or 'marquetry', in which different coloured, sometimes discrete, areas of glass were applied over the surface. The latter

CARVED RED GLASS OVERLAY WATER POT, QIANLONG PERIOD, 1736–95 (D11.7cm/4½in)

Carved in unusually high relief with five-clawed dragons, this water pot is a fine example of the vigorous 18th-century style. (BELOW LEFT)

GLASS OVERLAY SNUFF BOTTLES, 1780–1850 (H*c*.6.5cm/2½in)

By far the most numerous products in glass were snuff bottles, which exhibit the entire range of techniques and colours. (BELOW)

allowed the carver to use the colours that were appropriate to his design and as such is reminiscent of a technique used by Chinese jade carvers, who retained portions of the differently coloured 'skin' of the jade pebble to pick out elements of the design. These more complicated techniques tend to be found on small, earlier pieces, which were often intended for the scholar's table.

COLOURED GLASS

CARVED IMPERIAL-YELLOW BOWL, QIANLONG PERIOD, 1736–95 (D27cm/10⅝in)

The rich yellow of this bowl alludes directly to the yellow-glazed porcelain reserved for use by the imperial family. (LEFT)

Plain and mixed coloured glass wares maintained their popularity throughout the lifetime of the imperial glass workshop, and indeed the substitutional notion of the function of glass retained its strongest hold on such pieces. Red and yellow glass suggested realgar, a poisonous arsenical material beloved of Daoist adepts; brown glass with scattered

tiny chips of metallic copper resembled aventurine quartz; deep blue glass echoed lapis lazuli; and various muted monochrome glasses are reminiscent of Song Dynasty celadon glazes on ceramics. Perhaps the best-known monochrome colour is 'imperial yellow', adapted from the colour of the glaze used on wares reserved for the emperor's personal use; a good eighteenth-century

example should be a rich egg-yolk yellow.

Many pieces of Chinese glass bear reign marks, usually located on the underside of the base. These marks come in many forms, by far the most common of which is a wheel-cut four character mark. Constrained by the cutting wheel the characters are made up of short straight lines without any curves, which gives a rather rough effect.

THE NINETEENTH
CENTURY

*I*n glass, as in other manufacturing industries in the nineteenth century, Britain was a world leader. In 1851 the organizers of the Great Exhibition at The Crystal Palace in London set indigenous products alongside those of other countries to high praise from the reviewers and judges.

Ralph Nicholson Wornum won a prize from the Art Journal for 'an essay on the best mode of rendering the Exhibition of the Works of Industry of all Nations . . . practically useful to the British Manufacturers'. Of the glass section he singled out British manufacturers for high praise, with Rice, Harris & Son of Birmingham surpassing Bohemia (except in cheapness). To Apsley Pellatt, 'the art is largely indebted, and to his exertions we may, in a great degree, attribute the prominent position it has held, of late years, in Great Britain, defying the competition of the world and excelling, in most particulars, the works of the old Venetians.' The review was somewhat partial, as the French, Germans and Bohemians were all making glass to a high standard.

Following the Franco-Prussian War, an influx of Bohemians, Germans and French injected further new ideas into the art and science of glass-making. The developments in cameo glass, acid-etching and rock crystal engraving met with universal acclaim. By the end of the century, in common with the British ceramics industry, the impetus had disappeared, moving to North America and the Continent.

FRENCH OPALINE GLASS, 1820–5

*The Neoclassical gilt-metal mounts, forms and strong hues of these pieces
reinforce the suggestion of semiprecious stone inherent in the quality of the glass.*

BRITISH GLASS

The last three quarters of the nineteenth century witnessed major developments in British table glass. In the 1830s the introduction of press-moulded glass brought cheap wares to a wide public for the first time. More significant was the repeal of the hundred-year-old excise tax on glass in 1845, which boosted production and encouraged experiment throughout the industry. The results of this were evident in the rich and varied show made by British manufacturers at the Great Exhibition of the Industry of All Nations, held in the so-called Crystal Palace in London's Hyde Park in 1851.

During the second half of the century, competition for markets at home and abroad stimulated growth. From the 1860s to about 1890, the range of glassware produced in Britain, and the technical and aesthetic qualities of its best pieces, were extraordinary. By the 1890s the labour-intensive methods often adopted by major manufacturers were proving costly, and the final decade of the century was marked by a decline in quality. Nevertheless, the contribution of British glass-makers to the history of European glass during this period remains of the greatest significance.

A NEW CUT-GLASS STYLE

From the mid-1820s to the late 1840s almost all British luxury table glass was cut, as it had been during the previous two decades. Around 1825, however, a new style of cut glass appeared. To the current Regency style of cutting, based on horizontal bands or panels of deeply cut motifs such as relief or strawberry diamonds, was added a style of flat cutting, typically in arrangements of tall, vertical flutes. The flutes were often slender, perhaps 15 around a decanter body. During the later 1830s and early 1840s, however, they were usually cut broadly, from which the term 'broad flute' is derived.

The new style may have been introduced in the provinces rather than in London, the traditional centre for British cut glass. The earliest documented glass with vertical flutes, for example, is known from two designs in the 1823 pattern-books of the Birmingham silversmith and manufacturer, Matthew Boulton (1728–1809). This glass may well have been cut in Boulton's own workshop or at one of the many cutting shops known to have been operational in Birmingham at that time. There is also evidence of the emerging style in sheets of pattern drawings attributable to a factory in the West Midlands, possibly in Dudley. These drawings, which date from the mid-

WOOD ENGRAVING OF A GLASS-CUTTER, 1849

Like most cutters by this date, the craftsman is working at a steam-powered machine in a large factory workshop. The image is from Curiosities of Glass Making, *by Apsley Pellatt.*

1820s, show broad flute and diamond-cut glass to have been in production simultaneously. Broad flute cut glass appeared routinely in the pattern-books of the Stourbridge firms of Webb & Richardson (later W.H., B. & J. Richardson) and Thomas Webb & Sons, through the 1830s and early 1840s. Otherwise there is documentary evidence of it in Ireland in around 1830 and in a price list of the London glass manufacturer, Apsley Pellatt, published in 1838. The style was probably common to most British cut-glass centres by the mid-1830s.

The introduction of broad flute cutting reflected less a change in taste than a need to widen the market for cut glass. This is clear from the fact that broad flute glass was cheaper than diamond-cut work, alongside which it was produced. The pattern sheets mentioned above show prices for both kinds of decoration, and a traveller's diary for 1832 confirms that fluted wares were sold for less than diamond cut. Gradually, however, the Regency style became unfashionable, and manufacturers brought in variations on the basic broad flute patterns, probably with the luxury market in mind.

By around 1840 thicker, heavier blanks were used for the best-quality glass, deeply cut in bold but simple designs. The 'Gothic arch', a deep, inverted V-shaped cut, and the 'broad hollow', a circular or oval hollow cut on a broad flute, were typical. Large hollows could be combined in simple ways and pillars, flutes in relief with rounded sides, were much used on expensive glassware. Pillars were particularly difficult to cut on a curve, and glasses which have pillars twisted in series around their bodies are among the most spectacular products of the period. The process of frosting parts of glass was also popular by the 1840s, a dulled surface being achieved by rubbing with an abrasive. All these developments are seen in the pattern-books of Stourbridge manufacturers but probably occurred in most areas.

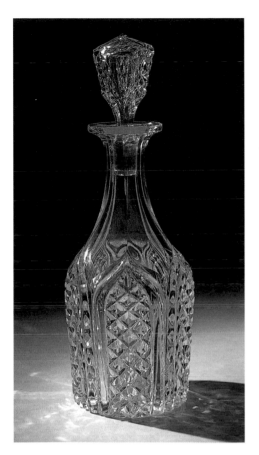

CUT-GLASS DECANTER, *c.*1845–50 (H33cm/13in)

The 'Gothic' arches framing diamonds and the heavy stopper are typical of ornate British cut glass at the time of the 1851 Great Exhibition.

THREE WINE GLASSES, *c.*1830 (Tallest: H17.8cm/7in)

Glasses for white wines such as hock were normally coloured – green being particularly popular in the 1830s and 1840s. The shape of the tall glass in the middle was associated at this period with ale or champagne.

PILLAR-CUT JUG, WEBB & RICHARDSON, *c.*1830–5 (H25.5cm/10in)

Broad flute glassware seems not to have been normally available in services, although most of the types of glass familiar from the Victorian table service were in production by the 1820s. Contemporary factory and retail records refer to types, not services, the latter perhaps supplied only on commission. Wine glasses sometimes have names, such as 'Princes', 'Beautiful' or 'York', and may also be associated with a specific drink: glasses for claret wines, liqueurs, hocks, champagne and ale are all recorded by the 1830s. It is likely that the practice of dining in separate courses, which stimulated demand for a complete series of wine glasses sized for particular drinks, was still insufficiently familiar for manufacturers to market services with real success.

The broad flute style lasted into the early 1840s. Diamond-cutting was gradually reintroduced, and, by the time of the Great Exhibition of 1851, the best cut glass was marked by a profusion of patterns expressive

DETAIL FROM A SHEET OF FACTORY DRAWINGS, *c.*1825–30

This Regency-style decanter was probably drawn in a West Midlands factory. The weight and cutting cost are noted to the left.

of conspicuous consumption. Shapes, too, developed; the often austere lines of broad flute glasses were replaced by glassware with generous curves – even on the stoppers of decanters. Cut glass, however, remained the touchstone of quality. The glass fountain by F. & C. Osler of Birmingham, the centrepiece of the Great Exhibition, was inevitably dependent upon cutters' skills for its appeal.

OPALINE
BOTTLE,
W.H., B. & J.
RICHARDSON,
*c.*1850
(H31.75cm/12½in)

*The bottle features
transfer-printed
decoration made up of
comic figures arranged
to form the name of a
drink. Examples are
known for whisky,
gin and rum.*

ENAMELLED
WATER JUG,
W.H., B. & J.
RICHARDSON,
*c.*1845–50
(H24.1cm/9½in)

*From a set including
goblets for dessert, the
jug is decorated with
hand-painted water
irises suggestive of the
vessel's function.*

COLOUR AND EXPERIMENT

The removal of the excise tax on glass in 1845 allowed manufacturers to attempt new techniques and promote new lines. The most obvious signs of this freedom were an increase in coloured ornamental wares during the late 1840s and a greater use of skilled decorators for enamelled and engraved tableware.

Certain kinds of coloured glass had been introduced prior to 1845. For example, some two-colour cased glass was made by Stourbridge firms in the late 1830s and 1840s, and opal and turquoise vases and toilet bottles were in production at the Stourbridge firm of Thomas Webb around 1840. The majority of such pieces, however, were probably made in the late 1840s or 1850s, their source of inspiration French and Bohemian glassware. Prominent British manufacturers of these types were George Bacchus & Sons of Birmingham; W.H., B. & J. Richardson of Wordsley, near Stourbridge, and J.F. Christy of Lambeth, London. Bacchus produced vases with transfer-printed enamelled classical figure scenes, while Richardson made hand-painted and transfer-printed enamelled wares alongside their cased vases, sometimes in three colours with added enamelled decoration. Among the most striking of Richardson's enamelled glasses are the painted water jugs and pairs of goblets intended for dessert. These have naturalistic designs symbolic of water, in accordance with a contemporary theory that decoration should be in sympathy with the function of the object.

Engraving, too, became more common, and from the 1850s onward it featured as the hallmark of luxury glassware. Some engravers undoubtedly worked within the factories, but many of the best seem to have been independent, working on commission from factories or retailers. Routine factory engraving in the 1840s and 1850s consisted of stylized floral or fruit motifs, or simple ornamental designs such as the Greek key pattern. For quality glasses such as exhibition pieces, naturalistic designs might be produced, with richly modelled motifs engraved to various depths. Most glass-making areas probably had their engravers by the middle of the century; London and Stourbridge certainly had, as did the northeast of England, where there was a long tradition of engraving on glass.

Glass-makers experimented with a variety of techniques in the mid nineteenth century. In his *Curiosities of Glass Making*, published in 1849, the London manufacturer Apsley Pellatt (1791–1863) mentions many he claims to have tried. How far these went

into commercial production is uncertain, but the book well conveys the spirit of innovation characteristic of the time. Traditional, particularly Venetian, methods offered one starting point. An interesting example of the use of a technique derived ultimately from Venice is found in a wine glass with an opaque-twist stem, made by F. & C. Osler as part of a set to commemorate the opening of the Albert Dock in Liverpool in 1846. The stem closely resembles those of eighteenth-century English wine glasses but is delicately cut with thin flutes. A greater innovation was silvered glass, patented by F. Hale Thomson and Edward Varnish of London in 1849. Double-walled vessels containing a sealed silver deposit, usually colour cased, were made in a variety of forms; the manufacturer is thought to have been James Powell & Sons of London. Great hopes were expressed for the future of the technique, and it was popular for a while. However, like the enamelled and coloured wares of these years, it did not survive much beyond the Great Exhibition.

RUBY-CASED GOBLET, W.H., B. & J. RICHARDSON, 1851 (H19.7cm/7¾in)

Designed and possibly engraved by W.J. Muckley, this goblet appeared at the Great Exhibition. The roses are engraved through cased ruby glass. (LEFT)

PRESSED-GLASS FRUIT DISH, PROBABLY GEORGE BACCHUS & SONS, c.1850 (H18.4cm/7¼in)

Made by press-moulding, the dish imitates pillar-cut glass of the 1830s and 1840s. (BELOW)

THE FIRST
PRESSED GLASS

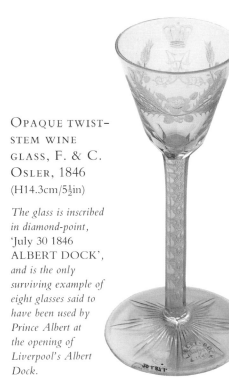

OPAQUE TWIST-STEM WINE GLASS, F. & C. OSLER, 1846 (H14.3cm/5½in)

The glass is inscribed in diamond-point, 'July 30 1846 ALBERT DOCK', and is the only surviving example of eight glasses said to have been used by Prince Albert at the opening of Liverpool's Albert Dock.

The example of cut glass has shown how glass manufacturers differentiated market levels. The major instance of this during the nineteenth century was the introduction of press-moulded glass in the 1830s. Press-moulding, which in fact originated in the United States, involved the use of a hand- (and later steam-) operated press to force hot glass into a mould made up of one or more parts. The relative cheapness of pressed glass greatly increased the availability of glassware. The earliest datable examples of pressed wares for the British buying public are the commemorative plates made from 1837 to 1841, celebrating the accession and coronation of Queen Victoria, her marriage to Albert and the birth of the Prince of Wales; some of these may actually be American in origin.

Much early pressed glass imitated cut glass and was made from high quality lead crystal. Birmingham and the West Midlands, to which later accounts attribute the origins of press-moulding in Britain, probably produced most of it; Rice Harris & Son exhibited pressed wares at the Great Exhibition, and Bacchus & Sons was certainly in pressed manufacture at this time; both Birmingham firms also made blown glass. Birmingham was also an important centre for mould-making, or die-sinking, the highly skilled part of press-moulding. It is thought that some die-sinkers worked independently from the various glass factories, possibly supplying their moulds to several establishments. From 1842 onward design patents could be taken out, and many pressed-glass manufacturers in Britain eagerly availed themselves of this opportunity to protect their new designs from being copied by other makers.

THE GLASS TABLE SERVICE

In the mid-1850s mention is made in factory records of services of glass, and they are illustrated in the earliest known trade catalogues. This seems to have been the period when large services of glass, at a range of prices, were first marketed commercially. A full service contained sets of glasses (for liqueurs, sherry, port, claret, champagne, wine and water), quart and claret decanters, finger bowls, ice plates, carafes, tumblers and other items. The service suited the method of dining in a series of courses adopted by Victorian society during the mid nineteenth century, with different glasses specified for the wines taken at each course.

The services of the 1850s and 1860s were

generally light in weight and decorated by cutting, engraving or etching. Cut glass became less fashionable but remained a staple; most services were either engraved or etched. Shapes now favoured were simple, such as the shaft and globe decanter with tall neck and globular body, and the wine glass with rounded bowl and thin, often plain stem. The thinner shapes encouraged the use of ornamental or pictorial designs; every piece in a service had matching designs, and a full engraved service was expensive.

ENGRAVING, ETCHING AND THE GRECIAN STYLE

By the 1860s the best-quality tableware was usually engraved. Britain attracted a number of skilled master engravers from Bohemia to work for London retailers and, increasingly, for the provincial factories. Among the best known are Paul Oppitz in London, Frederick E. Kny in Stourbridge, Wilhelm Pohl in Manchester, H. Keller in Glasgow and Franz Tieze in Dublin. These men brought with them a repertoire of Bohemian themes and motifs, such as stags among trees, and they also adapted with ease to the designs required by the British. Alongside the Bohemians local craftsmen grew in number; by around 1870 it is likely that every glass-manufacturing centre had sufficient engravers to meet demand.

The most fashionable style for engraved work during the 1860s and 1870s was the Grecian. A critic had commented that 'the most beautiful forms' of tableware in the Great Exhibition were 'Greek shapes', something which manifestly did not apply to the vast majority. From the late 1850s, when Greek ornament began to appear with frequency in the Stourbridge factory pattern-books, to the late 1870s, the forms and ornament of Greek pottery strongly influenced glass design. Glass engraved in the Grecian style was much in evidence at the International Exhibition in London in 1862. Apsley Pellatt & Co., whose glass was made at the Falcon Glassworks, Southwark, London, put on a rich show and included glasses simply engraved with lines, in a

loosely Grecian manner, adapted to the requirements of factory production. The London retailers W.P. & G. Phillips, to whom Thomas Webb of Stourbridge supplied glass for engraving, were also prominent exhibitors of Grecian glassware.

The Grecian designs shown in the *Art Journal* catalogue of the 1862 exhibition were expensive to produce, and it is unlikely that complete services were ever engraved with scenes of figures throughout. Rather, matching was achieved through the ornamental work. Thomas Webb's pattern-books in the 1870s, when Frederick Kny engraved for the firm, illustrate figure scenes only on claret decanters and water sets for dessert. The books also reveal the eclectic nature of Victorian design, for the engraved Grecian figures and patterns often decorate glasses with ribbed handles and other features derived from Venetian models.

CUT DECANTER, MOLINEAUX, WEBB & CO., 1850s (H30.5cm/12in)

COVERED BOWL, ENGRAVED BY FRANZ TIEZE, *c.*1870 (H15cm/5⅞ in)

For middle and lower markets acid-etching replaced or was combined with engraving, but Grecian figures and motifs were often still employed. A great contribution to the etching technique was made by John Northwood (1836–1902) in Wordsley, near Stourbridge, who in 1861 developed a template machine for outlining figures or ornament and in around 1865 a geometric etching machine for producing complex linear designs. On the template machine outlines were marked by a needle in a wax coating covering the glass to be decorated, a template acting as a guide; an acid dip etched the outline into the glass surface. In 1867 Northwood devised an acid-alkali mix that further frosted the interior of the design to reproduce the effect of an engraving. Free-hand line work and polishing were done on the best-quality etched pieces. Many of these figure scenes were Grecian, and some were taken from the *Outlines* of the Neoclassical sculptor John Flaxman (1755–1826), published in 1793 and reprinted throughout the nineteenth century as a design source. Richardson's pattern-books show etched Flaxman figures on jugs and goblets probably decorated in the Northwood workshop.

PRESSED GLASS FROM 1850 TO 1880

By the 1850s the pressed-glass industry was becoming established. The West Midlands factories now concentrated on blown wares, and it was in the northeast and northwest of England that most later nineteenth-century pressed glass was made, mainly at Gateshead, Sunderland and Manchester. Pressed-glass factories tended also to make blown glassware, and the influence of blown glass style is often seen in pressed wares. Molineaux, Webb & Co. of Manchester, for example, made blown and pressed glass in the Grecian style.

Little is known of pressed glass in the 1850s. Joseph Webb of Stourbridge registered several designs which imitate the then

WATER JUG AND PAIR OF GOBLETS, PROBABLY W.H., B.&J. RICHARDSON, *c.*1870 (Jug: H31.9cm/12⅔in)

PRESSED GLASSWARE, MANCHESTER, 1860s–80s (Biscuit barrel: H19.5cm/7¾in)

From left to right are: greyhound paperweight, John Derbyshire, design registered 1874; biscuit barrel, Molineaux, Webb & Co., registered 1867; swan flower vase, Burtles, Tate & Co., registered 1885.

fashionable simple cut patterns. A sugar bowl and milk jug registered in 1856 by Robinson & Bolton of Warrington, Lancashire, have large diamonds on the bodies and scalloped rims, again following cut-glass styles. These may be typical of the decade.

There is more information for the 1860s. One trend in pressed glass is exemplified by Molineaux, Webb's Grecian-style glassware. This firm registered a series of designs during the 1860s, often using a Greek key pattern (registered in 1864) and a partially frosted surface. The frosting sometimes functioned as a ground for the main motif and sometimes, as on a comport design of 1868, a striped effect was achieved. These pressed lines ran parallel to the firm's blown production, in which a pattern such as the Greek key would be engraved. Percival Vickers & Co. and James Derbyshire were other Manchester firms producing glass in similar style and technique.

A frosted effect was also employed by Henry Greener of the Wear Flint Glass Works in Sunderland during the 1860s.

Greener's 1860s pressed glass is particularly notable for its stipple grounds of small raised dots readily suited to the press-moulding technique. The other major northeast factories were Sowerby's Ellison Glassworks and George Davidson & Co. (at the Teams Glass Works), both of Gateshead-on-Tyne.

Coloured wares and figures were perhaps the major innovations in pressed glass during the 1870s. The trend toward colour is also found in blown art and fancy glass and continued to the end of the century. The press-moulded figures were occasionally of high quality, their subject matter appealing to sophisticated tastes; more often they are intended for a popular market.

The range of coloured glass made by Sowerby's was particularly rich. 'Vitro-porcelain', in translucent turquoise or a semi-transparent milky opal, was introduced in 1877. In the same year the opaque 'Patent Ivory Queen's Ware', probably imitating Wedgwood's pottery 'Queensware', also appeared. Marbled glass seems to have been patented in 1878, termed 'malachite' when coloured green and white and now often misnamed 'slag' glass when white and purple. Other colours were developed early in the 1880s, notably two rubies, two types of amber and 'blanc de lait', an opaque white glass sometimes decorated with flowers in relief and painted in cold colours. Other northeast and Manchester firms also

employed colours similar to those of Sowerby's, but the 'Aesthetic' designs of that firm, often based on artistic book illustration, are distinctive.

A number of Manchester firms introduced figures during the 1870s. John Derbyshire registered a lion, based on Sir Edwin Landseer's design for the base of Nelson's Column in Trafalgar Square, in 1874. Other popular subjects, such as Queen Victoria and Britannia, were made by Derbyshire, while Molineaux, Webb registered perhaps the finest of these pressed-glass figures, a black sphinx resembling Wedgwood's basaltes ware, in 1875. Many figures were made in a variety of colours or in colourless, frosted glass; the colours are sometimes strident, as in the chromium green and uranium yellow Britannia and Victoria of Derbyshire.

Although relatively little is known of it at this date, ordinary tableware must have been produced by all the pressed-glass firms in large quantities. Tumblers and goblets were a staple product, while celery vases, sugar bowls, creamers, butter dishes, comports and round or oval dishes were among the other popular pressed items, often advertised to the public in services. To judge by advertisements and trade catalogues of the early 1880s, many of these followed simple cut-glass designs.

LATER LUXURY
TABLE SERVICES

By the late 1870s the Stourbridge area had unquestionably become the leading British centre for luxury table glass. Building on its established reputation for manufacturing and cutting glass, the district had now attracted immigrant decorators of great skill and trained many local craftsmen to the highest standards. Glass for lower markets was produced in the area – for example, an 1890s trade catalogue of the Smart Brothers firm shows ordinary cut, etched and engraved services and glassware, often in mid-century styles – but it was its luxury glass that distinguished Stourbridge from other glass-manufacturing towns.

Two main types of luxury tableware were made in Stourbridge from the late 1870s to the end of the century, 'rock crystal' and 'brilliant' cut. Rock crystal was a Stourbridge speciality, otherwise produced in Britain only at the Edinburgh & Leith works. Brilliant cutting was widespread in the late nineteenth century, originating in the United States and spreading throughout Europe by the 1880s; it was also to influence the styles of the pressed-glass manufacturers of northern England.

ROCK CRYSTAL GLASS, STEVENS & WILLIAMS, 1895 (Jug: H20.3cm/8in)

The engraving on these vessels is Japanese-inspired. (LEFT)

ROCK CRYSTAL BOWL, THOMAS WEBB & SONS, *c.*1884 (H8cm/3in)

Engraved on the bowl is a Chinese bat amid floral scrolls. (BELOW)

ROCK CRYSTAL GLASS

Rock crystal glass was first produced by Thomas Webb & Sons of Stourbridge in 1878. The name refers to a decorative technique rather than a style; rock crystal glass was actually made in a number of styles. There are several distinctive features of this type of glass, the main one being engraving which is brightly polished in the manner of cut rock crystal. In the best rock crystal glass the engraving is deeper than normal and may be interwoven with cut patterns and, sometimes, etching. The interweaving of cut and engraved motifs, all bright-polished, gives the glass a sumptuous appearance reminiscent of carvings in natural rock crystal.

Webb's rock crystal glass is arguably the best ever made. The technique was used for ornamental vases as well as table services, and the latter are truly remarkable for the amount of skilled labour required to decorate the large number of glasses needed for a full late Victorian service – well over a hundred. How many services were manufactured in each pattern is unknown, but the frequency of patterns suggests very few; it may well be that many rock crystal services were simply supplied on commission, sometimes, as the pattern-books indicate, to the east coast of the United States.

The earliest Webb rock crystal has shallow engraving and naturalistic designs. These were often engraved in the workshop

of Frederick Kny, whose strength was figurative work, which he had executed for Webb, particularly in the Grecian style, during the early 1870s. In the 1880s Kny was joined at Webb by two other Bohemian master engravers, F. Kretschmann, of whom little is known, and William Fritsche (*c.*1853–1924). Fritsche was responsible for the development of rock crystal at the factory in the 1880s and 1890s, working in ornamental rather than figurative styles and developing the blending of cut and engraved decoration, the hallmark of Webb's best rock crystal. Fritsche's signature is sometimes found, even on tableware.

During the mid-1880s Webb made a number of Chinese-style vases, inspired by the stylized ornament published in Owen

Jones's *Examples of Chinese Ornament* of 1867. Fritsche, perhaps with Kny, modified the style to suit tableware, and luxuriant services in an Anglo-Chinese manner resulted. Later in the 1880s and the early 1890s, Fritsche produced some extraordinary swirled designs, employing richly cut and engraved rococo scrollwork and Indian pine motifs, the latter familiar from Paisley shawls. By the early 1890s, however, much Webb rock crystal was made using thin blanks, and cut effects were to an extent replaced by mould blown patterns. A need to reduce production costs is evident and was paralleled by a similar development in Stourbridge art glass in around 1890.

The Brierley Hill firm of Stevens & Williams was the other major producer of rock crystal glass, beginning in 1879. The factory made a series of deeply cut and engraved services and vases during the 1880s and early 1890s, using acid-etched effects to a greater extent than Webb. The company appears to have been particularly aware of advanced taste, its early rock crystal using naturalistic Japanese-style decoration, with floral designs sometimes traversing cut pillars in flowing rhythms. In around 1900, when Frederick Carder (who later started Steuben Glass in New York) was its art director, Stevens & Williams adopted the Art Nouveau style, which was scarcely seen in Webb glass. Stevens & Williams' Japanese-style glass was frequently produced to the designs of Joseph Keller, an independent Bohemian engraver working in the Stourbridge district; the Englishman, John Orchard, and a man named Miller, possibly a Bohemian, were the main factory engravers of the firm's rock crystal.

Two other Stourbridge firms, Webb, Corbett and Stuart & Sons, also made some rock crystal glass in the 1890s, although of lesser quality.

BRILLIANT CUT GLASS

Although cut glass continued in popularity in the 1860s and 1870s, no distinctive new style of the period can easily be recognized. By the late 1870s, however, the 'brilliant' style emerged, its name aptly describing its effect. At its most complex brilliant cutting involved covering the glass surface with intersecting cuts that created innumerable, often fragmentary shapes making up larger patterns. Basic motifs used were stars, hob-

BRILLIANT CUT WATER JUG AND PAIR OF GOBLETS, F. & C. OSLER, 1883 (Goblets: H19.9cm/7⅝in)

A set of two water jugs and four goblets was presented by the Birmingham Liberal Association to John Bright to mark his 25th year as Member of Parliament for the borough. A dessert service was also presented, the centrepiece for which survives in the Rochdale Museum.

BRILLIANT CUT BASKET, STEVENS & WILLIAMS, c.1880 (H17.5cm/6⅞in)

The variation of patterns of deep cutting within panels and the notched rim exemplify one type of brilliant cutting, derived from the cut-glass style of the late 1840s.

nail or polygonal diamonds, strawberry diamonds and fan scallops, out of which a dazzling surface effect was achieved.

The origins of brilliant cutting are thought to lie in American cut glass shown at the Philadelphia Centennial Exhibition of 1876. An early documented example in Britain is a 'brilliant cut' set advertised by Philip Pargeter (1826–1906) of the Red House Glassworks in Stourbridge in a trade catalogue of about 1880. This set of dinnerware is relatively simply cut with a band of large relief diamonds, each further cut with a star. During the 1880s more complicated designs were produced. F. & C. Osler of Birmingham, who specialized in cut-glass furniture and lighting equipment for the overseas market, made a brilliant cut water set for John Bright, a Member of Parliament, in 1883. This presentation set is particularly complex, its panels of cutting being overlaid with a strip of floral engraving, introducing a variety of composition and texture typical of late Victorian design.

As of yet British brilliant cut glass has

scarcely been researched. From the amount surviving and the extent to which it was imitated by pressed-glass manufacturers, it can be presumed to have been made in most if not all manufacturing areas.

LATER ENGRAVING AND INTAGLIO

After Thomas Webb & Sons and Stevens & Williams turned their attention to the production of rock crystal glass, they largely abandoned traditional matt engraving until the early twentieth century. Other Stourbridge firms continued to engrave as before, and outside Stourbridge the tradition seems to have remained strong. Quality engraving is known to have been done in Scotland during the 1880s: in Edinburgh at John Ford's Holyrood glassworks and in Glasgow at John Baird's factory. The Bohemian J.H.B. Millar ran a workshop in Edinburgh which seems to have been closely associated with the Holyrood works, and another Bohemian, H. Keller, engraved for Baird. They may have worked in the Grecian style for some years after its abandonment in the Stourbridge factories. Floral engraving probably remained common into the 1880s, as evidenced by a claret jug with ferns, which was engraved by Emanuel Lerche, another Bohemian working in Scotland, and survives in the Royal Museum of Scotland. More research, however, is needed to establish the strength of the tradition of matt engraving over this period.

A new technique, intaglio, was introduced at Stevens & Williams in 1890. Allied to engraving, intaglio was used in the 1890s and beyond for producing motifs similar to those common on engraved glass. The method requires a small lathe like an engraver's, but one to which stone, not copper, wheels are fitted. The stone wheels grind the glass quite deeply, and the intaglio design is always polished bright. As well as appearing on its own or in conjunction with copper-wheel work, intaglio was employed on some of the cheaper Stourbridge rock crystal glass of the 1890s.

PRESSED GLASS AFTER 1880

Early Victorian pressed-glass styles continued to some extent into the 1880s and 1890s. The expense of mould-making probably explains in part the degree of conservatism in pressed-glass design. Commemorative lines increased in popularity: most firms, for example, responded to Queen Victoria's golden and diamond jubilees. More figures appeared, some marketed extremely cheaply, like the small busts of the monarch in black glass made by Thomas Kidd of Ancoats, Manchester, for the 1897 jubilee.

Nevertheless, there were significant new developments, particularly in tableware design. Most noticeable during the 1880s was the extensive following of the brilliant cut style by all the pressed-glass manufacturers. A range of tastes was catered for,

WATER JUG, JOHN BAIRD, *c*.1876–80 (H33.3cm/13in)

The classical form of this Scottish jug is derived from ancient Greek pottery; the engraving is attributed to H. Keller. (ABOVE LEFT)

TANKARD JUG, JOHN FORD, PROBABLY 1880s (H24.8cm/9¾in)

Fern designs were popular in the late Victorian era. Perhaps mostly executed by local engravers, the designs rarely show the modelling skills associated with immigrant Bohemians. (TOP)

PRESSED GLASS, TYNESIDE AND WEARSIDE, 1860s–*c*.1900 (Mafeking dish: D25.7cm/10in)

From left to right are: dish commemorating the relief of Mafeking, 1900; comport in 'pearline' glass, George Davidson, 1903; ruby vase, Sowerby, 1877; dish, McDermott (Gateshead), 1866. (ABOVE)

from restrained to more exuberant versions of the style. Davidson & Co. of Gateshead produced some relatively conservative glass, as in a registered design of 1881 consisting simply of alternate pillars and vertical panels of rows of three raised dots; variations on this pattern were brought out at intervals during the decade. In 1889 Davidson introduced a set of tableware with pillars alternating with relief diamond panels topped by fans, more in keeping with the richer versions of brilliant cut glass. This set was made in 'Pearline', a shaded glass in either blue or primrose, one of the most notable colour innovations of the 1880s.

Executed in a manner truly 'brilliant' were designs such as Molineaux, Webb's 'Duchess' service of 1883. Apart from the stems of vessels such as the celery vase and salad bowl, or the necks of cruets, all of which were fluted, glasses in this service were covered with a rich relief pattern of alternating squares and four-pointed stars in a chequerboard effect. A Henry Greener design of 1897 was richer still, with clusters of multi-pointed stars, octagons and fans covering the surface. Yet the 1881 pressed-glass catalogue of Percival Vickers & Co. of Manchester offers a reminder that tables of the period might be dressed with far different glassware; from that year Percival Vickers' 'St Petersburg' service was available, decorated with just a row of sprigs in the Neoclassical taste.

Certain pressed-glass manufacturers produced highly original designs, fully utilizing the possibilities of the technique. Perhaps most distinctive are the jugs and other tableware of W.H. Heppell & Co. of Newcastle-upon-Tyne, comprising fish and shell forms of great charm, registered in the early 1880s. Edward Moore & Co. of South Shields produced superbly moulded wares, specializing in a range of gadrooned patterns reminiscent of English silver of the eighteenth century; these date from the 1880s.

Although the northeast firms and those of Manchester continued to be the major producers of pressed glass, other towns also made pressed wares. Glass from the Warrington firms of Robinson, Son & Skinner

and Edward Bolton has now been identified. Bolton advertised a boat-shaped flower trough in a supplement to *The Pottery Gazette* in 1877, and a creamer and other vessels with simple frosted pillars are known from the firm's pattern-book covering the years 1871 to 1897. John Ford's Holyrood works in Edinburgh had also been making pressed glass since the 1870s.

ART AND FANCY GLASS

The 'art' glass of the late nineteenth century is quite distinct from glass of the contemporaneous Arts and Crafts Movement. Made by the factories producing luxury tableware, notably those of Stourbridge, art glass was produced for a wealthy public of conservative taste. It embraced decoration, which Arts and Crafts glass-makers largely abandoned in favour of the qualities of the material itself. Occasionally pieces are marked 'Art Glass', but the term covers a wide range of high-quality ornamental vases and other vessels usually lacking even a factory mark. The spirit of art glass is perhaps best caught in a phrase heading an advertisement for the Stourbridge firm of Thomas Webb & Sons in 1889: 'Works of Art in Sculptured Glass'. 'Fancy' glass is essentially cheap art glass, and the term refers to both blown and pressed decorative ornamental wares.

Numerous types of art glass were developed from the mid-1870s to the 1890s. Some were entirely furnace-made, and these occurred in three main varieties – those with applied ornament, those reliant on colour effects and those with internal or surface decoration. The three categories are not always distinct, as much of the glass shows a rich variety of treatment. Other examples of art glass were cold-decorated, utilizing the skills of engravers, carvers or enamellers; again, cold techniques were sometimes employed in combination with decorative treatments at the furnace.

APPLIED ORNAMENT

Glass with applied ornament was particularly suited to late Victorian taste. It appealed to all levels of the market, so much of this type of glass merits the term 'fancy' rather than 'art'. Much ruby glass was made in the 1880s and 1890s with applied and often stamped colourless ornament, on rims and feet especially; simple scallops with fan- or shell-like mouldings are typical. The major Stourbridge firms of Webb, Stevens & Williams and Richardson made more lavish examples. Vases were ornamented with floral, animal or grotesque additions, pincered to shape by the glass-makers.

Occasionally a type of art glass was named. In 1884 John Northwood developed 'Matsu-no-ke' glass for Stevens & Williams, colourless 'rustic' stems being trailed over a coloured body and flower forms stamped with a patent stamping device. During the 1880s Stevens & Williams also added rustic work to bowls with crimped rims that had been internally decorated with air channels from a mould, the surface finally being acid-

BOWL WITH APPLIED DECORATION, STOURBRIDGE, 1880s (H10.2cm/4in)

The opalescent glass features silver leaf decoration beneath the surface. The amber-coloured fish have been tooled and pinched to shape, then applied to the body of the vase.

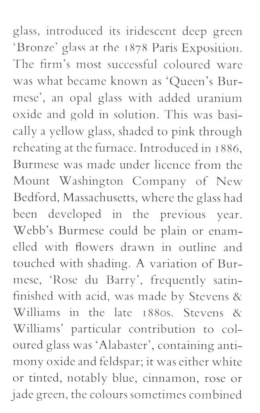

CENTREPIECE,
HODGETTS,
RICHARDSON &
SON, 1878 OR
LATER
(H63.5cm/25in)

*Used for flowers, the
centrepiece is decorated
with machine-threaded
ruby trails. The design
of such pieces was
influenced by Venetian
chandeliers, examples
of which were imported
into Britain in the later
Victorian period.* (FAR
LEFT)

FLOWER STAND,
THOMAS WEBB
& SONS, 1880s
(H19cm/7½in)

*Enamel-painted floral
decoration was often
used by Webb on his
Burmese ornamental
glassware.* (LEFT)

treated for a satin finish. This combination of craftsmanship and mechanical inventiveness raised applied-work pieces to an extraordinary height. It is further seen in the machine-threaded glassware produced by Hodgetts, Richardson & Co. from 1876 and Stevens & Williams from 1877. Threading machines enabled trails of coloured glass to be mechanically wound around a glass body with great precision. The technique was used for tableware as well as art glass. A glass type on which this threading was sometimes employed to effect was the centrepiece for flowers, which provided an artistic focus for the late Victorian dinner table.

COLOURED WARES

The new colour effects of art glass relied chiefly on the addition of metallic oxides to the glass mix, heightened in some cases by internal or surface treatments. Thomas Webb & Sons, well known for coloured glass, introduced its iridescent deep green 'Bronze' glass at the 1878 Paris Exposition. The firm's most successful coloured ware was what became known as 'Queen's Burmese', an opal glass with added uranium oxide and gold in solution. This was basically a yellow glass, shaded to pink through reheating at the furnace. Introduced in 1886, Burmese was made under licence from the Mount Washington Company of New Bedford, Massachusetts, where the glass had been developed in the previous year. Webb's Burmese could be plain or enamelled with flowers drawn in outline and touched with shading. A variation of Burmese, 'Rose du Barry', frequently satin-finished with acid, was made by Stevens & Williams in the late 1880s. Stevens & Williams' particular contribution to coloured glass was 'Alabaster', containing antimony oxide and feldspar; it was either white or tinted, notably blue, cinnamon, rose or jade green, the colours sometimes combined on stemmed or handled vessels. A further technique for achieving colour was used by many factories – the inclusion of gold or silver metallic foil in the body of the glass giving a shimmering, crazed effect. Most remarkable of this type was Stevens & Williams' 'Silveria' of the late 1890s. This included silver foil, which sometimes was partly oxidized to a golden hue, and trails of green glass disposed over the surface.

INTERNAL AND SURFACE DECORATION

Internal and surface treatments of art glassware were usually based on traditional glass-making techniques, but often utilized skills and inventiveness in a wholly Victorian manner. A good example is the diamond air-trap technique developed by Stevens & Williams in the mid-1880s. The hot glass was inserted into a mould with crossed ribs, then covered by a further gather of glass. Air

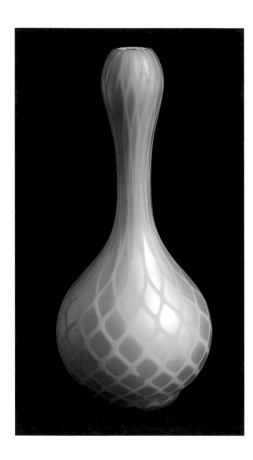

DIAMOND AIR-TRAP VASE, STEVENS
& WILLIAMS, *c.*1885 (H25.5cm/10in)

*A moulded diamond pattern of air is trapped
between an inner layer of opaque white and an outer
layer of transparent turquoise glass, and the surface
is satin-finished with acid.*

was trapped in the impressions made by the
ribs, its diamond pattern softened by an acid
satin finish. The technique has affinities with
historic Venetian practice. More directly
Venetian in inspiration was the *latticino* glass
developed by John Northwood for the same
firm, including white and colourless glass
canes in the glass body; this was used for
certain tableware forms. The Edinburgh &
Leith Flint Glass Works, which was taken
over by Alexander Jenkinson (1821–80) in
1865, was also producing Venetian-type
cane-work glass and mottled glassware by
the mid-1870s. Stevens & Williams' 'Moss
Agate' was perhaps the most adventurous of
such art glass. Crackled internally by the

action of sprayed water, it was irregularly
streaked with colours picked up on the
marver and then cased in colourless glass. It
relied, therefore, to quite an unusual extent
on accidental effect.

Among surface treatments enamelling re-
emerged as a significant form of decoration
in the late 1880s and 1890s. The Frenchman,
Jules Barbe, working first at Webb and then
independently, enamelled and gilded vases
and tableware. At Stevens & Williams
another Frenchman, Oscar Pierre Erard,
designed 'Tapestry' glass, combining
painted floral decoration and machine
threading to produce effects of rare delicacy.

COLD DECORATION

Of all the types of art glass of the 1880s and
1890s those decorated in the cold state have
provoked the greatest admiration. The techniques used for this glass were labour-
intensive, and certain high-quality pieces are
known to have taken two to three years to
produce. The main type is cameo glass, a
speciality of the major Stourbridge firms.
Other cold-decorated art glass was engraved
and carved in high relief, and many examples were also made in the rock crystal
technique used for luxury tableware.

The first cold-decorated art glass had been
produced as early as 1873. The Elgin Vase
was commissioned by J.B. Stone (later Sir
Benjamin Stone) in the 1860s, and a blank
for it made in his Birmingham works of
Stone, Fawdry & Stone. A colourless two-
handled vase inspired by Greek pottery was
provided for John Northwood, then an
independent decorator, to carve and
engrave. The major effort required was to
work a frieze of horsemen from the British
Museum's Elgin marbles in high relief
around the body. A smaller vase without
handles, similarly worked, was made at
Thomas Webb & Sons in around 1875; this
was decorated by Frederick Kny. The production of this second piece illustrates the
competitive spirit of quality art-glass manufacture. The Webb vase was most likely
shown at the 1878 Paris Exposition, where it
acted as an advertisement for the firm.

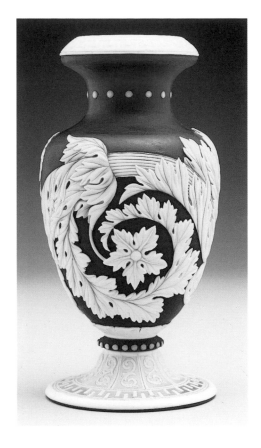

CAMEO-GLASS VASE, HODGETTS,
RICHARDSON & SON, *c.*1878
(H19cm/7½in)

*The balance of colour on this vase suggests a
connection with the contemporary figurative cameo
pieces made for Richardson by Alphonse Lechevrel.*

CAMEO GLASS

More influential on commercial art-glass
production was John Northwood's 1873
commission, from Philip Pargeter of
Wordsley, to make a replica of the Roman
cameo-glass Portland Vase, which was completed in 1876. Much difficulty was experienced in making the two-colour blank,
owing to the problem of fusing two different glasses. There was then the exacting task
for Northwood to work the white casing to
reveal the blue ground underneath, and
engraving and carving with hand tools to
create the design. Around the same time
Joseph Locke (1846–1936) also produced a

CAMEO-GLASS PLAQUE, THOMAS
WEBB & SONS, 1880s (D32cm/12⅝in)

The plaque, representing two dancers, is attributed to George Woodall. Classical subjects with a mildly erotic content appear often on his vases. (BELOW)

CAMEO-GLASS VASES, STOURBRIDGE, 1880s (Tallest: H30.4cm/12in)

Made either at Thomas Webb & Sons or Stevens & Williams, these vases show the formal and naturalistic styles of floral cameo made by the two firms in the 1880s. (ABOVE)

Portland Vase replica for Richardson, and at the Paris exhibition of 1878 the same firm showed figurative cameo pieces by Alphonse Eugène Lechevrel (b. 1850). Lechevrel's cameo work is distinguished by a sensitive awareness of the relationship between the design and ground – his few cameo productions well convey the austere atmosphere of classical myth and legend.

By around 1880 both Webb and Stevens & Williams were seizing the opportunity to turn cameo glass into a commercial success. Certain labour-saving methods were adopted, notably the use of acid to take down the ground. Figure designs were largely rejected as too complex, except for exhibition or commissioned pieces. Webb's cameo production was in the hands of the Woodall brothers, George (1850–1925) and Thomas (1849–1926), while Stevens & Williams' was produced either by John Northwood or by a team of carvers, including John Northwood II (1870–1960), Joshua Hodgetts (1857–1933), who specialized in naturalistic floral designs, William Northwood (1857–1937) and James Hill (1850–1928). Most of the vases were in two colours, although Webb made some superb examples in three. A rare version of cameo glass had silver-deposit designs laid onto the floral work: this was the speciality of Oscar Pierre Erard at Stevens & Williams. Designs on the whole are not easy to attribute, although some pieces are marked. By 1890, production was proving too costly in the face of cheaper Continental imitations, and attention was switched to intaglio work. High-quality figurative cameo glass continued to be made, especially by the Woodalls, into the early years of the twentieth century.

END OF AN ERA

There is some evidence – in the abandonment of the commercial production of cameo glass and in the decline in quality of rock crystal tableware – of difficulties in the luxury glass market at the end of the nineteenth century. To an extent the achievements of the Victorian glass-makers did survive into the Edwardian era, with men like William Fritsche still engraving quality tableware up to the First World War. However, competition from overseas may have been a major factor in causing a certain decline. The pressed-glass trade also lost some of its impetus, probably for the same reason. The years from around 1860 until about 1890 had seen an efflorescence of glass-making in Britain under particular social and economic conditions which perhaps was impossible to sustain. Those three decades can fairly be described as a golden age for British glass.

AMERICAN GLASS

The questions surrounding early American glass are by no means answered. Few of the objects made in the New World prior to the invention of the pressing machine in the 1820s were distinctively different in shape, colour or ingredients from glass made elsewhere. Until recently, books were filled with illustrations of foreign glass confidently labelled American as a result of naïveté or wishful thinking.

American Glass, by George S. and Helen McKearin, did not appear until 1941, long after the old craftsmen and all who remembered them had gone to their graves. Although the book is in need of revision to reflect current scholarship, and has been superseded by more specific studies, it remains the definitive work on the subject of American glass.

Thus, while anyone in the United States could easily assemble an impressive collection of native examples from the Victorian era, a collector might not in a lifetime, even with unlimited funds, be able to acquire enough authentic American glass from the eighteenth century to fill a vitrine.

THE EARLIEST GLASS-MAKERS

Although glass-making was attempted in North America during the seventeenth century, notably at Jamestown, Virginia, the Colonies were dependent upon England for everything from bottles and window glass to fine lead tableware in the latest London styles. It was, however, German immigrants, trained in the non-lead manufacturing methods of the Continent, who established the most successful American glasshouses in the century that followed.

Three are of special significance: the Wistarburgh glassworks, near Alloway, New Jersey, built by Caspar Wistar and continued by his son Richard, from 1739 to 1777; the glasshouse operated by Henry William Stiegel at Manheim, Pennsylvania, from 1764 to 1774; and the New Bremen glassworks, in Frederick County, Maryland, which were organized in 1785 by a group from old Bremen, headed by John Frederick Amelung, and kept in operation, intermittently, for about ten years.

TYPES OF EARLY GLASS

While the Wistars relied on an output of unrefined green glass, Stiegel and Amelung introduced fancy colourless tableware. With the publication of *Stiegel Glass*, in 1914, Frederick William Hunter led the way to misidentification of this material and launched two generations of Americans on a quest for questionable glass.

The largest group consists of colourless, non-lead, mallet-shaped decanters, tumblers and wine glasses, copper wheel-engraved with tulips, sunflowers and baskets of flowers. Originally prized as Stiegel or Amelung, depending upon whether they had descended through families in Pennsylvania or Virginia, it was not until Dwight P. Lanmon published his 1969 study of glass imports into the port of Baltimore from 1780 to 1820 that they were called into question. Lanmon pointed out that glassware of this description had come into Baltimore by the shipload from the Continent. He used well-documented illustrations from a catalogue presumed to have been sent to an American retailer by the agent of a German glass manufacturer.

'ENAMELLED' GLASS

Misinterpretation of the word 'enamelled', as found in 1772 advertisements for Stiegel's glass, led collectors to seek out any drinking vessels, decanters and the like which were painted with gaudy designs in red, white, blue, yellow and black, of the sort found scattered across the length and breadth of western Europe. Most desired were those on which appeared a sentiment in English, such as 'We two will be true', or a phrase in pidgin German, assumed to have been created in Manheim for local families of German descent, the 'Pennsylvania Dutch'. In the absence of evidence to suggest that American or European manufactories ever employed glass painters, it is possible that independent American decorators may have utilized blanks from the same German or Bohemian factories as the *Hausmaler* of Europe.

On the other hand, in eighteenth-century glass terminology the word 'enamel' referred to opaque white glass, and 'enamelling' was used to describe the embedding of opaque white threads into the stems of wine glasses.

Recently, it has been shown that during the last two years of his production, Henry William Stiegel was manufacturing lead-glass tableware in imitation of the finest English imports. The discovery of an engraved lead-glass goblet, with a white enamel-twist stem – made to celebrate the wedding of Stiegel's daughter, Elizabeth, to William Old in 1773 – may finally have put the lie to the concept of Stiegel as a maker of 'peasant glass'.

NON-LEAD GLASS

Careful examination of presentation glass engraved with the words 'New Bremen', together with analysis by energy-dispersive X-ray fluorescence, has made it possible to

LEAD-GLASS WINE GLASS, ATTRIBUTED TO HENRY WILLIAM STIEGEL, 1773 (H17cm/6¾in)

The glass is copper-wheel engraved with the initials of Elizabeth Stiegel and William Old. (FAR LEFT)

DARK AMETHYST NON-LEAD GLASS SUGAR BOWL, ATTRIBUTED TO THE NEW BREMEN GLASS-MANUFACTORY, c.1785–95 (H20.4cm/8in)

The bowl displays copper wheel engraving. (LEFT)

attribute more than fifty surviving examples to the Amelung factory. Most are of a lightweight, non-lead glass of greyish tint, exhibiting a greater degree of sophistication in form and decoration than the German imports mentioned above. A few rare examples exist in deep amethyst and, based on the evidence of a single shard found at the factory site, it is believed objects were also made in cobalt blue.

LEAD GLASS

Fine lead-glass tableware was being produced early in the nineteenth century in Boston and Philadelphia, but it was Pittsburgh, Pennsylvania, that became the centre for elegant services cut in the English manner and saw the creation of some of the country's first ornamental glass. The French engraver, Alexis Jardell, one of the most influential, if not the first, of the city's truly skilled glass cutters, arrived in Pittsburgh in

March 1818. The renown of the city's heavy, brilliant clear glass, cut in cross-hatched diamonds with blaze, or with the ever-popular strawberry diamond and fan, appears to date from this time. By 1823 drinking glasses were being engraved to order with 'crests, cyphers or designs', and decorated as gifts with monograms and symbols of fidelity, such as a greyhound or two hearts burning on the altar of love. By 1825, the Bakewell company was advertising sets of cut-glass tumblers, each with a sulphide portrait of an American patriot embedded in the base. A mantelpiece ornament enclosing a sulphide bust of George Washington was also made.

BLOWN-MOULDED GLASS

The process of blowing glass into hinged moulds of three or more parts to fashion tableware in imitation of Anglo-Irish cut glass may not have originated in the New

World, but 'blown-three-mould' glass, as it is called, was made in far greater quantity and variety in the United States than anywhere else.

For more than 20 years, in the early part of the nineteenth century, a wide range of objects, from toy wine glasses to table centrepieces to punchbowls, usually of colourless glass, were variously patterned with vertical and horizontal ribs, bands of diamond quilting effect, sunbursts, bull's-eyes and the like, and, later, rococo plumes and scrolls. Examples found in coloured glass are highly valued.

As the American population moved westward at the beginning of the nineteenth century, the settlement of each new community increased the demand for window glass, dry goods containers and bottles for wine, whisky, porter or even home brew. Glasshouses sprang up along the Ohio River from Pittsburgh southward to Louisville, Kentucky. The technique of

'BLUE COLUMBIA' FLASK,
ATTRIBUTED TO KENSINGTON UNION
GLASS WORKS, PHILADELPHIA,
c.1820–30 (Cap. 1 US pint/0.47litre)

LACY, PRESSED LEAD-GLASS COMPORT, PROBABLY THE
BOSTON & SANDWICH GLASS COMPANY, *c*.1835–50
(H14.3cm/5⅝in; bowl: D18.5cm/7¼in)

patterning bottles by dip-moulding, as practised by Stiegel and others in the early
Eastern manufactories, was carried to the
fledgling glass concerns and transformed
into an art. In this process, gathers of glass
were inserted into small, brass rib moulds,
then removed and blown into brilliant
bubbles of aquamarine, green or amber that
were swirled left or right.

By 1817, the glasshouses had begun to use
full-sized moulds to make pocket flasks with
relief decorations of sunbursts or masonic
arches on their sides. These were followed
by bottles patterned with symbols of historical and patriotic significance, from presiden-
tial portraits to ears of corn beneath the
slogan 'Corn for the World' (protesting
against the English Corn Laws, which were
repealed in 1846). Such bottles were made in
many sizes and colours, and are now avidly
collected. Every example known has been
described, assigned a number and valued.

PRESSED GLASS

The most significant contribution of the
United States to glass production was the
invention and perfection of machinery to
press lead glass into metal moulds in the
1820s. By mid-century factories had pro-
liferated in New England and the Midwest,
at first producing heavy sugar bowls,
creamers and other table articles in 'lacy
glass', so called because the intricate stippled
designs pressed into the surface broke up
reflected light. On master salts and 'cup
plates' (used to hold hot handleless cups
while people drank tea or coffee from their
saucers), one may find an entire vocabulary
of early Victorian ornament. Before long
complete table services became available in
non-stippled patterns, made to resemble fine
cut glass; they had names like 'Excelsior',
'Horn of Plenty' and 'New England Pine-
apple'. The fierce competition fostered an

RUBY-FLASHED AND CUT-GLASS
LAMP WITH MATCHING STANDARD ON
A MARBLE BASE, ATTRIBUTED TO THE
BOSTON & SANDWICH GLASS
COMPANY, *c*.1860–80 (Lamp: H71cm/
28in; shade: H24cm/9½in)

extraordinary variety of designs and a dazzling array of colours. The Boston &
Sandwich Glass Company of Sandwich,
Massachusetts, and later the New England
Glass Company, specialized in whale-oil
lamps and candlesticks with tops of one
colour and bases of another. Czechoslovakian reproductions were made during the
1920s and are very deceptive.

Although it would revive briefly for the
nation's Centennial in 1876, the American
Civil War, and labour unrest and competition from abroad, soon brought to an end
the heyday of American pressed glass.

CONTINENTAL GLASS

The Industrial Revolution was to transform glass-making in the nineteenth century, bringing greater organization to the manufacture of glass and a more scientific approach to its production. Glass furnaces were improved and standardized, their higher heat capabilities enabling manufacturers to produce finer quality glass of a consistent nature, more suitable to the increased demands of mechanical cutting. Moreover, the involvement of chemists in the industry successfully assisted the development of a greater variety of coloured glass.

Shapes and patterns were influenced by increasing numbers of books illustrating designs from antiquity, by international trade and, in the first half of the century, by the introduction of national trade exhibitions promoting each country's industrial and artistic products. In 1851 the Great Exhibition, held at Hyde Park in London, heralded a period of greater international awareness of art and science. A number of Bohemians, as well as other Europeans and Americans, displayed their glass alongside the exhibits of major British glass-makers and glass retailers. It led to similar events, such as that in Paris in 1855, where over half of the displays were of French manufacture. It was at this exhibition that the revived Venetian style made its first major appearance. At the London exhibition of 1862 the Viennese firm of J. & L. Lobmeyr displayed its glass to much acclaim; it was natural, therefore, that it should have had one of the largest displays at a similar event in Vienna in 1873. These exhibitions were on an enormous scale and continued around the world throughout the century.

At the beginning of the nineteenth century western Europe was widely influenced by the classical arts of Egypt, Greece and Rome. This is reflected in the Empire style in France and the 'massiveness' apparent in the British decorative arts at this

time. While the Neoclassical style was revived in Britain in the middle of the century, it was the Neo-Renaissance styles, based on fifteenth- and sixteenth-century European designs, which were preferred by the Europeans. Indeed, Lobmeyr commissioned many designs in the High Renaissance, Oriental and Islamic styles, whose ornament appeared in dictionaries and encyclopedias of the 1860s and 1870s.

CUT GLASS

Cut table glass and lighting continued to be popular into the first quarter of the century. With the introduction of steam-powered cutting machines at the beginning of the century, the industry had been revolutionized, enabling the manufacturers slowly to change

PLATE FROM THE CATALOGUE OF THE LONDON 1862 EXHIBITION, SHOWING GILDED AND ENAMELLED GLASS FROM THE IMPERIAL MANUFACTORY OF ST PETERSBURG, *c*.1860

their designs, from the shallow, flat cut diamonds of the late eighteenth century to a more heavy, deeply cut style in the 1820s, which culminated in the monumental, over-cut exhibits at the Great Exhibition in 1851. This change in style was quite gradual, and the styles were international, so it is often difficult to differentiate between items made in Britain, Ireland, France or Bohemia. For example, one French glasshouse, St Louis (founded in Lorraine in 1767), was making glass in the English manner in 1781 under the instruction of English cutters. In 1802 Aimé-Gabriel d'Artigues (1778–1848), the former manager of St Louis, purchased the Vonêche factory at Namur in the Low Countries. He began production of cut lead crystal there and later, in 1816, at the Baccarat factory, which he also acquired. By 1826 the Val St-Lambert factory, near Liège in Belgium, was employing a skilled, supervisory force of English workers.

SULPHIDES

While the French continued to produce cut glass, they perfected another technique to add to their repertoire – that of including white ceramic medallions into glass, commonly known today as 'sulphides'.

Glass portrait medallions had been made fashionable in the late eighteenth century by James Tassie (1735–99) in Scotland, and later in London by his nephew, William Tassie (1777–1860). They modelled wax portraits of popular figures, often politicians or the aristocracy, that were then cast in plaster, the wax removed, and molten glass poured into the mould. When cooled, the medallions were mounted on to sheets of glass and framed. Bohemians had also tried to encrust glass with greyish clay figures at this time but without much success.

The French succeeded where the Bohemians had failed. Pierre-Honoré Boudon de Saint-Amans (1774–1858) patented the improvement of flat medallions for inclusion in glass in 1818, implying that they had been made before, possibly by Barthélemy Desprez (fl.1773–1819), a sculptor for the Sèvres porcelain factory who, with his son, became famous for the production of sulphides. In his *Memoir on the Origin, Progress, and Improvement of Glass Manufactures . . .* (1821), London glass-maker Apsley Pellatt (1791–1863), who patented 'crystallo-ceramie' (sulphides) in England in 1819, remarked that the French '. . . having expended a considerable sum in the attempt, at length succeeded in encrusting several medallions of Bonaparte, which were sold at an enormous price . . . . The French have, however, not succeeded in introducing encrustation into articles of any size, such as decanters, jugs or plates'. This statement was untrue, however, as many early French

items (other than paperweights) exist. The best description of this encrustation technique is found in Pellatt's *Curiosities of Glass Making* (1849). He also mentioned coloured inclusions, but these are now often attributed solely to the French.

Besides plaques and paperweights, which are occasionally marked by makers or medallists, the most common items are perfume bottles and tumblers; jugs and decanters were also manufactured, predominantly bearing formal portraits, coats of arms, religious subjects and occasionally landscapes. These sulphide items were sometimes produced to accompany large cut vases and candelabra. The technique survived throughout the century and, though not confined to French and English manufacturers, they probably provided the main inspiration for other European glasshouses.

CUT-GLASS OBELISK ORNAMENT WITH SULPHIDE INCLUSION OF THE MADONNA AND CHILD, *c.*1830–40 (H27.2cm/10¾in)

As it bears no maker's or medallist's mark, this representation of a popular subject is difficult to attribute, but is probably French. (LEFT)

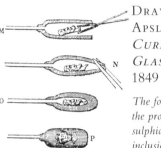

DRAWING FROM APSLEY PELLATT'S *CURIOSITIES OF GLASS MAKING*, 1849

The four steps show the production of a sulphide pocket for inclusion in a vessel.

COLOURED GLASS AND TRANSPARENT ENAMELS

The cutting of clear glass was in decline by the middle of the century, especially with the change in taste toward the newly developed coloured and enamelled glass produced by the many Bohemian glasshouses. In the eighteenth century the Bohemians were famous for their engraved glass, but by the nineteenth they had concentrated on the development of transparent enamels, which led to the production of stained, coloured cased glass. In France at this time a milky-looking glass, known as 'opaline', was developed.

Johann Joseph Mildner had introduced enamelled decoration on glass in the late eighteenth century, but the technique's importance lay in the early part of the following century. Samuel Mohn (1762–1815), a porcelain painter, started his experiments in 1806, painting enamel portraits on

TRANSPARENT ENAMELLED BEAKER,
ANTON KOTHGASSER, *c.*1820–30
(H11cm/4¼in)

The classical floral centrepiece, along with the cherub in a landscape, illustrates the movement toward naturalistic design. The cut cogwheel base was stained yellow prior to cutting.

to glass. By 1807 he had established a studio at Leipzig. He moved two years later to Dresden and by then had announced his discovery of the lost art of transparent painting on glass. His skills were passed on to his son, Gottlob (1789–1825), who had received formal training in the studios at Leipzig and Dresden before moving to Vienna in 1811. The younger Mohn continued to run the Dresden factory from Vienna and by 1815, having gained the knowledge and skills of church and castle window painting, was appointed palace painter at Schloss Laxenburg. It was probably due to Gottlob Mohn that Anton Kothgasser (1769–1851) was encouraged to include transparent enamelled decoration of glass in his repertoire.

Anton Kothgasser was a decorator at the Royal Vienna Porcelain Manufactory until 1816, when he opened a decorating studio in Vienna where he employed other important decorators, each with his own distinctive style. Their products were sold in Nuremberg as well as in Vienna.

The early items were often solid, straight-sided or flared tumblers, decorated with such diverse subjects as portraits, town scenes, palaces, churches, landscapes,

flowers, birds and insects. The transparent enamels give the impression of soft, romantic watercolours on glass. Their later tumblers followed the then popular, middle-class Biedermeier style, which was prevalent between *c.*1820 and *c.*1840 and which, with its plain, provincial Neoclassical elements, loosely followed the Empire style. Although principally used to refer to furniture, the term Biedermeier may also be applied to the porcelain and glass that complemented such furniture.

Mohn and Kothgasser were not the only exponents of the enamelling art. They inspired many other *Hausmaler* (independent decorators of both porcelain and glass), especially the Bohemian Friedrich Egermann (1777–1864), who later changed his speciality from the art of enamelling to the development of coloured glass.

THE COLOURING OF GLASS

Friedrich Egermann, from Blottendorf (Polevsko), near Haida, in southern Bohemia, was a trained glass-blower and decorator of glass with a sound knowledge of chemistry. In 1818 he was responsible for the development of a yellow stain, which was attained by using silver chloride, and by the 1830s he had perfected a ruby stain. Until the time of these discoveries, virtually no pale glass tints had been made or developed. The vessel could be either painted or dipped into the stain, which was fixed by being fired at a low temperature in a kiln, giving the appearance of a solid pale colour throughout the glass. The staining technique was suitable for the decorating workshops as it required the same heat as that of the enamel-firing kilns. More elaborate glass could combine both staining and enamelling.

Experiments to make solid coloured glass were conducted in southern Bohemia by Count von Buquoy. He produced opaque black glass in 1817 in emulation of Wedgwood's popular eighteenth-century 'black basaltes' ceramic wares, which was followed by a similar red glass, called 'Hyalith' in 1819. Egermann was experimenting along similar lines at the same time; his work

GROUP OF BIEDERMEIER GLASSES, *c.*1830–50 (Tallest: H16.7/6½in)

These show the variety of colours used during this period, as well as the progression of shapes, from simple tumblers to goblets.

GROUP OF
AGATE GLASS,
*c.*1830–40 (Beaker
at right:
H10.5cm/4¼in)

*The three perfume
bottles and beaker on
the right are good
examples of marbled
'Lithyalin' glass, while
the blue goblet has the
appearance of lapis
lazuli. The example
on the left was
enamelled prior to
being decorated with an
exotic landscape.*

culminated in his 1829 patent for marbled 'Lithyalin' glass, which, in its imitation of agates, satisfied the discerning public's desire for rare, curious natural phenomena. Examples of Lithyalin included vases, beakers and, frequently, perfume bottles, which, concurrent with the development of the fragrance industry, were in great demand. Pieces were often cut and polished, sometimes enamelled or gilded. As the French firm of St Louis also produced agate glass, it is often hard to distinguish their work from that of the Bohemian glass-makers.

During the 1820s and 1830s most European glasshouses were experimenting with various types of coloured glass, resulting in great strides in this burgeoning area of glass manufacture. The Harrach glassworks in northern Bohemia, for example, claimed to have rediscovered the secret of 'Kunckel red', the fine translucent ruby colour originally developed by Johann Kunckel at the Potsdam glasshouse in the late seventeenth century. Perhaps one of the most interesting discoveries was made by Josef Riedel (*fl.*1830–48), who in the 1830s developed attractive yellowish-green (*Annagrün*) and greenish-yellow (*Annagelb*) glass, made by adding uranium to the colourless glass batch (both glass types were named after Riedel's wife). These colours were also made by the Harrach glassworks (which was taken over by the Riedel factory in 1887).

'SPECIMENS OF
CUT GLASS',
EXHIBITED BY
W. HOFFMAN
OF PRAGUE AT
THE GREAT
EXHIBITION,
LONDON, 1851

*The central vase was
white over a colour,
while the remainder
were matt opaline,
some with applied
snakes. All show a
lack of restraint, a
characteristic
not seen in earlier
items.* (LEFT)

FRENCH OPALINE

The French, too, were experimenting with colour. They directed their energies in particular to the production of a fine white and semi-opaque coloured glass known as 'opaline'. Milk white glass had been made by the Venetians, the French and the British in previous centuries, but the earlier glass was much denser in colour, imitating Oriental porcelain. The French opalines were more translucent, while remaining opaque,

and when held up to the light revealed a fiery red tint due to the addition of bone ash. Opaline was produced in a wide range of colours, the most popular being a turquoise blue not unlike the *bleu-céleste* of Sèvres porcelain. The rarest but most desirable variety was a wonderful pink known as *gorge-de-pigeon*, named after the iridescent throat feathers of a pigeon.

The manufacture of opaline glass was not confined to tableware. It is more frequently found in the form of Neoclassical vases,

CASED GLASS

ENGRAVED GLASS

caskets and perfume bottles, as well as columns for lighting. Many of these items can be dated from the style of their elaborate ormolu mounts. Opaline was made both by free- and mould-blowing; sometimes pieces were cut and, occasionally, like the agate wares, they were press-moulded. It is not uncommon to find jugs, goblets or butter dishes with an applied trailed snake wound around their bodies.

As the century progressed opaline glass was produced in many countries. The Russian factories, for example, exhibited much opaline glass in St Petersburg in 1828–9. By the middle of the century glasshouses in Bohemia and Britain were producing opa-

The development of solid pale colours led to the reintroduction of the Roman technique of casing, a layering process which was not available to earlier glass-makers, with their less scientific approach to glass manufacture. The coloured glass used had to be prepared carefully, with identical coefficients of expansion and contraction, otherwise the vessels would crack. A cased vessel was produced by blowing a bubble of coloured glass (for the exterior), which was then opened up into the shape of a deep bowl and placed in a

With the exception of the introduction of copper-wheel engraving machines, the technique of engraving glass has changed little since the seventeenth century. Styles of design, however, have altered with each succeeding century. At the end of the eighteenth century, for instance, Neoclassical French and Bohemian engraving had become very stiff and formal. But in the period of peace that followed the long Napoleonic wars, a period of middle-class prosperity blossomed in Europe, which

PAIR OF OPAQUE WHITE VASES, MONOT & CIE, *c.*1855
(H69.5cm/27¼in)

These 'Medici shape' vases are gilded and enamelled. They were made by the Monot firm of La Villette, France, for the 1855 Paris Exposition.

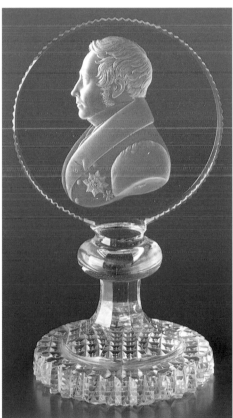

line glass, but their products rarely had the fine, lustrous surface of the early French wares. Their choice of decoration consisted largely of gilt or gilt and enamelled swags and leaf designs, later developed into superb polychrome-enamelled floral arrangements, often covering the surfaces of large white vases. French opaline glass was an influence on some Bohemian glasshouses, but the latter's often unattractive creations, examples of which were to be seen at the Great Exhibition of 1851, were matt finished.

warm metal stand. Another glass-maker prepared the inner layer by blowing a second bubble of a different colour into the original bowl. The whole item was then reheated, blown again and formed into the required shape. This could be done a number of times, thus creating several layers (double casing was mentioned as early as 1836). Besides producing a thicker coating than staining achieved, the technique also allowed a much greater scope for both cutting and engraving.

BOHEMIAN ENGRAVED DESK ORNAMENT DEPICTING COUNT FRIEDRICH VON SACHSEN-WEIMAR, DOMINIK BIEMANN, *c.*1835
(H13.3cm/5¼in)

BOHEMIAN
ENGRAVED
GOBLET, *c*.1860
(H58.5cm/23in)
(RIGHT)

LOBMEYR
ENAMELLED
GOBLET, MID
19TH CENTURY
(H14.5cm/5¾in)

*In the form of a
'Dutch' Roemer
decorated in the Islamic
manner, the goblet is a
good example of the
combination of styles
during the Renaissance
Revival.* (CENTRE)

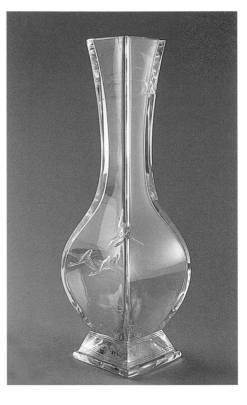

BACCARAT VASE, *c*.1878 (H28.5cm/11¼in)

*The birds-in-flight design on this vase reveals a
strong Japanese influence.* (ABOVE)

created a stimulating environment for the decorative arts generally. In this environment engraved and coloured glass in particular prospered.

The Bohemian tradition for high-quality engraved glass survived through the work of the Sachr and Pohl families of engravers, among others. Franz and Johan Pohl in turn taught Dominik Biemann (1800–57), one of the most famous engravers of the first half of the nineteenth century. Biemann had studied drawing at the Prague Academy of Painting in 1826, a tuition reflected in his excellent portrait engravings. Biemann settled in Prague, and from 1825 he regularly travelled to Franzensbad for 'the season', when he produced portraits of visitors, and views of the town and its environs.

Among the thousands of engravers working in Europe in the nineteenth century there were many important individuals, and even families. Besides the Sachrs and the Pohls, there were August Böhm (1812–90), the Pelikans of Meistersdorf (Mistrovice), the Simms of Gablonz (Jablonec), notably Anton, and Franz Anton Riedel (1786–

1844), a member of the Riedel manufacturing family in Isergebirge. A school formed around Andreas Mattoni (1779–1864) in Karlsbad (Karlovy Vary), where Ludwig Moser (1833–1916) was trained. Moser was later to establish the company of Ludwig Moser & Söhne at Meierhöfen (Nové Dvory) near Karlsbad. While artists such as Biemann remained in their own countries, many others travelled across Europe, some, such as August Böhm, even making their way to the United States.

Engraving in the early nineteenth century was devoted to formal portraiture and landscapes of a style similar to those on the enamelled beakers. However, the development of stained and cased glass, as well as the introduction of a greater variety of shapes, including vases and large goblets with covers, allowed engravers greater scope. Idealized landscapes, often with stags or horses in scenes reminiscent of the artists' environs and the growing passion for hunting, replaced the topographical scenes. Invariably, the better-quality cutting was reserved for the better-quality object; the

poorest engravings of the 1870s and later were on stained rather than cased glass.

Most engravers in the middle of the nineteenth century seem to have become stuck in an endless groove of producing stags in landscapes and the like, but this design tedium was broken by Ludwig Lobmeyr (1829–1917). Founded by Josef Lobmeyr (1792–1855) in 1822, the firm flourished under his sons, Josef (1828–64) and Ludwig. Lobmeyr's glass, often made to commissioned designs from major contemporary artists and architects, was supplied by Wilhelm von Králik, of Winterberg (Vimperk) in southern Bohemia, to whom the family was related by marriage. Their decoration consisted not only of fashionable Neo-Renaissance styles, which included a revival of glass cut and carved to imitate rock crystal, but also Islamic and Oriental

OPALESCENT GOBLETS AND COVERS,
VENICE AND MURANO GLASS
COMPANY, *c.*1878
(Taller: H51.5cm/20¼in) (RIGHT) AND A
PLATE FROM A SALVIATI PATTERN-
BOOK, *c.*1875 (FAR RIGHT)

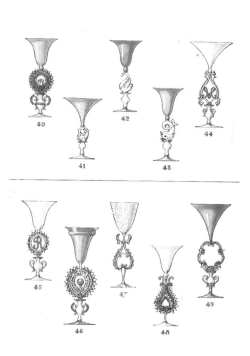

DRAWING FROM
APSLEY
PELLATT'S
*CURIOSITIES OF
GLASS MAKING,*
1849

*An old Venetian
technique, for making
'Vitro di Trino', is
shown.* (RIGHT)

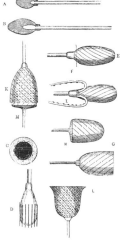

designs, both engraved and enamelled. Lobmeyr remained at the forefront of fashion and its central position within a large empire gave it a wide sphere of influence.

Like the French, British, Americans and others, Austrian designers were greatly influenced by Japanese art, to which they were exposed in the 1860s.

While remaining popular, the engraving of glass was joined in the 1860s by another decorative technique, acid-etching, which in turn led to the use of acid to polish the matt surfaces of both cut and engraved glass.

HISTORISMUS

Alongside the preference for items decorated in the style of the High Renaissance, there emerged a demand for reproduction objects of other periods. This production covered a number of early styles, especially Venetian and German, and has more recently come to be known as 'Historismus'.

THE VENETIAN REVIVAL

The mid nineteenth-century interest in works of art of earlier periods, as well as the publication of catalogues and presentation of exhibitions featuring early pieces, including glass, stimulated manufacturers to re-create those works on a large scale. The Venetian glass industry was revived as a result of this interest. At his Choisy-le-Roi factory, George Bontemps (1799–1884) produced *latticinio* glass in 1838 and in the following year, in northern Bohemia, Count Harrach also adopted this typically Venetian technique. British glass-makers, too, were to play an important part in the resurgence of the Venetian glass industry.

In 1850 the Society of Arts held an influential exhibition in London of 'Ancient and Medieval Art', which won high praise from the art critics. This acclaim may in part have prompted the revival of Venetian glass. One of the more important figures in this revival, Dr Antonio Salviati (1816–90), who established a glass company at Murano in Venice, was mentioned at length in Charles

Eastlake's *Hints on Household Taste*, published in 1868. In particular, Eastlake praised Salviati's encouragement of the Venetian glass industry. Salviati formed a partnership with Lorenzo Radi in 1859. Like many other European glass-makers, Radi had been experimenting with earlier Venetian techniques. In 1862 Salviati exhibited a large arrangement of Venetian-style glass at the International Exhibition at South Kensington in London and by 1866 the British-backed Salviati & Co., Ltd, had showrooms both in the English capital and in Venice. The firm took part in the Paris Exposition in 1867 and in the next year it opened new showrooms at 30 St James's Street, London, trading as the Venice & Murano Glass & Mosaic Co., Ltd.

While Salviati's firm was arguably the most influential, there were other important Venetian glasshouses, including Barovier, Borella, Moretti and Toso, which were revitalized or created by the rising demand for Venetian glass. Not only were these manufacturers producing drinking glasses with complicated stem formations, but they

FRENCH CANE-
WORK ITEMS IN
PSEUDO-
VENETIAN
REVIVAL STYLE,
*c.*1850 (Tallest:
H20cm/7⅞in)

*The jug is cased on the
inside, giving it an
opalescent appearance.*

OLD GERMAN

From the 1870s in central and northern Europe various glass-makers favoured another Historismus trend, producing a flood of *Humpen, Roemers, Kuttrolfs* and *Daumenglas.* These imitated the originals, and often bear sixteenth- or seventeenth-century dates. A main exponent of 'Old German' glass was the Rheinische Glashütte of Ehrenfeld, which was formed in 1879. Another was Meyr's Neffe of Bohemia and Vienna, which in the 1890s produced marvellous copies of *Hochschnitt* goblets. These Historismus pieces can be distinguished from the originals through differences in material, complexity or style.

BOHEMIAN ENAMELLED *HUMPEN,*
*c.*1880 (H15.3cm/6in)

*Some late vessels of this type are difficult to
distinguish from the originals; this colour, however,
would not have been used originally.*

also manufactured a wide range of table glass, tazzas, chandeliers, vases and mirrors, using old techniques in particular. These included chalcedony, which resembled the semiprecious stone; aventurine, which incorporated minute specks of oxidized metal simulating gold; opalescent glass, created by reheating one part or the whole of the item, turning it milky in colour; ice, or crackle, glass, produced by plunging a very hot bubble of glass into cold water, immediately crazing the vessel, which was then reheated just sufficiently for it to remelt and remain stable.

Reports of the time indicate that it was very difficult to distinguish between the seventeenth-century originals and the new imitations, suggestions which were largely a marketing ploy. In many cases the items were manufactured in lead glass, which was never used in Venice in the sixteenth and seventeenth centuries, or they were made in a metal that was too brown in colour. Typically of the period, and making identification comparatively simple, the decoration was more complex, elaborate and/or excessive than that which would have featured on earlier glasses. Likewise, vessels were produced in colours unavailable to glass-makers in the earlier period, and in forms unknown to them. While these glass techniques were soon copied elsewhere, the Venetian originals are unmistakable.

SCANDINAVIA

In Scandinavia in the nineteenth century vast cut-glass table services were in production: Reijmyre in Sweden had 62 service designs in 1877, by 1882 Nuutajärvi of Finland advertised 72 services, and in Denmark Holmegaard, only established in 1825, was producing table glass within ten years. In Norway, although the state monopoly expired in 1803, it was not until 1852 under the ownership of the Berg family that the Biri factory became the centre for bottle making, Hurdals Verk for flat glass and Hadeland for table and decorated glass.

THE FINAL YEARS

Glassmaking flourished throughout Europe in the nineteenth century and, although some companies and factories continued to produce high-quality items, many turned to the mass-production of enamelled, etched and cut glass, particularly for the British market.

The Bohemians and Austrians were the main innovators of nineteenth-century Europe, but by the end of the century their supremacy was on the wane.

PAPERWEIGHTS

The classic period of paperweight production was short-lived, spanning about thirty years in the middle of the nineteenth century. Like many apparently new inventions its roots were centuries old, and in a year or two it had attained a high standard of production.

Prototypes were probably made by glass-workers experimenting at the end of the day and selling the results for their own benefit, as was common in the industry at the time. If indeed this was the source, it was not long before several factories in France and elsewhere were in the full flood of production.

The earliest weights are dated 1845, from which year examples by both Pietro Bigaglia in Venice and the Baccarat glassworks, near Nancy, France, are known. The latter, together with two other French factories, St Louis, near Bitche in Lorraine, and Clichy, outside Paris, were the three most important paperweight manufacturers.

Pietro Bigaglia benefited from the rich, four-hundred-year-old tradition of Venetian glass-making, which included, among others, the techniques of millefiori and *latticinio*, both of which were used extensively in paperweight decoration. Bigaglia was also well placed to take advantage of the demand from a wealthy European clientele to supply decorative objects for the writing table. He failed in his effort, however, and Bigaglia's paperweights fall short of the standards achieved by his talented French rivals, lacking their products' clarity of glass, high polish and bright colours.

IMPORTANT TECHNIQUES AND TERMS

Paperweight collectors concentrate on the three principal French factories, although the firms did not only produce weights: inkwells, rulers and scent bottles, among other objects, were made. Like paperweights, they incorporated the patterned rods, or 'canes', which were formed by grouping together short, fat rods of coloured glass, fusing them and then, while the glass was still molten, pulling them out to a length of, perhaps, 9 m (30 ft). The pattern was maintained, but instead of the rod being several centimeters in diameter, its diameter was now in millimeters. These canes could then be assembled in an iron ring, heated and finally encased under a blob of clear glass, whose purpose was to magnify the design.

Many paperweight-related terms can be found in the Glossary, but some frequently used words follow:

Bouquet. A paperweight with two or more flowers.

St Louis
CROWN, c.1845
(D5.6cm/2¹³⁄₁₆in)
(TOP LEFT)

BOHEMIAN
DOUBLE
OVERLAY
MUSHROOM,
c.1845
(D5.6cm/2¹³⁄₁₆in)
(TOP RIGHT)

CLICHY
MAGNUM
CHEQUER, c.1845
(D11.1cm/4⅜in)
(CENTRE)

CLICHY DOUBLE
OVERLAY
CONCENTRIC
MUSHROOM,
c.1845
(D8.2cm/3³⁄₁₆in)
(BOTTOM LEFT)

CLICHY SWIRL,
c.1845
(D7.6cm/3in)
(BOTTOM RIGHT)

Carpet ground. A field of densely packed small canes predominantly of the same type and colour, but with a pattern formed of varied and contrasting canes.

Garlands. Chains of canes interlinked to form a set pattern.

Ground. The flat or slightly domed patterned background in a paperweight; sometimes solid-coloured, but generally detailed, i.e., comprising many canes or *latticinio*.

Jasper ground. A ground formed of tiny chips of two colours of glass, resulting in a speckled appearance.

Lampwork. The process of manipulating glass at the lamp, that is, shaping it from rods and tubes of ready-made glass by heating and softening, and then decorating it in a variety of ways. Some of the rarest paperweights were made using this technique, with flowers, fruits, butterflies and snakes among the subjects created.

Magnum. A paperweight with a diameter of about 2.5 cm (1 in) larger than the average diameter of 8 cm (3⅛ in).

Mushroom. A paperweight comprising a tight gathering of canes that spring out, in the form of a mushroom, from the base and spread to a domed top in either a concentric or close millefiori pattern.

Overlay. A paperweight encased in one or more layers of coloured glass, and cut with circular windows, called printies or facets, which reveal a decorative motif within. A few are further embellished with gilding. Bases are polished or cut with stars or diamonds.

Pedestal. A paperweight supported by a stem resting on a spreading circular foot.

Silhouette. An outline of a subject, usually filled in with black, which is made of glass in a mould and inserted into canes to make millefiori glass. Silhouettes in paperweights largely take the form of animals (birds, insects and mammals), but a few floral and human forms – including a dancing devil – also exist. Clichy did not use silhouettes, but Baccarat and St Louis did.

Swirl. A paperweight with a central cane from which curved spokes radiate.

Torsade. A ribbon of one or more glass-spiral threads enclosing a central design.

BACCARAT

The Baccarat glass factory, founded in 1764 under the patronage of Louis XV, tended to use strong colours for its distinctive flower and millefiori paperweight designs, which it began to produce in around 1846. Millefiori weights signed with a 'B' and the date are not uncommon. The date most frequently found is 1848, followed by 1847. Rarer are 1846, 1849, 1853 and 1858. The factory's lampwork designs are never signed or dated.

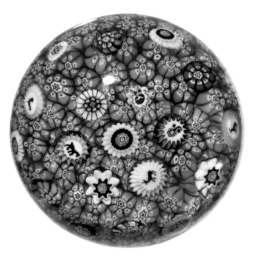

BACCARAT CARPET GROUND, 1848
(D7.6cm/3in)

Baccarat was renowned for its coloured carpet grounds, such as this red example, whose canes include silhouettes of a goat, deer, bird, horse and rooster. It is signed and dated 'B.1848'.

Baccarat is famed for its magnificent coloured carpet grounds, such as those in blue, white, green, red and the more rare examples of yellow.

The canes include one of a very distinctive arrowhead shape – easily identifying the factory – as well as butterflies, honeycombs, trefoils, quatrefoils, roses, shamrocks and whorls. Occasionally two motifs make up a single cane, such as the example featuring a shamrock above a pelican.

Silhouette canes are dispersed evenly within the carpet grounds. Such canes feature birds (crane, pelican, pheasant, pigeon, rooster, stork and swan), domestic and wild animals (dog, goat, horse, squirrel, deer, monkey, elephant and kangaroo), and insects (butterfly), as well as a dancing devil and a man holding a rifle.

Millefiori designs are often close-packed, scattered, patterned or in the form of a mushroom.

Garland weights are typical Baccarat products and are mainly in clear glass, although coloured examples are known.

Baccarat mushroom weights are dominated by blue and white colour combinations, whereas green and salmon pink are rare and strong shades are exceptional. The base of the mushroom can be encircled by a torsade, which in a Baccarat weight runs anti-clockwise, while those of St Louis run clockwise. As the mushroom weights of the two factories are very similar, this is a useful method of identification.

Mushrooms can also be encircled by a garland, often translucent red or green. The overlay may be in blue, turquoise, pink or red. Very rarely there may be gilding.

Baccarat made pedestal weights, with either a concentric or millefiori-scattered pattern. These range in diameter from 6.5 to 10 cm (2½ to 4 in).

The factory also produced sulphide weights and related objects, the embedded medallion featuring portraits of well-known persons and mythological scenes.

The most common Baccarat flower weights are pansies, sometimes with a bud.

The factory made fruit weights, but it did not mix the fruits, as did St Louis. In descending order of rarity, the fruits are apricots, apples, cherries, peaches, strawberries and pears, all of which are naturalistic.

A Baccarat butterfly is colourful and often placed in the centre of the clear glass, which usually has a star-cut base. It can also be found hovering over a muslin ground or over a flower, such as a clematis, rose or wheatflower (rarely a pansy). The insect normally covers about a third of the bloom but occasionally shades it entirely.

The factory produced snake and lizard weights, both of which are rare. The reptiles are found on a white muslin ground (comprising close-packed *latticinio* rods) or a cream speckled, greenish-brown rock ground. Snakes are spotted green, deep red or shades of brown and pink.

One of the rarest Baccarat weights is 'Ducks-on-a-Pond'. The ducks are usually in shades of yellow, red, brown and blue, with accurately detailed features, and they float on speckled green water. All are hollow weights cut with printies and all rest on a glass foot, making these weights altogether exceptional.

The 'Newel Post' weight is characterized by its massive globe. This is set on a short stem in a metal mount and encloses numerous canes, among which are the signature 'B' (for Baccarat), animals and flowers, and sometimes the date 1848.

Baccarat weights range in diameter from miniatures of 5 cm (2 in) up to magnums of anything over 10.2 cm (4 in). Their bases may be faceted with stars comprising five or more points, a typical feature of this factory, and the sizes vary from small to those reaching the edge of the glass.

BACCARAT WHEATFLOWER AND BUTTERFLY, *c*.1845
(D7.6cm/3in)

The colourful insect hovers over one third of the flower, which is surrounded by leaves. The base is star-cut. (TOP LEFT)

BACCARAT SNAKE, *c*.1845
(D7.6cm/3in)

The coiling red serpent rests on an opaque muslin ground. The factory's snake weights are rare. (TOP RIGHT)

BACCARAT 'NEWEL POST', 1848
(H21.3cm/8⅜in; D15.2cm/6in)

The massive dome of this unusual weight is set with a multitude of canes, including silhouettes – a reindeer, swan, goat, butterfly and man – as well as stars, arrowheads, trefoils, shamrocks and whorls. Set on a short stem in a metal mount, the weight is signed and dated. (RIGHT)

CLICHY

Clichy's paperweights are discernibly different in both colour and style from those made by the Baccarat and St Louis factories.

Founded in 1837, the Clichy glassworks first began making paperweights in the mid-1840s and from 1849 the firm dominated the paperweight market. Production ceased in 1885, when the company was taken over by the Lander family, makers of coloured glass, and became the Cristalleries de Sèvres et Clichy.

Unlike Baccarat and St Louis, which used lead crystal, Clichy employed a special kind of glass known as boracic glass. This had the effect of sharpening the internal design and its presence is therefore a useful guide today to identifying the output of the factory.

Clichy was the only French paperweight factory to take part in the 1851 Great Exhibition in London, where it was awarded a special prize for its wide-ranging overlay colours. The factory also produced the only known commemorative millefiori weight, which was engraved on the base with a 'V.A.' monogram (for Victoria and Albert) under a crown and the inscription 'Londres 1851'. Otherwise, Clichy weights are rarely signed or dated.

Clichy weights are generally softer in colour than those of Baccarat and St Louis, and are fractionally lighter in weight. There is one distinctive cane – the 'Clichy rose' (although occasionally such a cane can be found in Baccarat weights). While the rose is generally pink and green, it is also known in blue, green, yellow, purple and white, and usually comes enclosed by four green sepals. It can be found in swirls, millefiori and, rarely, as a full bloom in bouquets.

Some rare bouquets are tied with a pink or blue ribbon. They are encased in clear glass and occasionally rest on a *latticinio* ground. More uncommon still is a moss green ground.

Millefiori weights can be close-scattered or concentric, and may include the Clichy rose. Concentric millefiori weights often include the rose in abundance and sometimes in alternating colours. These millefiori weights are often cased at the base with elongated staves, usually in white with blue, green, pink or purple.

Clichy also made mushroom weights, the designs generally on a smaller scale than those of their rivals. Mushroom stems are often striped in a similar manner to the millefiori weights with striped baskets. The mushrooms are either encased in clear glass or in overlays. Overlay colours include eggshell white, pink, blue and dark moss green. In all double overlays, the strong outside colour encloses opaque white, which is revealed as a thin frame around the printies. There are usually five, or occasionally six, of these around the sides and one other on the top. The diameters range from 5.1 cm (2 in) to 10.2 cm (4 in), and the bases can be plain or strawberry-diamond cut.

Clichy also produced attractive pedestal weights decorated with close, chequered, carpet ground and concentric millefiori patterns. The canes are striped and run vertically. The foot may be decorated with *latticinio* or a circle of rose canes.

Like Baccarat, Clichy produced sulphide weights and related glass, often featuring cameo portraits of prominent historical or literary figures, such as Napoleon and Queen Victoria.

Swirls, which are characteristic of Clichy, appear fairly frequently in various colours, of which combinations of opaque white and either cobalt blue, green, purple and pink predominate. The rarest examples are white with two or more colours. The central cane

CLICHY MAGNUM CONCENTRIC, *c.*1845 (D10.8cm/4¼in)

The weight consists of pink, white and purple canes, and the centre section features pink, green and blue Clichy rose canes. It is set in a green and white striped basket. (BELOW LEFT)

CLICHY PANSY, *c.*1845 (D7.3cm/2⅞in)

Resting on an opaque white latticinio *ground, this rare weight features both pansy and bud, the two purple petals with striped markings.* (BELOW)

CLICHY MAGNUM BASKET, *c.*1845 (H6.7cm/2 9/16in; D10.8cm/4¼in)

This is Clichy's most impressive weight. At the periphery of its waisted dome are 15 cane groups, comprising pastry moulds, cogwheels, whorls, stardusts and composite canes. Around the rim and base are twisted torsades. (LEFT)

or canes may incorporate either a millefiori cluster, a pastry mould (with a scalloped rim) or, most desirable of all, the Clichy rose. Sizes can range from approximately 5 cm (2 in) to 10.2 cm (4 in) in diameter.

Clichy occasionally made flowers. Its very rare pansy is beautifully and delicately formed, with a softer palette than Baccarat's. Possibly its most attractive flower is a stylized clematis, which, like the convolvulus, can be found either double or single. The petals are usually ribbed in a soft colour such as pink, blue, purple or rusty red. The ground can be either clear, coloured, muslin or *latticinio*. The flower is sometimes found within a bouquet of stylized or natural flowers in various colours, including white, pale pink, blue or yellow. When the convolvulus appears in clear glass weights that have diameters of 6.5 to 9 cm ($2\frac{1}{2}$ to $3\frac{1}{2}$ in), the base is usually star-cut.

Clichy fruits are among the rarest weights and include apples and strawberries. The factory does not appear to have produced vegetable weights.

The most important – and impressive – weight ever made by Clichy was a realistic magnum basket originally (but no longer extant) with a handle.

ST LOUIS

Founded in 1767, the St Louis factory, like Baccarat, was set up under the aegis of Louis XV. The first dated St Louis paperweight is from 1845, although the quality suggests that some years must have passed in experimentation. Other dates exist, including 1847 and 1848; rarer are 1845 and 1849. The factory name, which can be signed 'SL' for St Louis, may appear above the date, and the colours of both date and name can vary.

Concentric and mushroom weights are the types most likely to bear dates and signatures. Scrambled weights (comprising a mass of assorted millefiori canes in a haphazard pattern) may include a cane with the initials 'SL' and/or a date.

The factory's designs are more limited in scope than those produced by Baccarat and Clichy, but their sense of colour is coherent. An idiosyncratic colour is a salmon pink, which is found frequently in pastry-mould canes and on the fruits.

Silhouettes used by St Louis include a dog, duck, turkey, camel, stylized flower and assorted dancing figures: a devil, man, lady and couple.

The millefiori weights take different forms, one of the most interesting being a carpet ground cross set in pale colours. Otherwise, they appear as concentric or close-scattered weights. While silhouettes are often distributed evenly throughout the

weight, a single silhouette may occasionally be found in the centre. The concentrics range in size, their diameters anywhere from 5 to 10.2 cm (2 to 4 in).

Mushroom weights are usually composed of concentric or scattered millefiori canes enclosed by a torsade with a clockwise twist.

St Louis produced some of the best single and double overlay paperweights, among which may be found gilt examples with floral and leaf designs. Colours are often dark blue, green and pink and, more exceptionally, white. They are usually cut with six printies to the side and one on top, but rarer examples include smaller printies. Sizes range from 6.5 to 9 cm ($2\frac{1}{2}$ to $3\frac{1}{2}$ in) in diameter (no miniature weights are known to have overlays). Bases are either star-, grid- or strawberry-cut.

The factory's most characteristic design is the crown, which was made in all sizes and various colours. Crown weights are hollow and typical colours combine blue, red and white; green, red and white; and yellow, blue and white, the twisted ribbon of coloured glass alternating with white *latticinio*. The design is centred on a single or cluster of millefiori canes. Usually the design fills the glass, but occasionally more clear glass surrounds the crown. These weights are never faceted.

St Louis specialized in flowers, fruits, vegetables and reptiles, with flower weights,

ST LOUIS CROWN, *c.*1845 (D7cm/$2\frac{3}{4}$in)

The crown was typical of St Louis, but such a colourful design is rare. (TOP)

ST LOUIS MUSHROOM, 1848 (D7cm/$2\frac{3}{4}$in)

The concentric millefiori mushroom is surrounded by a cobalt blue torsade. (LEFT)

St Louis fruit, *c*.1845 (D6.3cm/2½in)

Three cherries, two oranges and a lemon are set between leaves and rest on a double swirling opaque white latticinio ground. Such vividly coloured fruit weights were typical of the French factory. (TOP)

St Louis snake, *c*.1845 (D5.7cm/2¼in)

The red-eyed mottled green serpent coils around itself on an opaque white muslin ground. The edge of the glass is faceted. (ABOVE)

both natural and stylized, comprising about a third of the factory's output. The flowers are found singly and in flat and upright (or standing) bouquets, all containing leaves. They can be found on colourless or colour-tinted ground glass as well as on muslin and *latticinio* grounds.

The dahlia is one of the most common blooms and usually appears in blue, red, purple or mauve. Rarer examples are yellow with black dots (very similar to wheatflower weights). Other St Louis flowers are the primrose and convolvulus (both very rare), anemone, camomile, clematis, fuchsia, pelargonium, rose and pansy. The St Louis pansy is less naturalistic than that in the Baccarat weights, and can be found lying on a clear, coloured or jasper ground. Occasionally it forms part of a small bouquet and can also be included among stylized flowers. The bases of the pansy weights are normally diamond-cut, whereas dahlia weights occasionally have star-cut bases.

St Louis bouquets are either flat or upright. Intricate patterns are formed by intertwining leaves and flowers, the colour being strongly contrasted within the bouquet. They can be found in clear glass and sometimes cut with printies, faceted or domed; they were produced in sizes whose diameters range from 5 to 10.2 cm (2 to 4 in).

Vividly coloured fruit and vegetable paperweights are typical of the St Louis factory and are usually arranged in a group set on a *latticinio* ground in clear glass. Fruits include apples, strawberries, cherries, oranges, pears and grapes, while the rarer vegetable weights include carrots, radishes and turnips. Weights may be of single species or in a combination; sometimes a fruit may appear with a blossom. Examples of single plums, oranges or lemons are the rarest. Vegetables may be found in groups of six or seven, these set within a *latticinio* basket. Like the bouquet weights, they may be cut with printies or diamonds.

St Louis snakes are usually either green or pink with mottled markings and generally have red eyes and a red nose. They coil around on a bed of muslin.

OTHER FACTORIES

Although Baccarat, Clichy and St Louis produced weights to the highest standard in the nineteenth century, other factories in France, Britain and the United States also made some very good weights.

BOHEMIA

Along with Venetian examples, Bohemian paperweights helped to inspire the early paperweight movement, with the French developing and perfecting some Bohemian techniques to produce high-quality paper-weights. The main patterns used in Bohemian weights are millefiori, and their weights tended to be rather inelegant.

FRANCE

One of the most intriguing paperweight manufacturers was Pantin, a French factory founded in *c*.1850 on the outskirts of Paris. Pantin did not produce paperweights until 1878, after the major makers had ceased production. Its reptile and other animal designs were far more realistic than those of other factories.

BRITAIN

The Whitefriars factory in London, trading under the name of James Powell & Sons, made weights from the mid nineteenth century. Weights dated 1848 may be spurious. In comparison with the output of its French rivals, Whitefriars weights are crude in execution and colouring, and the canes are larger and less complex. One identifying cane is a seated white rabbit. The factory's most famous objects are candlesticks and inkwells of rather lumpish design incorporating close-packed and concentric designs in both stopper and bottle.

George Bacchus & Sons of Birmingham specialized in domestic glassware, but paper-weights were also a part of the firm's output, albeit a very minor one. Bacchus weights were in production by 1848 and may have been included in the 1851 Great Exhibition in London, where the firm had a stand. The weights produced by the English factory are larger, heavier and of less transparent glass than French examples.

Bacchus concentrated on millefiori work, of which the best are concentrics. The canes are larger and cruder than those of the French factories, with many irregularities. Several are specific to the factory, including a female head in profile, and star, cog and ruffle canes.

The most attractive characteristic of the Bacchus weights is their strange, ethereal coloration which, on concentric weights, seems to radiate light from the centre. This feature more than compensates for the poor formation of the individual canes.

Paul Ysart (b. 1904), who came from a family of Barcelona-born master glass-makers, was apprenticed with the St Louis factory before moving to Scotland with his family in 1915. He was employed by several Scottish factories, including Moncrieff and Caithness. His paperweights comprise mainly the millefiori type, but he also created flowers, bouquets, fish and other sea creatures, and butterflies. Many of his weights rest on translucent coloured and mottled grounds. They are signed 'PY', with both initials placed side by side.

UNITED STATES

From 1850 the New England Glass Company of East Cambridge, Massachusetts, made millefiori, flower and fruit paperweights, the latter of which were the most successful. However, the quality of production does not approach that of the three major French factories; among other things, its colours are more strident and the weights suffer from unclear glass and air bubbles. New England produced small crown weights and a few overlays and scrambled weights, but it concentrated on flowers and fruit. Flowers include camomile and buttercup blossoms, as well as the rarer clematis, rose, wheatflower and poinsettia. The distinctive leaves of the New England weights

are bright green, with their spine and veins clearly drawn.

The Boston & Sandwich Glass Company of Sandwich, Massachusetts, made weights from about 1852 until 1888, when the factory closed. The glass was flint-based, light in weight and somewhat blurred. Canes include a bee, running rabbit, eagle, heart and cross, and usually form the centre of a flower. Flower weights include poinsettias and roses. The quality of the lampwork is generally undistinguished but some examples are exceptional.

Also in Massachusetts, the Mount Washingon Glass Company, founded in East Boston by Deming Jarves in 1837, made very large weights. These range from 10 to 11.5 cm (4 to $4\frac{1}{2}$ in) in diameter and were probably made from the 1870s, by which time the firm had moved to New Bedford. Mount Washington's output comprised fruits and flower paperweights; these were not very naturalistic, but their assemblages were more ambitious than those of other factories. Unfortunately, the weights suffered from various imperfections, including bubbled glass.

The Gillinder & Sons factory in Philadelphia was founded in 1861 by English-born William T. Gillinder (1823–71), who had worked for George Bacchus & Sons. The firm produced millefiori and flower weights, as well as clear glass weights moulded with portraits of statesmen.

RELATED OBJECTS

Along with paperweights, the various glass factories made much rarer tazzas, shot glasses, tumblers, candlesticks, hand coolers, scent bottles, rulers, decanters, inkwells and dressing-table sets using the same techniques. The decoration was included in finials, stoppers and bases, and usually took the form of clustered canes or closed-packed, scattered or scrambled millefiori. Examples are found from all the factories and there is almost always some characteristic cane to aid with attribution.

BACCHUS CONCENTRIC, *c.*1850
(D8.9cm/3½in)

The central cane, a large white ruffle, is specific to Bacchus. Such millefiori concentrics were among the finest weights by the English firm. (TOP)

ST LOUIS VASE, *c.*1845 (H10.8cm/4¼in)

The vase's base is formed as a crown weight and consists of red, green and white twists interspersed with opaque white latticinio twists. The vase has a blue and white torsade around the rim. (ABOVE)

ART AND CRAFTS
AND ART NOUVEAU

The excesses of Victorian glass – epitomized by the giant exhibition pieces smothered in gilding and colour and cut with thousands of shimmering facets – were already being condemned by contemporary critics. Out of this antipathy toward the mechanical production of the Industrial Revolution grew a desire to return to more natural sources. The revolutionary effect on design following the opening up of Japan to the West and the publication of pattern-books illustrating ornament from around the world, aided by theorists such as William Morris advocating the role of the craftsman, led to the evolution of a completely new style, Art Nouveau.

The craftsmen working on Victorian glass were artisans – blowers, cutters, enamellers and gilders – all creating pieces of breath-taking complexity and all subservient to a predetermined pattern laid down by the designer. In Art Nouveau glass an artist conceived an idea and, working closely with the blower, the dream was made manifest. A highly skilled artist-cutter may then have worked on the piece, carving away to give life to the final form. The nature-based roots of Art Nouveau flowered organically. Internal colours, accidental effects and a misty softness clouded the surface, quite unlike the brilliant finish so important thirty years earlier.

A TIFFANY FAVRILE, JACK-IN-THE-PULPIT VASE
AND FOUR IRIDESCENT VASES ATTRIBUTED TO LOETZ, c.1900

The organic forms and ornament of these vases reflect the Art Nouveau
preoccupation with nature as a source of inspiration.

EUROPEAN ART NOUVEAU

TERMS AND VARIATIONS

The terms 'Art Nouveau' and 'Arts and Crafts' are generally used to describe a multitude of different decorative styles which emerged in Europe and the United States in the 1880s, peaking around 1900, the year of the Exposition Universelle in Paris. The motifs employed – usually natural forms – were largely treated in an unrealistic manner, arranged either in asymmetrical compositions of swirling curves or in more rigid patterns of simplified, sometimes almost geometric shapes. In most cases, there is a marked tendency toward abstraction, and often the subject, whether plant, bird, animal or human figure, is more or less unrecognizable.

Called Art Nouveau in France and Belgium, the style was known as Jugendstil in Germany, Secessionstil in Austria and Arts and Crafts in Britain; in fact, each country had a different name (or even two) for its own variation(s) of the style: for instance, in Italy there was Stile Liberty, after the floral textiles sold by the London retailer Arthur Lasenby Liberty, as well as Stile Floreale. However, even within the decorative arts of any one nation, there were usually several different versions, often connected to cities or regions, or to certain influential designers. So, rather than treating Art Nouveau glass in terms either of the countries producing it or of formal categories, it is probably more appropriate to describe it according to the technical processes used in its manufacture and decoration, processes which nearly always contributed to its particular style. The principal techniques employed were cameo carving, iridescent decoration, enamelling and free-form blowing. The importance of tableware and stained glass of the period are also surveyed below.

CAMEO GLASS

The commercial and artistic success of Emile Gallé's cameo glass spawned imitations all over Europe and in the United States. The wheel-carving of cased glass, which earlier in the nineteenth century had been a craft requiring great care and dexterity, had by 1900 become, thanks to the introduction of hydrofluoric acid, a much more straightforward industrial process. This innovation, together with improved communication and a vastly increased amount of technical literature, enabled glass manufacturers throughout the West to emulate Gallé's achievements.

FRANCE

At Münzthal, situated in the part of Alsace and Lorraine that was ceded by France to Germany at the end of the Franco-Prussian War (1870–1), the St Louis glassworks began to make cameo glass during the 1890s. It was decorated with floral motifs or landscapes, the latter sometimes incorporating animals. Often the landscapes are contained within panels surrounded by abstract decoration. Apart from vases and bowls, the firm made lampshades mounted on metal bases in the form of a wild animal. St Louis cameo glass was marked 'D'Argental', the French name for Münzthal.

The Muller brothers and their sister established, c.1895, a decorating studio at Lunéville, a few miles from Nancy. The eldest brother and the sister had been apprenticed at the St Louis factory, but they had fled to Lunéville after the Franco-Prussian War. Five of the nine Muller brothers had learned their skills at the Gallé workshops in Nancy. The pieces that they decorated at their Lunéville studio were made to their specifications at a glassworks in the neighbouring town of Croismare.

The decoration – floral subjects, birds and landscapes, sometimes with Symbolist allusions – was wheel-carved and acid-etched, and the brothers developed their own original technique which they called *fluogravure*. This method involved the use of hydrofluoric acid to etch both the body of the vessel and the areas of applied enamel decoration, giving an effect of rich, glowing colour. The *fluogravure* technique attracted the attention of the manager at the Val St-Lambert glassworks near Liège in Belgium. In about 1895 this firm had produced cased-glass vases with deep-cut, abstract Art Nouveau decoration in the style developed by the Belgian architect–designer Henry Van de Velde. From 1906 to 1908, Désiré and Henri Muller worked for Val St-Lambert, designing over 400 models, most decorated by *fluogravure*; their subjects were similar to those on the Lunéville work.

By 1900 Auguste Legras had established two glassworks, at St-Denis and Pantin, both suburbs of Paris. Most of the glass he manufactured had few artistic pretensions. It was intended to appeal to popular taste, and it may be a measure of Gallé's success that a purely commercial firm decided to manufacture cameo glass. The Legras version was made in various styles, the most distinctive imitating carved carnelian. Layers of opaque glass, shading from beige to pink, were acid-cut with patterns of flowers, fruit or seaweed that were then enamelled, usually red or brown, with the leaves in green.

In about 1910, another Pantin glasshouse, run by Stumpf, Touvier, Viollet & Cie, introduced a line of cameo glass designed by Camille Tutré de Varreux, the firm's artistic director (who used the pseudonym 'de Vez' when he signed his work). Iridescent glass was generally used, and the acid-cut decoration took the form of flowers, landscapes, animals and birds. Although this combination of cameo carving and iridescence – the two principal categories of Art Nouveau

CAMEO-GLASS
SHADE FOR A
HANGING LAMP,
MULLER FRÈRES,
c.1900
(D39.5cm/15⅝in)

*Lampshades like this
cast a diffused, coloured
light much favoured
when Art Nouveau
was in vogue. This
shade would have been
designed for a bedroom,
the poppy decoration
symbolizing sleep.* (LEFT)

glass was acclaimed when first shown to
the public in 1910, it came too late to
command any significant following.

One of the earliest artists to exploit the
revived technique of carving cased glass was
Eugène Rousseau (1827–91), whose combined workshop–retail premises were
situated in the rue Coquillière, Paris. The
vessels Rousseau designed were made at the
glasshouse of Appert Frères in Clichy. In
Rousseau's atelier they were carved in
cameo or intaglio with decoration inspired
by Japanese art. The carving was done
mostly by Eugène Michel, a glass engraver
who had worked for Rousseau since 1864,
and Alphonse-Georges Reyen, a master
craftsman who joined Rousseau in 1877.
The following year examples of Rousseau's
carved cameo glass were exhibited at the
Exposition Universelle in Paris. The outer
layer of glass on Rousseau's vases was often

CAMEO-CARVED VASE, EUGÈNE
ROUSSEAU, 1884 (H20cm/7⅞in)

CAMEO-GLASS VASE, VAL ST-
LAMBERT, *c*.1900 (H44.5cm/43⅜in)

*Three layers of different coloured glass are
incorporated in this piece. The Val St-Lambert
factory was situated near Liège in Belgium, and
under Georges Deprez, its general manager from
1894 to 1908, various Art Nouveau styles were
produced.* (ABOVE LEFT)

CAMEO-CARVED VASE, LEGRAS,
c.1900 (H46.5cm/18⅜in)

*At the turn of the century, Auguste Legras
responded to Gallé's enormous commercial success by
producing his own cameo-carved glass at his factory
in the suburbs of Paris. This example possesses
qualities of design and technique considerably above
the average for the factory.* (ABOVE RIGHT)

opaque, and when carved it looked like lacquerwork, adding to the Japanese effect. When his assistant Ernest Léveillé (*fl*.1885–1900) took over Rousseau's workshop in 1885, he continued to produce his former master's designs. In the 1890s, Reyen left to establish a workshop at Rueil where he made similar vessels, some decorated with Art Nouveau plant forms and female nudes. Early in the twentieth century, Michel set up his own studio and made, among other types of glass, intaglio- and cameo-carved vessels in the style of Rousseau.

Appert Frères, the firm which made Rousseau's blanks, also supplied vessels to Pannier Frères, with premises on the corner of the rue Auber and rue Scribe in Paris. The Panniers' cased-glass vases were generally carved with birds and insects in a Japanese manner related to Rousseau's work. The gallery run by the Panniers, which was at the same address as their workshop, was called the Escalier de Cristal (Crystal Staircase) and the brothers stocked Gallé pieces as well as their own work.

At his gallery called Au Vase Etrusque, Louis Damon sold cased-glass vases made for him by Daum and decorated in his workshops. The vases, introduced in the late 1890s, were pear-shaped with two applied glass teardrops running down the sides. They were decorated with fine cameo and intaglio carving and depicted, among other subjects, plants, fish or scenes from classical mythology. Later Damon had other shapes decorated in his workshops, and he briefly employed Auguste Heiligenstein, who became well-known in the 1920s for his glass enamelled in the Art Deco style.

Another Paris gallery, called A la Paix, sold art glass made by a number of manufacturers, including work produced by the proprietor, Jules Mabut, in his workshop in the rue Vieille-du-Temple. His cased and cameo-carved vessels were designed by the painter Henri Laurent-Desrousseaux, who also created ceramics that were sold at the same outlet. In about 1909, gallery and workshop were sold to Georges Rouard, who in the 1920s became the leading dealer in Art Deco glass, ceramics and silver.

BOHEMIA

Many of the Bohemian glasshouses made cameo-carved cased glass vessels using hydrofluoric acid and imitating Gallé's late industrial glass. The firms of Goldberg, Harrach, Králik and Reich all produced such glass in addition to other lines for which they are more celebrated. An interesting variation on the theme of cameo glass is found in the decorative treatment of some vessels by Ludwig Moser & Söhne of Karlsbad (now Karlovy Vary, Czechoslovakia). In this method the clear crystal body was overlaid with blobs of coloured glass which then were cameo carved into flowerheads or leaves; other leaves and stems were intaglio carved in the surface of the clear body, and the base was often internally coloured and gilt.

CAMEO-GLASS VASE, EUGÈNE MICHEL, *c*.1890 (H31cm/12⅜in)

Michel started working for Eugène Rousseau in 1864. This vase, with its gilt touches and decoration carved in both cameo and intaglio, has the appeal of luxury which characterized glass and china sold by Rousseau at his Paris shop. (ABOVE LEFT)

CAMEO-GLASS VASE, IMPERIAL RUSSIAN GLASSWORKS, 1899 (H32cm/12⅝in)

This vase is an early example of cameo-carved glass produced at the Imperial Russian Glassworks in St Petersburg. The factory was sponsored by Nicholas II, and this vase is engraved on the base with the letter 'N' below a crown. (ABOVE)

OTHER COUNTRIES

In England cameo-carved vases in a more or less Art Nouveau style were made by Thomas Webb & Sons, but generally the firm's output of this type of glass was decorated with naturalistic renderings of flowers or classical figures. More interesting was the work produced at the Reijmyre glassworks in Sweden. Cased-glass vessels, often with applied pads, were cameo carved with subjects such as flowers, dragonflies and underwater scenes. Designs were commissioned from Alf Wallander, Ferdinand and Anna Boberg, and other Swedish artists. Cameo glass was also made in Sweden by Kosta Boda, which used some of the same designers as Reijmyre. At Kosta Boda, however, hydrofluoric acid was used widely, with little hand carving, and each model was produced in a series.

The farthest-flung outposts of cameo-carved glass made in the manner of Gallé were in Russia and the United States. The Imperial Russian Glassworks at St Petersburg began to produce superbly crafted pieces in about 1900. The outer layer of most vessels was opaque, giving them the appearance of carved hardstone. The decoration was inspired by both French and Swedish design. In the United States, cameo glass was made by Tiffany Studios in New York. The Honesdale decorating studio in Honesdale, Pennsylvania, and Steuben Glass in Corning, New York, used hydrofluoric acid for carving and neither achieved a standard of design higher than ordinary.

ENGRAVED GLASS

Glass engraving and wheel-cut ornament were both alien to the spirit of Art Nouveau, a style which precluded clarity and sparkle. Tertiary tones and very low relief or smooth decoration were preferred because they could best express the indeterminate, mysterious quality favoured by Symbolist artists and writers. Some engraving was done at Eugène Rousseau's workshop, and it was one of the many decorative techniques used in the Bohemian glass industry at this time, although little of it was Art Nouveau in style. Similarly, deep, wheel-cut patterns were generally reserved for the more traditional designs and styles of glass, although they occasionally accompanied Art Nouveau motifs in enamelling.

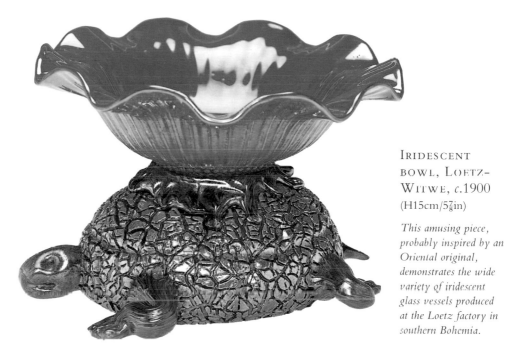

IRIDESCENT
BOWL, LOETZ-
WITWE, *c.*1900
(H15cm/5⅞in)

This amusing piece, probably inspired by an Oriental original, demonstrates the wide variety of iridescent glass vessels produced at the Loetz factory in southern Bohemia.

IRIDESCENT GLASS

Iridescent glass became an important Art Nouveau medium, lending itself particularly well to subtle nuances of colour and irregular, flowing patterns. The technology behind it was developed in response to interest aroused by archaeological discoveries of ancient glass. The iridescence seen in glass which has been buried for centuries is caused by carbonic acid in the soil corroding its surface. Light rays falling on it are split, creating a prismatic effect. The iridescent glass manufactured in the later nineteenth century was produced by coating coloured glass with metallic oxides. The Austrian firm of J. & L. Lobmeyr showed examples at the Vienna International Exhibition of 1873. That might have been the end of the craze, but for Heinrich Schliemann's sensational discoveries at Mycenae in 1876. Two years later at the Paris Exposition, modern iridescent glass was displayed by Lobmeyr, Thomas Webb & Sons and the Pantin glassworks of Monot, Stumpf. In the 1880s the attraction of iridescent glass was gradually transformed from archaeological interest to aesthetic appreciation. Its origins were credited in some of the names given to it: one type produced by Tiffany was called 'Cypriote', Fritz Heckert made 'Cyprus glass', Steuben used the name 'Tyrian' and Loetz dubbed one of its lines 'Kreta'.

LOETZ-WITWE

During the 1890s, Max von Spaun, director of the Johann Loetz-Witwe glassworks at Klostermühle in southern Bohemia, undertook an extensive programme of experiments in iridescent glass, and in 1898 the firm held an exhibition in Vienna where its successful results were shown. Over the next decade Loetz produced a wide variety of

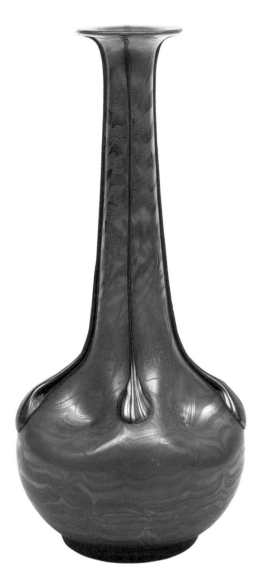

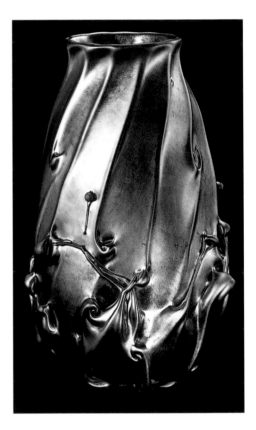

IRIDESCENT VASE, LOETZ-WITWE, *c*.1900 (H48.5cm/19⅛in)

An exceptionally large piece for Loetz, this vase is otherwise typical of the factory's production. The decorative, iridescent ribbons stand out well from the amber ground. (ABOVE)

IRIDESCENT VASE WITH SILVER OVERLAY, LOETZ-WITWE, *c*.1905 (H16cm/6⁵⁄₁₆in)

The ovals incorporated in the design of the overlaid silver decoration echo the blue oval splashes of iridescence in the glass. The indentations in the walls of this vase are a feature frequently found in vessels by Loetz. (RIGHT)

'AURENE' VASE, STEUBEN GLASS, *c*.1910 (H17.3cm/6⅞in)

Frederick Carder, Steuben's artistic director, introduced the 'Aurene' line of iridescent glass in 1904. It was either blue or gold and was sometimes given lightly engraved surface decoration. (ABOVE)

IRIDESCENT VASE, LOETZ-WITWE, *c*.1900 (H25cm/9⅞in)

Much of the iridescent glass produced by Loetz was inspired by the work of the American Louis Comfort Tiffany. Quantities of unmarked Loetz pieces, such as this one, were exported to the United States, where they were sold at a much lower price than Tiffany glass. (ABOVE CENTRE)

decorative effects using iridescent spots, ribbons and threads of gold, silver, blue, purple and amber. The glass varied in form from simple onion- and mallet-shaped vases to vessels with attenuated goosenecks, exotic handles, indentations and applied trailing pads. Vases were occasionally twisted or given irregular rims, and sometimes they were gourd-shaped. Several were decorated with silver overlay.

Max von Spaun designed many pieces himself and he also commissioned designs from leading Viennese designers. In 1902, Koloman Moser and students in his class at the Vienna School of Applied Art designed a number of simple shapes with iridescent wave forms and spirals as decoration. Designs were also commissioned from the architects Josef Hoffmann and Otto Prutscher. In 1903, Loetz engaged the artist–craftswoman Maria Kirschner (1852–1931) to design iridescent glass vessels. Her pieces have straight or slightly curved contours and often include angular handles, but they are without any surface decoration. They are usually in semi-opaque gold or purple iridescent glass.

The wide range of shapes and decoration produced at this time corresponds to the development of the Art Nouveau style in Austria. The writhing plant forms and studied asymmetry which Viennese artists copied from French and Belgian prototypes gave way early in the twentieth century to a more formal, geometric manner inspired by the work of the Scottish architect–designer Charles Rennie Mackintosh and the English designer Charles Robert Ashbee.

BOHEMIA

A number of the Bohemian glasshouses imitated Loetz and Tiffany iridescent glass. Carl Goldberg's workshop at Haida (present-day Nový Bor, Czechoslovakia) also sometimes used silver overlay or gilding on its iridescent glass, which was made there from about 1900.

Wilhelm Králik Sohn, a firm with factories at Eleonorenhain and Ernstbrunn in southern Bohemia, made iridescent glass in irregular shapes; often the rim of the semi-molten vessel has been cut with shears and turned back to form handles. Most of the output from Pallme-König & Habel's factory near Teplitz comprised iridescent glass, which was usually decorated with glass threads wound around the vessel.

GERMANY

Ferdinand von Poschinger's glassworks at Buchenau in Bavaria produced iridescent glass in typical Art Nouveau shapes, with subtly curved profiles and pinched rims. Some of them had enamelled and gilt decoration designed by Karl Schmoll von Eisenwerth of Darmstadt and Julius Diez of Munich; motifs included lizards, flowers, insects and female heads. The iridescent glass made by the firm of Fritz Heckert in Petersdorf, Silesia, was also decorated with enamelling and gilding. The designers were Max Rade (1840–1917), whose motifs were usually flowers, birds and animals, often within borders composed of ribbons, leaves, stars and geometric shapes, and Ludwig Sütterlin (1865–1917), who favoured floral or abstract ornament.

FRANCE

The only notable iridescent glass produced in France was made by Turkish-born Amédée de Caranza. From about 1900, de Caranza made iridescent glass vessels using a method adapted from techniques employed by Clément Massier to produce ceramics decorated with metallic lustres. De Caranza had worked at Massier's pottery in Vallauris (Alpes-Maritimes) before establishing his own studio in Paris. He perfected red, blue and yellow iridescence, which he applied to vessels of opaque glass. Decoration consisted of fruit or flowers and sometimes fish swimming among reeds. In 1903, he joined the firm of H. A. Copillet & Cie at Noyon (Oise). A wide range of tableware and ornamental glass was manufactured and decorated using de Caranza's techniques and designs. Some pieces were designed by Edouard de Neuville.

ENAMELLED GLASS

The bright, clear colours of most enamels made them an inappropriate medium of decoration for Art Nouveau glass. However, as the technique was comparatively simple and the results popular, many manufacturers used it (although it is noticeable that the output of enamelled glass in France was declining by the 1890s). The emphasis placed on nuance and suggestion by the French Symbolists deterred Art Nouveau craftsmen and designers from using enamelled decoration, which is too well defined. French glass-makers only returned to it when Art Nouveau was on its way out, and it became a prominent feature of Art Deco glass decoration. But the dawn of Art Nouveau had been illuminated by Japanese art, and the colourful, shorthand style of the Japanese draughtsmen was reflected in the enamel decoration of much of Gallé's early glass.

FRANCE

As early as 1866, Eugène Rousseau had commissioned a ceramic service decorated with designs of birds, animals and plants drawn by Félix Bracquemond after illustrations in Japanese albums. The service sold well in Rousseau's Paris shop and he arranged to have glass vessels enamelled in a similar style. As happened in the case of his cameo glass, he had vases and tableware made by Appert Frères of Clichy, which were then enamelled in his own workshops. Most of the designs, which were probably copied or adapted from Japanese prints and drawings, featured birds, fish, insects or flowers. Sometimes the enamelling was combined with delicate carving by Alphonse-Georges Reyen.

The technique of enamelling on glass had been brought to a high pitch in France by Joseph Brocard (d. 1896), who had made a close study of mosque lamps from the Middle East. His vases, dishes and ewers reproduced the brilliance of the enamels and gilding found on the lamps, but they hardly

VASE WITH ENAMELLED
DECORATION, EUGÈNE ROUSSEAU,
1880s (H26cm/10¼in)

fall within the bounds of Art Nouveau. However, Brocard's work inspired not only Gallé but also Auguste Jean, who made clear glass vases enamelled and gilt with ornament derived from both Persian and Japanese art. These belong to the earliest stages of Art Nouveau in France.

BOHEMIA

Art Nouveau enamel decoration of a very different character was practised in Bohemia. The development in Austria of a more geometric version of Art Nouveau has already been mentioned, and not long after the turn of the century this style became prevalent among students at the technical schools at Steinschönau (present-day Kamenický Šenov, Czechoslovakia) and Haida in Bohemia. Both schools marketed work by their instructors and students, and the local manufacturers bought their designs, as well as commissioning work from well-known figures of the Wiener Werkstätte (Vienna Workshops), founded in 1903 by Koloman Moser and Josef Hoffmann. Johann Oertel & Co. of Haida bought designs from Josef Hoffmann, and Carl Schappel, another Haida glass-maker, commissioned work from Hoffmann, Otto Prutscher and Max Rade.

At Steinschönau, the manufacturer Friedrich Pietsch made glassware enamelled with decoration designed by the students at the local technical school. In about 1912, one of these students, Karl Massanetz, set up a workshop at Steinschönau, where he decorated vases in black enamel with intricate patterns. Massanetz's abstract, geometric style was probably influenced by the enamelled patterns designed by Hoffmann for glass manufactured by J. & L. Lobmeyr. This decoration was called *bronzit dekor* and involved in its application a technique invented by Professor Hugo Max, an instructor at the Steinschönau technical school. Ornament in *bronzit dekor* was also designed by other Wiener Werkstätte artists, including Ludwig Jungnickel, whose repeating patterns featured simplified animal forms within a geometric framework. Animals and birds also appeared in the enamelled decoration designed by Adolf Beckert (1884–1929) for a range of frosted and clear glass tableware made in about 1910 by Loetz. Between 1909 and 1911 Beckert was artistic director at Loetz; he had studied at the Haida technical school and later was director of the school at Steinschönau.

GERMANY AND ITALY

In Germany, the technical school at Zwiesel in Bavaria produced quantities of enamelled glass. Its director from 1910 was Bruno Mauder (1877–1948), who designed and decorated glass with elaborate and gilt ornament. In 1905, the German artist Otto Vittali started making pottery and glass which he decorated with enamels. His clear glass vases are covered with ornament, which is sometimes of Islamic inspiration, sometimes botanical and often incorporated gilding and silver.

In 1913, the Italian painters Teodoro Wolf Ferrari and Vittorio Zecchin designed simple glass vessels, which were made by the Artisti Barovier glassworks of Murano and which they decorated with enamels and gilding. Wolf Ferrari's ornamental designs were abstract, and Zecchin's were influenced by the work of the Art Nouveau artists Jan Toorop and Gustav Klimt. Only these antecedents bring his work within the orbit of Art Nouveau glass.

FREE-FORM VESSELS

The attention focused by the theory of the Art Nouveau style on organic form pushed some glass artists in the direction of creating unconventional, but natural, shapes. They exploited the full potential of blowpipe and furnace. Moulds were discarded in favour of free-form vessels, and heat was used to create decorative distortions. The natural phenomena of the process of manufacture became, in some cases, the principal ornament of a vessel. Bubbles and oxides in the molten glass were allowed to form their own decorative designs. Nature was not only the artist's theme, but often the artist itself.

An example of an almost idolatrous devotion to nature is seen in the glass of the German artist Karl Koepping (1848–1914). His early training had been in chemistry but he turned to art, for about twenty years following a career as an etcher and engraver. In 1895 he began to experiment in glass, at first making stemmed cups from simple blown tubes. But his keen interest in Japanese art fostered a desire to make more elaborate floral forms. He turned for help to Friedrich Zitzmann (1840–1906), an experienced glass-blower who had worked at Murano. Together they made stemmed cups in floral forms. The stems meandered or spiralled up to the bowls, which were shaped like flowerheads. From the stems sprang leaves and tendrils, curling and twisting in imitation of real plants. The glass was coloured naturalistically and sometimes iridescence was also applied.

The two men quarrelled after about a year, and Zitzmann started making similar pieces on his own. Koepping turned to a school for glass instrument-makers at Ilmenau in Thuringia to execute his designs. Josef Emil Schneckendorf (1865–1949) made vases and bottles in a style similar to that of Koepping before becoming director of the Darmstadt glassworks owned by Ernst Ludwig, Grand Duke of Hesse, where he made vessels in more conventional shapes decorated with iridescence.

The Vallérysthal glassworks was situated in the part of Alsace Lorraine annexed by Germany after the Franco-Prussian War. In 1898 the firm commissioned designs from Charles Spindler, F. A. Otto Krüger and Bruno Paul, all of whom had gained reputations as Art Nouveau designers in Munich – although none of them had previously worked in glass. Vallérysthal made free-form vessels to their designs, decorated with pulled threads, internal bubbles and opaque colours forming irregular patterns in the translucent glass.

Similar decorative effects were achieved by the glassworks of James Couper & Sons in Glasgow. The tinted, transparent glass used for its vessels was rolled while still semi-molten on a marver sprinkled with powdered coloured glass and small bits of mica. The pieces were then blown into shapes designed by Christopher Dresser and George Walton, who were both designers in several different media. Sometimes opaque white glass, combed into feathery shapes, was used as additional decoration; pieces of silver foil and streaks of aventurine were often included in the body of the vessel. Couper called the glass 'Clutha'. Some of the shapes, particularly those designed by Dresser, were quite outlandish, with long, thin tubular necks and rims in the form of wide, curled flanges.

The glass vessels designed by the half-Norwegian, half-German Hans Stoltenberg-Lerche (1867–1920) and made by Fratelli Toso in Venice had some aspects in common with Clutha glass. Stoltenberg-Lerche was a sculptor who had designed silver, jewellery and ceramics before turning

VASES, JAMES COUPER & SONS, c.1895
(Taller: H36.8cm/14½in)

This Glasgow firm specialized in internally decorated glass, which was called 'Clutha', an old name for the river Clyde. Many Couper pieces, including these two, were designed by Christopher Dresser.

to glass during the first two decades of the twentieth century. A few of the vessels he designed resembled pieces of Clutha glass designed by Dresser. Others were reminiscent of Koepping's work, of classical antiquity or the Venetian tradition. Powdered coloured glass provided internal decoration, and bubbles in the glass were allowed to burst on the surface. Sometimes coloured glass snakes or fish were applied to the vessels.

Like Stoltenberg-Lerche, the French artist and craftsman Jules Habert-Dys (1850–1928) only turned to glass toward the end of his career. In 1910 he exhibited a clear glass bottle into the surface of which, while it was still semi-molten, he had pressed red glass in a chequered pattern. When the glass had annealed, it was polished and the decoration was left flush with the surface of the vessel. Subsequently Habert-Dys made glass vessels from layers of alternately coloured and clear transparent glass. Metal was then applied to the surface of the vessel in irregular patterns of flowing lines, and the glass could only be seen in the interstices of

the metal. Some pieces were completed with a layer of clear glass.

An even greater achievement than his enamelled glass was a group of free-form vessels produced by Auguste Jean. These were turned into wild, irregular shapes by twisting, pressing and prodding the semi-molten glass. Made in clear glass and void of decoration, they stand in their own right as sculptural expressions of Art Nouveau.

From 1909, the Val St-Lambert factory at Jemeppe-sur-Meuse in Belgium produced a series of onion-shaped vases with extenuated necks. They were designed by the manager of the factory, Romain Gevaert (1875–1981), and his wife, Jeanne Tisehon (1875–1955). The vases were made of opaque coloured glass and decorated with irregular patterns of different coloured glass rolled on to the surface. The decoration was either confined to the bulbous lower part of the vase, or it was extended in long, tapering lines up the neck. The vases were treated with hydrofluoric acid, which gave them a matt, slightly rough-textured surface.

CENTREPIECE, JAMES POWELL &
SONS, 1906 (H36cm/14¼in)

*This centrepiece was part of a large service made for
the Italian diplomat Count Minorbi, whose family
crests are enamelled on the shields mounted on the
silver wirework handles. The inlaid glass-thread
decoration was used extensively by the Powell firm
on its tableware during this period.* (ABOVE)

TAZZA, OTTO PRUTSCHER, *c*.1905
(H20.5cm/8⅛in)

*Koloman Moser and Otto Prutscher, two of the
leading designers associated with the Wiener
Werkstätte, designed tableware that was
manufactured by the Bohemian firm of Meyr's
Neffe. The geometrical decoration is characteristic of
the Vienna Workshops' style.* (ABOVE CENTRE)

SHERRY JUG, KOLOMAN MOSER,
c.1900 (H24cm/9½in)

*With its cleverly designed electroplated silver mount
that combines elegance with practicality, this jug
was designed by Moser for the Vienna firm of
Bakalowits.* (ABOVE RIGHT)

TABLEWARE

Through the great number of art
periodicals that were published in
Europe during the time when Art
Nouveau flourished, several designers established international reputations. As a result,
many large manufacturers wanted the
better-known names associated with their
products. The area where the ploy was
particularly effective was tableware, a competitive market in which the designer's
name could give a firm's product an edge
over the opposition. The services were
nearly all made in clear, colourless glass,
with a minimum of decoration, usually in
enamels or gilding. Most pieces were of
simple, elegant form, which affirms the
claim often made for the Art Nouveau style,
i.e., that it introduced the Modern Movement in architecture and design.

The English architect Philip Webb
designed tableware made by James Powell &
Sons and sold by Morris & Co. at its shop in
London. Both the Baccarat and Pantin
glasshouses manufactured services designed
by the Dutch architect H. P. Berlage.

Tableware by the German architect–
designer Peter Behrens was produced at the
Rheinische Glashütten at Ehrenfeld, near
Cologne, and sets of drinking glasses by the
same designer were made by Benedikt von
Poschinger at Oberzwiesel in Bavaria. Von
Poschinger also manufactured drinking
glasses designed by Richard Riemerschmid,
Albin Muller and Adalbert Niemeyer of
Munich. Hans Christiansen of Darmstadt
designed sets of decanters and glasses for
Egon von Poschinger's Theresienthaler
works. Koloman Moser and Otto Prutscher
both designed tableware which was made at
the Meyr's Neffe glasshouse in Bohemia.
The designs were commissioned by Bakalowits, a retail firm with a shop in Vienna
from which glass was sold throughout
Europe and North America. Bakalowits also
commissioned Joseph Maria Olbrich, an
architect and designer working in Vienna
and Darmstadt, to design crystal candlesticks. The plain tableware in geometric
shapes designed by the Prague architect Jan
Kotěra for Count Harrach's glassworks was
an early manifestation of the Modernist style
that developed during the years between the
two world wars.

STAINED-GLASS
PANEL, *c*.1900
(H146cm/57½in)

*The stylized mask
adorning the fountain
suggests this panel was
designed in Germany
or Austria.* (FAR LEFT)

STAINED-GLASS
PANEL, *c*.1900
(H110.5cm/43¼in)

*This panel has been
attributed to the
workshop of Carl
Geylings Erben in
Vienna, which supplied
public buildings
throughout the
Austro-Hungarian
Empire.* (LEFT)

WINDOWS AND
PANELS

Stained- and coloured-glass windows and panels were a feature of much Art Nouveau interior decoration, being ideal media for the subdued light favoured by the style's adherents. William Morris contributed enormously to the revival of the technique and artistic effects of Medieval windows. He designed many of the windows that were made by his firm, and others were the work of Pre-Raphaelite painters such as Dante Gabriel Rossetti, Ford Madox Brown and Edward Burne-Jones. The latter also designed windows for James Powell & Sons, whose chief designer was later another Pre-Raphaelite painter, Henry Holiday.

Following the success of the stained-glass windows designed by the Nabis painters, manufactured by Tiffany's and shown at the opening of Siegfried Bing's Paris gallery, La Maison de l'Art Nouveau, firms all over Europe sought new designs from artists and architects. Gebrüder Liebert in Dresden commissioned designs from Hans Christian-

sen, while in Vienna the firm of Carl Geylings Erben made stained glass to designs by several of the Wiener Werkstätte artists, including Leopold Forstner, Karl Witzmann and Otto Prutscher.

But Glasgow, perhaps, had the most thriving stained-glass industry. The firm of J. & W. Guthrie commissioned designs from the English artists Christopher Whall and Robert Anning Bell, as well as from some of the leading Scottish painters. George Walton designed stained-glass windows for many of the interiors he created in Glasgow, and another Glaswegian, Oscar Paterson, designed and made numerous windows. Stained glass designed by Charles Rennie Mackintosh, among other leading Glasgow artists and designers, was made in the studio of Hugh McCulloch, the most prolific producer of stained glass in Scotland.

The stained glass of Dublin artist Harry Clarke (1889–1931), who learned his art in his father's church-decorating firm, combined elements of Celtic Revivalism, Art Nouveau, Symbolism, even Art Deco. His visionary works were densely detailed, deeply coloured tapestries featuring distinctive, mystical figures in ornate settings.

DETAIL OF STAINED-GLASS WINDOW,
MORRIS & CO., 1882

*The angel with dulcimer is part of a window made
for the parish church at Cattistock, Dorset.*

EMILE GALLÉ

PORTRAIT OF
EMILE GALLÉ,
BY VICTOR
PROUVÉ, 1892

*Prouvé, friend and
collaborator of Gallé,
has depicted him in the
midst of his creative
process, drawing
inspiration from plants
to create the decorative
motifs of his glass.*

(1846–1904), made the town of Nancy in Lorraine a centre of creativity and production in the applied arts to rival the capital.

The artists of Nancy achieved distinction in many areas, but the craft for which Nancy became internationally celebrated was that in which Emile Gallé made his reputation, the challenging and magical medium of glass, and the style with which the town became associated was the naturalistic version of Art Nouveau that Gallé had evolved. His creative vision and his commercial acumen combined to expand a small family business into a flourishing concern with international outlets and to establish a template for a successful local *industrie d'art*. The flowering of the decorative glass industry in and around Nancy in the late nineteenth and early twentieth centuries owed everything to Gallé's remarkable artistic ambitions. The story of his aesthetic formation and the mutiplicity of his achievements – he also produced furniture and ceramics – provides a rewarding case study in the predominant aesthetic problems of the decorative arts and in the struggle toward the reconciliation of art and industry in the late nineteenth century.

From the first major international display of its kind, the Great Exhibition of 1851 (held in the so-called Crystal Palace, which was constructed in Hyde Park, London), up until the 1900 Paris Exposition Universelle, the second half of the nineteenth century was marked by a sequence of exhibitions held all over the world that fulfilled a dual celebratory and didactic purpose. The occasions brought together the fruits of contemporary art and industry and provided a forum for the exchange of ideas and for debate on such problems as the preservation of artistic integrity in the age of the machine and the identification of styles appropriate to design for industrial manufacture. Questions of form, function and decoration were up for consideration.

The Paris Exposition Universelle of 1900 celebrated the achievements of the arts and industries of many nations. For the host country in particular it provided the occasion to celebrate the triumphs of the decorative arts in a new style. This new style became known as Art Nouveau and its two most distinctive characteristics were its rupture with the traditional patterns of stylistic evolution and

historical reference, and its debt to nature as the primary source of inspiration, albeit often abstracted into highly stylized forms.

The 1900 exhibition featured the work of Paris's foremost designers, craftsmen and decorators, many working in this new mode. It also provided an important international showcase for the work of a provincial school of artists who, under the influence of their guiding light, Emile Gallé

The need for satisfactory solutions to such questions was central to Emile Gallé's aesthetic quests. He was a frequent exhibitor at the regular Paris Salons in the last quarter of the nineteenth century and used the major exhibitions in 1884, 1889 and 1900 as occasions to present extensive exhibits which demonstrated the virtuosity of his craft and defined his philosophical stance as an artist and a manufacturer.

EARLY WORK

Gallé's education was broadly based, embracing a rich tradition of French literature and art history, as well as the scientific and technical apprenticeship that was essential training for his destined career as head of the family business manufacturing decorative glass and faience. Throughout his life he continued to broaden his culture, particularly in the realms of literature and horticulture, two disciplines that were to serve his art to great effect.

The range of Gallé's study of art history is shown in the many historical references in his creations. These were more numerous in the early phases of his career and as such reflect the prevalent patterns of historicism to which Art Nouveau and, in Gallé's case, his personal naturalistic version of Art Nouveau, provided so dramatic a reaction in the closing years of the century. Gallé's early essays included imitations of eighteenth-century styles, and inspiration was also provided by engraved glass or rock crystal vessels of the Renaissance. He also fashioned pieces on Medieval themes, including figurative subjects, which were usually rendered in enamels, and was sufficiently intrigued by ancient Middle Eastern enamelled glass to make a variety of vessels that were derived directly from Islamic models, most notably a series of vases in the form of traditional enamelled mosque lamps. These were also copied by another contemporary French glass-maker, Joseph Brocard.

THE INFLUENCE OF ORIENTAL ART

In the late 1860s and early 1870s Gallé studied the glass collections of the Louvre, the British Museum and the South Kensington Museum (now the Victoria and Albert Museum). He was captivated by techniques he found there, which from the mid-1870s he proceeded to develop and push to extraordinary limits. Chinese cased-glass bottles suggested motifs, colours and contrasts; ancient glass proposed rich effects of surface iridescence. Within this complex web of influences, one strand deserves particular attention. Like so many artists of his generation, Gallé experienced the impact of the arts of Japan, introduced to France, Britain and the United States in the 1860s. In Japanese art Gallé and many of his contemporaries discovered a new vernacular of two-dimensional expression, with its emphasis on the stylization of motifs derived from nature by the use of emphatic line, silhouette, deliberate and elegant asymmetry, and flat blocks of colour. Japanese art provided the basis of a graphic language owing nothing to conventional Western art, and enabled a new, resolutely modern style to find full and sophisticated expression.

Emile Gallé made numerous pieces in specific homage to the arts of Japan. On a more pervasive level, much of his mature work owes a debt to Japan, notably in his elegant stylization of plant motifs. Confronted with so many stylistic options, Gallé came to recognize the perils of devotion to form rather than content. He turned to nature as the richest source of inspiration for his art. In England author and critic John Ruskin had encouraged the methodical observation of nature as the basis for all artistic endeavour. By the late nineteenth century there was a widespread movement away from historicism toward nature as a source of inspiration. This, combined with the strong impact of Japanese art, led to the fluid, stylized, organic forms of Art Nouveau. Very rapidly, however, Art Nouveau became little more than a fashionable impasse, the convoluted extremes of which came to be scorned by Gallé.

NATURE AS SOURCE

Gallé's exploration of nature as a source for his art was a deeply considered process. He formulated his own ideas on how to use nature as the basis of a richly symbolic art with the power to touch the human soul. He was a passionate horticulturist and planted and tended gardens of exotic plants to provide specimens for his studio. He photographed, sketched and took detailed notes on his own plants and those observed on his travels.

Gallé realized that within the plant and insect world were motifs that could be developed as symbols with a profound expressive value. He had the motto '*Ma racine est au fond des bois*' ('My roots are in the depths of the woods') carved into the oak doors of his studio as a fundamental credo. In 1900 he read a paper before the Académie de Stanislas in Nancy entitled *Le décor symbolique*, in which he set forth his philosophy. He regarded the symbolism of nature as a spontaneous idiom to which any heart could respond. He saw in the infinite manifestations of nature an inexhaustible fund of motifs through which the artist could express a mystical exaltation before the miracle of creation, and through which he could evoke the mystery and the glory of the universe, the joy and the tragedy of the human condition. Nature furnished a lexicon of sublime symbolism.

In 1889, in the notes he composed to accompany his contribution to the Paris Exposition Universelle, Gallé defined his aim as an artist. He described his personal mission as the evocation in glass of delicate or dramatic moods. He imagined himself an alchemist, whose mastery of technique ensured every chance of dazzling success within the hazardous, critical processes of work at the glass furnace. As far as was possible he imposed in advance on the volatile material the precise colours and forms which he had conceived as most appropriate to embody his ideas and visions.

APPLIED GLASS PINE VASE, EMILE GALLÉ, 1903 (H17.9cm/7in)

A technically complex piece, this case involves internal, surface and applied decoration.

TECHNIQUES

Gallé greatly extended the boundaries of glass as a medium of artistic expression. The artistic commitment he made to this most challenging medium depended on his development of a depth of technical knowledge and practical skills which made possible hitherto unknown levels of glass-working virtuosity. His earliest works involved the application of enamelled decoration, often incorporating naturalistic grisaille landscapes, to the cold surface of thin-walled vessels fashioned of blown glass.

Anxious to extend his palette and to incorporate colour and decoration within the body of the glass itself, however, Gallé was soon experimenting, searching for formulae that could give glass the rich lustres of ambers, agates or other semiprecious stones. He devised internal effects, as did two other contemporary French experimental glassworkers, Eugène Rousseau and Ernest

Léveillé, trapping flights of chemical inclusions within thick walls of glass. In Gallé's creations such effects could evoke moss, tongues of flame, aquatic plants, a sky. He made extraordinary dichroic glass, the tint of which could change according to the angle of the light, from, for instance, a cloudy opalescent blue to the deepest amber glow. A crucial development was his introduction of cameo techniques by the early 1880s, wherein the initial glass gather was cased in one or more layers of different colours which could then be cut back, leaving a decoration in relief in one colour against a contrasting ground. The majority of these pieces were decorated with stylized floral motifs, and other popular subjects included landscapes and insects, in particular butterflies and dragonflies. Gallé's team included highly accomplished engravers able to interpret his designs in cameo carving of the greatest subtlety. In 1889 he began to make extensive use of hydrofluoric acid as an etching agent to achieve cameo reliefs with

greater speed on the production line. Sometimes a line of poetry would inspire the decoration of a piece, the text being incorporated within the decoration to produce what is known as *verrerie parlante*.

The year 1897 saw the introduction of Gallé's *marqueterie-sur-verre* technique, which involved applying and pressing pieces of semi-molten glass into the surface of a still hot vessel according to a predetermined design. These inlays would then be carved to render the details of a stem, petal or leaf. In the last years of his life, between 1900 and his death in 1904, Gallé pushed his team of master glass-workers to even greater challenges, working glass in high relief at the furnace, leaving his engravers then to render detail through their laborious cold bench work. His greatest *tours de force* were often reserved for exhibition pieces or for major commissions. An exemplary masterpiece from this culminating phase of Gallé's career is his glass hand. Rising from the sea, encrusted with shells and dripping with

ACID-ETCHED CAMEO-GLASS VASE, MULLER FRÈRES, *c*.1900
(H42cm/16¼in)

Its technique may be commonplace, but this vase is unusual for its decoration, which pays homage to the decorative arts of Japan. (LEFT)

SCULPTED AND APPLIED GLASS HAND, EMILE GALLÉ, *c*.1900–4
(Lifesize)

A tour de force of invention and glass-working skills, this hand is unusual in Gallé's oeuvre in that it serves no practical function. (RIGHT)

seaweed, this is an evocative sculpture laden with symbolism, a complex work of art which takes the medium far beyond merely decorative or functional concerns and indeed into the realm of fine art.

COMMERCIAL SUCCESS

As Gallé's artistry found even greater scope and his reputation increased, so too did the popular demand for decorative glassware bearing his name. By 1900 Gallé was head of a factory employing some three hundred people. He was the firm's creative director, and there was a design studio to assist the master in adapting his ideas for interpretation in large series of vases produced by semi-industrialized methods. The gulf had greatly increased between the everyday production of decorative vases and the far more costly experi-

VASE PARLANT, EMILE GALLÉ, 1890s
(approx. H50cm/19¾in)

This long-stemmed vase with stopper bears the engraved lines 'La Silence des Nuits panse l'âme blessée. La bonté de la nuit caresse l'âme sombre'. These words provided Gallé's inspiration for the decoration. (LEFT)

GROUP OF ACID-ETCHED CAMEO-GLASS VASES, EMILE GALLÉ, *c*.1900
(Tallest H34.8cm/13¾in)

These pieces reflect the standard production of the Gallé factory after the introduction of acid-etching techniques in 1889. Such pieces were produced long after Gallé's death in 1904. (ABOVE)

PÂTE-DE-VERRE AND CARVED WOOD CASKET, DAUM, *c*.1905 (H18.5cm/7¼in)

APPLIED AND CAMEO-GLASS DRAGONFLY AND WATERLILY VASE, DAUM, *c*.1900 (H12.5cm/5in)

These motifs were evidently popular, to judge from the number of surviving examples and variations on this Art Nouveau theme as interpreted by Daum.

mental endeavours to create unique objects or very small works of art in glass which, with a subtlety born of extraordinarily fine-tuned skills, expressed the full depth of Gallé's sensibility as an artist.

Commercial success and industrial expansion inevitably led to a dilution of artistic quality in the majority of decorative works manufactured for the broad retail market. One of Gallé's most refined patrons and admirers, Count Robert de Montesquiou, accused him of having *'fait pipi à l'esthétique'* (urinated on his aesthetic standards) by using acid-etching to facilitate mass production. Undeniably, the factory-made, acid-etched works lack the finesse and the evocative, Symbolist layers of poetry present in Gallé's finest, more complex and more intimate creations. In reaching a wide public he was obliged to make sacrifices and to some extent compromised his art in order to achieve this end. Although he enjoyed great success as an industrialist, it is open to debate whether he satisfactorily resolved his aim of uniting artistic and industrial ambitions. It should be noted that many of the most conventionalized pieces bearing his name were in fact produced after his death, for the factory continued production well into the 1920s on the momentum of its founder's reputation. What cannot be disputed is the integrity of Gallé's ambitions and resolve to

create a set of aesthetic principles. It was the strength of this vision that was instrumental in galvanizing so many local artists into a school, at first a loose-knit endeavour but, in 1901, formally unified as the Alliance Provinciale des Industries d'Art.

OTHER NANCY GLASS-MAKERS

This group, known as the Ecole de Nancy, applied Gallé's naturalistic aesthetic to its various crafts. Foremost among its artists were the Daum brothers, Auguste (1853–1909) and Antonin (1864–1930). Following Gallé's lead, they too expanded a family glassworks, making decorative table and domestic vases into a thriving *industrie d'art*. Producing good-quality decorative vases in a modern idiom, with nature as their repertoire, the Daum brothers experimented in order to be able to produce breathtaking works which, at their very best, rivalled Gallé's achievements technically, though they were never imbued with Gallé's inimitable, profound and mysterious sense of poetry. The Daum workshops experimented with complex internal polychrome effects and mottled colour sur-

face effects in overlays, which made charming painterly decorations possible, even on pieces with only one layer of acid-etching. They devised their own variants on the *marqueterie-sur-verre* and high-relief processes, achieving particular success with certain designs, including a series of vases on the theme of dragonflies and lily ponds, both of which were archetypal Nancy motifs. The Daum works collaborated with Louis Majorelle (1859–1926), the leading Nancy furniture-maker and metalworker, on a wide variety of decorative lamps, the glass shades, usually floral forms, in elegant naturalistic iron or bronze mounts.

Among the numerous other glass-makers working in and around Nancy, few managed more than to echo Gallé's endeavours. The names of Arsall, d'Argental, de Vez and Muller Frères are found on derivative decorative cameo glass. Désiré Christian (1846–1907), working at Meisenthal in Lorraine, had collaborated very closely with Gallé yet managed to produce inventive, independent works. Jacques Gruber (1870–1936), a key figure in the Ecole de Nancy as an architect and furniture designer, applied the principle of cameo glass popularized by Gallé to the creation of attractive glass panels, which he incorporated into furniture. He also produced stained-glass doors and windows within architectural schemes.

AMERICAN ART NOUVEAU

Soon after the advent of curvilinear, nature-inspired Art Nouveau on the Continent, American designers were given the opportunity to become a significant part of an international movement. They proceeded to interpret this innovative European style in a colourful, vibrant manner that was distinctively American.

TIFFANY GLASS

The leading exponent of American Art Nouveau was Louis Comfort Tiffany (1848–1933). Born in Connecticut, he was the son of Charles L. Tiffany, founder of Tiffany & Company, the influential New York jeweller. At an early age, Louis Tiffany showed an interest in the arts, particularly painting, and he studied with both George Inness in New York and Léon Bailly in Paris.

INTERIOR DESIGNS

In 1881, Tiffany and three associates formed Louis C. Tiffany and Associated Artists, an interior-design firm that quickly became New York's premier avant-garde society decorator, furnishing the homes of many prominent citizens, including Cornelius Vanderbilt II. Through these projects Tiffany became interested in the uses of architectural and decorative glass, and more and more Tiffany interiors incorporated coloured glass in windows, fireplace surrounds and lampshades.

Tiffany's first complete domestic project was commissioned by George Kemp for his New York residence. The 1879 interior included possibly the earliest example of flat Tiffany glass: a panel depicting autumn gourds, fruits and vines, which was designed to echo an elaborate painted frieze situated in Kemp's dining room.

Sadly, most of Tiffany's interiors are no longer extant, including several rooms in the White House, redecorated at the request of President Chester A. Arthur in 1882–3. Much of this interior reflected popular contemporary taste, but its distinguishing feature, in the ground-floor vestibule, was a large stained-glass screen covered with geometric designs and motifs illustrating American history. The screen, which included an early use by Tiffany of opalescent glass, was destroyed early in the twentieth century.

PARISIAN INFLUENCE

On a trip to Europe in 1889, Tiffany first saw the glass vases of Emile Gallé. At the time Tiffany was still producing commissioned windows and panels incorporating his glass, and no doubt he was impressed by Gallé's highly personal vision of nature. On this same visit, Tiffany also met Siegfried Bing (1838–1905), whose Paris shop gave Art Nouveau its name. Bing commissioned Tiffany to create stained-glass windows based on drawings by artists such as Pierre Bonnard, Henri de Toulouse-Lautrec and Félix Vallotton. On completion, Bing then exhibited the windows alongside Tiffany iridescent glass and, later, included his lamps and metalwork. The fruitful Bing-Tiffany collaboration, along with the realization that the industrial production of artistic glass could be critically accepted – and widely acclaimed – propelled Tiffany's designs, and those of other talented Americans as well, into the international arena.

EGGPLANT, TIFFANY LEADED FAVRILE GLASS PANEL, DESIGNED FOR THE GEORGE KEMP RESIDENCE, 1879 (H74cm/29in; L99cm/39in) *This panel was among Tiffany's earliest works using leaded glass. An identical panel was shown in an 1899 exhibition at the Grafton Galleries, London.*

IRIDESCENT GLASS

Many assume that Tiffany was responsible for the development of iridescent glass in the late nineteenth century. Certainly this type of glass is closely identified with Tiffany Studios – as his design company was known from 1900. But other artists and scientists in glass manufacture, such as the Viennese Ludwig Lobmeyr in the 1870s, had been experimenting in re-creating the iridescent patina found on ancient glass.

Tiffany's iridescent glass – which he called 'Favrile' – first appeared in 1894. The largely traditionally shaped vases, with their shimmering patina, won praise for their impressionistic movement of line and colour.

Tiffany was a naturalist and, like Gallé, he attempted to transform flowers into vases. Tiffany's floriform vases were never intended to hold flowers, but to *be* flowers. The Jack-in-the-Pulpit Vase, for example, combined vivid blue iridescence and the unusual form of a widely flaring flower face perched on a tall, slender stem.

OTHER INFLUENCES AND TECHNIQUES

Although Tiffany did not actively pursue the manufacture of cameo glass, he was influenced by eighteenth- and nineteenth-century Chinese cameo glass, as well as by the interpretation of this ancient technique in England. Tiffany was a serious collector of Chinese and Japanese works of art, Oriental carpets and early Roman glass, among other things, and displayed them in Laurelton Hall, his opulent Long Island, New York, mansion. The motifs, techniques and shapes of his glassware were often inspired by *objets-d'art* in his possession.

Among Tiffany's finest accomplishments was paperweight, or reactive, glass, so named because it responded to changes in temperature in the furnace. Usually of simple shapes inlaid with various coloured oxides, these vases depicted flowers, leaves or marine growth – or sometimes they simply created an impression of moving colours enclosed in slightly iridescent or opalescent grounds.

TIFFANY LAMPS

Tiffany's leaded-glass lamps were not manufactured on a large scale until 1899, when the construction techniques developed for stained-glass windows were adapted to produce multiples of each design. Thus, every individual style of Tiffany lampshade comprised the same number of pieces forming an identical pattern.

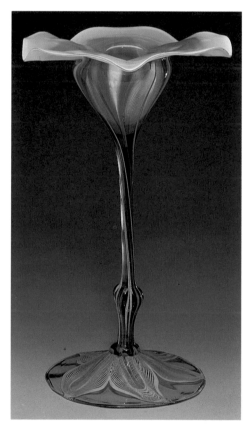

TIFFANY FAVRILE GLASS FLORIFORM VASE, 1899–1920 (H36.5cm/14¼in)

This is the most successful of Tiffany's floriform vases. The colours of the petals and leaves ascending from the bowl reinforce the impression of a growing, undulating flower. (LEFT)

TIFFANY FAVRILE CAMEO-GLASS 'TEL EL AMARNA' VASE, c.1915 (H21.9cm/8⅝in)

The vase represents an unusual coupling of the ancient technique of cameo glass on an Oriental shape, further enhanced by iridescent Egyptian decoration on the collar. (ABOVE LEFT)

TIFFANY FAVRILE GLASS AND BRONZE PEONY LAMP, 1899–1920 (H80cm/31½in; D55.9cm/22in)

All Tiffany shades in a specific pattern were constructed using identical patterns. The choice of colours and types of glass differentiated one shade from another. The bases were interchangeable and produced strikingly different effects. (ABOVE)

TIFFANY FAVRILE GLASS AND BRONZE LABURNUM LAMP, 1899–1920 (H68.6cm/27in; D54.6cm/21½in) (ABOVE RIGHT)

STEUBEN GLASS

The Steuben Glass Works was founded in 1903 in Corning, New York, by English-born Frederick Carder (1863–1963). Steuben's high-quality glass, produced to Carder's own designs, made it Tiffany's closest competitor.

Carder had been apprenticed at the family pottery in Staffordshire and then employed as an artist at Stevens & Williams before moving to the United States in 1903. Throughout his years at Steuben and well into his nineties he designed, carved, blew and modelled glass. Unlike Tiffany, Carder was intimately involved in all aspects of glass-making and was responsible for many technical and artistic innovations.

As well as iridescent 'Aurene' glass, pro-

QUEZAL AND VINELAND FLINT

In 1901 Martin Bach (1865–1924) and Thomas Johnson set up the Quezal Art Glass & Decorating Company in Brooklyn, New York. Both had worked for Tiffany and at Quezal they produced high-quality, innovative iridescent glassware. Quezal also manufactured Jack-in-the-Pulpit vases decorated with striated feathering reserved against an opalescent ground, and the company's reputation lay in its original decoration as well as in its virtuosity in the handling of the molten glass.

After his father's death, Martin Bach, Jr., went to work for Victor Durand at Vineland Flint Glass Works in New Jersey. With Bach's 1925 arrival, Durand Art Glass was set up, and even though Art Nouveau had long gone out of favour, Durand produced iridescent glass until 1931.

HANDEL AND PAIRPOINT

Many companies tried to produce leaded-glass lamps. With two exceptions, most made vastly inferior copies of Tiffany's designs.

Handel & Company in Meriden, Connecticut, made decorative art glass, but the firm is best known for leaded-glass and reverse-painted glass lamps. The moulded shades of the latter were simple domed forms, often with chipped or sandblasted exteriors that produced a frosted effect when illuminated, and distinctive interior surfaces painted with flowers, birds or landscapes.

The Pairpoint Manufacturing Company of New Bedford, Massachusetts, produced glass lamps reverse-painted with landscapes and still lifes and introduced mould-blown, or 'Puffy', lamps, in 1907, which were moulded in frosted glass and painted on the inside with a variety of flowers or animals.

What made Tiffany lamps so superior to others of the time were the choice of colours, their placement within the confines of the pattern and the glass tiles used. Not all the glass used in Tiffany lamps was made by Tiffany Studios, but that which was made elsewhere conformed to Tiffany specifications and was not available to other firms. Special types of Tiffany glass included drapery glass (thick, folded glass used to depict lush flowers, such as magnolia and peony blossoms), fractured or confetti glass (with pieces of coloured glass pressed into moulds to create depth in the lamps) and mottled glass, which added depth and colour variation. A wide range of lamps was available, from those with simple geometric shades to elaborate, expensive models. Except for rare instances when a base was integral to a specific shade (i.e., the Wisteria Lamp and its tree-trunk base), lamps and shades could be purchased separately.

Tiffany's designs were at the height of popularity during the first decade of the twentieth century. The First World War and changing tastes of the firm's clientele forced Tiffany Studios to close in 1928, although very little was in fact produced in the last ten years of the company's existence.

STEUBEN MILLEFIORI GLASS CHARGER, 1926 (D27.9cm/11in)

Millefiori glass was produced at Steuben from 1909 until the mid-1920s in very limited quantities.

duced from *c.*1904, Carder developed many varities of art glass, including 'Millefiori', named after ancient mosaic glass; etched 'Intarsia' and crackled 'Moss Agate', types of cased glass; translucent 'Mandarin Yellow', inspired by Chinese porcelain; and silky surfaced 'Ivrene' and 'Verre de Soie'.

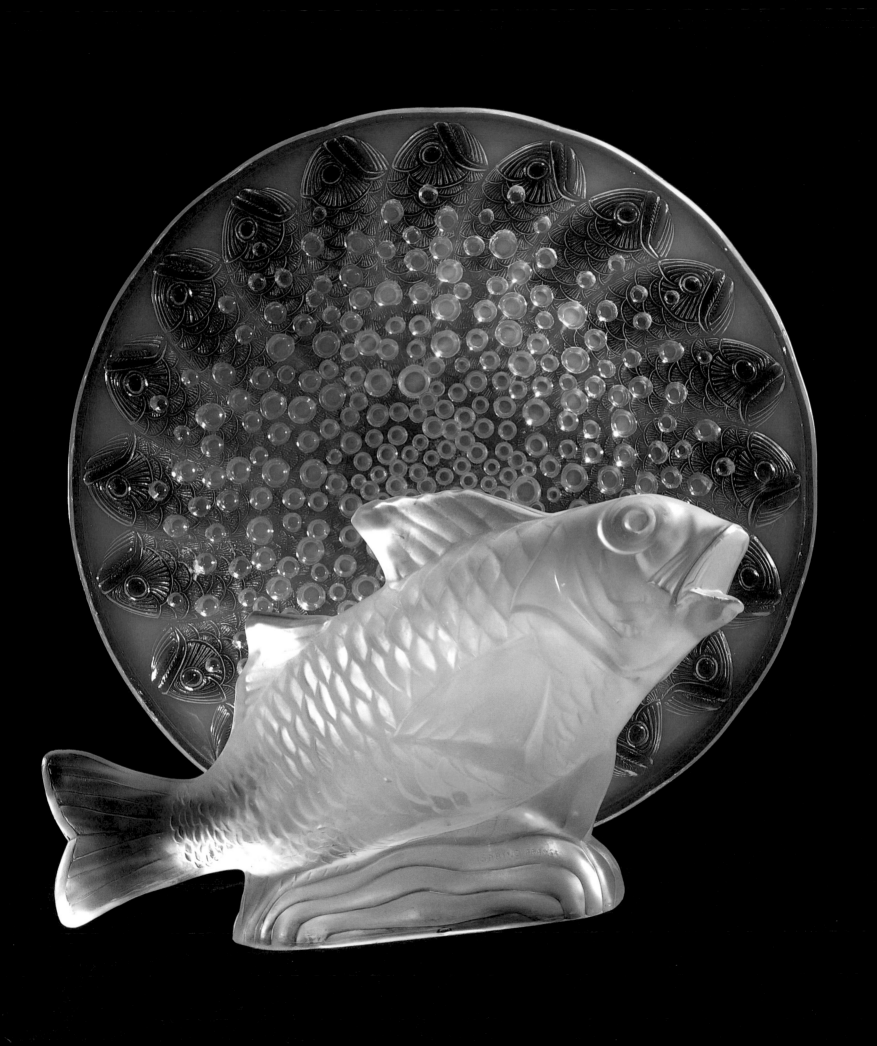

TWENTIETH-
CENTURY
DEVELOPMENTS

The excitement and technical developments of glass by Emile Gallé, Louis Comfort Tiffany and other innovators were to survive the First World War and the Depression. The convoluted sinuousness of Art Nouveau, however, was replaced by a more rectilinear and simplified approach to design, loosely referred to as Art Deco.

Perhaps the best-known name from the early twentieth century is that of René Lalique, whose wide-ranging production encompassed a plethora of mass-produced pieces, as well as the occasional one-off. His matt and opalescent moulded glass was copied by many other manufacturers in both Europe and the United States.

The farther south in Europe one moved, the greater part colour and surface played in glass-making. In Italy in the 1930s, the Venini factory was creating classically shaped vases with dramatically contrasting black and red patterning and gold streaking, among other decoration. The collective Venetian repertoire of shapes encompassed both the traditional and the organic — and the distinctive 1950s Venini handkerchief vase.

Across the Atlantic, the 1960s witnessed a revolution in glass-making and the ascent of the studio artist, who produced technically and aesthetically innovative, largely sculptural, works. The international Studio Glass Movement, with Harvey Littleton as its high priest, spread across the United States and to Europe.

A SABINO OPALESCENT GLASS FISH LAMP AND LALIQUE
OPALESCENT GLASS COUPE, 1930s

*Two examples of the technique introduced by Lalique for series-production
moulded glass objects typical of the inter-war years.*

163

BETWEEN THE WARS

AN ERA OF INNOVATION

The quarter century roughly bridging the two world wars was a rich, exciting period for glass production in Europe and, to a lesser extent, North America. Not only were there singular examples of art glass, created in both studios and sympathetic factories, but there was much glass of the mass-produced variety, whose methods of manufacture were ever evolving and improving.

Traditional methods, forms and decoration were still being applied to and widely accepted in glass, but it was the taste for innovative and exciting shapes, colours, motifs and techniques, first formed at the turn of the century by the Art Nouveau style and close to unquenchable by the 1910s, that led to the immense popularity of glass *objets* between the wars. From René Lalique's myriad perfume bottles, made for a host of *parfumeurs*, to Wilhelm Wagenfeld's glass-cube containers for the Bauhaus, to Steuben Glass's limited-edition, artist-designed vessels, to Orrefors' Swedish Modern vessels, the spectrum of interwar glass satisfied the needs of many.

FRANCE

Besides the traditional cut-glass wares of firms such as Baccarat, which made concessions to *le style moderne* by producing some objects in a contemporary vein, French glass from the 1910s to the 1930s can be divided roughly into two types: the mass-produced, usually mould-blown or press-moulded variety, and the one-off or limited-number *objets-d'art*. The variety of modern French glass,

most of which can be called Art Deco (the term derives from the trendsetting 1925 Exposition des Arts Décoratifs et Industriels Modernes in Paris), makes the output of France at this time arguably the richest and most influential glass of all.

ART NOUVEAU PRECURSORS

Since 1900 Art Nouveau had been on the decline. Although the Gallé factory continued to produce glass until the mid-1930s, the taste for its mainstay of ornate, nature-inspired objects had waned markedly. There was, however, one type of glass, 'rediscovered' in the late nineteenth century and still being made in the 1930s, whose pieces comfortably spanned both Art Nouveau and Art Deco: *pâte-de-verre*.

PÂTE-DE-VERRE

Sculptor, painter and ceramic artist Henri Cros (1840–1907) is credited with reawakening interest in *pâte-de-verre*, or glass paste. His first *pâte-de-verre* creations, from the mid-1880s, were sculptural, and included Greek and Roman bas-reliefs and statuettes. Among his contemporaries working with *pâte-de-verre* in France during this period were the Belgian-born Georges Despret (1862–1952), Albert-Louis Dammouse (1848–1926), and Amalric Walter (1869–1959) and his longtime collaborator, designer-sculptor-teacher Henri Bergé (1868–1936). Dammouse, Walter and Bergé worked in the nature-inspired, Art Nouveau mode, oblivious to the geometric, stylized Art Deco repertoire; Despret preferred making human likenesses.

However, two later *pâte-de-verre* artists, Gabriel Argy-Rousseau (1885–1953) and François-Emile Décorchement (1880–1971), were highly attuned to the contemporary style. Although Argy-Rousseau created a significant number of lyrical pieces

decorated with floral and other organic motifs reminiscent of Art Nouveau, much of his work is unmistakably modern, with its geometric and stylized floral and bird designs, its elegant gazelles and classical, notably Egyptian-style, figures in dramatic poses. He first exhibited *pâte-de-verre* glass in 1914, after the war going into business with Paris retailer Gustave-Gaston Moser-Millot, for whom he created numerous *pâte-de-verre* vases, bowls, boxes, trays, lamps, pendants, and perfume bottles and burners. He also produced attractive figurines, among them sensuous females modelled by Marcel Bouraine; they were of *pâte-de-cristal*, which had a greater lead content and was heavier and more highly polished than *pâte-de-verre*.

Argy-Rousseau's wares were sold both at home and abroad, and proved to be hugely popular in the 1920s, with their varied, often modern motifs and subtle attractive gradations of colour. The factory closed in 1931 due to the Depression, but Argy-Rousseau continued to work on his own, making religious plaques as well as boldly geometric, faceted vases throughout the 1930s.

Décorchement, first a painter and ceramist, turned to *pâte-de-verre* early in the century. He experimented for some years, his initial thin-walled, Art Nouveau-style vessels giving way in the early 1910s to bolder, thicker pieces decorated with relief masks and simpler organic and animal motifs. After the war, his *pâte-de-verre* and *pâte-de-cristal* vases and bowls, which were exhibited the world over, became even heavier and simpler, as well as larger; their decorations were both classical and contemporary, and their colours were deep, rich and jewel-like, often with inner bubbles and streaks. Geometric forms and motifs characterized most of Décorchement's work in the late 1920s, though in the 1930s he turned much of his attention to stained glass, including windows for the church of Ste-Odile in Paris.

*PÂTE-DE-VERRE
VASE, HENRI
CROS, LATE
19TH CENTURY*
(H23cm/9¼in)

*Neoclassical figures are
portrayed on this vase,
whose paste-glass
technique Cros revived
in the 1880s. Cros also
made pâte-de-verre
masks, plaques and
figures, and the method
was used by other
French glass-makers
into the Art Deco
period.* (ABOVE)

**BOOKENDS AND
COVERED DISH,
AMALRIC
WALTER, 1920s**
(Bookends:
H17cm/6¾in)

*Animals often decorate
the pâte-de-verre
pieces created by
Walter. The stylized
fish bookends were
modelled by André
Houillon, the
honeycomb and bee
dish by Henri Bergé*
(ABOVE RIGHT)

**VASE, FRANÇOIS-EMILE
DÉCORCHEMENT, 1925** (H24cm/9½in)

*Décorchement's thick-walled pâte-de-verre vessels
were largely bold, simple pieces with Neoclassical or
moderne touches. This vase features scrolled
handles and has a mottled appearance resembling
that of marble.* (ABOVE)

**LIZARD VASE, GABRIEL ARGY-
ROUSSEAU,** *c.*1920 (H28.6cm/11¼in)

*This dramatic sculpture is of pâte-de-cristal, whose
lead content is higher than pâte-de-verre (it is also
heavier and more highly polished). The vessel's
geometric faceting and triangles are in stark contrast
to the lifelike reptile.* (LEFT)

MAURICE MARINOT

The leading maker of French Art Deco studio glass was Maurice Marinot (1882–1960). Born in Troyes, he studied painting at the Ecole des Beaux-Arts in Paris, returning in 1905 to Troyes, where he remained most of his life. Marinot, a Fauve painter, displayed canvases in the Salon d'Automne and Salon des Indépendants until 1913. But it was a visit to the small Bar-sur-Seine glassworks of his friends, the brothers Gabriel and Eugène Viard, in 1911 which changed his life. There and then he became enamoured with the medium of glass.

At first Marinot designed clear-glass vessels which were then blown by a gaffer, leaving Marinot to decorate them with figurative, floral and other motifs in enamels. Eventually he taught himself to blow glass so that he could manipulate the basic chemical mixture of silica and potash or soda in its malleable, molten state, then transform it into a pure, solid object ready for decoration. Marinot's enamelled-glass vessels were painted with female heads and nudes, birds, flowers, fruits and other decorative motifs, arranged in bands or swags or featured singly in medallions, and rendered in bright, opaque hues.

Upon his return to work in 1919, after war service in the medical corps, Marinot continued to create and then decorate glass, but more and more he was drawn to the medium *per se*, pure and unpainted, and his later work shows this shift in interest to decoration inherent within the substance itself. From the 1920s until the beginning of the Second World War, Marinot produced single-handedly some 2500 glass vessels: bowls, vases, flacons and stoppered bottles. From about 1923 his pieces were void of exterior enamelled motifs and unabashedly featured interior decoration, such as chemically induced metallic and coloured streaks, veins and trails, rich crackled effects and masses of trapped air bubbles.

Though relatively small in scale, generally well under 30 cm (12 in) tall or wide, these pieces took on a monumentality with their thick, heavy walls and bold but pure

shapes. The forms generally comprised one of two types, either sleek and smooth, whether globular, ovoid or squared-off, or partially grainy and acid-engraved, perhaps with a ribbon band or encircling geometric design. The stoppers on jars and bottles usually ended in small, clear-glass orbs, though some featured the same coloured internal decoration as the vessel itself. From 1927 Marinot created pieces with an organic, at times asymmetrical, quality, though he still produced well-formed, rounded pieces. Unfortunately, a great deal of Marinot's work was destroyed in 1944 during the liberation of Troyes, and thereafter he concentrated on painting.

THURET, NAVARRE AND OTHERS

Following in Marinot's footsteps were André Thuret (1898–1965), an engineer whose vessels were both free-blown and blown into asymmetrically shaped moulds, as well as formed directly at the kiln, and

VASE, MAURICE MARINOT, 1918–20
(H44.25cm/17¾in)

The clear body of this vase is internally strewn with bubbles and streaks, and it is vividly painted with three dancers. By the mid-1920s Marinot abandoned enamelling altogether, concentrating on various types of internal decoration. (LEFT)

DESIGN FOR GLASS, MAURICE MARINOT, 1928

The drawing shows a variety of flacons of strong, simple form, their stoppers tiny orbs and their intended interior decoration taking on a shape often contrasted to that of the bottle itself. (BELOW)

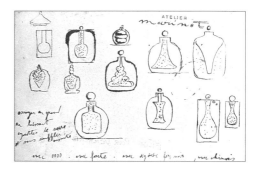

BOTTLE WITH STOPPER, MAURICE MARINOT, c.1925 (H12cm/4¾in)

The red and yellow intercalary decoration captured within this handsome Marinot flacon and stopper is complemented by the bottle's faceted, irregular surface, which suggests a geological specimen. (ABOVE)

sculptor Henri Navarre (1885–1971), whose moulded sculptures and vessels were known for their internal decoration, generally achieved by applying powdered metallic oxides to the parison on the marver before applying a layer of clear glass. This decoration, literally sandwiched between two layers of glass, is called intercalary, and it was also employed by other Art Deco glassmakers, among them the brothers Ernest and Charles Schneider, whose Epinay-sur-Seine glassworks produced acid-etched, internally decorated art glass, as well as cameo, carved, layered, applied and other glass appealing to a wide-ranging clientele.

ENAMELLED GLASS

Enamelled glass, such as Marinot created early in his career, was also produced by Marcel Goupy (1886–1954), long employed by Maison Rouard in Paris. He used stylized floral motifs on the inner and outer surfaces of his clear-glass carafes, bottles and goblets, whereas his one-off vases and bowls, some in pale, cloudy hues, featured classical figures (such as archers or nymphs), fashionable 1920s ladies, deer, floral garlands, even verdant Cubist landscapes.

Some of Goupy's designs were executed by Auguste Heiligenstein (1891–1976), who joined Maison Rouard in 1919. He left that firm in 1923, after which time he designed ceramics and glass commercially, as well as for private clients. His finest *objets* are distinctively enamelled, often with mythological scenes centred within medallions or frames, the rest of the vase, bowl or box painted and often gilded with floral, geometric, wave or other rich patterning. He also designed thick-walled vessels, often internally decorated and acid-etched, for the Legras Pantin glassworks in the 1930s.

DAUM AND OTHER FACTORIES

Of the firms founded in the Art Nouveau period which still made glass after the Second World War, Daum of Nancy was the most successful. Gallé's production largely reflected the firm's earlier nature-

inspired, *fin-de-siècle* glory. Exceptions include superb Art Deco cameo-glass creations such as an Egyptian-style vase of *c.*1920, with stylized acid-etched lotus leaves and applied-glass scarabs; an early 1920s vase catering to the popular taste for African exoticism, with a bas-relief frieze of elephants under palm trees and clouds; and a *c.*1925 turquoise vase overlaid in white and acid-etched with polar bears.

The Nancy glassworks of the brothers Daum thrived in the Art Deco period under the inspired guidance of Auguste Daum's son, Paul (1888–1944). Paul changed the company's artistic tack, concentrating on single-colour thick-walled vessels, acid-etched or wheel-carved, some with trapped air bubbles, mottling or metal-foil inserts. Collaborations with metalworkers, among them Edgar Brandt, resulted in wrought-iron and bronze-mounted *objets-d'art*, whose glass was often blown into openwork metal armatures featuring scrolls, stylized leaves and other Art Deco motifs.

The finest Daum pieces of the period are those lamps, bowls and vases which feature allover acid-etched or wheel-cut motifs on monochromatic grounds, the latter ranging from the subtlest icy white, butterscotch yellow and candy-floss pink to the most vibrant emerald green, turquoise and royal blue. Their subjects might be bold stylized blossoms, simply rendered birds on branches or in flight over waves, starkly silhouetted deer or gazelles in landscapes, lush palm fronds or a variety of Art Deco geometric or abstract configurations. The surfaces could be sleek and shiny, mottled and frosted, or a combination of both. There were also those vessels which in part harked back to Art Nouveau with their applied floral and fruit motifs; yet more often than not these were undeniably *moderne* in both the stylization and application of the decoration, either in bands or pendent along the necks and down the sides of a simply shaped vase or bowl.

Established French glass firms followed the Art Deco movement, including Baccarat. Among its Art Deco-style output during the long (1916–70) artistic leadership of Georges Chevalier were liqueur services (decanters and glasses), dressing-table sets and perfume bottles cut in and/or enamelled with bold geometric shapes. There were also clocks, centrepieces and lamps, some with stylized floral and swag patterns.

Jean Luce (1895–1964), a ceramics and glass designer, created glass of a decidedly Cubist bent. Around 1925 he abandoned enamelled surfaces and turned to bold geometric, or even simple horizontally lined, patterns etched and engraved on monumental vases. Occasionally he would contrast rough, sandblasted sections on a vessel with segments of smooth, mirrored glass.

LALIQUE'S MASS-PRODUCED GLASS

A significant French Art Deco glass-maker whose roots in the medium did not hark back to the Art Nouveau period was René Jules Lalique (1860–1945). His *fin-de-siècle* fame was founded on his genius as a goldsmith but his interest in glass began early in the twentieth century. His first creations were not mass-produced but one-off pieces of *cire-perdue* glass.

The mass production of Lalique glass began in earnest in the early 1910s, with the collaboration between Lalique and François Coty, the former at first designing but

before long also producing bottles for the latter's scents. The fragrance industry was transformed by this joint effort: previously perfume had been sold in unattractive pharmaceutical vials and transferred to a cutglass or other fancy flacon by the owner. From this time on, until his death in 1945, Lalique devoted his life to the production of high-quality, mass-produced, reasonably priced glass, with occasional one-off, limited-edition, large-scale and/or exhibition pieces (including fountains for the 1925 and 1937 Paris expositions).

There were over 300 scent-bottle designs, both for perfume companies and, sold empty, retail purposes, as well as atomizers and powder boxes. Other wares included vases, bowls, platters, centrepieces and other mostly decorative *objets*; table and wall lamps, chandeliers and other lighting devices; animal, bird and human figures, some used as bookends, automobile mascots and paperweights; jewellery; useful items, such as inkwells, seals, ashtrays, blotters,

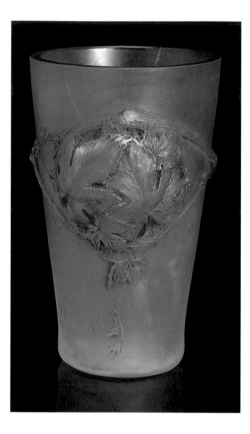

CIRE-PERDUE VASE, RENÉ LALIQUE, 1913 (H21.5cm/8½in)

The two relief bosses of ivy leaves joined by stems give this simply shaped cire-perdue *vase a strong sculptural quality.* (ABOVE)

12 FIGURINES AND *COQS ET RAISINS* VASES, RENÉ LALIQUE, 1920s (Taller: H29.5cm/11¾in)

Many of Lalique's mass-produced pieces feature Neoclassical themes, like the vase at left, moulded with nudes; it was designed in 1920, and the vase at right in 1928. (LEFT)

DOUBLE SUZANNE, MARIUS-ERNEST SABINO, 1930s (H27cm/10¾in)

Sabino produced two opalescent-glass lamps on the biblical theme of Suzanne. These two nudes stand on a bronze base pierced with peacocks. (BELOW)

TOURBILLONS VASE, RENÉ LALIQUE, 1926 (H20cm/8in)

One of Lalique's most dramatic Art Deco vases, Tourbillons (Whirlwinds) was available in solid colours, such as turquoise and amber, as well as this black-enamelled version. (RIGHT)

BACCHANTES VASE, RENÉ LALIQUE, 1927 (H25cm/10in)

A crowded frieze of classical figures in various abandoned poses forms this highly sculptural, monumental vase. (ABOVE)

picture frames, mirrors and clocks; and of course tableware, including goblets, tumblers, trays, pitchers, carafes, candlesticks, and menu and place-card holders.

Lalique's repertoire of motifs, used on objects as small as pendants and as huge as doors, ranged from vestigial Art Nouveau patterns, such as ribbon-tendrilled gourds and curved-tail mermaids, to Neoclassical subjects and Art Deco motifs in the geometric and stylized-blossom modes, as well as serpents, deer and gazelles.

The methods of manufacture and decoration tested, perfected and then used commercially by Lalique were as varied as the objects created. Glass was blown into a mould (resulting in, for example, the big round vases) or simply press-moulded. Internal colours were clear or monochromatic, though some cased vases sandwiched a white layer between two layers of another colour, resulting in rich, luxuriant greens, blues or reds. Many of the large, important vases came in vivid hues, including turquoise, jade green, scarlet and purple.

OPALESCENT GLASS BY LALIQUE AND OTHERS

Lalique's opalescent glass, whose complicated chemical formula was a closely guarded secret, was extremely popular (at one time comprising some 90 per cent of his output). Its milky-white 'pearliness' took on blue or yellow sheens, depending on how it caught the light. Some pieces were also available in opalescent yellow.

Following Lalique's success with this glass, other European factories began making opalescent (variously called opaline or opalique) pieces. These decorative pieces were either subtly inspired by or blatantly (and invariably poorly) copied from the French master. Most successful in his efforts, however, was the Sicilian-born Parisian Marius-Ernest Sabino (1878–1961).

Some of his vast output was too close to that of Lalique for comfort, several vases with shells and swallows, for instance, and two *Suzanne au bain* statuettes. Other pieces, like the vase *La Ronde*, with four modish nude dancers, held their own. In contrast to Lalique's Neoclassical women, Sabino's subjects were often models of the period, with slim, androgynous shapes, helmet haircuts and high-arched, pencil-thin eyebrows. Edmond Etling, Verlys, Pierre d'Avesn (who worked for Lalique for over ten years) and future film-maker André Hunebelle also produced opalescent glass.

STAINED GLASS

Jacques Gruber and Gaëtan Jeannin were the leading makers of stained and leaded glass in Art Deco France. Stylized floral motifs, geometric patterns, modishly dressed figures and painterly, often Cubist and/or streamlined, images were among the subjects they depicted.

BRITAIN

James A. Jobling & Co. in Sunderland, which produced decorative coloured and opalescent pressed glass (as well as Pyrex), was a large glassworks in inter-war Britain. In the main its 'art glassware', though at times exhibiting a *moderne* flair with geometric and stylized-floral designs, was safely traditional or baldly imitative of popular Continental models.

Moncrieff Glassworks of Perth, Scotland, made internally decorated vessels, called Monart glass, in the 1920s and 1930s, under the direction of Mrs Moncrieff and Barcelona-born glass-maker Salvador Ysart. Monart glass sold well in both Britain and the United States.

New Zealand-born architect who designed both ceramics and glass in the Art Deco period. He created a variety of handsome, utilitarian glassware, both clear and coloured, plain and engraved, cut and moulded, before the Second World War (after which he went back to architecture).

A characteristic Murray design in glass or ceramics comprised parallel horizontal grooves; such architectonic fluting was used for vases, decanters and other tableware, as well as for a limited quantity of mid-1930s flacons and powder boxes with ivory stoppers and lids. His rectangular crystal decanter, wheel-carved with a solitary cactus, is boldly Modernist, wholly original and somewhat akin to Viennese and Scandinavian glass, which Murray had seen at the 1925 Paris Exposition.

BACCARAT CLOCK, 1925 (H16.3cm/6½in)

Under Georges Chevalier's direction, Baccarat produced glass in the Art Deco vein. The case of this pendulette, created by Chevalier for the 1925 Paris Exposition, is moulded with stylized blossoms flowing from two cornucopias. (ABOVE)

MONART VASE, 1920s (H33.6cm/13¼in)

Moncrieff Glassworks in Perth, Scotland, made Monart vases from the 1920s to c.1950. They were characterized by their internal decoration, in this example iridescent coloured veins spreading over this vase's pale green body. (RIGHT)

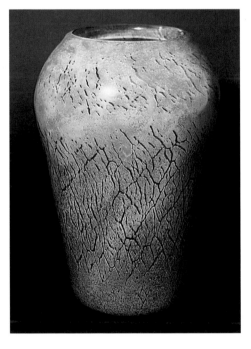

In the 1930s Stevens & Williams, at Brierley Hill near Stourbridge, England, included a great deal of simple but refined, often engraved, lead-crystal and cut-glass tableware in its output. The man most closely associated with this company was not a technical-oriented glass-maker but a designer: Keith Day Murray (1892-1981), a

ADVERTISEMENT FOR KEITH MURRAY GLASS, 1933

Murray designed glass for both James Powell & Sons and Stevens & Williams. His creations usually comprised simple engraved motifs on plain but elegant forms. (ABOVE)

SCANDINAVIA

Much Swedish glass produced during the interwar years was admired and imitated the world over. Orrefors Glasbruk, founded in 1898 and thriving today, began by producing window glass, ink bottles and other simple, useful wares. However, its decorative art glass, whose production Johan Ekman pursued vigorously after buying the firm in 1913, turned Orrefors into a highly productive, innovative glassworks. This art glass, created largely under the direction of painters Simon Gate (1883–1945) and Edvard Hald (1883 1980), who joined the firm as designers in 1916 and 1917 respectively, included vases, bowls, dishes and other pieces of great craftsmanship.

In addition to highly creative artists, Orrefors employed talented master craftsmen, like glass-blower Knut Bergqvist, who was instrumental in the development of 'Graal' glass, a type of glass with internal decoration, cased in clear glass. Graal glass, designed by Hald, Gate, Vicke Lindstrand (1904 83) and others, came in various colours and designs and, unlike the sharply defined motifs on the engraved pieces, its decoration was subtle and muted, almost mysteriously contained within the medium.

Several other Swedish factories produced fine glass, including the Kosta Boda, Eda and Elme glassworks. At Kosta Boda – Sweden's oldest surviving glass-maker, set up in the 1740s – Edvin Ollers, Ewald Dahlskog and Elis Bergh were the principal designers. Their creations comprised both blown, undecorated, useful wares, often pale-coloured, and more ambitious pieces engraved with *moderne* and Neoclassical motifs, both geometric and figurative.

Finland's Riihimäki and combined Karhula–Iittala factories produced significant Modernist glassware, including the former's 'Bubuki' line of rectilinear moulded vessels and Karhula's undulating, proto-biomorphic 'Savoy' glass, originally designed for the eponymous Helsinki hotel by architect Alvar Aalto in 1936 (and still produced

ORREFORS FIREWORKS BOWL, EDVARD HALD, DESIGNED 1921 (H20.3cm/8in, D27.6cm/11in)

Hald was associated with the Swedish firm Orrefors for over 50 years. The fairground-with-fireworks theme of this vase, one of which was featured at the 1925 Paris Exposition, is executed with a painterly verve (the vase shown was engraved by Karl Rössler in 1930). (LEFT)

ORREFORS VASE, VICKE LINDSTRAND, 1930 (H14.1cm/5½in)

Called Think No Evil, Hear No Evil, See No Evil, *this vase is etched and painted with three female nudes amid stylized blossoms.* (ABOVE)

ORREFORS DECANTER AND GLASS, SIMON GATE, DESIGNED 1922 (Decanter: H38.2cm/15¼in)

The decanter's stopper and the goblet's stem are the only decoration on these vessels, parts of two classic Orrefors ranges in production until 1965. (LEFT)

'BÖLGEBLICK'
GLASS, AINO
MARSIO–AALTO,
1932

*This range of pressed
glass, designed in 1932
by the architect wife of
Alvar Aalto, was
made until 1956 by
Karhula. Recently
some pieces have been
produced again.* (LEFT)

LEERDAM VASE,
CHRIS LEBEAU,
1923

(H23.5cm/9¼in)

*With its elegant
internal decoration, this
thin-walled, blown-
glass vase is a fine
example of art glass
made by the Royal
Dutch Glass Works in
Leerdam.* (BELOW)

today). In 1932 architect Aino Marsio–Aalto (1894–1949), Alvar's wife, created the widely praised 'Bölgeblick' range of functionalist pressed glass for Karhula: these bowls, plates, pitchers, tumblers, creamers and sugar bowls in both pale and bold hues are characterized by overall moulded ribbing, most strikingly on the upright conical, horizontally ribbed pieces.

The Hadeland Glasverk in Norway, founded in 1762, produced both elegant engraved tableware and later, in the 1930s, thick-walled architectonic pieces, partly inspired by the Bauhaus. Many important Hadeland pieces were designed by its art director, Sverre Pettersen, who introduced sandblasted decoration to the factory; the sculptor Ståle Kyllingstad also contributed significant monumental forms. In Denmark, architect Jacob E. Bang designed Swedish-*moderne*-style engraved and etched vessels and tableware for Copenhagen's Holmegaard Glasvaerk from 1925 to 1942.

BELGIUM AND THE NETHERLANDS

Functionalism was the key word in glass design in Belgium and the Netherlands during the interwar years, although decorative art glass was also a significant production.

The Royal Dutch Glass Works in Leerdam made use of the talents of several Dutch architects and designers, among them H.P. Berlage, Karel P. C. de Bazel and Cornelis de Lorm. A wide variety of elegant mass-produced tableware emerged from *c.*1916, and in the early 1920s the firm opened its Unica Studio, devoted to the design of one-offs ('Unica') and limited editions ('Serica') of modern glass; among its designers were Chris Lebeau and Andries D. Copier.

Unica and Serica pieces could be delicate or heavy; enamelled on the outside or

internally decorated; clear crystal or coloured; smooth or faceted. Copier's designs ranged from simple, thin-walled ribbed vases to perfect glass orbs to thick-walled, bubble- and streak-decorated vessels.

At the 1925 Paris Exposition, Cristalleries du Val St-Lambert, the Belgian glassworks, unveiled art glass called 'Arts Décoratifs de Paris'. Designed by Léon Ledru and Joseph Simon, the line included cased-glass coloured vessels, either intaglio-cut or acid-etched, and pieces with applied-glass decoration or alternating smooth and matt segments; all bore strong overall geometric patterns. Also at Val St-Lambert, master engraver Charles Graffart achieved renown for producing vessels with Neoclassical-*moderne* figures in Art Deco surrounds. Later, in the 1930s, Lalique-inspired moulded opalescent and coloured glass in the Luxval 'series' was produced.

pieces by Wagenfeld and others, and ornate art glass. Karl Wiedman created several lines of thin-walled, iridescent glass. From 1926 internally decorated 'Ikora' vessels were made, and in the mid-1930s Wiedman introduced opaque 'Lavaluna' glass, with external whorled motifs and crystalline touches. WMF also made clear glass with engraved motifs, cased coloured glass, and mould- and free-blown vessels.

BOWL, JOSEF HOFFMANN, *c.*1915
(H12.2cm/4¾in)

Several Wiener Werkstätte members designed glass vessels, most of which were made in Bohemian factories. Despite its relatively small size, this thick-walled, cut-glass bowl of deep violet glass appears quite monumental. (BELOW)

'KUBUS' CONTAINERS, WILHELM WAGENFELD, 1938

Bauhaus designer Wagenfeld designed this eminently practical, stackable range of modular pressed-glass containers for the Vereinigte Lausitzer Glaswerke. The pieces fit together to form a cube. (RIGHT)

GERMANY

The Bauhaus contribution to glassware was eminently simple, functional and clear-cut. Wilhelm Wagenfeld (b. 1900), a teacher, metalworker and industrial designer, created a variety of glass from the early 1930s onward. There were elegantly rounded drinking glasses, as well as the 'Kubus' range of starkly rectilinear, easily stackable storage containers. There was also the vaguely zoomorphic Pelikan ink bottle of 1938. His tea service (1930–4) for Jenaer Glaswerke, Mainz, was easy to handle, pleasing to look at and heat-resistant, combining beauty with utility. Most of his 1930s glass was produced by Jenaer or the Vereinigte Lausitzer Glaswerke in Weisswasser.

WMF (Württembergische Metallwarenfabrik) had begun to make glass in the 1880s. Its range spanned utilitarian clear-glass

AUSTRIA AND CZECHOSLOVAKIA

Around the turn of the century in Austria, glass-makers, both in established factories and in newly founded studios, were thriving, creating both iridescent, curvilinear Art Nouveau glass and a great deal of glass in novel, exciting styles that forsook the historicism and decoration of the mid nineteenth century and looked to the future. In fact, much Austrian *fin-de-siècle* glass, notably that connected to the Wiener Werkstätte (the Viennese Workshops founded in 1903 by Secession members Josef Hoffmann and Koloman Moser), was so geometric, stylized and/or proto-*moderne* that it could easily be mistaken for later glass and, indeed, such thoroughly modern glass continued to be produced for several decades.

Among the older firms embracing the new taste was J. & L. Lobmeyr of Vienna, which in 1918 included a Bohemian branch, J. & L. Lobmeyr Neffe Stefan Rath. Josef Hoffmann (1870–1955) was named Lobmeyr's artistic director in 1910, and its other designers during this fertile period included Adolf Loos, Michael Powolny, Dagobert Peche, Otto Prutscher and others connected to the Wiener Werkstätte. There were also non-Werkstätte designers and engravers – Marianne Rath, Ena Rottenberg and the Czech Jaroslav Horejc among them – who created impressive, heavy-walled pieces engraved with mythological, biblical and other figures. Lotte Fink's enamelled-glass vessels were decorated with similar subjects in densely rendered images more akin to the glaze on pottery.

Josef Hoffmann was responsible for developing *bronzit* glass for Lobmeyr: its clear- or coloured-glass vessels were painted in black or dark grey (often highlighted with

ETCHED AND ENAMELLED CZECHOSLO-VAKIAN VASES, 1925–30 (Tallest: H16.4cm/6½in)

The abstract motifs on these vases relate to styles of 1920s Paris and Vienna. They were made at the Specialized School of Glass-making at Kamenický Šenov. The vases at left and centre came from the studio of A. Dorn and P. Eiselt.

gold) with ornate repeating patterns – geometric, stylized-floral and the like – usually provided by another designer.

E. Bakalowits & Söhne was another Viennese factory producing Wiener Werkstätte glass. The black-and-white 'Zebraware' of Koloman Moser (1868–1918) originated in *c.*1903 in the medium of glass, although bold Wiener Werkstätte ceramics in black and white are better known.

From 1915 the Wiener Werkstätte bought blanks, usually of blown glass, from mostly Bohemian sources, which were then decorated by hand in their studios. The resulting pieces, painted by Hoffmann, Mathilde Flögl, Hilda Jesser, Dagobert Peche, Vally Wieselthier et al., were covered in rainbow-hued, simply rendered motifs of leaves, flowers, clouds, stars, animals and other objects. The Werkstätte began cutting their own glass in 1919.

The republic of Czechoslovakia, formed in 1918, included the former kingdom of Bohemia, long a glass centre. Members of Prague's Artěl group, set up in 1908 and devoted to simple, functional design, often Cubist-inspired, created useful and decorative glassware, but on a small scale and for a select group. Jaroslav Horejc, as well as Josef Rosipal and other architects, designed Artěl

glass, some of it made by the Dobronín Glassworks, like Rosipal's architectonic *c.*1910 vase of clear, cut glass overlaid with small diamonds and large zigzags in blue.

Two specialized schools of glass-making, at Nový Bor and Kamenický Šenov, made handsome Art Deco pieces. From the studio of A. Dorn and P. Eiselt at Kamenický Šenov, for example, came vases with two or three different types of surface finishes, etched and enamelled with colourful geometric and abstract motifs.

ITALY

Italian glass-making between the wars was concentrated, as in the distant past, on the island of Murano. From the mid-1910s and throughout the 1930s, a plethora of *objets-d'art*, some wholly original, others partly based on earlier pieces, emerged from Italian studios and factories. Many glassworks during this period came and went, their names often changing and their design personnel moving from one firm to another, but their combined repertoire of techniques was ever improving and growing, as was their cumulative international reputation.

The most significant names in glass-making were Paolo Venini (1895–1959) and Ercole Barovier (1889–1974), who came from families with long histories in glass production and who employed innovative methods and talented designers in their factories. The Murano glassworks of Venini & C. and Ferro Toso–Barovier & C. (later Barovier & Toso) produced glass during the interwar period which manifested a distinct form of bold Italian Modernism, although both strove to revive traditional techniques, maintain high standards of production and introduce new glass types.

When, in 1921, Paolo Venini, a Milan lawyer, and Giacomo Cappellin (1887–1968) pooled finances to buy a glass factory, they shared a love of glass and a dissatisfaction with the overdecorated pieces being made in Murano. Aiming to make simple yet classical glassware, they named Vittorio Zecchin (1878-1947) art and technical director; his pure, elegant colourless or pale-hued decorative and useful ware (including chandeliers) was much admired in Italy as well as at the 1925 Paris Exposition.

After breaking with Cappellin in 1925, Venini brought Francesco Zecchin and sculptor Napoleone Martinuzzi (1892-1977) into his new company, which from the start experimented widely with established and novel glass-making and decorating methods. In the 1920s and 1930s, besides making traditional millefiori and filigree glass, Venini created *vetro battute* ('beaten glass', whose surface has small indentations, like those on hammered metal), *vetro corroso* (with a crackled appearance produced by applying hydrofluoric acid to a resin-covered surface), *vetro pulegoso* (a bubbled glass whose air bubbles often extended to the surface of a piece, giving it a blistered, pockmarked look), *vetro sommerso* ('submerged glass', a type of coloured cased glass) and *vetro tessuto* (with vertical threads of white or coloured glass on its surface).

In 1928 Martinuzzi introduced the 'Novecento' style; early examples were largely opaque and undecorated vessels, possessing a post-Deco sobriety and severity, but later pieces had subtle and at times irregular surface decoration, such as bubbles, gold leaf, iridescence and interior 'veils' of colour (*bullicante*). Architect Carlo Scarpa (1906–78) took over Venini's art direction in 1932, and until the 1940s he provided the firm with strong Novecento designs.

In the 1930s architect Tomasso Buzzi worked for Venini, introducing, among other things, free-form, more fluid vessels and surfaces of *lattimo* glass speckled with gold leaf, the latter often adorning monumental amphora-type vases. Such vases and other classically shaped vessels of *vetro pulegoso* were Martinuzzi's trademark, and he applied a variety of distinctive, ornate handles to their sides: from ribbons of loops, reaching from neck to bottom, to serpentine shapes, like errant toothpaste.

Rossi e neri (red and black) was a distinct Novecento-style glass made by Venini, the Zecchin Martinuzzi glassworks and others. These dramatic vases, generally spherical and baluster- or amphora-shaped, comprised black bodies highlighted with red, either as blobs of scarlet applied overall, as tendril-handles or as outlines on the rims, stems and bases. Silver-leaf inclusions often appeared, and the globular models especially recalled the lacquered-metal vessels created in 1920s Paris by Jean Dunand.

Second only to Venini in reputation was Barovier. In 1919, when Ercole, his brother Nicolò and their cousin Napoleone joined the family firm, its output changed, with both *murrine*-decorated and monumental opaque, blown-glass vessels in the Art Deco vein being produced. Chief designer Ercole introduced new types of glass, including Marinot-inspired vessels coloured by means of heat but without fusion and in *c*.1927 'Primavera' glass, thin-walled and elegant,

VASES AND BOTTLE, MURANO, *c*.1930
(Tallest: H30cm/12in)

The vases are by Venini, the amethyst bottle is by M.V.M. Cappellin. (TOP)

VASES, MURANO, *c*. 1925–30
(Tallest: H30.5cm/12¼in)

The rossi e neri *vase at left is by Napoleone Martinuzzi for Venini, the millefiori vase is by Fratelli Toso and the green example is attributed to M.V.M. Cappellin.* (ABOVE)

with an opaque surface that looked like cracked ice and was often complemented by handles, rims and feet of a contrasting solid hue. There were also glass figures such as a *c.*1930 puffed-up pigeon in white glass with gold-leaf highlights and black eyes and beak. Designed by Ercole Barovier, the bird resembled the stylized bird sculptures by Jan and Joël Martel of Paris. In the 1930s Barovier glass tended to be of the heavy, thick-walled variety, often with coloured applications, and during this period Ercole Barovier continued working with glass coloured by heat without fusion.

UNITED STATES

Throughout the 1920s iridescent, curvilinear and nature-inspired Art Nouveau-style glass continued to be made, though its popularity had waned and many makers were forced to close down. Surprisingly little outstanding, original art glass of the types made in France, Scandinavia and Italy came out of the United States, despite the fact that several major exhibitions of European glass occurred there after the 1925 Paris Exposition. There was, however, handsome tableware with Jazz Age appeal.

Arguably the most popular type of glass was mass-produced, moulded 'Depression' glass, a recently coined term applied to a huge variety of useful and fancy, traditional and Modernist wares which were cheap, cheerful and commercial. Depression glass was generally translucent and coloured, but clear and opaque varieties were also available. Makers included Anchor Hocking, Diamond, Federal, Hazel Atlas, A. H. Heisey, Indiana and Jeannette. Three handsome patterns were Indiana Glass's Number 610 line (1926–32), also known as 'Pyramid' because of its zigzag motif, the same firm's Cubist-inspired 'Tea Room' line (1926–31) and Anchor Hocking's elegant, concentric-ringed 'Manhattan' pattern (1938–41), similar to Aino Marsio–Aalto's 'Bölgeblick' range of 1932.

'CINTRA' VASE, STEUBEN GLASS, 1920s (H17.8cm/7in)

Colourless glass has been rolled in pink and blue, cased in colourless glass and then cut to create this stunning example of 'Cintra' glass, developed by Frederick Carder. Note the glass-orb feet, a touch akin to Marinot's globe stoppers.

The terms 'Carnival' and 'Depression' glass are often used interchangeably, but the former is more correctly applied to those inexpensively produced *c.*1900–25 pressed, iridescent vases, bowls and platters often given as funfair prizes. Such glass, much of it by Imperial Glass in Ohio and Fenton Art Glass in West Virginia, largely harked back to the Victorian style. The iridescence was sprayed on and heated to fix it.

The Steuben Glass Works of Corning, New York, which became a division of Corning Glass in 1918, was arguably the most important American maker of decorative and table glass at the time. Designer, marketing man and technical adviser Frederick Carder (1863–1963) had appealed to Art Nouveau taste in the early years of the century, and in the 1920s he created glass that proved attractive to those drawn to Paris's *le style 1925*. Examples include a frosted-glass, Chinese lotus bowl, acid-etched with a stylized chrysanthemum; cased alabaster- and rose-glass jars and vases featuring *moderne* blossoms; and an array of

thick-walled, clear-glass or single-coloured vessels, some of cased cut crystal, with internal bubbles (including the 'Cintra' and 'Cluthra' lines). Carder also introduced 'Silverine' glass, embellished with chips of mica stone, and the 'Intarsia' line, similar to Orrefors' Graal glass. Apparently Carder disliked the Art Deco style, so it is not surprising that through the 1920s Steuben still made the iridescent Art Nouveau-style glass he favoured, for which there was still a market, albeit a limited one.

From the early 1930s Steuben began to produce clear, often engraved and etched glass with an appeal that was chic and contemporary. In 1932 industrial designer Walter Dorwin Teague (1883–1960) was hired to create tableware for Steuben: his mostly geometric designs for the engraved and etched 'Empire', 'Riviera', 'St Tropez' and 'Spiral' patterns were simple but elegant, modern yet classic (he also designed Streamline Moderne radios for Sparton, with peach- and blue-glass fronts).

In the mid-1930s sculptor Sidney Biehler Waugh (1904–63) designed outstanding monumental pieces for Steuben in crystal, including Gazelle Bowl, Mariner's Bowl, Zodiac Bowl and Europa Bowl, most engraved by Hungarian-born Joseph Libisch with stylized Art Deco subjects drawn from the French and Swedish design repertoires. After the 1937 Paris Exposition, the company commissioned famous artists and sculptors, including Salvador Dali, Aristide Maillol, Henri Matisse, Eric Gill and Georgia O'Keeffe, to design motifs (and in a few instances, shapes) for limited-edition, engraved Steuben crystal.

A. Douglas Nash worked for Tiffany Glass until 1928, when he bought out the Art Nouveau master's firm to start up his eponymous corporation, which lasted only until 1931, a victim of the Depression. His best-known creation was 'Chintz' glass, which comprised an alternating pattern of wide and narrow ribbed stripes of different hues. From 1932 to 1935, Nash worked for Libbey Glass in Toledo, Ohio, designing etched and engraved glass, as well as a short-lived range of cut and engraved luxury

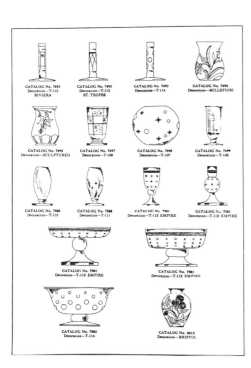

DESIGNS FOR
STEUBEN GLASS,
WALTER
DORWIN
TEAGUE, 1932

*This catalogue page
shows the industrial
designer's preference for
geometric motifs (the
floral patterns are not
his).* (FAR LEFT)

'BLUEBIRD'
RADIO, WALTER
DORWIN
TEAGUE, 1937–
40 (H115cm/45½in)

*Teague designed this
and other radio cases
with geometric
coloured-glass fronts for
Sparton of Jackson,
Michigan.* (LEFT)

pieces: the 'Libbey–Nash Series' of stemware (over eighty patterns in four colours) and of clear- and coloured-glass limited-edition ornaments. A unique Libbey–Nash cocktail glass of c.1933, called 'Syncopation', featured an off-kilter glass-cube stem on a low, pyramid foot.

Fostoria Glass of Moundsville, West Virginia, maker of relatively affordable glass, employed talented outside designers to create new products in the modern vein, including in the 1920s George Sakier, a New York interior designer. Among his designs for the firm, in what he called the 'classic modern' mode, was an elegant cylindrical, fluted vase, which came in three sizes and a variety of evocatively named hues, including amber, ebony, topaz and wisteria.

The most unusual, even futuristic, glass made in the United States at this time was the 1928 'Ruba Rombic' pattern of the Consolidated Lamp & Glass Company of Coraopolis, Pennsylvania. The oddly shaped, multi-angular, asymmetrical tableware in amber, grey, green and lavender was

unlike anything that had come before. Consolidated also made conventional or boldly imitative glass, as did Phoenix Glass in Monaca, Pennsylvania. Both firms marketed bowls and vases which blatantly copied Lalique designs.

Standing alone among American glassmakers in the 1920s and 1930s was the pioneering studio-glass artist Maurice Heaton (b. 1900). In the late 1920s he displayed the results of a long apprenticeship: sheets of bubbled glass decorated with white and coloured spirals, circles, triangles and other patterns of enamel glaze, the effects achieved by turning glass on a kind of potter's wheel.

Heaton was drawn to the Bauhaus philosophy that useful, everyday objects could be well-designed and pleasing to look at. He adhered to this maxim as much as he could, notably in his designs for multiple objects, mostly lighting fixtures, including shades for floor lamps with shiny steel bases (made for the American Designers' Gallery co-operative in 1928) and lamp shades in the 1930s for the Lightolier firm.

'RUBA ROMBIC' CANDLESTICK,
c.1928–33 (H6.6cm/2½in, D12.3cm/5in)

Consolidated Lamp & Glass produced 'Ruba Rombic' pressed glass, whose name, the Pennsylvania firm advertised, came from 'Rubaiy (meaning epic or poem) Rombic (meaning irregular in shape)'. It was available in amber, grey, lavender and the dark green shown. (ABOVE)

POST-WAR: 1945–70

The style of the 1950s, based on largely asymmetrical forms and patterns found in the natural world, was perhaps best expressed in glass. The lightness and malleability of the material lent itself to the creation of shapes and decoration which reflected the designer's search for vitality, fluidity and abstraction. 'Biomorphism', or Organic Modernism, as the style has become known, was in part a reaction against Modernism, which, in the hands of some Bauhaus pupils and admirers, had atrophied in a meaningless, geometric morbidity. The new style represented the artist's and designer's response to shapes and structures in nature, discovered under the latest, powerful microscopes. The atom and the cell fuelled the post-war artistic imagination. The unadorned, geometric forms of the 1930s were replaced by the more vital irregularity of the natural world.

VENICE

In Venice, war had been kept at arm's length. By mutual consent, both sides had avoided the destruction of the city. On the small island of Murano, which lies in the bay some 3–5 km (2–3 miles) from Venice, the glass-making industry that had been revived less than three-quarters of a century earlier was allowed to remain, and during the years following the end of the war it consolidated its strengths. The emphasis on the role of the glass-blower in the creation of artistic pieces was stressed. Applied decoration, for centuries one of the most highly regarded features of Venetian glass, declined until it almost disappeared (although it still flourished in production for the less discerning tourist market). Engraving was used sparingly, and cutting – so unlikely if not impossible on the thin soda glass generally used in Venice – was rare.

The importance of the glass-blower made cooperation between him and the designer essential. The relationship between the two was developed and refined to the extent that studios would build teams of artists and craftsmen with the utmost care, patience and determination. In an address given to the 1956 International Glass Conference in Paris, the Venetian glass-maker Ercole Barovier spoke of 'master blowers whose duty is faithfully to reproduce and interpret the soul of the artist rather than the drawings he has given them'. Each piece of artistic glass made in Venice is an expression of the designer's personality interpreted by the glass-blower, a unique rendering of the designer's theme.

In Venetian glass the theme was usually colour. Dishes, vases and bowls were primarily conceived as vehicles for compositions of different coloured elements. Colour was deployed not only for its tint, but also for its depth. The refractive powers of each tone were exploited. Opacity and translucence were factors which had to be carefully considered.

VENINI GLASS

At the Milan Triennale of 1948, whose theme was 'Shapes for Utility', Venini, the leading firm of Venetian glass-makers, showed a group of objects, including an umbrella, a pair of gloves and a revolver, all made of glass. Such irony had been typical of Surrealist resistance to functionalism throughout the 1930s, and Venini's art director, Carlo Scarpa, had been appointed in 1932. Another reprise of the 1930s in Venini's post-war output was the Neo-Romanticism of the glass obelisks designed by the Russian-born American artist, Eugène Berman (1899–1972). But the firm's designers did not only look back to the pre-war years. During the 1940s, Carlo Scarpa designed vases and bowls decorated with enclosed interwoven bands of coloured glass (*tessuti*) and others decorated with *murrine* (thin slices of multi-coloured glass rods).

The leading figure at Venini during the post-war years was Fulvio Bianconi (b. 1915). Among his early achievements for the firm were vessels decorated in the technique known as *zanfirico* (based on *vetro a retortorli*), which combined thin threads of glass in different colours twisted into spiral patterns; *pezzati*, vessels decorated with patches of different coloured glass; and one of the classics of post-war glass, the handkerchief vases (*vasi fazzoletti*). The latter were made by preparing a square of thin glass internally decorated with *latticinio* and coloured rods, and then draping it semi-molten over the top of a post. As the glass fell around the post in folds, it annealed and formed an inverted vase in the form of a patterned handkerchief. It was a brilliant expression of the lightness of Venetian glass and the delicacy of its decoration. Imitations were made all over the world but none captured the brio of the original. The variety of decorative techniques devised by Bianconi was rivalled only by the wide range of shapes he designed. Simple, traditional vase forms were complemented by tall bottle shapes; there were also irregular, globular vessels with arbitrarily placed openings.

Paolo Venini, the firm's founder and director, contributed designs himself and kept a close eye on everything made in his workshops. Until he died in 1959, Venini glass had a distinctive style of its own, without ever becoming as uniform as the products of Gallé, Tiffany or Lalique. In 1956, Venini, Bianconi and architect Gio Ponti (1891–1979) designed a series of bottles called 'Morandi', inspired by the still-life paintings of the Italian artist Giorgio Morandi (1890–1964), which featured groups of tall, slender bottles and other vessels. Another triumph of Venini post-war glass was the *occhi* ('eyes') decoration which was

'HANDKERCHIEF' VASE, VENINI, *c*.1955 (H28.3cm/11⅛in) (BELOW)

VASES AND DISH, VENINI, *c*.1950–60 (Taller vase: H20cm/11in, dish: L37cm/14½in)

The c.1950 dish was designed by Carlo Scarpa in 1940, but did not prove popular until after the war. The c.1960 vases, featuring occhi ('eyes') decoration, were designed by Tobia Scarpa. (ABOVE)

VASES, PAOLO VENINI, *c*.1955 (Tallest: H39cm/15⅜in)

Paolo Venini approved all the designs manufactured in his glasshouse, giving the firm's products a stylistic uniformity akin to that achieved by Tiffany and Lalique. (ABOVE)

'SCOZZESE' VASE, FULVIO BIANCONI, *c*.1954 (H28.6cm/11¼in)

Bianconi was Venini's premier post-war designer. This decoration was called Scozzese (Scottish) because of the tartan-like effect made by crisscrossing inlaid rods of coloured glass. (ABOVE)

VASES, VENINI, 1951–64 (Tallest: H41cm/16⅛in)

The two vases at left are decorated with coloured glass bands, the others with murrine. *The two Tobia Scarpa vases at right feature* 'occhi'.

developed by Tobia Scarpa (b. 1935): here, *murrine* with a clear, colourless core cased in red glass are fused together, giving the effect of an irregular net spread over the vessel. Tableware was also made by Venini, and the firm produced a few figures, usually humorous, some of birds and others of characters from the commedia dell'arte.

BAROVIER, SEGUSO & TOSO GLASS

The Barovier family has been prominent among Venetian glass-makers since the fifteenth century. During the post-war years Ercole Barovier was artistic director at the firm of Barovier & Toso. He was responsible for an endless flow of technical and decorative innovations. In 1947, his son Angelo

FISH, VENINI, 1960–6 (Longer: L47cm/18½in)

Designed by Ken Scott, these purely decorative pieces reflect a brilliant use of colour as well as shape.

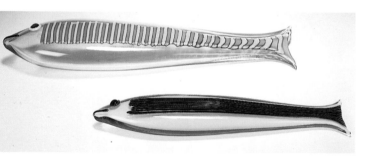

(b. 1927) joined him; as well as assisting his father, he created his own designs and decorative effects. Many of Ercole Barovier's techniques involved corrosion in the furnace; layers of gold or coloured glass decoration were allowed to split open in the heat, and surfaces were often roughened. He wanted his glass to have a primitive look, a desire reflected in the names which were given to some of the effects he invented, such as *barbarico*, *neolitico* and *aborigino*. The colours of the glass made by Barovier & Toso are usually softer than Venini's, but a

richness is often achieved through the use of gold. Shapes are generally undistinguished, although some vessels are enlivened by handles and spouts in the form of sketchily modelled animals or birds.

In 1937, the firm of Barovier, Seguso & Ferro was reorganized as Seguso Vetri d'Arte, and Flavio Poli (b. 1900) was appointed artistic director. Poli introduced a series of vessels whose surfaces were treated with hydrofluoric acid; they were called *corrosi*. Then, in the early 1950s, he moved on to *sommersi* vases, which are constructed

in layers of different coloured glass. Using this technique he created a series of vases called *valve* ('shells'), their shape inspired by the shells of mussels. Most of Poli's forms pertain to the biomorphism found in the work of so many artists and designers active during the 1940s and 1950s. Some of his vessels have irregular, curved shapes with large holes in their sides, reminiscent of some of Henry Moore's sculpture. Poli's designs are always precise, usually with gently curving profiles. Perhaps more than any other Venetian designer, Poli was influenced by designs emerging from Scandinavia.

In 1945, Archimede Seguso (b. 1909) left Seguso Vetri d'Arte, where he had worked as a master blower, and the next year he set up his own glassworks. He was both designer and manufacturer of his glass, and, although his shapes often show the influence of Flavio Poli's biomorphic style, he developed a repertoire of his own original decorative techniques. In 1950, he created his *merletto* ('lace') form of decoration, first presented to the public in the following year. Thin threads of glass were blown into the walls of the vessel, in more or less irregular patterns. In some instances, the jumbled threads would be thinned out in certain areas, leaving patches of almost clear glass; in others, thicker streaks of coloured glass would run arbitrarily across the *merletto* pattern. Another of Seguso's decorative techniques was *a piume*, wherein thin threads combed into the form of feathers were enclosed in the blown glass. A *composizione lattimo* ('milky composition') was a vase or bowl decorated with a herringbone pattern of opaque white glass which writhes over most of the vessel, leaving an irregular band of clear glass at the lip.

OTHER FACTORIES

The *Oriente* series of vases and bowls, designed by the painter Dino Martens and made by the glassworks of Aureliano Toso, provide a contemporary equivalent in glass to Abstract Expressionist painting. The clear glass vessels are internally decorated with irregular areas of brightly coloured opaque glass fused with pieces of *zanfirico* and a large white *murrina* marked with black radiating lines. Many of the shapes Martens designed have a baroque luxuriance which is complemented by the powdered gold often included in the decoration. For Arte Vetraria Muranese (AVEM), Giulio Radi (1895–1952), the firm's artistic director, created vessels that are opaque, decorated internally with a layer of gold or silver which has split up, pieces of coloured glass and *murrine*. Radi obtained colour gradations through the reaction of chemicals spread over the surface of the vessel.

Gino Cenedese designed many of the pieces made in his factory. Some of his sculptures – more or less realistic models of, for example, a horse's head or a male torso – were treated with hydrofluoric acid to give them a rough texture. He also made three-dimensional compositions of threads and thicker pieces of coloured glass embedded in blocks of clear, colourless glass. Many of them were entitled *Acquario astratto* ('Abstract Aquarium').

In 1950, Alfredo Barbini (b. 1912) left Gino Cenedese's factory and established his own workshop. He started making large animal figures, and later made vases with an internal layer of coloured glass inside a thicker layer of colourless glass engraved with thin, horizontal lines.

VASE, ALFREDO
BARBINI, *c.*1955
(H25cm/9⅞in)

Barbini left Gino Cenedese's glasshouse in 1950 and set up his own workshop. This vase, however, was designed for the firm of Pauly & C. (RIGHT)

VASE AND
CARAFE,
ERMANNO
TOSO, *c.*1960
(Both: H30cm/11⅞in)

From 1939 Toso was art director at Fratelli Toso on Murano. The carafe is decorated with a large murrina *in the base.* (RIGHT)

SCULPTURE, BRUNO DE TOFFOLI, *c.*1954 (H53cm/20⅞in)

This piece demonstrates the suitability of glass to the representation of forms suggested by the natural world. (RIGHT)

Such was the success of post-war Venetian glass that when some of the most prominent painters and sculptors were invited to submit designs for manufacture the response was remarkable. At least three different pieces were made in small editions to designs by Pablo Picasso. A two-handled vase entitled *Il Burlesco* ('The Burlesque') was made at the glassworks of Aureliano Toso; *Portatrice d'acqua* ('Water Carrier'), a bottle-shaped vase in the form of a woman carrying a much smaller vase in one of her arms, was manufactured by the Mazzega workshop; the firm of Dalla Venezia & Martinuzzi produced a figure of a centaur (Francesco Martinuzzi, who was responsible for making this figure, was the son of Napoleone Martinuzzi). Mazzega made a glass plaque designed by Marc Chagall, and another designed by Georges Braque. An abstract sculpture entitled *Armonie architettoniche* ('Architectonic Harmonies') was made by Ferro & Lazzarini to a design by Le Corbusier. The same glassworks manufactured a bowl designed by Oscar Kokoschka called *Baccanti* and a hanging sculpture by Alexander Calder entitled *Colomba volante* ('Flying Dove'). However, the imposition of such powerful artistic personalities on the Venetian glass-workers seems to have inhibited their own creativity. All these specially produced pieces lack the spontaneity usually so apparent in Venetian glass. The glass-blower's improvisation, which often invests a vase or a bowl with the essential characteristics of the medium, is here missing.

SCANDINAVIA

The character of the glass produced in Scandinavia during the post-war period was determined by considerations of style as much as by respect for the qualities of the material. A conscious effort was made by designers' organizations in Sweden, Finland, Norway and Denmark to nurture the concept of a Scandinavian style which had been germinating in the mind of consumers since the 1930s. Signifi-

cant reviews of the style included the exhibition 'Design in Scandinavia', which toured Canada and the United States from 1954 to 1957, and Ulf Hård af Segerstad's *Scandinavian Design* (Stockholm, 1961), whose introduction was headed 'Four Countries – One Aesthetic Culture'. The style which had emerged might be described as an amiable, playful version of functionalism. As a result of the Second World War, in which only Sweden had not felt the Nazi scourge, the German intellectualism associated with Bauhaus design had become repugnant. Moreover, natural forms had always inspired Scandinavian designers, and the abstract geometry of 1930s functionalism was alien to peoples who had little experience of the modern urban environment. One of the early classics of biomorphism was the amoeba-shaped 'Savoy' glass bowl, designed in 1936 by the Finnish architect Alvar Aalto. Natural shapes dominate Scandinavian post-war glass. Colour is much less important than it is in Venetian glass, and the more watery tones of the far north prevail. The crystal-clear nature of Scandinavian flint glass makes it suitable for engraved and cut decoration. In the post-war period the engraved designs were often wistful, almost sentimental, reflecting the utopian optimism of those years.

SWEDEN

In 1940, Vicke Lindstrand had left the Swedish firm of Orrefors. Edvard Hald was still there, but in a less commanding position. The designers who came to the fore during the post-war period were Edvin Öhrström (b. 1906), Sven Palmqvist (1906–84) and Nils Landberg (b. 1907). The last two had both been trained at the Orrefors engraving school and had acquired most of the glass-maker's skills. Öhrström had been trained as a sculptor, but he had been involved in the development of the 'Ariel' technique in 1936 and he used it in some of his post-war work. Sometimes the enclosed decoration was figurative, but more often abstract patterns accentuate the form of the vessel. He also designed vases and bowls

decorated with very shallow engraving of lines or spattered dots, giving a textural effect. Sven Palmqvist created some vessels which were engraved with figures – for example, circus performers – represented in a personal version of the Cubist style. Palmqvist, however, is better known for his decoration in the 'Ravenna' technique that he developed in the late 1940s. Enclosed coloured glass is formed into patterns between channels of trapped air sprinkled with sand. Nils Landberg was an accomplished glass-blower and his designs often reveal his knowledge of this particular skill. Drinking glasses in the 'Tulip' series, for instance, have trumpet-like feet tapering to long, thin stems which support the elegant bowls. Tall, bottle-shaped vases made in glass tinted with subtly gradated colours, with tiny feet and lips in the form of discs, are another typical Landberg design. Another designer at Orrefors, Ingeborg Lundin (b. 1921), who joined the firm in 1947, created vases in the form of two cones, one inverted on the other, which were made in 'family' groups, much of the artistic effect resulting from the formal and spatial rela-

'RAVENNA' BOWL, SVEN
PALMQVIST, *c.*1955 (W15.2cm/6in)

*Palmqvist developed the 'Ravenna' decorative
technique while working at Orrefors. The red
patches have been forced into air pockets created in
the blue body of the bowl.*

'ARIEL' VASE, INGEBORG LUNDIN,
*c.*1975 (H18.5cm/7¼in)

*The 'Ariel' technique of decoration had been
developed at the Orrefors factory during the 1930s.*

'ARIEL' VASE, INGEBORG LUNDIN,
1978 (H19cm/7½in)

tionships between the pieces. Lundin, like
Öhrström, often used very shallow engraving to create textural effects. Some vessels
were given patches of cloudy tinting, often
in a soft pink tone. She designed several vases
decorated in the Ariel technique, most with
animals or abstract patterns.

In 1950, Vicke Lindstrand was appointed
art director of the Kosta Boda glassworks.
Neither he nor Erik Höglund (b. 1932), the
other principal designer employed by the
firm during the 1950s, had been trained as a
glass-maker, and both worked in other
media – Lindstrand in ceramics and textiles,
Höglund in metalwork and wood-carving.
The vessels they designed for Kosta Boda are
very stylish but less influenced by glass-making techniques than by a predetermined
image of the product to be marketed.
Lindstrand's vases often have a flattened oval
section, with streaks or spirals of coloured
glass cased in a thick layer of clear, colourless
glass. Höglund's shapes are often square or
oblong in elevation, with rounded corners.
For the Gullaskruf glassworks, Hugo Gehlin
(1889–1953) designed vases and bowls with
elaborately wrought outer surfaces. Twisted

or crumpled relief decoration gives his
vessels an impressive vitality. The designs of
Arthur Carlsson Percy (1886–1976) for the
same firm are more restrained – sometimes
quite traditional – and decorated with
simple engraved lines or modest fluting.

The Reijmyre and Strömbergshyttan
factories both made well-designed, usually
utilitarian glass. In contrast, the Flygsfors
glassworks produced vases designed by Paul
Kedelv (b. 1917) and Viktor Berndt
(b. 1919) which are on the borderline
between vessel and sculpture. Kedelv
favoured abstract, asymmetrical shapes, and
Berndt designed vases moulded with relief
decoration of faces inspired by tribal masks.

FINLAND

In Finland, designers worked in many
different media, and as a result Finnish glass
lacks the spontaneity and improvisation of
the Venetian article. On the other hand,
practically every piece is a clear stylistic
statement. The possibilities of biomorphism
were relentlessly explored, and the Finnish
craftsmen proved themselves again and

again the designers' able accomplices. In the
two or three years before her death, Gunnel
Nyman (1909–48) designed a number of
vessels for the Finnish glasshouses. Although
she had spent the earlier part of her career
designing furniture, she showed that she had
a natural sympathy with glass and a profound understanding of biomorphism.
Some of her vases have soft, organic shapes.
Others are cut so that they appear to have
been made from a rolled-up sheet of glass,
and they resemble the furled petals of a
flower. Decoration consists of tiny bubbles
lined up in regular patterns, or more simply
of the effects of refraction caused by the
cutting. Inlaid colour is occasionally used.

Gunnel Nyman designed for the three
leading Finnish factories: Iittala, Nuutajärvi
and Riihimäki. After her death Tapio Wirkkala (1915–85) was made chief designer at
Iittala, and in 1950 Timo Sarpaneva
(b. 1926) joined the firm. These two took
over where Gunnel Nyman had left off,
creating a range of work which brilliantly
combines allusions to nature with the techniques of manufacturing glass vessels. Wirkkala designed dishes in the form of a leaf and

Although in the form of a vase, this piece, made by Iittala, is referred to as a sculpture.

'TAPIO'
DECANTER AND
GLASSES, TAPIO
WIRKKALA,
1954 (Decanter:
H19.5cm/7¾in)

This set was called 'Tapio' after a character from Finnish mythology whose name the designer shared. It was manufactured by the Iittala glasshouse.

VASE, TAPIO WIRKKALA, 1946
(H19.5cm/7¾in)

The Iittala glassworks produced two series of 50 vases each to this design. It was part of Wirkkala's display of glass that won him a grand prix at the 1951 Milan Triennale.

'FINLANDIA' VASE, TIMO SARPANEVA, 1965–9 (H28cm/11in)

Sarpaneva designed ceramics, textiles and cast-iron cooking pots as well as glass. The Iittala glassworks manufactured the 'Finlandia' series of vases.

BOTTLE VASE, KAJ FRANCK, c.1955
(H19cm/7½in)

This unusually coloured piece was designed for Nuutajärvi in Finland. Franck won the grand prix for his glass designs at the 1957 Milan Triennale.

bowls in shapes evoking the conch shell. Other vases, made in frosted glass and called 'Medusa', have sides which recall the waving 'legs' of a jellyfish. Some of Wirkkala's vases were shaped in moulds to look like melting blocks of ice. He designed a series of vessels in clear, colourless glass engraved with thin, vertical lines, some with bud-like tops and narrow mouths, others widely flared with undulating rims; they represent the gradual blossoming of the arum lily. Sarpaneva, too, tried to capture natural processes in glass. He designed several vases in the form of a cylinder, sometimes flanged, which were made in wooden moulds. In the mould, the hot, molten glass received the impression of the charred wood. Other vases designed by Sarpaneva were asymmetrical, with undulating profiles and small wells sunk in the thick walls.

Kaj Franck (b. 1911) designed for the Nuutajärvi glasshouse from 1950. His vases were thin-walled and often in globular shapes with tiny openings. They were usually made of clear glass, sometimes tinted. Other forms he designed were more angular: for example, a squat vase in the form of an arrowhead. The vases and tableware designed by Nanny Still (b. 1926) for Riihimäki have strong, clear shapes, often featuring spheres or hemispheres. The work of Franck and Still is less biomorphic in style than that of Wirkkala or Sarpaneva, and closer in feeling to the austere geometry of Bauhaus functionalism.

DENMARK AND NORWAY

There are parallels between the designs of Per Lütken (b. 1916) for the Danish firm of Holmegaard and those of Arne Jutrem (b. 1929) for the Hadeland factory in Norway. Both tended toward simple, symmetrical shapes, but both produced more fanciful work for a few years during the 1950s. Lütken designed a number of vases with the neck and mouth twisted, giving an appearance of flames. Jutrem designed vases with strange, applied nodules, looking like suckers; generally his work was more orthodox – vases of simple shape decorated with

CZECHOSLOVAKIAN VASE, DESIGNED BY JAN KOTIK AND ENGRAVED BY CESTMÍR CEJNAR, 1957 (H27cm/10⅝in)

enclosed dots or spirals of colour, or bubbles of air. Herman Bongard (b. 1921) designed vases for Hadeland decorated with enclosed colour in abstract patterns.

CZECHOSLOVAKIA

In 1948, the Czechoslovakian glass industry was nationalized, but production of both decorative and utilitarian wares continued. However, isolation from the West resulted in a stylistic conservatism which was seldom breached. Jaroslav Horejc (1886–1983) continued to create the elaborately cut and engraved pieces that he had been producing since the 1920s, and in much the same robust, painterly style, reminiscent of Rubens. During the 1950s, he worked at a studio in Kamenický Šenov, where he continued the Bohemian tradition of heavily cut

and engraved crystal. Věra Lišková (b. 1924) was another designer who worked at this studio; her work is less grand, often incorporating subjects from nature, such as wild flowers. Subsequently, Lišková made abstract and figural sculptures which she modelled by hand over an oxyacetylene flame. Sculpture and sculptural vessels are among the most impressive pieces of postwar Czechoslovakian glass. Stanislav Libenský (b. 1921) and his wife, Jaroslava Brychtová (b. 1924), made vases and bowls moulded with figural subjects in high relief. They also created some large architectural pieces for public buildings. Their style gradually became more abstract, but their works have always retained links with the natural world. 'Harrtil' glass was developed at the Harrach factory in the mid-1950s by Miloš Pulpitel. Free-form blown vessels were decorated with thin lines of inlaid coloured glass arranged in intricate abstract patterns. It is similar to some Venetian glass and certainly stands comparison with it.

GERMANY

German post-war glass is notable for work by two of Wilhelm von Eiff's pupils, Konrad Häbermeier (b. 1907) and Hanns Model (1908–83). Häbermeier had been von Eiff's assistant at Stuttgart and was himself an accomplished glass cutter and engraver. He produced vases and bowls in the biomorphic style engraved with abstract decoration. For the Göppingen Gralglashütte he designed simple, undecorated vessels in tinted, clear glass. Hanns Model started making carved glass vessels in Stuttgart in 1933. During the postwar years he made large, irregularly shaped dishes and vases with abstract decoration intaglio-cut through layers of coloured glass. At the Zwiesel technical school, some of the instructors designed interesting pieces of cut or engraved glass. Hans Mauder, the son of Bruno Mauder, who had been a director of the school, designed vases with simple cut decoration in a biomorphic style.

Rudolf Rothemund, an architect on the staff of the Zwiesel school, generally chose figural subjects for engraving, and Stefan Erdös, who joined the staff in the mid-1950s, designed vases and bowls with engraved decoration of animals drawn in a primitive style, or alternatively abstract ornament.

BRITAIN

Helen Monro Turner (1901–77), a pupil of Wilhelm von Eiff, opened the Juniper Workshop in Edinburgh in 1956; there factory blanks were decorated with cut, engraved or sandblasted designs. Her style was naturalistic, inspired by classical art. Another British glass engraver, Laurence Whistler (b. 1912), continued to decorate pieces in the Neo-Georgian style he had developed before the Second World War. More innovative was the work of John Hutton (1907–78), who carried out extensive architectural commissions for engraved glass panels at the cathedrals in Coventry and Guildford. Thomas Webb & Sons produced a series of vases decorated with engraving by Hutton of sketchily drawn angels, based on his designs for Coventry Cathedral. During the 1950s, James Powell & Sons produced thick-walled vases designed by Geoffrey Baxter (b. 1922) in a restrained biomorphic style, which were comparable to pieces of Scandinavian glass being produced at that time.

THE

NETHERLANDS

At the Leerdam glassworks, Andries Dirk Copier and Floris Meydam (b. 1919) continued to make vessels for the firm's 'Unica' series. Copier's style remained as individual as it always had been. Shapes were often ovoid, sometimes with high shoulders. At the end of the war, he developed a decorative technique of enclos-

FREE-FORM SCULPTURE, ANDRIES DIRK COPIER, *c.*1968 (H34.5cm/13⅝in)

The non-functional pieces created by Copier at Leerdam during the 1960s inspired the nascent Studio Glass Movement in the United States.

ing enamelled designs, usually of fish and seaweed, between layers of coloured glass. He also produced pieces with layers of coloured glass which burst open in the heat of the furnace and were then cased in clear glass. He also developed a technique of forming irregularly shaped bowls by sucking air out of the vessel and creating a vacuum. Toward the end of the 1950s, he began to experiment with non-functional, free-blown shapes. Meydam worked mainly with internal decoration of coloured glass and metallic oxides.

UNITED STATES

In the late 1960s Copier was visited in his studio by the American glass artist Harvey K. Littleton (b. 1922), who recognized that the Dutchman had long treated glass as a means of pure artistic expression. Littleton had suggested to a

conference of American craftsmen, held in 1959 at Lake George, New York, that 'glass should be a medium for the individual artist'. Littleton's father was a glass scientist at the Corning works, and Harvey had been an apprentice there in 1945 before going to art school in England. He then became involved in ceramics, so when he put forward his proposition at Lake George he had very little practical experience of glass-making. However, the strength of his belief in the idea of glass as a medium for the artist, like painting or sculpture, induced the Toledo Museum of Art to organize two workshop-seminars. Here, the inexperience of Littleton and the other students made it impossible to realize the glass pieces they envisaged. Dominick Labino (1910–87), at that time vice president in charge of research at the Johns-Manville Fiber Glass Corporation, was called in to help. He developed a glass with a melting point at a low temperature which could be obtained in a furnace small enough to be used in a studio, and he also invented such a furnace. Labino became one of the pioneer Studio Glass artists, specializing in pieces with subtle colour effects. Littleton has made abstract sculptural pieces, some of them designed as ironic comments on the functionalist's prejudice against purely artistic values. For instance, one of his pieces is an elongated 'vase' bent into a C-curve and placed on a glass plinth.

LATER

STUDIO GLASS

During the 1960s the Studio Glass Movement gathered momentum and reached many countries in Europe. Some of the larger glassworks encouraged their designers to create pieces of artistic glass which were then issued in small editions. For example, in 1969 the Finnish designer Oiva Toikka (b. 1931) created a sculpture called 'Lollipop Isle', which was produced by Nuutajärvi. The title of this unusual piece is a punning

'FOURSQUARE', HARVEY K. LITTLETON, 1975
(H13.4cm/5¼in)

Littleton achieved greater artistic and intellectual expression as he mastered the technical problems associated with glass-making. (RIGHT)

'EMERGENCE FOUR-STAGE', DOMINICK LABINO, 1975
(H22.4cm/8⅞in)

This piece incorporates trapped air and internal gold and coloured veiling. (BELOW)

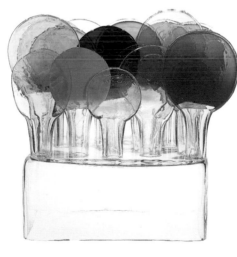

'LOLLIPOP ISLE', OIVA TOIKKA, 1969
(H45.7cm/18in)

Made at the Nuutajärvi glassworks, this sculpture incorporates elements of both moulded and free-blown glass, and marks Toikka's progression from functional to purely artistic.

reference to the strong influence of the Pop Art movement in painting, to which the sculpture has a greater affinity than to any traditional category of glassware.

The Toledo Museum of Art workshop seminars, held in 1962 in the United States, were an important turning point in the history of glass. Never before had the material been considered a worthy medium for an artist endeavouring to make a statement – or pose a question – about the human condition. Such large issues had always been the province of the painter or sculptor but not the craftsman. Since 1962, however, many art students have turned to the medium of glass in order to express themselves, or just to create beautiful objects.

Few artists of the international Studio Glass Movement began their careers working in glass, because only in the quite recent past have art schools begun offering instruction in the subject, or providing the necessary equipment and facilities.

During the late 1960s and the 1970s, however, the situation was more than adequately remedied, so that several artists became obsessed with design, decoration and technique and endlessly experimented to create new and beautiful effects. Klaus Moje (b 1936), for instance, a glass artist who worked until recently in Germany, mastered several traditional techniques and used them to achieve many aesthetic innovations in glass. On the other hand, Erwin Eisch (b. 1927), another German glass artist and no less a craftsman than Moje, used glass to express himself in first Pop and then Funk idioms.

A similar divergence arose in the United States. Dale Chihuly (b. 1941) followed Littleton in his concern to promote the purely formal, aesthetic potential of glass objects, whereas Marvin Lipofsky (b. 1938) and Sam Herman (b. 1936) always tended to let their imagination create amorphous but expressive pieces.

From 1975, the international Studio Glass Movement has expanded rapidly and its talented, innovative artists have achieved an enormous variety of styles and techniques in almost as many different countries.

FAKES AND FORGERIES

Fake: to tamper with, for the purpose of deception.

Forgery: the making of a thing in fraudulent imitation of something; that which is forged, counterfeited or fabricated.

Reproduction: an honest recreation of an earlier object.

Since the end of the nineteenth century there have been many attempts to reproduce antique glass. This reproduction of earlier forms, however, was rarely an attempt to deceive but a tendency in sympathy with revivalist fashions. Many of the pieces reproduced in the past have today become confused with originals.

Nevertheless, the rise in value of certain types of glass has inevitably attracted the forger. Thus, in the 1930s, when there was much new literature on eighteenth-century English glass, it was this type of glass that was copied; today, forgers are making close copies of the works of Gallé, Daum and Lalique, and are undoubtedly forging some modern studio glass.

To make their productions more believable, forgers often deliberately 'distress' their copies. The simplest way to achieve this is to add wear, particularly to feet or bases. Old wear is a fine, grey haze of minute scratches; false wear produces deep parallel lines. A magnifying lens should reveal the telltale scratches of emery paper – especially covering areas of feet or bases which do not come into regular contact with the surface. Acids are used on ancient glass to create artificially the much admired iridescence that occurs naturally through burial in the ground. Such chemicals can also be used on modern reproductions to remove the brilliance of new glass and give a piece a vintage appearance. Metallic oxides, such as gold, are generally used to create the iridescence.

'ISLAMIC' GLASS BOWL, 14TH CENTURY
(H21.5cm/8½in)

This may have been made in c.1880 by Samson in France. The decoration is very thickly enamelled, unlike that on the originals. The 'Arabic' inscription around the central panel is made up of imaginary script.

ANCIENT GLASS

Deliberate copying of ancient glass has occurred since the beginning of this century and many pieces are today produced in the Middle East, especially in Damascus and Israel. Unlike the originals, ancient glass reproductions are frequently complete; and although the methods of manufacture are similar to those of antique pieces, the raised edges of badly fitting modern metal-mould joints are often more apparent. A visit to a specialist museum will reveal just how little complete material has survived.

Modern pieces can also be broken and repaired or even be buried to make the copy more believable. Some original, but insignificant, pieces may also have been reworked in this century, with the addition of engraving or other decoration making them more valuable. Iridescence on the outer surface of a vessel, but not on the inside, is very often an indication of a deliberate forgery. It is also the case that some examples made from modern glass are heavier than the original early potash glass products.

CONTINENTAL GLASS, 1500–1900

In Germany in the 1860s, there was keen interest in earlier historical styles. This revival, known today as 'Historismus', resulted in the widespread reproduction of, among other types of glass, sixteenth- and seventeenth-century enamelled *Humpen*. Many of these elaborate drinking vessels, bearing appropriate dates and coats of arms from the Holy Roman Empire, have become confused with the originals. Indeed, some were deliberate forgeries. The metal is, however, often different in colour – occasionally pinkish rather than the usual green tint, and often containing air bubbles. The enamel painting on Historismus examples is generally more stiff and formal than on genuine *Humpen*.

The characteristic trumpet-shaped feet of early German *Roemers* made of *Waldglas* were created by building up spiral trails of glass, the ribbing apparent on both sides. Nineteenth-century reproductions, however, are generally mould-blown; consequently, their undersides are smooth.

Roman, Islamic and Venetian glasses were all copied in the nineteenth century, many of these reproductions merely inspirations rather than direct copies. Early Venetian glass is usually light in weight, whereas nineteenth-century copies are distinguished by the use of heavier soda-lime metal or lead crystal. Later reproductions of seventeenth- and eighteenth-century Baroque engraved glass goblets, especially beakers decorated in the *zwischengold* and *Schwarzlot* techniques, were widely manufactured. These are often made with such fine craftsmanship that it is difficult to believe they were intended to deceive.

Early nineteenth-century-style Bohemian cased glass is still made today. Most of these modern copies should be viewed as a continuing tradition of a popular style, but their gilding is generally brighter and the glass more brilliant. Similarly, decalcomania glass has a flawless finish and, unlike original examples, its interior paint is intact.

ENGLISH DRINKING GLASSES

Of all English glass, eighteenth-century drinking glasses have most commonly been forged, reproduced and faked, especially in those cases where the values could be increased significantly by engraving. Since much eighteenth-century engraving was of average quality, it is easily imitated. Plain eighteenth-century glasses with later engraved decoration are today all but indistinguishable from the original.

Bohemian engravers working in Dublin in the 1890s produced Williamite glassware in the style of glass of the 1720s and 1730s, to commemorate the two-hundredth anniversary of the Battle of the Boyne. Engraved glass with Jacobite emblems was made for the hundredth anniversary of the Jacobite Rebellion in 1845, but, like the many forgeries that were produced in the 1930s, most examples combined too much, and usually incorrect, detail. Some glasses, how-

PAIR OF BOHEMIAN *ZWISCHENGOLD-GLAS* BEAKERS, 19TH CENTURY (H12cm/4¾in)

The faces have a late 19th-century feel to them, unlike the profiles on original beakers of this type, which date from a century earlier. Engraved scenes on the reverse of the portraits bear an obvious resemblance to Victorian book illustrations. (LEFT)

GERMAN *JAGDHUMPEN*, 19TH CENTURY (H28cm/11in)

Made in the 1860s in response to a revival of historical styles, this vessel is misleadingly dated 1624. Originals would not display numerous oval-shaped bubbles, as can be seen on the detail of this example, and the glass and enamels are of the wrong colour. (LEFT AND ABOVE LEFT)

ONE WILLIAMITE
AND TWO
JACOBITE
GLASSES OF
RECENT DATE
(Williamite glass:
H16.3cm/6⅜in)

*The Williamite wine
glass on the left is
based on an 18th-
century prototype. The
two Jacobite glasses are
20th-century
interpretations of 18th-
century examples.*

ever, were advertised and sold as reproductions, but today, with ever higher prices commanded by Jacobite glasses, to the untrained eye, copies and originals have become confused.

Enamelled glass resembling the mid eighteenth-century output of the Beilby workshop is also being reproduced, some of which is of high quality. It may be coming from the Continent, where the enamelling tradition is considerably stronger than in Britain. On some of the poorer quality examples, the gilding on the rims is flat and bright and possesses none of the grainy features of the originals.

E 8436	**E 7175**	**E 8512**	**E 7176**
AIR TWIST STEM	SPIRAL STEM	SPIRAL STEM ENGRAVED	AIR TWIST STEM WINE
FIAT GLASS	VINE ENGRAVED WINE	WINE	Height 7″
Engraved Tudor Rose	Height 7″	Height 5¾″	Dia. 3″
Height 6″	Dia. 2⅝″	**13/6** each	**9/−** each
15/− each	**15/−** each		

PAGE
ILLUSTRATING
REPRODUCTION
18TH-CENTURY
DRINKING
GLASSES, 1934

*The illustration is from
the Hill-Ouston Gifts
Catalogue. The glasses
of this firm, based in
Birmingham, are
sometimes passed off as
genuine examples.*

GROUP OF 19TH-CENTURY ENGLISH
DRINKING GLASSSES IN 18TH-
CENTURY STYLE (Colour-twist glass:
H16.5cm/6½in)

*The left-hand wine glass has an opaque twist that
goes the wrong way for it to be an 18th-century
original. The others have flat feet, and the colour-
twist of the glass on the right is top-heavy.*

Forgeries occur among opaque-twist and air-twist glasses, especially those with drawn trumpet bowls. The quality and colour of the glass, its bright, shiny appearance and the absence of tool marks on feet and bowls are useful indicators. The absence of a pontil mark under the foot might also suggest a twentieth-century reproduction. This rough mark is simply the scar that is left when the completed glass is broken off from the glass-maker's pontil iron. Almost all handmade glass, either contemporary or antique, will bear a pontil mark and it is not a guarantee of age. Indeed, in the early twentieth century a firm in the English Midlands employed a man full-time to apply pontils on to press-moulded glass in an attempt to disguise this machine process. Most facet-cut glasses, decanters and bowls have the pontil ground off.

Unwitting collectors may be deceived by the 'marriages' of two separate glasses. The joining of a bowl from one glass on to the stem of another can be successfully disguised if the sticking occurs at a definite joint – such as at the top or the bottom of the stem. Such methods are employed today, because of the recent advances made in the use of adhesives in glass restoration. The removal of a stem can also turn a bucket-shaped goblet or rummer into a tumbler, the original stem joint, like the pontil, being ground away.

Lead crystal can be distinguished from soda glass by using an ultraviolet lamp. Under this light lead crystal fluoresces light blue tinged with purple, while soda glass fluoresces green-yellow. This may not differentiate between English and Continental examples, however, since during the eighteenth century lead crystal was also produced by glass-makers in the Low Countries and in Scandinavia.

DECANTERS

Decanters have often been copied. Some early nineteenth-century English coloured examples were reproduced in Czechoslovakia in the 1930s. However, they are often too shiny and the gilding is of poor quality. Irish decanters of the late eighteenth and early nineteenth centuries are popular with forgers, especially those moulded with the name of a Cork glasshouse. They are generally bright in colour and, unlike on the originals, their lettering is quite legible.

CUT GLASS

Almost the same techniques for cutting glass were maintained from 1800 until quite recently, whereas a new technique for polishing, using acid, was introduced at the end of the nineteenth century. While polishing with putty powder on a cork wheel retains the crispness and grain marks of the earlier stone wheels, the technique of acid-polishing gives a dull finish and tends to round off the edges of the cuts. However, some close replicas are still polished with a cork to give the authentic texture and finish of early nineteenth-century examples.

The quality and colour of the glass have also improved considerably, from the slight greyish tinge of old glass toward a greater brilliance and whiteness in new glass. Victorian and Edwardian cut-glass styles were still produced by some Stourbridge firms into the 1930s. Press-moulded copies of cut glass can be distinguished by the mould seam lines.

TWO 19TH-CENTURY ENGLISH DRINKING GLASSES IN 18TH-CENTURY STYLE AND ONE ORIGINAL 18TH-CENTURY GLASS (Tallest: H23cm/9in)

The glass on the right is an original 18th-century wine flute or ale glass whose bowl and foot have been cut in the 19th century. (ABOVE)

MARKED 'CORK' DECANTER, c.1900 (H25cm/9¾in)

The vessel was made from a 20th-century mould, a hundred years after the heyday of Irish glass.

PAPERWEIGHTS

As with most collectables, paperweights are popular targets for the forger. Modern French examples rarely show the wear of the originals and faceted edges are likely to be smooth, unlike their earlier fire-polished counterparts. Some Scottish weights from the workshop of Paul Ysart have been widely forged, the canes and signatures being recognizably uncharacteristic and the signature 'PY' cane often has the second letter dropped slightly.

PRESS-MOULDED GLASS

Although it is known that several nineteenth-century manufacturers of English pressed glass have reintroduced old moulds throughout the twentieth century, some of the more recent forgeries in this class appear to have been produced in the Far East. Comparison with original examples reveals a marked lessening of quality in the copies and, where coloured opaque glass is concerned, a more plastic, less bold character to the finish of the metal.

ART NOUVEAU AND ART DECO GLASS

The dramatic rise in value of Gallé, Daum and Lalique glass has led to a spate of forged material appearing on the market, much of it of high quality, whose sources are thought to be Belgium and France. Only the sharpness of the cutting is unlike the original, and many pieces have been sandblasted. Signatures on these glasses are often incorrect. Likewise, a (modern) fake signature can appear on Lalique-style opalescent glass of the 1930s – which was produced in England, France, Belgium and the United States, but not passed off as Lalique at the time of its manufacture.

Loetz glass is now widely reproduced or often just misattributed; it can be distinguished from its many Austrian copies by the high quality of its iridescence, the thickness of the glass and the smoothing off of the pontil. Scottish Monart glass has

'DAUM' ETCHED AND ENAMELLED GLASS VASE (H28cm/11in)

The rise in prices of Art Nouveau and Art Deco glass has led to a spate of forged material on the market, much of it – such as this example – of high quality. Only the sharpness of the cutting distinguishes it from the original. (LEFT)

MODERN AMERICAN LOETZ-TYPE IRIDESCENT VASE AND REPRODUCTION AMERICAN MOULD-BLOWN RUBY CREAM JUG (Vase: H12cm/4¾in)

The vase is of a style popular in the first half of the 20th century, but was made recently from the volcanic ash of Mount St Helens. The jug, in 19th-century style, was made in Virginia. As neither item is marked, it could be possible to pass them off as originals. (BELOW)

recently been reproduced, modern copies bearing forged manufacturer's paper labels. However the forged labels are screen-printed and the print rubs off easily. Good forgeries of Italian Venini glass are also known, produced in Venice and bearing more recent acid-stamped trademarks.

CONTEMPORARY STUDIO GLASS

Plain, insignificant examples of contemporary studio glass have been engraved with the signatures of leading artists. Comparison with the known work of those artists and their signatures will help to expose the fakes.

SELECT BIBLIOGRAPHY

PRE-ROMAN GLASS

Cooney, John D.: 'Glass', *Catalogue of Egyptian Antiquities in The British Museum*, vol. 4, London, 1976

Fossing, Poul: *Glass Vessels before Glass-blowing*, Copenhagen, 1940

Goldstein, Sidney M.: *Pre-Roman and Early Roman Glass in The Corning Museum of Glass*, New York, 1979

Grose, D.F.: *Early Ancient Glass*, The Toledo Museum of Art, New York, 1989

Glass at The Fitzwilliam Museum, exhibition catalogue, Cambridge, 1978

ROMAN GLASS

Harden, D.B.: *Roman Glass from Karanis Found by the University of Michigan Archaeological Expedition in Egypt 1924–29*, Ann Arbor, 1936

Harden, D.B.: 'Ancient Glass, II: Roman', *The Archaeological Journal*, vol. 126, London, 1969, pp. 44–77

Harden, D.B., Hellenkemper, H., Painter, K. and Whitehouse, D.: *Glass of the Caesars*, exhibition catalogue, Milan, 1989

Newby, M.S. and Painter, K.S. (eds.): *Roman Glass: Two Centuries of Art and Invention*, Society of Antiquaries of London, Occasional Papers (new series) 13, London, 1991

ISLAMIC GLASS

Fukai, Shinji: *Persian Glass*, New York, Tokyo and Kyoto, 1977

Jenkins, Marilyn: *Islamic Glass: A Brief History*, New York, 1986

Lamm, Carl J.: *Mittelalterliche Gläser und Steinschnittarbeiten aus dem Nahen Osten*, Berlin, 1929–30

MEDIEVAL GLASS

Baumgartner, Erwin and Krueger, Ingeborg: *Phönix aus Sand und Asche*, Munich, 1988

Brisas, Catherine: *A Thousand Years of Stained Glass*, Garden City, New York, 1984

Foy, Danièle: *Le verre médiéval et son artisanat en France méditerranéenne*, Paris, 1988

Foy, Danièle and Sennequier, Geneviève: *A travers le verre du moyen âge à la renaissance*, Rouen, 1989

Grodecki, Louis: *Le vitrail roman*, 2nd edn, Fribourg and Paris, 1983

THE RENAISSANCE PERIOD
Venice

Charleston, Robert J.: 'Glass', *Glass and Enamels, The James A. de Rothschild Collection at Waddesdon Manor*, London, 1977

Egg, Erich: *Die Glashütten zu Hall und Innsbruck im 16. Jahrhundert*, Innsbruck, 1962

Mentasti, Rosa Barovier et al.: *Mille Anni di arte del vetro a Venezia*, exhibition catalogue, Venice, 1982

Tait, Hugh: *The Golden Age of Venetian Glass*, The British Museum, London, 1979

The Venetian Influence

Buckley, W.: *European Glass*, London, 1926

Chambon, Raymond: *L'histoire de la verrerie en Belgique du IIme siècle à nos jours*, Brussels, 1955

Frothingham, Alice Wilson: *Barcelona Glass in Venetian Style*, New York, 1956

Germany

Klesse, Brigitte and Mayr, Hans: *European Glass from 1500–1800, The Ernesto Wolf Collection*, Vienna, 1987

Von Strasser, Rudolf and Spiegl, Walter: *Dekoriertes Glas*, Munich, 1989

THE EIGHTEENTH CENTURY
Continental Glass

Baumgärtner, Sabine: *Sachsisches Glas*, Wiesbaden, 1977

Drahotova, Olga: *European Glass*, London, 1983

Dreier, Franz-Adrian: *Glaskunst in Hessen und Kassel*, Kassel, 1969

British Glass

Bickerton, L.M.: *Eighteenth Century English Drinking Glasses*, Woodbridge, Suffolk, 1986

Charleston, Robert J.: *English Glass and the Glass Used in England, circa 400–1940*, London, 1984

Truman, Charles: *English Glassware to 1900*, London, 1984

Warren, W. Phelps: *Irish Glass*, London, 1981

Westropp, M.S. Dudley: *Irish Glass*, Dublin, 1978

Chinese Glass

Brown, Claudia and Rabiner, Donald: *Chinese Glass of the Qing Dynasty 1644–1911, The Robert H. Clague Collection*, Phoenix, 1987

Brown, Claudia and Rabiner, Donald: *Clear as Crystal, Red as Flame: Later Chinese Glass*, New York, 1990

Moss, Hugh M.: *Enamelled Glass Wares of the Ku Yueh Hsuan Group*, Baltimore, 1978

Europaisches und Aussereuropaisches Glas, Museum für Kunsthandwerk, Frankfurt am Main, 1973

THE NINETEENTH CENTURY
British Glass

Morris, B.: *Victorian Tableglass and Ornaments*, London, 1978

Slack, R.: *English Pressed Glass 1830–1890*, London, 1987

Wakefield, H.: *Nineteenth Century British Glass*, London, 1982

Woodward, H.: *Art, Feat and Mystery, The Story of Thomas Webb & Sons, Glassmakers*, Stourbridge, 1978

American Glass

Barlow, Raymond E. and Kaiser, Joan E.: *The Glass Industry in Sandwich*, vols. 2, 3 and 4, Windham, New Hampshire, 1983, 1987 and 1989

Innes, Lowell: *Pittsburgh Glass 1797–1891*, Boston, 1976

McKearin, George and Helen: *American Glass*, 1st edn, New York, 1941

Schwartz, Marvin D. and DiBartolomeo, Robert E. (eds.): *American Glass*, 2 vols., New York, 1973

Spillman, Jane S.: *American and European Pressed Glass in The Corning Museum of Glass*, New York, 1973

Wilson, Kenneth M.: *New England Glass & Glassmaking*, New York, 1972

Continental Glass

Pestova, Zuzana; *Bohemian Engraved Glass*, London, 1968

Polak, Ada: *Glass and Its Makers*, London, 1975

Spillman, Jane S.: *Glass from the World's Fairs 1851–1904*, Corning, New York, 1986

Paperweights

Hollister, Jr, Paul: *The Encyclopedia of Glass Paperweights*, New York, 1969

Jokelson, Paul: *Antique French Paperweights*, privately published by Paul Jokelson, 1955

Rossi, Sara: *The Letts Guide to Collecting Paperweights*, London, 1990

ARTS AND CRAFTS AND ART NOUVEAU
European Art Nouveau

Arwas, Victor: *Glass, Art Nouveau to Art Deco*, London, 1987

Bloch-Dermant, Janine: *L'art du verre en France 1860–1914*, Lausanne, 1974

Neuwirth, Waltraud: *Das Glas des Jugendstils*, Munich, 1973

Philippe, Joseph: *Le Val Saint-Lambert*, Liège, 1974

Emile Gallé

Charpentier, Françoise Thérèse and Thiébault, Philippe: *Gallé*, Paris, 1985

Charpentier, Françoise Thérèse et al.: *Art Nouveau, L'Ecole de Nancy*, Lausanne, 1987

Daum, Noël: *Daum Mastery of Glass*, Lausanne, 1985

Garner, Philippe: *Emile Gallé*, London, 1976

American Art Nouveau

Gardner, Paul V.: *The Glass of Frederick Carder*, New York, 1971

Grover, Ray and Lee: *Art Glass Nouveau*, Rutland, Vermont, 1967

Koch, Robert: *Louis C. Tiffany's Glass, Bronzes, Lamps and Metalwork*, New York, 1971

Koch, Robert: *Rebel in Glass*, New York, 1964

Neustadt, Egon: *The Lamps of Tiffany*, New York, 1970

Revi, Albert Christian: *American Art Glass Nouveau*, Camden, New Jersey, 1968

TWENTIETH-CENTURY DEVELOPMENTS
Between the Wars

Bayer, Patricia and Waller, Mark: *The Art of René Lalique*, London, 1988

Klein, Dan: *The History of Modern Glass*, London, 1984

Marcilhac, Félix: *R. Lalique, Catalogue raisonné de l'oeuvre de verre*, Paris, 1989

Opie, Jennifer H. (ed.): *Scandinavia: Ceramics & Glass in the Twentieth Century*, London, 1989

Czechoslovakian Glass, 1350–1980, The Corning Museum of Glass and the Museum of Decorative Arts, Prague, New York, 1981

Post-War: 1945–70

Aloi, Roberto: *Vetri d'Oggi*, Milan, 1955

Beard, Geoffrey: *Modern Glass*, London, 1968

Garner, Philippe: *Contemporary Decorative Arts*, London, 1980

Grover, Ray and Lee: *Contemporary Art Glass*, New York, 1975

Heiremans, Marc: *Murano Glas 1945–1970*, Antwerp, 1989

Polak, Ada: *Modern Glass*, London, 1962

Glass 1959: A Special Exhibition of International Contemporary Glass, The Corning Museum of Glass, New York, 1959

FAKES AND FORGERIES

Battie, David: *Fakes and Forgeries – an Exhibition incorporating Sotheby's 'Black Museum'*, London, 1990

Bly, John (ed.): *Is it Genuine?*, London, 1986

Spiegl, W.: *Glas des Historismus*, Braunschweig, 1980

Wilkinson, R.: *The Hallmarks of Antique Glass*, London, 1968

CARE AND CONSERVATION

Newton, Roy and Davison, Sandra: *Conservation of Glass*, London, 1989

CARE AND CONSERVATION

RESTORATION

In recent years conservators have made great strides in the restoration of glass. By matching the refraction of light through glass with modern glues and epoxy resins, almost perfect repairs can be achieved. The techniques, however, are expensive and in addition the adhesive will discolour and the damage becomes apparent in time.

Wax and silicone moulds used with polyester resins have revolutionized the restoration of ancient glass that requires an infill due to considerable loss.

Now that repairs to glass are so deceptive, vessels can easily be passed off as perfect. An example is the resticking of an undamaged foot from one glass on to the bowl and stem of another. The break may not be visible until the adhesive eventually discolours or the deception is discovered by means of ultraviolet light. Under ultraviolet the repair will fluoresce yellow, whereas the original will appear purple.

If the bowl or foot of a wine glass is slightly chipped, the rim may be ground down to lose the damage. Trimming can often leave the foot uncomfortably out of proportion to the bowl (it should be remembered that the bowl of an eighteenth-century English wine glass is generally smaller than the foot). To avoid trimming, a chip may be filled with an acrylic resin. Paperweights can also be reground and polished to disguise chips and bruises, thereby altering the original profile.

RECOGNIZING PROBLEMS

Some antique glass, especially sixteenth- and seventeenth-century Venetian glass and soda glass in general, can suffer from an irreversible condition known as crizzling, or 'weeping glass'. It is caused by an imperfect proportion of the ingredients in the original glass batch, particularly an excess of alkali.

The discovery that the addition of lead oxide to the batch provided a remedy has largely left eighteenth-century English glass free of this problem. In affected pieces the alkali weeps out, causing the internal structure of the glass to decompose and eventually disintegrate. Although a glass may be susceptible to this disease, it may never show signs of it until the humidity and temperature levels change significantly. Once the condition occurs it cannot be arrested, though it may be slowed down by placing the piece in a more stable dry environment.

A damp surface and a sour smell like that of ammonia provide the first signs that a glass is affected by crizzling. This is then followed by the appearance of a cobweb of fine internal cracks, which gradually cloud the surface. In some instances in Europe and in China in the seventeenth century this was used as a decorative effect. Crizzling has been observed in collections of late nineteenth-century English pressed glass and twentieth-century Scottish glass from Moncrieff (Monart) and Caithness. Even some examples of Italian glass from the Memphis design studio, made in the 1980s, have been found with this condition. Constant experimentation with different glass ingredients by industrial glass-makers, and novel effects sought by studio artists, will doubtless cause the problem to occur in the future.

HANDLING AND STORING

The iridescent surface on ancient glass, and some seventeenth- and eighteenth-century English bottles, can be very brittle. The handling of such pieces should be kept to a minimum as any form of surface treatment will only damage it. Pieces should, therefore, be kept in as stable an environment as possible. The heat from ordinary cabinet lighting can be detrimental to iridescence, and in fact, to glass in general. Low voltage tungsten lights, which provide an adequate light source with the minimum of heat build-up, are ideal for glass displays. When putting glasses away from view it is best not to store them upside down. The rims of wine glasses, for example, are more vulnerable to damage than their thicker feet and, besides, the upturned bowls can make wine taste musty.

CLEANING

Generally speaking, one should not immerse antique glass in hot water, since the rapid increase in temperature may cause the glass to crack. Paperweights, subject to internal stress inherent in their construction, have exploded due to thermal shock. Gentle wiping with warm, soapy water and drying with a soft cloth should be sufficient.

Old glass should not be put in a dishwasher. The temperature reached is very high and the swirling water jets abrade the surface, leaving glasses misty-looking.

To clean the outside of a wine glass, jeweller's rouge in liquid paste form, very gently rubbed on to the surface, can help. Wine stored in decanters for long periods can cause staining, with port one of the worst offenders. The storage of spirits such as brandy and whisky is not a problem, however. Vinegar or proprietary denture cleaners have been used to clean wine stains and 'tidemarks' from the inside of decanters. Anything more abrasive, like jeweller's rouge, will leave even deeper scratches which may exacerbate the condition. A jammed decanter stopper can be removed by holding the decanter horizontally over a soft surface – such as a bed or a very soft floor covering – and gently tapping the stopper with the handle of a wooden clothes brush in a movement away from one's body. The stopper should fly out.

If in doubt about the condition or repair of your glass, it is best to seek advice from a museum or recognized glass restorer.

PAPERWEIGHTS AND CANES

PAPERWEIGHTS

A range of important paperweight types from the Baccarat, Clichy and St Louis factories. LEFT TO RIGHT, TOP ROW: *St Louis carpet ground, Baccarat stylized bouquet, Baccarat 'Ducks-on-a-Pond'.* MIDDLE ROW: *Clichy swirl, Clichy overlay, St Louis flat bouquet.* BOTTOM ROW: *St Louis crown, St Louis cherry, Clichy spaced millefiori.*

CANES

LEFT TO RIGHT: *Baccarat trefoil, Baccarat flower silhouette, Baccarat goat silhouette, St Louis devil, St Louis dancers, St Louis star, Clichy rose, Clichy signature, Clichy whorl*

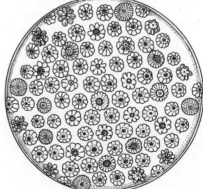

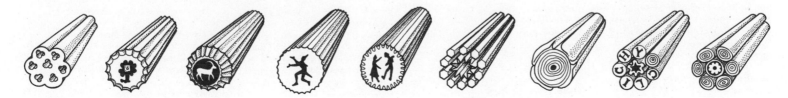

GLOSSARY

abrading Technique of grinding shallow patterns into a glass surface with a wheel.

acid-etching Technique developed in the 19th century to give glass a satin matt, shiny or frosted finish by exposing it to hydrofluoric acid. Areas not to be etched were covered by an acid-resistant protective layer (wax, varnish or oil) into which a design was scratched before the acid was applied. Also used on **cameo** glass to remove areas of the **overlay**.

agate glass See **calcedonio**.

air-twist See **twist**.

alabaster glass Type of translucent glass, usually white, first developed in Bohemia in the **Biedermeier** period. Frederick Carder produced iridescent Alabaster glass at Steuben. See *lattimo* and **opal**.

alabastron Small, cylindrical perfume flask of ancient Greece, made in **core-formed glass**, with a rounded base, broad rim and two small side handles.

albarello Italian; waisted, cylindrical jar, more usually made in tin-glazed earthenware, for holding medicines.

Aldrevandin Group Group of Medieval enamelled glass beakers made toward the end of the 13th century, their place of manufacture in doubt; named after an example in the British Museum inscribed 'MAGISTER ALDREVANDIN ME FECI[T]'.

alkali Essential ingredient in making glass, added to the **batch** in the form of potash (to make *Waldglas*) or soda (from **barilla**) to reduce the temperature at which the silica (in the form of sand and occasionally flint) would fuse.

Almorratxa or *almorrata* Spanish; type of **sprinkler** with many spouts for containing rose-water.

Amen glass Type of English glassware used for toasting the **Jacobite** cause (particularly the Old Pretender, James Stuart), decorated with verses of the Jacobite Hymn ending with the word 'Amen' and a crown executed in **diamond-point**, usually on a drawn-stem wine glass.

amphoriskos Small perfume jar of ancient Greece, sometimes made in **core-formed glass**, with a shouldered body, pointed base and two handles; a miniature amphora used for oil and wine.

amulet Glass ornament worn from Egyptian times to ward off evil.

Annagelb German; see **uranium glass**.

Annagrün German; see **uranium glass**.

annealing Process through which all glass vessels pass, wherein the finished hot object is cooled very slowly and evenly in an annealing oven to reduce any internal stresses that might have built up during its manufacture that would otherwise cause it to crack once cold.

art glass 1. Term applied to ornamental rather than functional glassware. 2. Types of American glassware dating from the 1870s onward, such as **Aurene glass**.

Aryballos Small globular bottle of ancient Greece, with two handles for suspension, made in **core-formed glass**; for cosmetic oils and balms.

Aurene glass Type of American **art glass** developed by Frederick Carder, its metallic surface obtained by spraying the glass with metallic chloride solutions through a flame.

aventurine Translucent glass with glittering metallic inclusions made in imitation of aventurine quartz; flakes of gold were used in 15th-century Venetian glass, copper from the 17th century.

balsamarium Small container of ancient Greece and Rome, usually a bottle; for perfumed oils, cosmetics or balms.

baluster Type of drinking glass, its stem in the form of a baluster (adopted from Renaissance architecture), which could be inverted or decorated with **knops**, internal **tears** and bubbles.

balustroid Type of **baluster** glass but with a lighter, more elongated stem. Although sometimes called 'Newcastle light balusters', they are now thought to have been produced mainly in Holland. (*Above*)

barilla (*Salsola soda*), salt-water marsh plant, the ashes of which were used as the **alkali** in making **glass**.

Baroque From the Italian *barocco*, a late Renaissance style dating from *c.*1660. Its exaggerated movement is reflected in the stem formations of Venetian glass and in German glass as *Laub- und Bandelwerk*.

basket 1. Glass in the shape of a basket, sometimes with an overhead handle. 2. Type of **paperweight** with a funnel-shaped lattice support, usually holding fruit and flowers.

batch Mixture of raw ingredients (generally **alkali**, lime and silica) that are melted and fused together in a pot or crucible to make glass. To this was added a proportion of broken glass, or **cullet**, and metal oxide colourants.

Berkemeyer German; 16th- and 17th-century *Waldglas* drinking glass, with a cylindrical lower part decorated with **prunts** and a flaring bowl.

bevelled Type of flat glass with a sloping edge to protect it from chipping, usually found on the edges of mirrors.

Biedermeier German, 'honest fellow'. The bourgeois style current in German decorative arts from *c.*1825 to 1840. In glass it takes the form of a change away from colourless to coloured glass (including **Hyalith, Lithyalin** and **uranium** glass), and **flashed** glass.

blank Any preliminary shape of a glass object that requires further forming or finishing processes.

Blankschnitt German, 'polished cut'. Style of engraved decoration, attributed to Georg Schwanhardt, found on German **potash glass**, particularly from Nuremberg, in which the relief effect is enhanced by polishing the ground part of the **intaglio**.

blowing Technique of shaping a molten mass of glass by blowing air into it through a **blowpipe**, either freehand or into a mould of two or more parts. It was first developed in the latter part of the 1st century BC.

blowpipe Hollow metal tube, about 1.5m (5ft) long and 2cm (¾in) in diameter, with a mouthpiece at one end and a thin ring fitted to the other that helps to retain the **gather** of molten glass from the pot. Air is blown through the mouthpiece to inflate and form the glass.

boracic Type of glass produced by Clichy in 1849 using borax, which, in the form of boric acid, was added to the **batch** as a **flux** in making **lead glass**. It was claimed to be free from bubbles and other impurities, and strong, being resistant to chips and changes in temperature.

brilliant cut Style of cut glass with very deep and highly polished complex cuts; developed in the United States during the second half of the 19th century.

cage cup Type of thick-walled late Roman glass that was undercut with an intricate openwork or figural pattern attached to the main body of the vessel by small hidden bridges. See **Lycurgus Cup**.

calcedonio Italian; marbled glass (with brown, blue, green and yellow swirls) made in imitation of banded semiprecious stones; originally made in Venice from the late 15th century and revived in the second half of the 19th century. Also known as **agate** and **chalcedony** glass.

came Grooved slip of lead securing glass in leaded- and stained-glass windows.

cameo Decorative **cased** or **flashed** glass with two or more different coloured layers, the outer layer(s) cut away so that the design stands out in relief against the background colour. First developed by the Romans from techniques used for banded stone and shell cameos at the end of the 1st century BC and revived in the 19th century. See also **Portland Vase**.

cane Slender, patterned rod formed by fusing together groups of coloured rods which, while still molten, were pulled out to reduce their diameter and to produce an internal polychrome design. Once cold, slices were cut, either to make **millefiori** and **mosaic** glass, or to incorporate into stems of drinking glasses. See **twist**.

casing Technique of forming two or more layers of glass to make **cameo** glass. A hollow **blank** of the outer layer is made before a gob of the inner background is blown inside it. The two then fuse as they are inflated together. Also used in **paperweights**, where the opaque coloured outer layer is cut away to form 'windows' through which the design can be seen.

cast glass Made from the 8th century BC by fusing powdered **frit** in single or interlocking moulds.

chalcedony See **calcedonio**.

cinerary urn Large container, sometimes lidded, with a spherical or ovoid body and a broad rim, used at first for storage purposes and later, from the 1st to mid 3rd centuries AD, as burial urns for ashes.

claw-beaker Tall Merovingian beaker, dating from the 5th to 8th centuries, with a body tapering toward a narrow foot and decorated with several rows of hollow, claw-like **prunts**. Called *Rüsselbecher* in German.

Clichy rose Cane made at Clichy resembling an open rose, with a pink central cylindrical motif surrounded by flattened tubes of green glass. Used in **millefiori paperweights**.

collar Circular ring of glass used at the junction of bowl to stem or between stem and foot on some wine glasses.

colour band Early Roman glass combining the techniques of **casting** and **blowing**, wherein globular bottles are formed from **mosaic canes** that were gathered on a **blowpipe** and inflated.

concentric Type of **millefiori paperweight** in which florets (slices from large **canes**) are arranged in concentric circles.

core-formed glass Type of glass dating from 1500 BC (before the invention of **blowing**), whose method of manufacture involves shaping trails of molten glass over a core of mud or clay (sometimes supported by a metal rod) and fusing them together in the furnace. After **annealing** the core was scraped out. Made in the form of *alabastra*, *amphoriskoi*, *aryballoi* and other vessels.

cristallo Italian; type of soda glass made with the ashes of **barilla**, which, with the addition of manganese oxide, produced a colourless glass that resembles rock crystal. First developed in Venice in the 15th century. See also **crystal**.

crizzling or **crisselling** Defect in **glass** caused by an imbalance in the **batch**, usually an excess of **alkali**, which makes the glass deteriorate; characterized by an internal network of fine cracks and sometimes surface dampness. It was corrected by George Ravenscroft in his development of **lead glass** in c.1676.

crown technique Technique for producing sheet glass wherein a bubble of **blown** glass was cut open, rotated rapidly and reheated frequently until it formed a flat disc attached to the end of the **pontil rod**. After **annealing** the glass could be cut to various sizes.

crown weight Hollow **paperweight**, made at St Louis, in which a pattern of twisted ribbons is arranged vertically and drawn together at the top.

crystal Colourless, transparent glass that resembles rock crystal. The word is derived from the Greek word for rock crystal, *krystallos*, or 'clear ice'. The term is now generally applied to high-quality cut glass. See also *cristallo* and **lead glass**.

cullet Fragments of raw or broken glass melted down with the new ingredients of a **batch** to act as a **flux** to reduce the time required to make **glass**.

cutting Decorative technique, employed since pre-Roman times, in which glass is ground away from an object's surface by a rotating wheel fed with water.

cylinder technique Technique for making flat or 'broad' glass for mirrors or windows. A large, elongated glass bubble is blown and then removed from the **blowpipe** so that both ends can be cut to produce a cylinder. This cylinder is slit lengthwise with shears and placed in a furnace, where the two sides uncurl (through mechanical force or gravity) to form a flat sheet of glass.

Daumenglas German, 'thumb glass'. Large cylindrical or barrel-shaped *Waldglas* beaker with circular indentations for the fingers and thumbs to grasp while drinking from it.

decanter Decorative bottle with stopper used for serving wine, spirits and even ale. The many shapes include bell, claret, club-shaped, cruciform, magnum, mallet, onion-shaped, Rodney, shaft and globe, ship's, shouldered, stirrup and whisky.

decanter jug Type of jug with a handle and stopper used as a **decanter**.

diamond air-trap Decoration wherein air pockets embedded in the glass are arranged in a diamond-shaped pattern, patented by W.H., B. & J. Richardson in 1857. A **gather** of glass is blown into a mould with projections of the desired design and covered by another **parison** so that the indentations trap air pockets.

diamond-cutting Decorative cut patterns: plain, strawberry or hobnail.

diamond or **diamond-point engraving** Linear drawing on a glass surface by means of a diamond or metal point, used since the second quarter of the 16th century across Europe. Later the technique of **stippling** with a diamond-point was developed.

diatretarius Latin; Roman glass-cutter or glass decorator, as opposed to *vitrearius*, glass-maker or glass-blower.

diatretum See **cage cup**.

dichroic Showing different colours when viewed in transmitted or reflected light. Achieved by adding metal to the **batch**, originally gold, later uranium or copper oxide, in a reducing atmosphere. See **Lycurgus Cup**.

dip-moulding Technique using a one-piece mould to achieve a pattern that can be further expanded on the **blowpipe**.

double ogee bowl Type of wine-glass bowl with a profile of two connected 'S's.

dromedary flask Type of post-Roman glass flask, found in Syria from the 6th to 8th centuries AD, decorated with heavy openwork trailing and shaped to resemble a dromedary.

enamelling Decorative technique wherein coloured powdered glass, mixed with an oily medium, is painted on to the glass surface and then reheated in the furnace to fuse the design. Practised since the 1st century AD.

engraving Technique of cutting into the surface of a glass by holding against the glass a rotating wheel of stone or metal fed with an abrasive.

faceting Technique of decorating curved glass surfaces by grinding to make shallow depressions that are flat or nearly so.

façon de Venise French, 'in the Venetian style'. Term used to describe high-quality glassware of Venetian influence, as opposed to **forest glass** or *Waldglas*, made throughout Europe in the 16th and 17th centuries.

faience Porous body of finely ground quartz (a form of silica) held together by a glassy 'connective tissue' and covered with a coloured vitreous glaze. It can be modelled or thrown on a wheel to achieve its final shape before being fired.

filigrana Italian, 'thread grained'. Type of glass originally made in Murano in the second quarter of the 16th century. Term covers all styles of decoration in which threads of glass (usually opaque white) are embedded in clear glass to form a very fine network pattern. The terms *latticinio* or *latticino* are also used. These designs include *vetro a fili*, *vetro a reticello* and *vetro a retortoli*. See also **filigree**.

filigree English term for *filigrana*, wherein a rod incorporating thin white or coloured threads is manipulated to give the appearance of lace.

flashing Technique of applying a thin glass layer of a contrasting colour to a glass object by dipping it into a pot of molten **metal** that can be cut away to leave a design in **cameo**.

flint glass Misused term for **lead glass**, wherein the silica is obtained from powdered flints (impure quartz) rather than from sand.

flute Very tall and slender flaring wine glass on a short stem.

flute cutting Pattern of parallel grooves on cut glass occurring in a variety of forms: mitred ('V'-shaped), round (concave semi-circular) and hollow (concave semi-elliptical).

flux Alkaline substance that is an essential ingredient in the **batch** to aid the fusion of the silica, added as potash or soda.

forest glass English term for glass with a strong greenish tint in which the **alkali** or **flux** in the **batch** is obtained from the ashes of burnt wood or ferns. The green is caused by iron alloys from the impure potash. Called *Waldglas* in German.

frit Term referring to some of the ingredients of glass that are pre-heated until they are red-hot but not fused; these are then cooled and ground into a powder and added to the other ingredients of the **batch**. This process removes moisture from the material and the gases that might result when heated, thus producing glass with fewer impurities.

gadrooning Continuous decorative pattern of short sections of ribbing either moulded, applied or deep cut; inspired by patterns on late 17th-century silver.

gaffer The head glass-maker, sometimes called a master blower, who does the most skilled work.

gather Blob or mass of molten glass attached to the end of a **blowpipe** or **pontil** before an object is formed from it.

gilding Technique of decoration wherein the surface or back of a glass vessel is covered with gold leaf, gold paint or gold dust mixed with a fixative and then fired. Alternatively, the gilding can be engraved with a design, cold-painted or sandwiched between another layer of glass (gold sandwich). See also *Zwischengoldglas*.

glass Homogeneous material which has a random, liquid-like (non-crystalline) molecular structure.

Glasschneider German, 'glass-cutter'.

gold-band glass Type of ancient **mosaic** glass with serpentine lengths of pre-formed **canes** of blue, purple, green and gold-sandwich glass.

gold-sandwich glass See **gilding** and *Zwischengoldglas*.

Graal glass Trade name for coloured mosaic-like glass developed by Orrefors in Sweden in 1916.

grisaille 1. Decorative painting in shades of grey on glass, sometimes used to imitate relief sculpture. 2. Brownish paint made from iron oxide, fused on to glass to define details in stained-glass windows.

hand cooler Small, egg-shaped glass object used either as a darning egg or to cool the palms of a lady's hand.

Hausmaler German, 'home painter'. A freelance or independent painter who decorated glass direct from the factory during the 17th and 18th centuries.

Hedwig beaker Type of thick-walled glass beaker of the 11th or 12th century, cut in high relief with stylized lions, griffins, eagles or palm-leaf patterns. Named after St Hedwig (d. 1243), because one of the surviving examples supposedly belonged to her.

Hochschnitt German, 'high engraving'. Technique of cutting glass in which the design stands out in high relief from the vessel body; opposite of **intaglio**.

Hofglasschneider German, 'court glass-cutter'. Highly skilled glass-cutter attached to a German court, especially in the 18th century.

Hofkristalschneider German, 'court crystal cutter'. As for *Hofglasschneider*.

Humpen German; tall, cylindrical beer or wine beaker made of *Waldglas* from the mid 16th to the 18th centuries.

huqqa Indian, 'hookah'. Globular or bell-shaped bottle, to which a long flexible tube for smoking tobacco is attached.

Hyalith Opaque black and, more rarely, opaque red glass in imitation of Wedgwood's basaltes ware, made in Bohemia from 1817 by the glasshouse of Count von Buquoy.

ice glass Decorative glassware with an outer surface resembling cracked ice, first produced in Venice during the 16th century. Made principally by plunging the hot glass briefly into water and then reheating it, or by rolling the hot glass over splinters and fragments of glass laid out on a **marver** and then reheating it to fuse the pieces to the surface. (*Above*)

incrustation Technique of inserting non-glassy matter, commonly ceramic, into glass, introduced in the last third of the 18th century. These encrusted pieces, also known as 'crystallo ceramie' and **sulphides**, were used in **paperweights**, pendants, decanters and jewel boxes.

inlay Any small, flat piece of glass fastened on to the surface of a larger object and cemented into place to form a component of a larger decorative design.

intaglio Technique of **engraving** or **wheel-cutting** a design below the surface of a glass object, in order to produce an image in relief whose background is in the highest plane; therefore, the opposite of *Hochschnitt*.

Intarsia glass A type of **art glass**, introduced by Frederick Carder, which has a layer of coloured glass with an etched design sandwiched between two colourless layers.

iridescence Rainbow-like effect found on the surface of excavated glass objects caused by a chemical attack on the surface of the glass resulting from its environment. This effect was artificially reproduced in Art Nouveau glass by the application of a metallic **lustre**.

Jacobite glass English glassware principally **engraved** (or, rarely, **enamelled**) with portraits, emblems (rose, star or thistle) or inscriptions ('Fiat', or 'Let it be done'; 'Redeat', or 'May he return') and verses from the Jacobite anthem – see **Amen glass** – to commemorate the Stuart cause of the Old and the Young Pretenders (James Stuart and Charles Stuart, or 'Bonnie Prince Charlie').

jelly glass Small vessel, usually of inverted conical or bell form on a flat foot, used for custards, jellies or syllabubs.

kick Conical indentation in the base of a glass vessel formed by the **pontil rod**, ranging from a slight concavity to a deep, conical hollow, to add stability and to collect sediment from the liquid inside.

knop Decorative blob or bulge on the stem of a glass; can be hollow or solid and comes in a variety of shapes, including acorn, annular, ball, bobbin, cylinder, drop, egg, flattened, melon, multiple, mushroom and winged.

Krautstrunk German, 'cabbage stalk'. Type of beaker, decorated with large flat **prunts**, made in *Waldglas* during the 15th and 16th centuries.

Kugler German; glass-cutter in the 18th and early 19th centuries who specialized in circular and oval cutting and other techniques in the **Biedermeier** style.

Kunckel red Type of glass coloured ruby red through the addition of gold chloride to the **batch**. Developed by the chemist Johann Kunckel, probably before 1679. Called *Rubinglas*, or *Goldrubinglas*, in German.

lacy glass 1. See **filigree**. 2. Type of American **pressed** glass in which the decoration of flowers or foliage is set against a diaper background, giving an overall sparkling lacy effect.

lampwork Glass either blown or manipulated from clear or coloured glass rods over a torch or blow lamp, used in **paperweights** and Nevers figures.

lathe-cutting Technique whereby **blanks** of glass are mounted and turned slowly with the aid of a bow or handled wheel while a tool fed with an abrasive is held against the glass in order to cut sharp profiles or to polish the overall surface.

latticinio or *latticino* Italian, from the word *latte*, 'milk'. Clear glass decorated with embedded threads of white glass to form network patterns. See **filigrana**.

lattimo Italian, from the word *latte*, 'milk'. Opaque white glass coloured by adding bone ash or tin oxide to the **batch** and sometimes by adding antimony or zinc. Known as *Milchglas* in German.

Laub- und Bandelwerk German, 'leaf and strapwork'. Term for a **Baroque** decorative pattern of intricate intertwined leaf and floral motifs.

lead glass Type of glass containing a large amount of lead oxide (24–30%), first made by George Ravenscroft as a remedy for **crizzling**. The resulting glass is more brilliant than *cristallo* and softer and better suited for cutting.

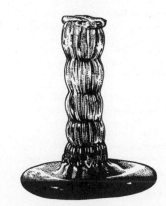

linen smoother Glass object with a heavy flat, rounded base and a handle used as a pressing iron. (*Above*)

Lithyalin Type of glass, invented by Friedrich Egermann, which is opaque (usually red) and marbled on the surface in imitation of semiprecious stones.

lustre painting Technique of producing an **iridescent** effect on the surface of glass by using metallic pigments that are fired in a reducing atmosphere.

Lycurgus Cup A cage cup of **dichroic** glass (opaque pea green in reflected light and red in transmitted light) made in the 4th century AD; cut with figures from the myth of King Lycurgus.

marbled Type of glass decorated with different coloured streaks resembling the patterns in marble.

marver Flat iron (probably originally marble) table upon which the **gather** is rolled into an evenly shaped mass.

marvering Technique of rolling hot, softened glass over a flat surface (a **marver**) in order to smooth out the vessel, to consolidate trailed decoration applied to the vessel or to pick up decoration in the form of blobs or fragments of glass.

matrix Mass of glass that encloses **mosaic** glass.

Matsu-no-ke glass Japanese-influenced design developed by Frederick Carder and registered by Stevens & Williams in 1884. Term also covers a Japanese style of decoration used in the latter part of the Victorian period.

merese Type of collar like a flattened **knop**, with a sharp edge generally applied to the stem, often in the form of a joint between the bowl and the stem. (*Above*)

metal Term describing glass while molten or cold, used to distinguish the material from the object.

Milchglas German, 'milk glass'. See *lattimo*.

millefiori Italian, 'a thousand flowers'. Term used to describe **mosaic** glass used in ancient and Venetian glass as well as in **paperweights**.

mosaic Pre-formed, sliced **canes** of glass placed around or in a mould, heated slowly until the elements fuse together to form the required shape and then polished when cold to smooth the surface.

mosque lamp Hanging lamp with bulbous body, flaring mouth and thick loop handles for suspension from mosque ceilings. First made in Syria in the 13th and 14th centuries, they were decorated in gilding and enamel, often with inscriptions from the Koran.

Moss Agate glass Type of **art glass** developed by John Northwood and Frederick Carder in the late 1880s. A gather of **soda glass** was cased in **lead glass**, coated in powdered coloured glass and again cased in **lead glass**, which was injected with water to cause the weaker soda glass to crack. After the water was emptied out it was reheated to leave a crackled network.

mould-blowing Technique of blowing a **gather** of glass, while attached to a **blowpipe**, into a wooden or iron mould in two or more parts; the decoration on the inside can be further inflated to reduce the sharpness of the design.

moulded pedestal stem Type of moulded stem that is ribbed and shouldered with generally between four and eight sides; made in England and Germany and popular from c.1715 to 1765. Sometimes called **Silesian stems**.

mould-pressing Technique of forcing or pressing hot glass into an open or multiple-part mould.

Nef Table ornament in the shape of a rigged sailing ship.

Neoclassicism Style from the latter part of the 18th century based on a renewed interest in the arts of Greece and Rome; largely inspired by the excavations at Pompeii and Herculaneum and the publication of the collections of ancient Greek vases belonging to the Comte de Caylus and Sir William Hamilton.

Nipt diamond waies Diamond-shaped network decoration made by nipping together ribs or trails of glass threads. A Venetian design but offered by Briton George Ravenscroft in his 1677 price list of new **lead glass**. (*Above*)

Nuppenbecher German, 'drop glass'. A *Waldglas* drinking glass decorated with applied **prunts**; made in northern Europe from the 14th century. See also *Krautstrunk*.

ogee bowl Bowl for a wine glass shaped with a double curve or an 'S'.

oinochoe Ancient one-handled jug, often with a trefoil mouth, made in **core-formed glass**.

opal glass Translucent white glass made by adding calcined bones to the **batch**.

opaque twist See **twist**.

overlay The outer layer of glass on **cased** and **flashed** glass.

pan-topped Shape of bowl on some drinking glasses and **sweetmeats**, in which the upper part of the bowl is wider than the curved lower part.

paperweight Small solid-glass decorative object used to hold down papers on a desk, originally made in France by Baccarat, Clichy and St Louis during the 'classic' period of paperweight manufacture (1845–55). Beneath a magnifying dome of clear glass (usually **lead glass**), an orderly **millefiori** or **lampwork** design was set low, near the base. The **pontil mark** on the underside was removed and the resulting slight concavity decorated with cutting (**star**, **strawberry diamond** or crosshatching). The dome could be **faceted** or **cased** with one or more colours through which windows were cut.

parison or **paraison** Bubble of molten glass formed on the **blowpipe** after air has been blown into it, expanded from the **gather**.

pâte-de-verre French, 'glass paste'. Ancient technique, revived in France during the second half of the 19th century, of melting in a mould ground glass, to which was added a **fluxing** medium and colouring agent (this was either powdered, coloured glass or metallic oxide).

phial Roman; small glass bottle used for ointments, medicines and perfumed oils.

phiale Greek; shallow bowl with a flat bottom or base-ring used as a wall ornament or for pouring libations.

piggin Glass with a small bowl and vertical handle that was used as a dipper for milk or cream.

pilgrim flask Type of bottle with a flattened bulbous body and four loop handles for suspension, intended for use

by pilgrims to carry water. The two flattened sides lent themselves to decoration, especially by Venetian enamellers. (*Above*)

pillar cutting Style of cut decoration with parallel vertical, convex ribs.

pincering Technique of pinching or squeezing the **trailing** or other ornamentation on an object for decorative effect by pincers.

Pokal German, 'goblet'. Usually applied to a late 17th- to mid-19th-century type of engraved, covered goblet with a flared bowl, for drinking toasts.

polishing Technique of giving a glass object an even finish, either by reintroducing it into the furnace or smoothing it against revolving wheels.

pontil or **punty** Solid iron rod to which the object from the **blowpipe** is transferred so that the rim may be finished, handle applied or any other final shaping carried out. Once the glass has cooled it is knocked off the rod, leaving a rough mark, the 'pontil mark', which, beginning in the 19th century, is usually ground away.

Portland Vase A dark blue **cameo** amphora with an opaque white **overlay**, carved on one side with Paris, his mother Hecuba and the goddess Athena, representing the Fall of Troy, and on the other side, the Rise of Rome with Augustus, his mother Atia (between whose legs rises a snake) and the god Neptune. Possibly made in Rome during the last quarter of the 1st century BC for the emperor Augustus. Formerly in the Palazzo Barberini in Rome and Sir William Hamilton's collection, then sold to the Duke of Portland and the British Museum. Lent to Josiah Wedgwood, whose Black Basalt it inspired.

potash glass Type of hard glass containing potash (potassium carbonate) derived from plant ash (**forest glass**); suitable for cutting, unlike *cristallo*.

press-moulding Technique wherein molten glass is poured into a metal mould and a plunger lowered into the mass, leaving a smooth centre with a patterned exterior. Fine pressed pieces are often finished by hand to obliterate the mould marks. May bear maker's marks.

printy Below-the-surface pattern of shallow concaves, circular or oval, made with a slightly convex cutting wheel.

prismatic cutting Decorative cut pattern consisting of long, straight mitred grooves cut horizontally in parallel lines.

prunt Blob of glass, sometimes in a contrasting colour, applied to the surface of an object for decoration (*Above*).

pyxis Greek; covered receptacle, usually cylindrical, used for cosmetics, ink or jewellery. Made in Roman times in **cast**, **blown** or **mould-blown** glass.

Queen's Burmese glass Type of **art glass** that changes shade from light rose at the top to greenish yellow at the bottom; developed by the Mount Washington Glass Company of Massachusetts and Thomas Webb & Sons in Stourbridge.

raised diamond-cutting Decorative cut pattern wherein diagonal grooves are cut close together and again at right angles to form four-sided diamonds in pyramidal form standing in relief. See also **strawberry diamond**.

reactive glass Type of **art glass**, introduced by Louis Comfort Tiffany, that changed colour when reheated.

relief-cutting Cutting on glass creating a design that stands in relief against the background, as on **cameo**, *Hochschnitt* and *Tiefschnitt* glass.

reticello See *vetro a reticello*.

reticulated glass Decorative glassware on which trails of glass are manipulated to form an open network. Originally a Venetian technique used from the 16th to 18th centuries.

rhyton Greek; unstable drinking glass, usually made in the form of a human or animal head tapering to a point.

rock crystal engraving Type of engraving, developed in England at the end of the 19th century by Thomas Webb & Sons and Stevens & Williams, wherein all the surfaces are polished.

Rococo Probably from the French *rocaille*, or 'rockwork'. An ornamental style, dating from *c.*1740 to 1760, that was marked by asymmetry and the use of abstract design suggested by shells, rocks, waves, flowers and foliage.

rod-formed glass Type of glass made by winding molten glass around a narrow metal rod to make beads.

Roemer German; traditional 15th- and 16th-century German *Waldglas* drinking vessel with an ovoid bowl, a hollow cylindrical stem decorated with **prunts** and a spreading coiled or blown foot.

Rubinglas German, 'ruby glass'. Glass colour with copper, gold or selenium. See **Kunckel red**.

ruby glass Related to *Rubinglas*, introduced by Frederick Carder, in either pink or brilliant red.

rummer Term usually applied to a 19th-century English low drinking goblet with a square or domed stemmed foot.

Rüsselbecher German. See **claw-beaker**.

salver Glass with flat bowl used for displaying foods such as fruit or for supporting **jelly glasses**.

Scheuer glass German; type of 15th-century German *Waldglas* drinking vessel with a wide, cylindrical neck and a bulbous body decorated with **prunts**, one of which is pulled out to form a handle.

Schwarzlot German, 'black lead'. Transparent enamel used during the Middle Ages for painting lines and shadows on stained-glass windows and in the 17th and 18th centuries by *Hausmaler* to decorate glass and porcelain.

Silesian stem See **moulded pedestal stem**.

silica Silicon dioxide occurring as quartz and as the principal constituent of sand used in the making of **glass**.

silvered glass Type of glassware popular in the second half of the 19th century, its silvery appearance created by pouring silver nitrate solution between the double walls of a vessel through a hole in the base, then sealed to prevent oxidization.

Silveria Type of **art glass** developed by John Northwood II in *c.*1900 with silver foil encased between two colourless or coloured layers of glass.

silver staining Technique of applying silver chloride in an acid solution to a glass surface to produce a yellow stain.

Skyphos Greek; hemispherical or semi-ovoid drinking cup with two handles.

snake thread Applied trailed decoration in an irregular, sometimes ridged, winding pattern resembling snakes; found on 3rd-century Roman glass from Cologne and the Near East.

snowflake glass 18th-century Chinese glass with white inclusions and bubbles.

soda glass Glass in which the **alkali** in the **batch** is obtained from soda (sodium carbonate) rather than potash. In Venetian *cristallo* the soda is derived from **barilla**.

sprinkler flask Glass flask which has a narrow or constricted neck so that the contents can only be poured out slowly or drop by drop.

stained glass Decorative windows, usually found in churches, made up of coloured glass panes further decorated by **staining** or **enamelling** and usually held in place by lead **cames**.

staining Colouring on the surface of glass achieved by the application of metallic oxides and reheating, like **silver staining**, to produce yellow or ruby colours by copper oxide. Used since the 14th century on window glass and from the beginning of the 19th century on decorative glass, notably by Anton Kothgasser and the Mohns.

stamnos Greek; wide-mouthed storage jar with an ovoid body and two loop handles attached at the shoulder.

Stangenglas German, 'pole glass'. Tall, cylindrical drinking vessel of the 15th and 16th centuries standing on a pedestal base.

star cut Type of cut decoration with grooves radiating from a central point and tapering outward. The earliest have six to eight points, while later examples have as many as 32.

stippling Technique of tapping a glass surface with a pointed implement to produce a pattern of tiny dots that build up to make a picture; practised by Frans Greenwood and David Wolff.

stopper Piece of glass acting as a cork to a bottle or decanter. Made in a variety of shapes and sizes, such as ball, bull's eye, conical, disc, mushroom and spire.

strawberry diamond Form of **raised diamond-cutting** wherein the flat areas between the high-relief diamonds are crosshatched to make a low-relief diamond pattern. Sometimes used on the bases of **paperweights**.

sulphide Silvery-looking opaque relief medallion or cameo (usually a portrait) made of a white porcellaneous material enclosed in transparent glass. Because of a thin layer of air under the glass the medallion acquires a silvery appearance.

sweetmeat Tall-stemmed container used to hold crystallized fruits and a variety of sweetmeats.

tazza Italian, 'cup'. Shallow ornamental cup or dish on a stemmed foot, used for fruits or sweetmeats, as a stand for other glasses or possibly for drinking.

tear Drop-shaped air bubble enclosed in a glass, usually in the stem. (*Above*)

trail Strand of glass, roughly circular in cross section, which has been drawn out from a small **gather** of glass and applied to the surface of a vessel.

trailing The laying of threads or **trails** of hot glass over a glass object to form a decorative pattern.

trulla Latin; ladle with a round bowl and a horizontal handle.

trunk beaker See **claw-beaker**.

turn-over rim Type of rim curved outward and downward; commonly found on late 18th- to early 19th-century Irish bowls and salt cellars.

twist Decorative device in the stems of 18th-century drinking glasses and **sweetmeats** produced by twisting a glass rod in which are embedded columns of air (**air-twists** and mercury twists), threads of white or coloured glass ('cotton-twists', 'colour-twists' or **opaque twists**) or a mixture of the three to give an elaborate multi-spiral.

uranium glass Yellowish-green (*Annagelb*) or green glass (*Annagrün*) made through the addition of uranium to the **batch**, introduced in Bohemia by Josef Riedel in around 1840.

Vandyke Scalloped decoration on the rims and edges of vessels, derived from the lace collars in Van Dyck's portraits.

verre églomisé Decorative technique in which gold or silver leaf is applied to the surface of glass (usually on the reverse), engraved and protected by varnish, metal foil or another layer of glass. So called after French mirror and picture framer Jean-Baptiste Glomy (d. 1786). Loosely used to describe types of *Zwischengold-glas* in jewellery and medallions.

vetro a fili Italian, 'thread glass'. Type of *filigrana* decoration in which clear glass has a pattern of continuous parallel lines.

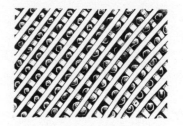

vetro a reticello Italian, 'glass with a small network'. Type of *filigrana* decoration in which clear glass has a pattern of embedded threads in a diagonal, crisscrossing arrangement trapping small air bubbles between them. (*Above*)

vetro a retortoli Italian, 'glass with a twist'. Type of *filigrana* decoration in which intricately twisted threads are embedded in clear glass in parallel lines.

vitrearius Latin; glass-blower or glass-maker (as opposed to a **diatretarius**, or glass-cutter).

Waldglas German. See **forest glass**.

wheel-cutting Process of decorating glass by means of a rotating wheel that grinds a pattern or inscription into the glass surface.

wheel-engraving See **engraving**.

wrythen Decoration of swirling vertical ribbing that gives a spiral effect.

Zwischengoldglas German, 'gold between glass'. Decorative technique, found on Bohemian glass (*c.*1730–40), wherein gold leaf applied to the outer surface of a glass vessel is engraved with a metal point and protected by being encased in another glass layer or sealed with transparent varnish.

GLASSHOUSES AND BIOGRAPHIES

Alexandria: city founded by Alexander the Great in 332 BC where glassware of the highest quality was produced until it was overrun by the Huns in the 4th century AD.

Altare: Italian glasshouse situated near Genoa, probably founded in the 11th century, rising to prominence during the second half of the 15th century to rival Venice. Glass-workers from Altare founded new glasshouses in France and the Netherlands.

Amelung, John Frederick (1741–98): born in Bremen, Germany, but travelled to the United States, where in 1784 he founded the New Bremen Glass Manufactory, in Frederick County, Maryland, producing finely engraved glass.

Argy-Rousseau, Gabriel (1885–1953): French Art Deco glass-maker specializing in *pâte-de-verre* and *pâte-de-cristal* vessels and figures, often classically inspired.

Baccarat: French town in Meurthe-et-Moselle; site of the Compagnie des Cristalleries de Baccarat, whose first glasshouse was founded in 1765. Known especially for its lead crystal and paperweights, the firm remains one of the leading French glass manufacturers.

Bacchus, George, & Sons: English glass factory in Birmingham which in the 19th century specialized in flashing, transfer-printing and paperweights.

Bakewell Company: American glasshouse founded in 1808 by Benjamin Bakewell (1767–1844) and Edward Ensell in Pittsburgh, Pennsylvania. In *c*.1813, on the acquisition of another glasshouse, it was renamed the Pittsburgh Flint Glass Manufactory; closed in 1882.

Barovier, Angelo: Venetian working in Murano who is supposed to have made the Barovier Cup, a dark blue enamelled wedding cup of *c*.1470–8, and to have contributed to the development of *cristallo*.

Barovier, Ercole (1889–1974): Italian glass-maker, descended from a long line of Murano masters; founded Barovier & Toso.

Beilby, William (1740–1819), **Thomas** (1747–1826) and **Mary** (1749–97): brothers and sister who in 1760 moved with their family from Durham to Newcastle-upon-Tyne, where they produced enamelled glassware until *c*.1778.

Bianconi, Fulvio (b. 1915): Italian glass designer who was leading post-war figure at Venini; created the classic handkerchief vase.

Biemann, Dominik (1800–57): born in Neuwelt, Bohemia. One of the most important glass engravers, especially of portraits on medallions, goblets and beakers, of the Biedermeier period.

Bigaglia, Pietro (*fl.*1845): Italian who worked in Murano and in 1845 exhibited the earliest millefiori paperweight in Vienna. His paperweights included some canes initialled 'P.B.'and bearing the date 1845.

Bishopp, Hawley (*fl.*1676–85): English glass-maker; worked at George Ravenscroft's Henley glasshouse from 1676; in 1682 he took over the Savoy glasshouse.

Böhm, August (1812–90): outstanding Bohemian glass engraver of the Biedermeier period.

Boston & Sandwich Glass Company: founded in 1825 at Sandwich, Massachusetts, by Deming Jarves, an agent for the New England Glass Company. Produced mould-pressed and lacy glass as well as paperweights; closed in 1888.

Böttger, Johann Friedrich (1682–1719): producer of stoneware, true porcelain and *Rubinglas* at the court of Dresden.

Bowes, Sir Jerome (d. 1616): English soldier and diplomat who in 1592 secured a monopoly, which became effective the following year, to make and import Venetian glass.

Briati, Giuseppe (1686–1772): glass-maker from Murano who specialized in *filigrana* and chandeliers.

Brussa, Oswaldo: Venetian who, with other members of his family, including his son, Angelo, decorated glass with polychrome enamel during the second half of the 18th century.

Caithness Glass Ltd: Scottish firm founded in 1960 specializing in paperweights; based in Perth.

Carder, Frederick (1863–1963): English glass designer and technician who studied with Emile Gallé and from 1880 to 1903 was a designer at Stevens & Williams before moving to the United States, where he founded the Steuben Glass Works.

Carré, Jean (d. 1572): glass-maker from Arras who moved to England in 1567. He first produced mirror glass in the Weald but in 1570 opened the Crutched Friars Glasshouse in London with Peter Briet, producing glass *à la façon de Venise* and later employing Giacomo Verzelini.

Clichy Glassworks: founded in 1837 by M. Rouyer and G. Maës at Billancourt before moving to Clichy-la-Garenne in 1839. From 1845 to 1857 it made paperweights of the highest quality.

Colinet: family who owned a glasshouse at Beauwelz, near Mons, Belgium, that produced glass *à la façon de Venise* from *c*.1506 to 1575.

Copier, Andries Dirk (b. 1901): Dutch glass designer long associated with the Royal Dutch Glass Works in Leerdam; created one-off 'Unica' and limited-edition 'Serica' pieces.

Cork Glass Company: Irish company founded in Cork in 1783, closing in 1818. Known especially for cut-glass decanters marked on the base 'Cork Glass Co.'

Corning Glass Works: multi-national glassworks producing industrial and domestic glass. Its headquarters are in Corning, New York, where the company moved in 1868. In 1918 it purchased the Steuben Glass Works and in 1951 established the Corning Glass Center, housing The Corning Museum of Glass (the most extensive glass museum in the world), the Hall of Science and Industry and Steuben Glass.

Couper, James, & Sons: Glasgow glasshouse that from *c*.1890 produced Clutha glass, with internal decoration of air bubbles, streaks and aventurine speckles. Some Clutha designs were provided by Dr Christopher Dresser, the noted theorist, botanist and designer in many media.

Crama, Elizabeth (*fl.* last quarter 17th century): diamond-point glass engraver who decorated goblets with calligraphy.

Cros, Henri (1840–1907): French glass artist who revived technique of *pâte-de-verre* in mid-1880s.

Crutched Friars Glasshouse: founded in 1568 by Jean Carré near Aldgate, London, to produce *cristallo* and glass *à la façon de Venise*. Giacomo Verzelini worked there, managing the firm after Carré's death.

d'Artigues, Aimé-Gabriel (1778–1848): from 1795 director of the St Louis Glass Factory. In 1802 bought the Vonêche glassworks in the Ardenne and in 1816 the Verreries de Sainte-Anne at Baccarat, renaming it Verrerie de Vonêche à Baccarat.

Daum Frères: French glassworks near Nancy (now called the Cristalleries de Nancy) operated by the Daum family since Jean Daum (1825–85) took it over in 1875. His two sons, Jean-Louis Auguste (1853–1909) and Jean-Antonin (1864–1930), produced glass in the Art Nouveau style influenced by Gallé.

Decker, Paul (1677–1713): German glass engraver influenced by the Rococo style seen in the form of *Laub- und Bandelwerk*.

Décorchement, François-Emile (1880–1971): French Art Deco glass artist working in *pâte-de-verre* and *pâte-de-cristal*.

de Lysle, Anthony (*fl.*1582): French glass and pewter engraver who came to London in 1582 and supposedly engraved glass from the factory of Giacomo Verzelini.

Desprez, Barthélemy (*fl.*1773–1819): Parisian sculptor who introduced the process of making sulphides.

Dorsch, Christoph (1676–1732): Nuremberg glass engraver.

Eder, Paulus (*fl.*1685–1709): Nuremberg glass engraver, especially in *Tiefschnitt*.

Egermann, Friedrich (1777–1864): born at Blottendorf, Bohemia. A glass-maker who decorated flashed glass, but best known for his Lithyalin glass.

Ennion (*fl.* first half 1st century AD): glass-maker who produced mould-blown glass of the highest quality, often signing his pieces.

Faber, Johann Ludwig (*fl.*1678–97): Nuremberg *Hausmaler* who painted stained glass and decorated glass vessels in *Schwarzlot* and transparent enamels.

Falcon Glassworks: two glasshouses in Southwark, London, supposedly founded by Francis Jackson and John Straw in 1693. They provided glass for James Giles and one glasshouse was run from 1803 by Green & Pellatt, who made sulphides from 1820.

Francisci, Nicolas (*fl.*1571): glass-maker producing glass *à la façon de Venise* at Liège.

Gallé, Emile (1846–1904): outstanding French glass-maker of the Art Nouveau period, producing vases, lamps, sculptures and other art glass at Nancy from 1874; also designed furniture and ceramics.

Gate, Simon (1883–1945): Swedish designer who worked for Orrefors from 1916 until his death; instrumental in developing Graal glass with glass-blower Knut Bergqvist.

Giles, James (1718–80): English decorator of enamelled porcelain who also decorated glass, usually coloured, with gilding and enamels.

Gillinder & Sons: glassworks in Philadelphia, Pennsylvania, founded in 1861 as Franklin Flint Glass Works by Englishman William T. Gillinder (1823–71). In 1863, when Edwin Bennett came to work with Gillinder, the company became Gillinder & Bennett, and in 1867, after the founder's two sons, James and Frederick, joined the firm, it traded as Gillinder & Sons. Known for paperweights.

Glass Sellers' Company: corporation of glass-makers and merchants granted a charter in 1635 and reincorporated in 1664 as The Worshipful Company of Glass Sellers of London. Originally imported Venetian glass from Murano. By 1674 George Ravenscroft was its official glass-maker.

Gondelach, Franz (1663–1726): glass engraver from Hesse who held the post of *Hofglasschneider* at Kassel, working mainly in *Hochschnitt* and intaglio.

Greene, John (d. 1703): member of the Glass Sellers' Company who corresponded and placed orders with a Muranese glass-maker, Alessio Morelli, from 1667 to 1673, for Venetian glass in English shapes.

Greenwood, Frans (1680–1761): Dutch glass engraver who excelled at stippling from the early 1720s.

Hald, Edvard (1883–1980): Swedish designer associated with Orrefors from 1917 until late 1970s.

Hall-in-Tyrol: Austrian glasshouse founded by the Augsburg glass-maker Wolfgang Vitl under the patronage of Archduke Ferdinand I in 1534, producing glass *à la façon de Venise*.

Handel & Company: glasshouse founded in 1885 in Meriden, Connecticut, by Philip J. Handel (1866–1914); mainly produced leaded- and painted-glass lamps.

Helmhack, Abraham (1654–1724): Nuremberg *Hausmaler*, a follower of Johann Schaper, who decorated both faience and glass in *Schwarzlot*.

Hill, John: glass-maker from Stourbridge who was sent to Waterford, Ireland, in 1783 to establish the glassworks financed by George and William Penrose.

Hoffmann, Josef (1870–1955): Viennese architect and handicraft expert, well known for his glass designs.

Horejc, Jaroslav (1886–1983): Czechoslovakian glass artist best known for his boldly modelled cut and engraved pieces; worked for Lobmeyr.

Iittala Glassworks: Finnish factory founded in 1881; has produced designs by architect Alvar Aalto, as well as by Tapio Wirkkala and Timo Sarpaneva.

Keith, James (*fl.*1750–87): glass-worker from Newcastle-upon-Tyne who worked at the Norwegian glasshouse at Nøstetangen.

Kiessling, Johann Christoph (d. 1744): court glass engraver in Dresden whose goblets were mainly decorated with hunting scenes.

Killinger, Georg Friedrich (*fl.*1694–1726): Nuremberg glass wheel-engraver.

Koepping, Karl (1848–1914): German artist who from *c.*1895 designed blown, often floriform, vessels, many with glass-blower Friedrich Zitzmann.

Kosta Boda: Sweden's oldest surviving glasshouse, founded in Småland in 1742.

Kothgasser, Anton (1769–1851): Viennese porcelain and glass decorator, introduced to glass painting by Gottlob Mohn. Typical work includes views of towns and landscapes painted in translucent enamels.

Kunckel, Georg Ernst (1692–1750): Thuringian glass engraver who was appointed court glass engraver at Gotha in 1721.

Kunckel, Johann (*c.*1630–1703): chemist and glass technician from an old glass-making family in Hesse. From about 1679 to 1693 he was in charge of the Potsdam glasshouse, where he developed ruby glass, also known as 'Kunckel-glass'.

Labhardt, Christoph (1641–95): gem- and glass-cutter from Switzerland who in 1680 went to Kassel, where he decorated glass in *Hochschnitt* and *Tiefschnitt*.

Labino, Dominick (1910–87): American glass artist and technician significant in the rise of the Studio Glass Movement.

La Granja de San Ildefonso: Spanish glassworks founded in 1728 near Segovia, under the patronage of Queen Isabella; produced plate glass for mirrors, chandeliers and vases.

Lalique, René Jules (1860–1945): French Art Nouveau jewellery designer and Art Deco glass-maker who established a glasshouse at Combs-la-Ville, near Paris, in 1908, and a second at Wingen-sur-Moder in 1918 which is still in operation.

Langer, Caspar Gottlieb (*fl.*1749): Bohemian-Silesian glass engraver from Warmbrunn, in Silesia.

Lauenstein: glasshouse founded in 1701 at Lauenstein, near Hamelin, in Westphalia; closed in 1870.

Lechevrel, Alphonse Eugène (b. 1850): glass engraver who made cameo glass at Hodgetts, Richardson & Co., Stourbridge.

Lehmann, Caspar (1563/65–1622): German gem-cutter, employed at the court of Prague under Emperor Rudolf II. Regarded as the first master of the art of glass engraving in modern history.

Libenský, Stanislav (b. 1921): influential Czechoslovakian designer and teacher whose glass ranges from small vessels to large-scale architectural pieces. Often works with his wife, glass-maker Jaroslava Brychtová (b. 1924).

Lindstrand, Vicke (1904–83): Swedish designer who worked for Orrefors (1928–40) and later Kosta Boda (1950–75).

Littleton, Harvey K. (b. 1922): highly influential American studio glass artist and teacher, in large part responsible for international Studio Glass Movement of 1960s and later.

Lobmeyr, J. & L.: Viennese glass manufacturer established in 1822. Successive managers of the firm were its founder, Josef Lobmeyr (from 1825 to 1855), Josef Lobmeyr, Jr (1855–64) and Ludwig Lobmeyr (1864–1902), who perpetuated the tradition of northern Bohemian glass engraving in their glasshouses at Steinschönau and Haida.

Locke, Joseph (1846–1936): English glass engraver and enameller who was a pupil of Alphonse Lechevrel, making cameo glass. After working in Stourbridge he moved to the United States, working for the New England Glass Company and later Libbey Glass.

Loetz-Witwe: glassworks founded in 1836 in southern Bohemia; renowned for its iridescent Art Nouveau glass made under the directorship of Max Ritter von Spaun.

Mansell, Sir Robert (1573–1656): English admiral who on his retirement acquired interests in glass and the development of coal as a fuel for furnaces. In *c.*1617 he built the Broad Street Glasshouse, which employed Italian craftsmen.

Marinot, Maurice (1882–1960): French Fauve painter who became the leading studio glass artist in the Art Deco period.

Mathesius, Johann (1504–65): parson who published the *Sarepta oder Bergpostill*, 15 sermons on glass-making which are the source of much important information about Medieval glass.

Mattoni, Andreas Vincenz Peter (1779–1864): glass engraver who founded a school of engraving at Karlsbad in Bohemia.

Mauder, Bruno (1877–1948): born in Munich, studied at the Kunstgewerbeschule and from 1910 was head of the Staatliche Fachschule für Glasindustrie, Zwiesel.

Mäuerl, Anton Wilhelm (1672–1737): Nuremberg glass engraver in the Rococo style who lived in England from 1699 to 1710.

Measey, Michael: member of the Glass Sellers' Company who, together with John Greene, corresponded with Alessio Morelli.

Menzel, Johann Sigismund (1774–1810): Silesian glass-worker who specialized in *Zwischengoldglas*.

Mildner, Johann Joseph (1763–1808): glass-maker who worked at the Gutenbrunn Glasshouse in Lower Austria producing *Zwischengoldglas* medallions.

Miotti family: Muranese glass-makers who operated from the Al Gesù Glassworks and were prominent in the 17th and 18th centuries.

Mohn, Gottlob Samuel (1789–1825): glass painter, son of Samuel Mohn, who taught Anton Kothgasser.

Mohn, Samuel (1762–1815): born in Weissenfels and died in Dresden. Known for his painting on glass in transparent enamels of city and landscapes.

Moncrieff Glassworks: factory in Perth, Scotland, founded in 1860s by John Moncrieff; produced internally decorated Monart glass from 1920s.

Morelli, Alessio (*fl.*1667–72): glass-maker from Murano who corresponded with John Greene and Michael Measey and produced Venetian glass in English styles for the Glass Sellers' Company.

Morris and Company: London furnishing and decorating firm founded in 1861 by William Morris et al. as Morris, Marshall, Faulkner and Company (Morris and Company from 1875). Produced much ecclesiastical and other stained glass to designs by Morris, painter Edward Burne-Jones and others.

Moser, Ludwig (1833–1916): glass engraver from Karlsbad who founded a glasshouse nearby at Meierhöfen.

Mount Washington Glass Company: American glasshouse founded in 1837 by Deming Jarves in South Boston, Massachusetts, producing paperweights and mould-pressed and cut glass.

Muller Frères: French glass-decorating studio established in *c.*1895 in Lunéville, near Nancy. Specialized in Art Nouveau cameo glass.

Neri, Antonio (1576–1614): priest and chemist who worked in glasshouses in Florence, Pisa and Flanders and who produced seven books on glass-making in 1612, *Arte Vetraria*.

Nevers: French city where glass was made from the 16th to 18th centuries, first by Italians from Altare. Most notable creations were small, highly detailed figures of opaque glass, made in the late 16th and the 17th centuries. Lampwork grottoes with Nevers figures were also produced.

New England Glass Company: American glass company incorporated in 1818 by Deming Jarves and others in East Cambridge, Massachusetts. Closed in 1888.

Northwood, John (1836–1902): English glass-maker who excelled in making cameo glass, including the first modern copy of the Portland Vase in 1876. He worked in Stourbridge, first for W.H., B. & J. Richardson and later for Stevens & Williams.

Northwood, John, II (1870–1960): son of John Northwood who, like his father, made cameo glass.

Öhrström, Edvin (b. 1906): Swedish designer employed at Orrefors (1936–57), where he helped develop Ariel glass (a cased glass with air bubbles) along with Knut Bergqvist and Vicke Lindstrand.

Orrefors Glasbruk: Swedish glassworks founded in 1898. Produced decorative glass from 1913, when it was acquired by Johan Ekman.

Osler, F. & C., Glasshouse: large English glassworks founded in 1807 in Birmingham. Specialized in glass furniture and chandeliers.

Palmqvist, Sven (1906–84): Swedish designer who worked for Orrefors, where in the late 1940s he developed Ravenna glass (heavy-walled vessels with brightly hued internal patterns).

Pantin Glassworks: French glasshouse that produced paperweights; founded in 1851 by E.S. Monot at La Villette and moved to Pantin in 1855.

Parker, William (*fl.*1765–71): glass-maker and glass seller whose London firm produced cut-glass chandeliers with glass provided by Whitefriars.

Pellatt, Apsley (1791–1863): best known for his perfection of the crystallo-ceramie (or sulphide) technique; also produced paperweights.

Pellatt, Apsley, Sr: father of Apsley Pellatt and founder of the Falcon Glassworks in Southwark, London, in *c.*1790.

Perrot, Bernard (d. 1709): Italian glass-maker who worked in France, first at Nevers (from 1649) and later from 1662 at Orléans, producing cast flat panels for mirrors and windows.

Poli, Flavio (b. 1900): Italian designer who was art director of Seguso Vetri d'Arte, Murano, where he developed new techniques and shapes, the latter largely biomorphic.

Potsdam: important German glasshouse transferred from near Drewitz in 1679. From then until 1693 it was run by Johann Kunckel. In 1736 it moved to Zechlin, where it continued until 1890.

Powell, James, & Sons: London glassworks acquired by James Powell in 1834; formerly known as the Whitefriars Glass Works.

Ravenscroft, George (1618–81): English glass-maker who founded a glasshouse in Savoy, London, in 1673 and in the following year obtained a patent for the production of lead glass.

Richardson, W.H., B. & J.: company founded in 1720 with a glasshouse at Wordsley, near Stourbridge. In 1829 it was taken over by Thomas Webb with William Haden Richardson and his brother Benjamin (Webb & Richardson). After a third brother, Jonathan, joined the firm, it became known as W.H., B. & J. Richardson.

Riedel, Josef (*fl.*1830–48): Bohemian glass-maker known for his greenish and yellowish *Annagrün* and *Annagelb* glass, made by adding uranium to the batch.

Rosbach, Elias (1700–65): glass engraver who worked at Potsdam from 1727 to 1736 and then at Zechlin.

Rousseau, Eugène (1827–91): French glass artist who experimented with many techniques, notably cameo carving; decoration much inspired by Japanese art.

St Louis Glass Factory: French glassworks founded in Lorraine in 1767. Made crystal glass from 1701, paperweights in mid 19th century. Still in operation.

Salviati, Dr Antonio (1816–90): versatile Venetian glass-maker who founded the Salviati & Co. glasshouse in Murano in 1859, which later opened a London showroom.

Sang, Andreas Friedrich (*fl.*1719–60): Thuringian glass engraver who was court engraver to Duke Ernest Augustus of Sachsen-Weimar. He later worked in the Netherlands.

Sang, Jacob (d. 1783): accomplished glass engraver who worked in Amsterdam on glass supposedly imported from Newcastle-upon-Tyne.

Sang, Johann Heinrich Balthasar (*fl.*1745–55): German glass engraver, son of Andreas Friedrich Sang, and court engraver at Brunswick from 1747.

Sarpaneva, Timo (b. 1926): Finnish designer in many media; from 1950 associated with Iittala Glassworks.

Schaper, Johann (1621–70): Nuremberg glass painter who worked in coloured enamel and occasionally *Schwarzlot*.

Schmidt, Johann Wolfgang (d. 1710): Nuremberg glass engraver who tended to depict battles and hunting scenes.

Schneider, Christian Gottfried (1710–73): master glass engraver at the court of Warmbrunn, in Silesia.

Schouman, Aert (1710–92): born in Dordrecht, he practised his art of stippling on glass there and in The Hague. A follower of Frans Greenwood.

Schwanhardt, Georg, the Elder (1601–67): Nuremberg glass engraver who studied under Caspar Lehmann and was the first to employ *Blankschnitt*.

Schwanhardt, Heinrich (1624–93): Nuremberg glass engraver, son of Georg Schwanhardt the Elder.

Schwartz, Samuel (1681–1737): glass-cutter and engraver employed at several Thuringian courts but worked mainly at Arnstadt.

Schwinger, Hermann (1640–85): Nuremberg glass engraver who was fond of idyllic rustic scenes.

Seguso, Archimede (b. 1909): Italian glass-blower and designer responsible for developing *merletto* (lace) and *a piume* (feathery) techniques.

Spiller, Gottfried (1663–1728): Potsdam glass engraver, nephew and pupil of Martin Winter.

Steinschönau: Bohemian city (now Kamenický Šenov, Czechoslovakia) renowned since the 19th century for its glass engravers; site of a Lobmeyr glasshouse and a technical school instrumental in the advancement of 20th-century Czechoslovakian glass.

Steuben Glass Works: founded in 1903 by Frederick Carder in Corning, New York, and taken over by the Corning Glass Works in 1918.

Stevens & Williams Ltd: glasshouse founded in the 18th century at Brierley Hill, near Stourbridge, as the Moor Lane Glass House. The name was changed when William Stevens and Samuel Cox Williams became principals of the firm in 1847.

Stiegel, Henry William (1729–85): born in Cologne. Emigrated to the United States, where he founded glasshouses in the 1760s in Pennsylvania, first at Elizabeth Furnace, then at Manheim.

Tassie, James (1735–99): Scottish sculptor who, with his nephew, William Tassie (1777–1860), made reproductions of engraved gems in glass paste and opaque white glass medallions. In 1781–2 he made sixty plaster copies of the Portland Vase; also made casts for Josiah Wedgwood.

Tiffany, Louis Comfort (1848–1933): Art Nouveau glass artist and painter who founded the Tiffany Glass and Decorating Company in New York; produced stained-glass panels and windows, leaded-glass lamps and blown glassware, among other objects.

Trümper, Johann Moritz (1680–1742): important glass engraver from Kassel, who went to Potsdam in 1713.

Val St-Lambert, Cristalleries du: Belgian glassworks founded in 1825 near Liège. Produced notable Art Nouveau and Art Deco glass, including designs by architect Henry Van de Velde.

van Heemskerk, Willem Jacobsz (1613–92): Dutch diamond-point glass engraver, known for his calligraphy on bottles and *Roemers*.

Venini, Paolo (1895–1959): most influential 20th-century Italian glass-maker who in 1926 set up the Venini glassworks in Murano, where he revived classical Murano methods and developed many new techniques and forms. Factory still in operation.

Verzelini, Giacomo (d. 1606): Italian glass-maker who founded the first glasshouse in England (in London) producing glass *à la façon de Venise* in 1575.

Visscher, Anna Roemers (1583–1651): accomplished amateur Dutch glass engraver from Amsterdam who decorated glass in diamond-point with calligraphy. Her younger sister, Maria, was also a glass decorator.

Wagenfeld, Wilhelm (b. 1900): German designer who taught at the Bauhaus; designed utilitarian glass from the 1930s.

Waterford Glass House: Irish glass company founded in 1783 and closed down in 1851. Waterford Glass Ltd was set up in 1951 and still produces glass today.

Waterloo Glass House (*c.*1815–35): factory founded by Daniel Foley in Cork. Produced glass similar to that of the Cork Glass Company but of a lesser quality.

Webb, Thomas, & Sons: Stourbridge glasshouse founded by Thomas Webb that most notably produced cameo glass in the late 19th century.

Whitefriars Glass Works: London glasshouse founded in 1680 in a former Carmelite monastery. Acquired by James Powell in 1834, it became James Powell & Sons and in 1962 resumed the name Whitefriars Glass Ltd.

Winter, Friedrich (d. *c.*1712): Silesian glass engraver who in 1690–1 set up a water mill for glass engraving in Petersdorf in the Hirschberg Valley.

Winter, Martin (d. 1702): glass engraver in the service of the Elector of Brandenburg; built a water-powered mill in Potsdam, near Berlin, to carve *Hochschnitt*.

Wirkkala, Tapio (1915–85): Finnish designer in many media; worked for Iittala from 1946 and for Venini from 1959.

Wistar, Caspar (1696–1752): German native who set up a glasshouse near Alloway, New Jersey, in 1739, producing mainly bottles and window glass in *Waldglas*; factory managed by his son, Richard, until it closed in *c.*1776.

Wolff, David (1732–98): foremost Dutch stipple-engraver on glass.

Woodall, George (1850–1925) and **Thomas** (1849–1926): brothers who were apprenticed to John Northwood and later worked for Thomas Webb & Sons producing cameo glass.

Ysart, Paul (b. 1904): Spanish-born glass-maker who made paperweights and other glass for Caithness and Moncrieff in Scotland after working at St Louis.

Zechlin: German glasshouse, situated to the north of Berlin, to which the Potsdam glass factory was moved in 1736.

Zwiesel: Bavarian city; site of the Staatliche Fachschule für Glasindustrie, which, under director Bruno Mauder, was instrumental in the development of 20th-century German glass.

INDEX

ACKNOWLEDGMENTS

The publisher thanks the following organizations and photographers for their kind permission to reproduce the photographs in this book:

1 Sheppard and Cooper, London/Mallett and Son Ltd; **4** The Corning Museum of Glass (Bequest of Gladys C. Welles); **4–5** Asprey PLC; **6** Broadfield House Glass Museum, Kingswinford; **9** above Edimedia (© ADAGP, Paris and DACS, London 1991); **12** Ken Adlard/Conran Octopus; **17** left Courtesy of the Trustees of the British Museum; **17** above right Courtesy of the Trustees of the British Museum; **17** below right The Corning Museum of Glass; **18** The Corning Museum of Glass; **19** left The Corning Museum of Glass; **19** centre Künstmuseum Düsseldorf – Glasmuseum Hentrich; **19** right The Corning Museum of Glass; **20** left Sheppard and Cooper, London; **20** right The Toledo Museum of Art; **21** left Antikenmuseum, SMPK – Berlin; **21** above right The Toledo Museum of Art; **21** below right Courtesy of the Trustees of the British Museum; **22** Yale University Art Gallery (photographer Michael Agee); **23** left The Brooklyn Museum, 49.61–1–4 Charles Edwin Wilbour Fund (photographer John Parnell); **26** left Courtesy of the Trustees of the British Museum (photographer Mario Carrieri); **26** right Sheppard and Cooper, London; **27** left Sheppard and Cooper, London; **27** right Fritz von der Schulenburg; **28** above The Metropolitan Museum of Art (Rogers Fund, 03.14.13); **28** below The Corning Museum of Glass (photographer Mario Carrieri); **29** The Toledo Museum of Art; **30** Sheppard and Cooper, London; **31** below Courtesy of the Trustees of the British Museum (photographer Mario Carrieri); **33** left Courtesy of the Trustees of the British Museum; **33** centre Römisch-Germanisches Museum (photographer Mario Carrieri); **33** right Sheppard and Cooper, London; **34** left Römisch-Germanisches Museum (photographer Mario Carrieri); **34** right Sheppard and Cooper, London; 35 left Museo Correr (photography Giacomelli); **35** centre The Corning Museum of Glass (Arthur Rubloff bequest); **35** right The Corning Museum of Glass; **36** left Sheppard and Cooper, London; **36** right The Hermitage, Leningrad; **37** above right Bridgeman Art Library (British Museum); **37** above left Yale University Art Gallery; **37** below Connaissance des Arts/Jacqueline Guillot/Edimedia; **41** above left The Metropolitan Museum of Art (Gift of Mrs Charles S. Payson 1969 69.153); **41** above right The Corning Museum of Glass; **41** below Courtesy of the Trustees of the British Museum; **42** above left The David Collection, Copenhagen, (Ole Woldbye); **42** above right The Corning Museum of Glass (Clara S. Peck Endowment); **42** below The Corning Museum of Glass; **43** left Courtesy of the Trustees of the British Museum; **43** right The Corning Museum of Glass (Collection of Ernesto Wolf); **44** above The Corning Museum of Glass; **44** below By courtesy of the Board of Trustees of the Victoria & Albert Museum; **45** The Cleveland Museum of Art (Purchase from the J.H. Wade Fund 44.235); **46** Sonia Halliday/Laura Lushington; **48** left Courtesy of the Trustees of the British Museum; **48** right The Corning Museum of Glass; **49** Statens Historiska Museer, Stockholm; **50** Scala, Florence (Treasury of St Marks); **51** Württembergisches Landesmuseum, Stuttgart; **52** Courtesy of the Trustees of the British Museum; **53** above Diozesanmuseum, Freising; **53** below left Künstmuseum, Düsseldorf; **53** below right Ursula Edelmann (Museum für Künsthandwerk); **54** left Museo Poldi Pezzoli, Milan; **54** above centre The Corning Museum of Glass; **54** below centre The Corning Museum of Glass (Gift, Funds from Alberta Stout); **54** right Rheinisches Landesmuseum, Bonn; **55** Künstmuseum Düsseldorf; **56** above left Josef Makovec, Luneburg; **56** above right Musée Départemental des Antiquités de Rouen; **56** below right Amt für Vor und Frühgeschichte, (Bodendenkmalpflege), Lübeck, Germany, Samlung der Bodenfunde; **57** left Museum for Decorative Arts, Prague (photographer Miloslav Sebek); **57** right The Corning Museum of Glass (Gift of The Ruth Bryan Strauss Memorial Fund); **60** above La Réunion des Musées Nationaux; **60** below right Courtesy of the Trustees of the British Museum; **61** above Courtesy of The Hispanic Society of America, New York; **61** below Scala, Florence (Galleria degli Uffizi); **62** above Sheppard and Cooper, London; **62** below left Sheppard and Cooper, London; **62** below right The Toledo Museum of Art; **63** above Reproduced by permission of the Trustees, The Wallace Collection, London; **63** below Courtesy of the Trustees of the British Museum; **64** above Ashmolean Museum, Oxford; **64** below The Corning Museum of Glass; **65** left By courtesy of the Board of Trustees of the Victoria & Albert Museum; 65 right Musée d'Archéologie et d'Arts Décoratifs, Liège, B/1061; **66** above Sheppard and Cooper, London; **66** below Sheppard and Cooper, London; **67** left Sheppard and Cooper, London; **67** right Prof. DDr.h.c. Hans Mayr, ABA, DGPH, oGPH; **68** Künsthistorisches Museum, Vienna; **69** above Scala, Florence (Galleria degli Uffizi); **69** below right Collection Fritz and Mary Biemann; **69** below left Courtesy of the Trustees of the British Museum; **70** above By permission of the British Library; **70** below Courtesy of the Trustees of the British Museum; **71** below Ashmolean Museum, Oxford; **72** above Reiner Zeitz Ltd, **72** below Museu d'Arts Decoratives, Barcelona; **73** left Sheppard and Cooper, London; **73** right Reproduced by permission of the Trustees, The Wallace Collection, London; **74** above left La Réunion des Musées Nationaux; **74** above right The Corning Museum of Art (Houghton Endowment Fund Purchase); **74** below Musée de l'Oeuvre Notre Dame de Strasbourg; **75** left Sheppard and Cooper, London; **75** right Courtesy of the Trustees of the British Museum; **76** left Courtesy of the Trustees of the British Museum; **76** right La Réunion des Musées Nationaux; **77** left Prof. DDr.h.c. Hans Mayr, ABA, DGPH, oGPH; **77** right The Toledo Museum of Art; **78** Prof DDr.h.c. Hans Mayr, ABA, DGPH, oGPH; **79** left Sheppard and Cooper, London; **79** centre Prof DDr.h.c. Hans Mayr, ABA, DGPH, oGPH; **79** right Sheppard and Cooper, London; **80** Collections of the Prince of Liechtenstein, Vaduz Castle; **83–5** Prof DDr.h.c. Hans Mayr, ABA, DGPH, oGPH; **86** below Prof DDr.h.c. Hans Mayr, ABA, DGPH, oGPH; **87–8** Prof DDr.h.c. Hans Mayr, ABA, DGPH, oGPH; **89** left Prof DDr.h.c. Hans Mayr, ABA, DGPH, oGPH; **89** right By courtesy of the Board of Trustees of the Victoria & Albert Museum; **90** Sheppard and Cooper, London/Mallet and Son Ltd; **91** above left Sheppard and Cooper, London/Mallet and Son Ltd; **91** above right Sheppard and Cooper, London; **91** below The Royal Collections, Rosenborg Palace, Copenhagen; **92** left By courtesy of the Trustees of the Victoria & Albert Museum; **92** right Asprey PLC; **93** left By courtesy of the Board of Trustees of the Victoria & Albert Museum; **93** right The Corning Museum of Glass; **94** Fitzwilliam Museum, Cambridge; **95** above Ken Adlard/Conran Octopus (Courtesy Delomosne & Son Ltd); **95** below By courtesy of the National Portrait Gallery, London; **96** centre Asprey PLC; **97–8** Ken Adlard/Conran Octopus (Courtesy Delomosne & Son Ltd); **99** above right and below Ken Adlard/Conran Octopus; **100** Delomosne & Son Ltd; **101** above left By courtesy of the Board of Trustees of the Victoria & Albert Museum; **101** above right Delomosne & Son Ltd; **101** below Ken Adlard/Conran Octopus (Courtesy Delomosne & Son Ltd); **102** Ken Adlard/Conran Octopus (Courtesy Delomosne & Son Ltd); **103** above left Ken Adlard/Conran Octopus; **103** above right Ken Adlard/Conran Octopus (Courtesy private collection); **103** below Ken Adlard/Conran Octopus (Courtesy Delomosne & Son Ltd); **104** Ken Adlard (Courtesy Asprey PLC/Delomosne & Son Ltd); **105** left Ken Adlard (Courtesy Jonathan Horne Antiques); **105** right Ken Adlard (Courtesy Delomosne & Son Ltd); **108** Connaissance des Arts/Roger Guillemot/Edimedia; **110** courtesy Curiosities of Glass Making by Apsley Pellatt; **111** above left Broadfield House Glass Museum, Kingswinford; **111** above right Asprey PLC; **111** below left Broadfield House Glass Museum, Kingswinford; **111** below right P. A. Burton; **112** left Pilkington Glass Museum; **112** right Broadfield House Glass Museum, Kingswinford; **113** above left Broadfield House Glass Museum, Kingswinford; **113** below left The Board of Trustees of the National Museums & Galleries on Merseyside; **113** right By courtesy of the Board of Trustees of the Victoria & Albert Museum; **114** left Manchester City Art Galleries; **114** right National Museum of Ireland; **115** above David Battie; **115** below The Trustees, The Cecil Higgins Art Gallery, Bedford; **116** Manchester City Art Galleries; **117** above Royal Brierley Crystal Ltd; **117** below Pilkington Glass Museum; **118** left Royal Brierley Crystal Ltd; **118** right Rochdale Museum Service; **119** above Huntley House Museum; **119** below left Glasgow Museums and Art Galleries; **119** below right Laing Art Gallery, Newcastle-upon-Tyne (Tyne & Wear Museums) and private collection; **120–1** Broadfield House Glass Museum, Kingswinford; **122** left The Board of Trustees of the National Museums & Galleries on Merseyside; **125** left The Corning Museum of Glass (Part gift of Roland C. and Sarah Katheryn Luther, Roland C. Luther III, Edwin C. Luther III and Ann Luther Dexter); **125** right Courtesy Winterthur Museum; **125** left The Corning Museum of Glass; **126** centre The Corning Museum of Glass (Gift of Louise Esterly); **126** right Courtesy of the Sandwich Historical Society Glass Museum; **127** David Battie; **130** below Mary Evans Picture Library; **131** left Musée National des Techniques; **131** right Künstmuseum Düsseldorf – Glasmuseum Hentrich; **132** right Musée des Arts Décoratifs, Paris; **133** The Corning Museum of Art (Bryan Strauss Memorial Foundation); **133** Collection Paolo Zancope, Venice; **134** above Angelo Hornak (Broadfield House Glass Museum, Kingswinford); **136** Spink & Son Ltd; **137** Spink & Son Ltd; **139** above Spink & Son Ltd; **140** Spink & Son Ltd; **141** above Spink & Son Ltd; **145** below Musée des Arts Décoratifs, Paris; **148** above right The Corning Museum of Glass (Gift of Corning Glass Works); **150** La Réunion des Musées Nationaux; **151** Haslam & Whiteway Ltd; **152** left Phillips Fine Art Auctioneers; **153** Sonia Halliday/Laura Lushington; **154** Philippe Garner (Musée de l'Ecole de Nancy); **155** left Philippe Garner; **156** Philippe Garner; **157** right Philippe Garner; **165** left Connaissance des Arts/Roger Guillemot/Edimedia; **165** below right Collection du Musée des Arts Décoratifs, Paris (© ADAGP, Paris and DACS, London 1991); **166** above right Collection du Musée des Arts Décoratifs, Paris; **170** left Compagnie des Cristalleries de Baccarat; **170** right Courtesy Tableware International; **171** By courtesy of the Board of Trustees of the Victoria & Albert Museum; **172** above Alvar Aalto Museum; **172** below Nordenjeldske Künstindustrimuseum; **173** left By courtesy of the Board of Trustees of the Victoria & Albert Museum; **173** right Austrian Museum of Applied Arts; **174** The Corning Museum of Glass; **176** The Corning Museum of Glass; **177** above Walter Dorwin Teague Associates Inc.; **177** below The Corning Museum of Glass (Gift of W.M. Schwind Antiques); **184** above left Iittala Nuutajärvi Oy; **184** above right Iittala Glass Museum; **184** below centre Iittala Glass Museum; **185** Museum of Decorative Arts, Prague; **187** above The Corning Museum of Glass; **187** below left The Corning Museum of Glass (Purchased with the aid of funds from the National Endowment for the Arts); **187** below right By courtesy of the Board of Trustees of the Victoria & Albert Museum; **190** above and below Jeanette Hayhurst Fakes Collection; **190** centre from Hill-Ouston Gift Catalogue 1934; **191** left Jeanette Hayhurst Fakes Collection; **192** below Jeanette Hayhurst Fakes Collection.

Sotheby's London/photographer Ken Adlard **2**, **24**, **38**, **58**
Sotheby's Amsterdam **10**
Sotheby's Chester **170** centre
Sotheby's Geneva **170** above left
Sotheby's Hong Kong **106**, **107** above left, **107** below
Sotheby's London **23** right, **31** above, **71** above, **86** above, **96** left, **96** right, **99** above left, **107** above right, **122** right, **123**, **128** left, **129**, **130** above, **132** left, **132** centre, **134** below, **142**, **145** above, **146–7**, **148** above left, **148** above centre, **148** below, **152** centre, **152** right, **153** above, **155** right, **157** left, **158** left, **162** (© DACS, 1991), **165** above right, **166** left, **166** below right, **167**, **168** (© DACS, 1991), **169** right, **175** above, **179** above right, **180–3**, **184** below left, **184** below right, **186**, **188–9**, **191** right, **192** above
Sotheby's Milan **175** below, **179** below
Sotheby's Monaco **158** right
Sotheby's New York **14**, **135**, **138**, **139** below, **141** below, **165** below left (© ADAGP, Paris and DACS, London 1991), **159–61**, **169** above left (© DACS, 1991); **169** below left Alastair Duncan (© ADAGP, Paris and DACS, London 1991).